The Psychology of Sports Coaching

This is the first book to offer a comprehensive review of current research in the psychology of sports coaching. It provides detailed, critical appraisals of the key psychological concepts behind the practice of sports coaching and engages with contemporary debates in this field. Organised around three main themes, it discusses factors affecting the coaching environment; methods for enhancing coach performance; and how to put theory into practice through coaching work.

Written by an international team of researchers and practitioners at the cutting edge of psychology and coaching, each chapter introduces a key concept, defines key terms, provides a comprehensive literature review, and considers implications for future research and applied practice. Encompassing the latest developments in the field, it addresses topics such as:

- the theory behind effective coaching
- creating performance environments
- promoting psychological well-being
- developing resilience through coaching
- transformational leadership and the role of the coach.

The Psychology of Sports Coaching: Research and practice is an indispensable resource for sport psychologists and sports coaches, and is essential reading for all students and academics researching sport psychology.

Richard Thelwell is Head of Department for Sport and Exercise Sciences at the University of Portsmouth, UK. Richard has amassed a portfolio of over 70 peer-reviewed publications including edited book chapters, international journal publications, and international conference papers. His current research interests lie within the area of coach psychology and in particular the themes of stress, emotion, coping and performance, psychological skills and behaviour change, and expectation effects. Richard also has a vested research interest in professional practice factors in applied sport psychology and is a Registered Psychologist of the Health and Care Professions Council. He also serves on the Editorial Board for the *International Review of Sport and Exercise Psychology*, the *International Journal of Sport Psychology*, and is Associate Editor for *Case Studies in Sport and Exercise Psychology*.

Chris Harwood is a Reader in Applied Sport Psychology and Sport Psychology Research Group Leader at Loughborough University, UK. He is a Registered Psychologist of the Health and Care Professions Council, a Chartered Psychologist of the British Psychological Society and High Performance Sport Accredited (Psychology) Practitioner with the British Association of Sport and Exercise Sciences (BASES). His research and teaching interests lie mainly in the psychological aspects of youth sport and athlete development with a particular focus on the psychology of parenting and coaching. He is also interested in professional practice factors in applied sport psychology.

Iain Greenlees is a Reader in Sport Psychology at the University of Chichester, UK. He is a Registered Psychologist of the Health and Care Professions Council and a Chartered Psychologist of the British Psychological Society. His research and teaching interests lie mainly in the psychological factors underpinning performance in sport and coaching settings. He is also interested in the efficacy of interventions in applied sport psychology. Iain is a former Associate Editor for *The Sport and Exercise Psychology Review* and he also now serves as an Editorial Board Member for *The International Review of Sport and Exercise Psychology*.

Routledge Research in Sports Coaching

The *Routledge Research in Sports Coaching* series provides a platform for leading experts and emerging academics in this important discipline to present groundbreaking work on the history, theory, practice, and contemporary issues of sports coaching. The series sets a new benchmark for research in sports coaching, and offers a valuable contribution to the wider sphere of sports studies.

Available in this series:

A History of Sports Coaching in Britain
Overcoming amateurism
Dave Day and Tegan Carpenter

Women in Sports Coaching
Edited by Nicole M. LaVoi

The Psychology of Sports Coaching
Research and practice
Edited by Richard Thelwell, Chris Harwood and Iain Greenlees

The Psychology of
Sports Coaching

Research and practice

**Edited by
Richard Thelwell,
Chris Harwood and
Iain Greenlees**

Routledge
Taylor & Francis Group

LONDON AND NEW YORK

First published 2017
by Routledge
2 Park Square, Milton Park, Abingdon, Oxon OX14 4RN

and by Routledge
711 Third Avenue, New York, NY 10017

Routledge is an imprint of the Taylor & Francis Group, an informa business

British Library Cataloguing-in-Publication Data
A catalogue record for this book is available from the British Library

Library of Congress Cataloging in Publication Data
Names: Thelwell, Richard.
Title: The psychology of sports coaching : research and practice / edited
by Richard Thelwell, Chris Harwood and Iain Greenlees.
Description: Milton Park, Abingdon, Oxon ; New York, NY : Routledge,
2016. | Includes bibliographical references and index.
Identifiers: LCCN 2016005957| ISBN 9781138917163 (hardback) |
ISBN 9781315689210 (ebook)
Subjects: LCSH: Coaching (Athletics)–Psychological aspects.
Classification: LCC GV711 .P79 2016 | DDC 796.07/7–dc23
LC record available at https://lccn.loc.gov/2016005957

ISBN: 978-1-138-91716-3 (hbk)
ISBN: 978-1-315-68921-0 (ebk)

Typeset in Times New Roman
by Wearset Ltd, Boldon, Tyne and Wear

Contents

Illustrations

Contributors

Calum A. Arthur, University of Stirling, UK

Jamie B. Barker, Staffordshire University, UK

Koen De Brandt, Vrije Universiteit Brussel, Belgium

Martin Camiré, University of Ottawa, Canada

Sarah Carson Sackett, James Madison University, USA

Pete Coffee, University of Stirling, UK

Matt Dicks, University of Portsmouth, UK

Andrew L. Evans, Salford University, UK

Sean G. Figgins, University of Chichester, UK

David Fletcher, Loughborough University, UK

M. Ryan Flett, West Virginia University, USA

Burt Giges, Springfield College, USA

Megan Gilchrist, The University of Queensland, Australia

Daniel G. Gould, Michigan State University, USA

Iain Greenlees, University of Chichester, UK

Chris Harwood, Loughborough University, UK

Camilla J. Knight, Swansea University, UK

Paul De Knop, Vrije Universiteit Brussel, Belgium

Sophia Jowett, Loughborough University, UK

Alan Lynn, Scottish Swimming, UK

Clifford J. Mallett, The University of Queensland, Australia

Andrew Manley, Leeds Beckett University, UK

Paul McCarthy, Glasgow Caledonian University, UK

Andrew Mills, Catalyst3, Melbourne Sports Institute, Australia

Peter Olusoga, Sheffield Hallam University, UK

Matthew Pain, The Football Association, England

Martin W. O. Rabjohns, The University of Queensland, Australia

Nathalie Rosier, Vrije Universiteit Brussel, Belgium

Steven B. Rynne, The University of Queensland, Australia

Mustafa Sarkar, Nottingham Trent University, UK

Christopher N. Sellars, University of Woverhampton, UK

Matt. J. Slater, Staffordshire University, UK

Matthew J. Smith, University of Chichester, UK

Juliette Stebbings, University of Birmingham, UK

Ian M. Taylor, Loughborough University, UK

Richard Thelwell, University of Portsmouth, UK

Mark Upton, English Institute of Sport, UK

Christopher R. D. Wagstaff, University of Portsmouth, UK

Paul Wylleman, Vrije Universiteit Brussel, Belgium

Sophie X. Yang, Sichuan University, China

Introduction

Richard Thelwell,[1] *Chris Harwood,*[2]
and Iain Greenlees[3]

Welcome to *The Psychology of Sports Coaching: Research and Practice*, a text that reflects both the development of psychology research focused on the sports coach, and the editorial team's extensive practitioner experience of working with such individuals. In addition to the increased research interest in the area in recent years, there is a developing acceptance that practitioners are spending more time working with, and through, sports coaches. Despite the maturing of the area, it is surprising that to date, no text or collection of works exists to comprehensively review and summarise the scientific literature in the area, or to direct future investigation and recommendations for applied practice. Our response is to provide a text that reviews the conceptual and theoretical components of the selected topic areas while also detailing how the research informs practice application. In doing so, the text moves beyond the existing available resources that focus on enhancing coaches' awareness of psychology (e.g. Burton & Raedeke, 2008), integrating psychology into coach practice (Nicholls & Jones, 2013), and outlining how coaches become more successful (Martens, 2012). The result is a distinctive three-part text comprising reviews of the most prominent thematic areas in which the majority of the coaching psychology research has been conducted. The first part addresses factors that affect the coaching environment and provides coverage of topics ranging from athlete-development phases, developmental environments, to parental involvement. The second part provides a focus for how coach performance can be enhanced, in which demands and development of high performance coaching, understanding of athlete expectations, and impacts of coach psychological well- and ill-being are among the topics covered. Attention in the final part is directed to how psychology practitioners work through coaches, with chapters covering, for example, transformational leadership, enhancing coach efficacy, and the integration of decision-making strategies in training.

As outlined, our intention was to assemble a collection of in-depth literature reviews on key areas that have emerged within the last decade to assist future research and practice within the fields of sport psychology and coaching science. Further to this, we also wanted to invite contributions from emerging researchers in addition to established international experts, so that fuller coverage of areas are presented with a distinctive conceptual, theoretical, and practical focus. It is hoped that the empirical evidence presented within each chapter, together with the dissemination of this body of research into practical implications for applied practice, offers a comprehensive, thought-provoking essential library for students, graduates, doctoral students, academics and professionals working in the fields of applied sport psychology and coaching science. The format of each chapter has been standardised as much as possible to resemble the works published in academic journals, with chapters divided into several sections: an introduction; a section clarifying and defining key terms; a comprehensive and contemporary review of literature; the directions for future research; and the implications of the work for applied practice.

The first part, *Factors that affect the coaching environment*, commences with Paul Wylleman, Nathalie Rosier, Koen De Brandt, and Paul de Knop who critique key coaching considerations through athlete development phases. The chapter details the transitions and stages athletes face in different domains of development using both a lifespan model and a holistic perspective to outline the development of the elite athlete career, before considering future research directions and implications for professional practice. In Chapter 2, Andrew Mills and Matt Pain critically review the creation of development and performance environments for adolescent athletes. Factors perceived by successful coaches to underpin optimal development environments are examined prior to critiquing the research findings that, when put together, highlight the importance of establishing cohesive player-centred environments guided by a clear vision and philosophy. Chapter 3, written by Megan Gilchrist and Cliff Mallett, reviews the theory behind effective coaching. Using self-determination theory as a framework, the authors unpack the complexity associated with why coaches coach the way they do, and provide direction on future research, and the relevance of this knowledge and understanding to coaching practice. In Chapter 4, Sophie Yang and Sophia Jowett use the 3 + 1Cs model to evaluate the understanding and enhancing of coach–athlete relationships in relation to individual differences, relationship characteristics, and environmental factors. In doing so, they explore key determinants of coach–athlete relationships, and how relationship quality associates with motivation, self-concept, team cohesion, and collective efficacy. In Chapter 5, Chris Wagstaff considers how sport psychologists can support coaches during organisational change, and provides a comprehensive review of research examining change in these domains. Given the increased focus of research in the area, the authors provide an insight to how coaches may seek to maintain effective performance during periods of substantial change. The final chapter within Part I by Camilla Knight and Daniel Gould reviews the coach–parent interaction and covers issues that coaches encounter with parents, and potential strategies to optimise parent–coach relationships. Given the paucity of literature examining coach–parent interactions, the chapter concludes with future research options focused around education and intervention strategies.

The second part, *Enhancing coach performance*, starts with Paul McCarthy and Burt Giges who, in Chapter 7, examine how the needs of coaches are met. The chapter highlights how coaches satisfy particular psychological needs through the coaching process and in particular how psychological needs are identified, satisfied, or unsatisfied. Having highlighted future research priorities, the authors comment on how practitioners may wish to integrate such material when consulting with coaches. Steven Rynne, Cliff Mallett, and Martin Rabjohns, in Chapter 8, consider research examining the work of high performance coaches, the factors that influence coach performance, and the qualities of successful coaches. The authors illustrate the concept of the coach as a learner, individual strategies to enhance coach performance, and organisational strategies to support coaches, prior to highlighting future research opportunities in the area with a focus on performance development. Chapter 9, written by Peter Olusoga and Richard Thelwell, reviews the literature examining coach stress and coping. In addition to reviewing the salient literature, the authors consider potential intervention strategies to manage stress experiences, before reviewing the implications for professional practice and future research. In Chapter 10, Andrew Manley, Iain Greenlees, and Richard Thelwell outline the key components associated with expectations that athletes have of coaches. The critique examines the subsequent effect of athletes' coach expectations on their attention, effort, and general behaviours prior to concluding with suggestions for applied practice and future research. Chapter 11, by Ryan Flett, Sarah Carson-Sackett, and Martin Camiré, reviews literature associated with the actions that coaches take to promote effective outcomes. In addition to critically reviewing the antecedents of effective coaching across the context of participation coaching, performance coaching, and high-performance coaching, the consequences and outcomes of both positive and negative actions are discussed in order to provide practitioner implications and future research directions. Juliette Stebbings and Ian Taylor bring Part II to a close with their chapter on coach well- and ill-being, and impacts on coach and athlete performance. Literature examining the influence of sporting environments on coach well-being is also reviewed, before the authors explore the often ignored processes for how athletes influence coaches' psychological health. The chapter concludes with suggestions as to how research can stimulate and improve applied practice.

The final Part of the text addresses issues associated with *Working through coaches* and starts with Calum Arthur and Alan Lynn, who review transformational leadership and how it may be used for, and by, the sports coach. A comprehensive review of the literature is presented, outlining how coaches can engage with the theory. Having identified a number of future research directions, the chapter closes with a detailed description of the potential applied implications within the sport, and, in particular, the coaching domain via use of the Vision, Support, and Challenge model. In Chapter 14, Chris Harwood discusses the concept of coaching efficacy with a specific focus on the importance of developing the confidence of coaches to integrate mental skills and psychological strategies into their daily coaching practice and philosophy. In addition to potential research directions, attention is given to the methods and behaviours by which coaches shape the psychosocial development of young athletes. Matthew Smith, Sean Figgins, and Chris Sellars, in Chapter 15, review the inspirational communication literature with a particular focus on how coaches interact with their athletes. Throughout, future research ideas to further our understanding of this process are offered in addition to practical suggestions on how coaches might inspire their athletes. Chapter 16, by Mustafa Sarkar and David Fletcher, synthesises the research evidence regarding the effectiveness of resilience training. Best-practice approaches to resilience development are presented in addition to explanations of how resilience training can enhance well-being and performance. The authors conclude by exploring what resilience training can achieve in the context of coaching, and what coaches should consider when developing resilience in athletes. Matt Dicks and Mark Upton, in Chapter 17, review decision-making research with a particular focus on coaching applications. Adopting an ecological psychology approach, the authors consider how the theory of affordances can be used as a framework for studying real-time decision making, with suggestions for future work to bridge the gap between theory, research, and practice presented. The final chapter by Andrew Evans, Matthew Slater, Pete Coffee, and Jamie Barker details how social identity theory can be used by coaches to enhance team functioning. In doing so, a discussion of the applied implications (e.g. creating team identities and contents) for coaches and practitioners is provided, with a narrative centred on future research opportunities.

Notes

1 Department of Sport and Exercise Science, University of Portsmouth, UK
2 School of Sport, Exercise and Health Sciences, Loughborough University, UK
3 Institute of Sport, University of Chichester, UK

References

Burton, D., & Raedeke, T. (2008). *Sport psychology for coaches*. Champaign, IL: Human Kinetics.
Martens, R. (2012). *Successful coaching* (4th edn). Champaign, IL: Human Kinetics.
Nicholls, A. R., & Jones, L. (2013). *Psychology in sports coaching: Theory and practice*. London: Routledge.

Part I

Factors that affect the coaching environment

1 Coaching athletes through career transitions

Paul Wylleman,[1,2] *Nathalie Rosier,*[2]
Koen De Brandt,[1] *and Paul De Knop*[2]

Introduction

While initially geared towards the topic of athletic retirement or 'end-of-career' transition, research during the past decades has lead to the current developmental and holistic perspective taken on a spectrum of transitions faced by talented and elite athletes. To be able to support athletes in achieving optimal development as well as maximum athletic potential, coaches need a good understanding of how talent development is influenced by multilevel transitions and the stages athletes face in different domains of development, such as athletic, psychological, psychosocial, academic. After reviewing some of the major lines of career transition research, the Holistic Athletic Career model (Wylleman, Reints, & De Knop, 2013a) will be used to provide a developmental and holistic perspective on one of the most important transitions, namely the junior-to-senior transition, as well as to identify three approaches coaches can use in order to optimize the development of athletes when faced with transitional challenges.

Key terms

As researchers studied the 'end-of-career,' a transition was defined as "an event or non-event which results in a change in assumptions about oneself and the world and thus requires a corresponding change in one's behaviour and relationships" (Schlossberg, 1981, p. 5). Continued research showed that transitions could be categorized by their degree of predictability, namely as normative transitions that are generally predictable and anticipated, or as non-normative transitions that are generally unpredicted, unanticipated, and involuntary in nature. Using a normative perspective on transitions, different 'within-career' transitions were identified, occurring from the start of the athletic career (initiation stage) up to its end (discontinuation stage), not only in the athletic development of athletes, but also in other aspects of athletes' development. Building upon research with talented athletes, elite student athletes, and former elite athletes, the Holistic Athletic Career (HAC) model was developed, reflecting the concurrent, interactive, and reciprocal nature of the development of athletes in five domains – athletic, psychological, psychosocial, academic/vocational, financial – as reflected in a conceptual normative framework combining a developmental perspective (i.e., from the initiation stage to the discontinuation stage) with a holistic perspective (i.e., athletes' development at different aspects of life). Using this model, the normative 'junior-to-senior' transition can be detailed in terms of the transitions athletes face at various levels: athletic, from the development to the mastery stage; psychological, from adolescence into young adulthood; psychosocial, from friends, coach and parents to national senior coach, support staff, partner; academic, from secondary to higher education or vocational, from secondary to semi-professional athlete; and financial, from support from family and sport governing body to support from sport governing body, national Olympic Committee, and sponsor. Using the HAC model, coaches and applied practitioners can take an educational approach by teaching their athletes from the end of the initiation stage transition-related competences such as knowledge, skills, attitude/experiences as part of their training, and an intervention approach, such as career support services, career transition programs to support their athletes' personal growth, balance their lifestyles, and optimize their post-athletic career lives.

Review of the literature

From athletic retirement to multilevel transitions

Interest in the occurrence of career transitions can be traced back to research in the 1960s and 1970s (e.g., Haerle, 1975; Mihovilovic, 1968) revealing that former professional athletes experienced a range of negative or traumatic experiences, such as alcohol and substance abuse, acute depression, eating disorders, identity confusion, decreased self-confidence, and attempted suicide during, as well as after, athletic retirement (e.g., Blinde & Stratta, 1992; Sinclair & Orlick, 1993; Wylleman, De Knop, Menkehorst, Theeboom, & Annerel, 1993). Interesting to note is that later research relativized the traumatic character of elite athletes' career termination (Alfermann, 2000; Wylleman et al., 1993). While athletic retirement was initially considered to be a singular, dichotic event (Lavallee, 2000), continued research revealed it actually to be a transitional process consisting of different stages – pre-retirement, retirement, and post-retirement – during each of which the effects of this transition could be moderated (e.g., Alfermann & Gross, 1997; Webb, Nasco, Riley, & Headrick, 1998).

The perspective that 'end-of-career' transitions can be seen as a process of change linked up with conceptual frameworks from outside of sport such as Schlossberg and colleagues' Model of Human Adaptation to Transition (Charner & Schlossberg, 1986; Schlossberg, 1981, 1984). By defining a transition as "an event or non-event which results in a change in assumptions about oneself and the world and thus requires a corresponding change in one's behavior and relationships" (Schlossberg, 1981, p. 5), Schlossberg could identify three interacting sets of factors (i.e., the athlete's characteristics, athlete's perception of the particular transition, and the characteristics of the pre-and post-transition environments) which influenced the process of transition. In its wake, sport-specific career transition models were also proposed which confirmed the 'end-of-career' transition as a process of change. For example, Taylor and Ogilvie (1998) described the transition process in terms of causal factors initiating the transitional process, developmental factors related to transition adaptation, coping resources affecting the responses to career transitions, the quality of adjustment to career transition, and the possible treatment issues for distressful reactions to career transition. Furthermore, models also described the influence athletes could have on the possible effects of this transition during this process. This is illustrated in Stambulova's (2003) Athletic Career Transition model, which states that, in order to cope with transitional challenges, athletes need to find an effective fit between the demands of the transition and their coping resources and strategies: the closer the fit, the higher the probability of athletes experiencing a successful transition; however, if athletes are ineffective in coping, have a lack of resources, or are unable to analyze the transitional situation, then a possible crisis transition awaits (Stambulova, 2000).

As research gathered momentum, so did the understanding that transitions should be distinguished by their degree of predictability. By considering normative transitions, which are generally predictable and anticipated (e.g., athletic retirement), and non-normative transitions, which are generally unpredicted, unanticipated, and involuntary in nature (e.g., an injury), researchers started to identify transitions occurring during, rather than at the end of, the athletic career. These normative 'within-career' transitions, such as the junior to senior transition, initiating a dual 'study and elite sport' career, a first-time Olympic participation (Wylleman, Lavallee, & Theeboom, 2004; Wylleman, Verdet, Lévêque, De Knop, & Huts, 2004) also enabled researchers to delineate specific normative career stages. This is reflected, for example, in Salmela's (1994) three-stage model of initiation, development, perfection, and in Stambulova's (1994) analytical athletic career model, which identifies five normative stages: preparatory stage, start of specialization, intensive training in the chosen sport, culmination stage, final stage and career end.

In line with this normative approach, and building upon research with talented athletes, elite student athletes, and former elite athletes (e.g., Wylleman, 2000; Wylleman, De Knop, Verdet, & Cecić Erpič, 2007; Wylleman, Verdet, et al., 2004), Wylleman introduced the Developmental Model of Transitions faced by Athletes (Wylleman & Lavallee, 2004). This model was found to take a significant step forward in understanding the importance of transitions to athletes (Alfermann & Stambulova, 2007) as it described not only normative transitions at athletic level, but also included normative transitions occurring in other aspects of athletes' development, such as the psychological. In this way, it combined a developmental (i.e., initiation into post-athletic career) with a holistic perspective (i.e., athlete's multilevel development) reflecting domain-specific normative transitions in athletes' psychological, psychosocial, and academic and vocational development. During the past years, the model was further developed, leading up to the current HAC model (Wylleman et al., 2013a) (see Figure 1.1).

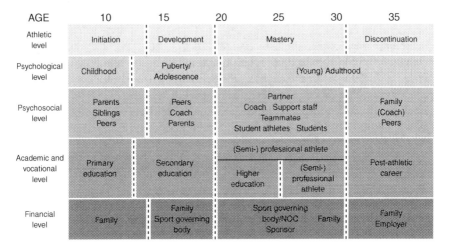

AGE	10	15	20	25	30	35
Athletic level	Initiation	Development		Mastery		Discontinuation
Psychological level	Childhood	Puberty/ Adolescence		(Young) Adulthood		
Psychosocial level	Parents Siblings Peers	Peers Coach Parents		Partner Coach Support staff Teammates Student athletes Students		Family (Coach) Peers
Academic and vocational level	Primary education	Secondary education	(Semi-) professional athlete			Post-athletic career
			Higher education	(Semi-) professional athlete		
Financial level	Family	Family Sport governing body	Sport governing body/NOC Family Sponsor			Family Employer

Figure 1.1 The Holistic Athlete Career model representing transitions and stages faced
by athletes at athletic, psychological, psychosocial, academic/vocational and
financial levels (Wylleman et al., 2013a).

Note
A dotted line indicates that the age at which the transition occurs is an approximation.

The Holistic Athletic Career model

The HAC model represents the concurrent, interactive, and reciprocal nature of
the development of athletes in five domains: athletic, psychological, psychosocial, academic/vocational, financial.

The top layer represents the transitions and stages athletes face in their athletic development, namely (a) the initiation stage during which young athletes
are introduced to organized competitive sports, from about six or seven years of
age, (b) the development stage, during which young athletes are recognized as
being talented, bringing with it an intensive level of training and competitions,
from about 12 or 13 years of age, (c) the mastery stage, reflecting athletes' participation at the highest competitive level, from about 18 or 19 years of age, and
(d) the discontinuation stage, entailing elite athletes' transition out of competitive sports, from about 28 or 30 years of age. The second layer reflects the
major transitions and stages in athletes' psychological development, including
childhood, adolescence, and young adulthood. The third layer is indicative of
transitions and stages occurring in athletes' psychosocial development and
denotes those individuals who are perceived by athletes as being most significant
during that particular transition or stage, such as parents, coach, peers, life time
partner. The fourth layer represents stages and transitions at academic (primary
education/elementary school, secondary education/high school, higher education) and vocational level. For elite athletes, vocational development may also
start after secondary education, and may involve a full- or part-time occupation

in the field of professional sports. The final layer illustrates the way in which the involvement of athletes may be financially supported throughout as well as after their athletic career. With family support being significant in the beginning, and for some elite athletes also again before and during retirement, the supportive role of sport governing bodies, national Olympic Committees, and/or private sponsors is clearly present from the end of the development into the mastery stage.

By presenting the concurrent, interactive, and reciprocal nature of these normative transitions, the HAC model shows that normative transitions do not only coincide, but also influence athletes' development and success at every level. It should be noted that, while normative in nature, the specific ages at which these transitions occur can vary. Its holistic lifespan perspective allowed sport psychologists to use this model in research (e.g., Bruner, Munroe-Chandler, & Spink, 2008; Debois, Ledon, & Wylleman, 2015; Pummell, Harwood, & Lavallee, 2008; Reints, 2011; Rosier, Wylleman, De Bosscher, & Van Hoecke, 2015; Tekavc, Wylleman, & Cecić Erpič, 2015; Wylleman, Reints, & Van Aken, 2012), as well as in the provision of athlete career support, for example in Scotland, France, the Netherlands, Belgium (e.g., Bouchetal Pellegri, Leseur, & Debois, 2006; Wylleman et al., 2013a) and in the development of the *EU Guidelines on Dual Careers of Athletes* (2012).

In order to illustrate the use of a 'whole career/whole person' perspective, the next section will describe the challenges faced by athletes in a normative within-career transition that can be considered essential in talented athletes' development, namely the junior-to-senior transition. The relevance of this transition is not only due to the fact that athletes face, during a relative short period, concurrent multilevel transitional challenges, but also because, on average, only one junior elite athlete in three is actually reported to make a successful transition into the senior elite ranks (Australian Sports Commission, 2003; Bussmann & Alfermann, 1994; Vanden Auweele, De Martelaer, Rzewnicki, De Knop, & Wylleman, 2004) with novice senior athletes taking on average 2.1 years to successfully complete this transition (Australian Sports Commission, 2003).

The junior-to-senior transition

At an athletic level, athletes face two specific challenges. First, as a final year junior, they will have a final opportunity to perform to their best level within their own age-category. This may lead to increased – perhaps self-imposed – performance expectations, which may entail increased frustration, anxiety, stress, and even burnout (e.g., Bruner et al., 2008; Pummell et al., 2008; Rosier et al., 2015; Schinke, 2014), as well as physical overload, overtraining, or athletic injury (Australian Sports Commission, 2003; Lorenzo, Borrás, Sánchez, Jiménez, & Sampedro, 2009; MacNamara & Collins, 2010; Orchard & Seward, 2002). Second, as a first year senior, athletes will face more mature and experienced senior athletes as teammates and as rivals and higher frequencies and standards of training and competition (Bruner et al., 2008; Lorenzo et al., 2009;

Pummell et al., 2008). Going from being one of the best as a junior to achieving lower levels of achievement as first year senior athletes (Bussmann & Alfermann, 1994) may have a strong impact on athletes' self-image and athletic identity (Brewer, Van Raalte, & Petitpas, 2000). The need for novice senior athletes to invest more time in their athletic involvement at senior level will also impact their development at other levels, such as social relationships or academic endeavors, possibly reducing athletes' feelings of enjoyment and motivation (e.g., Pummell et al., 2008; Stambulova, Franck, & Weibull, 2012). This may make them feel entrapped in rather than attracted to senior elite level (e.g., Cresswell & Eklund, 2007; Raedeke & Smith, 2001).

As athletes make the concurrent transition from adolescence into young adulthood, they face the challenge to develop their identity. This requires from them greater independence, responsibility and discipline (Rosier et al., 2015), as well as stronger self-regulatory and coping skills to cope with unexpected situations, higher expectations and pressures (Wylleman et al., 2013a) and the adoption of the lifestyle of an elite athlete, such as healthy food intake, recuperation, good sleeping habits, time management (e.g., Stambulova, Alfermann, Statler, & Côté, 2009).

At the psychosocial level, athletes' relations with significant others also develop or change: the involvement and expectations of coaches looking for, for example, more self-discipline and of training partners or teammates seeking high quality training may increase (Lorenzo et al., 2009). As athletes may move into a professional sport academy, private accommodation, or student housing, they will face the challenge of leaving family, friends, club and having to adapt to a new psychosocial environment with a new coach and new teammates. While parental roles and involvement may thus change (e.g., Wylleman et al., 2007), the reduction in daily parents–child interactions in combination with the maturation into young adulthood may actually improve parent–child relationships (Lefkowitz, 2005). Athletes' strong focus on, and involvement in, their elite sport career may impact negatively their friendships and lead to possible feelings of isolation (Pummell et al., 2008; Rosier et al., 2015). For these young adults, romantic relationships may become an important part of their lives (Wylleman & Lavallee, 2004) leading to an increase of support from a significant other, while at the same time possibly requiring athletes to cope with extra expectations and pressure (e.g., Stambulova et al., 2012).

Athletes will not only transit out of secondary education but many continue their dual career by combining an academic career in higher education with an elite athletic career (e.g., Wylleman, Reints, & De Knop, 2013b). The challenges at the academic level will be different from those in secondary education and could include, among others, taking more charge of their own academic career, being more self-regulated, for example by attending classes, re-scheduling exams, investing time in studying, or coping with changing social environments such as student life (e.g., De Knop, Wylleman, Van Hoecke, & Bollaert, 1999). The value attributed to an academic education in view of the risks and disadvantages of elite sport, such as a career-ending injury, or lack of financial stability, has led to increased importance being awarded to support systems providing elite athletes with the maximum possibility of developing the required competences in order to successfully start and complete a dual career (e.g., De Brandt, Wylleman, & Van Rossem, 2015; *EU Guidelines on Dual Careers of Athletes*, 2012; Stambulova & Wylleman, 2015).

Other athletes may, however, also discontinue their academic career and choose a vocational career as a professional, full-time athlete, or a dual career involving elite sport and another part-time occupation. In the first case, athletes will be faced with the transitional challenges of more and an increased focus on training sessions and competitions, which requires not only more time to recuperate, but leads – perhaps unexpectedly – to also being more available for social activities with family and friends (Rosier et al., 2015). In the latter case, athletes will need to find an occupational context which provides them with flexibilities allowing them to prioritize and plan their elite sport activities within their occupational activities such as time off from work for competitions or training camps abroad.

Finally, athletes will also face a transition at the financial level. More particularly, as not all first year senior athletes will have financial security via a contract as a semi-professional athlete, they may not be self-sufficient. In fact, many novice senior athletes will require continued financial support from significant others such as parents or partners (Reints, 2011), thus having a possible debilitating influence on elite athletes' self-perception and development into independence and self-control.

Implications for future research

While, up until now, a broader understanding of the occurrence of multi-level normative transitions has been gained, a clear need exists for researchers to focus on the occurrence of non-normative transitions. These idiosyncratic transitions, which do not occur to a set plan or schedule (Schlossberg, 1981), may include, from a holistic perspective, an athletic injury, an unexpected de-selection, an emotional breakdown, a sudden loss of a significant other, failing exams at university as an elite student athlete, or being offered a doctoral scholarship after graduation. It will be interesting to uncover in what way their generally unpredicted, unanticipated, and involuntary nature relates to the different normative transitions and thus also affect athletes' multilevel development.

As the HAC model represents a global, non-sport specific perspective on multilevel career transitions and stages, a second need for research consists of studying the sport-, gender-, organisation-, and cultural-specific characteristics that influence the transitional challenges faced by athletes. For example, as transiting from national to international level is a normative transition in all sports, its challenges may be perceived differently when occurring at different ages in early- and late-specialization sports (e.g., female gymnasts versus male rowers). In another example, researchers should also consider a gender-perspective and focus on the way female and male elite athletes face transitional challenges (e.g.,

Tekavc, Wylleman, & Cecić Erpič, 2015). Finally, researchers should also take heed of the significance of culture. As the holistic perspective is being amalgamated with approaches developed in cultural sport psychology (Stambulova & Ryba, 2014) the avenue is opened to conduct multicultural research by including, for example, culture-relevant variables.

In view of the provision of applied sport psychology services, the HAC model could be used to investigate the competences (i.e., knowledge, skills, attitude, experience) required to cope with multilevel transitional challenges. This could lead to the development of guidelines for coaches on how to educate and train their talented athletes to prepare for upcoming normative transitions, such as entering senior level, starting in higher education, or becoming a parent (e.g., De Brandt et al., 2015; Wylleman, 1999).

Finally, it is not only athletes who are confronted with career transitions and stages. Using the HAC model's developmental and holistic approach, researchers could investigate the transitional challenges faced by developing and elite coaches. In this way, a better understanding could be gained of the multilevel transitional challenges faced by young adult coaches developing into mastery level, or by former elite athletes initiating a coaching profession.

Implications for applied practice

Within the context of the developmental and holistic perspective provided by the HAC model, coaches can assist their athletes in preparing for, and coping with, transitional challenges using three different, yet complementary, approaches. In the first instance, coaches should take a knowledge-gathering approach by ensuring a good knowledge of the multilevel transitional challenges their athletes may face throughout the developmental, mastery and discontinuation career stages. Using the HAC model to gain a good overview of the occurrence of multilevel normative transitions, coaches can acquire a more in-depth knowledge by getting acquainted with research relevant to specific transitional challenges at the athletic level, such as the junior-to-senior transition (e.g., Stambulova et al., 2012), first time participation in Olympic Games (e.g., Wylleman et al., 2012), or the cultural aspects of influence on athletes' careers (e.g., Stambulova & Ryba, 2014). In order to ensure a holistic perspective, coaches should also look for – or be provided by sport psychologists with – information on (a) the developmental tasks and crises athletes will be confronted with during different life-stages (e.g., Newman & Newman, 2006), (b) the role and influence (or lack of influence) of interpersonal relationships and social networks on athletes during each of the athletic career stages (e.g., Wylleman et al., 2007), (c) the challenges created by combining an athletic career with an academic career (see Stambulova & Wylleman, 2015 for a special issue on dual careers of elite athletes), and (d) the possibility of developing a vocational career during (e.g., as member of the Armed Forces, or as a doctoral researcher) as well as after ending their athletic career (e.g., Bouchetal Pellegri et al., 2006). In order to get a better feel for the interactive and interdependent nature of multilevel transitions and stages, coaches can immerse themselves in athletes' biographies via research articles (e.g., Debois et al., 2015), books (e.g., Redgrave & Townsend, 2001; Wilkinson, 2006), or videos (e.g., Zidane, 2002).

In the second instance, coaches can take an educational approach by teaching their athletes from the end of the initiation stage transition-related competences (i.e., knowledge, skills, attitude/experiences) as part of their training (Wylleman, 2010). For example, the Life Development Interventions program (LDI; Danish, Petitpas, & Hale, 1995), which emphasizes continuous growth and development across the life span, makes an initial assessment of life events athletes may face, after which athletes are assisted in identifying those already developed, as well as new skills which will increase their ability to cope with the upcoming transitions. When coaches are prepared for, and supported by an expert, this LDI program could become part of the coaching provided to these athletes.

In another example (Wylleman, 1999; 2008), in first instance coaches should educate their athletes about future transitions, and also support them in identifying, as well as learning, those competences required at the time of the onset of a particular transition and career stage. Examples of competences delineated on the basis of the HAC model are related to time management (from age ten), coping with transitions (from age 14), media (from age 16), relationships (from age 18), financial management (from age 22), and networking (from age 26). In the second part, when athletes face actual transitional challenges, coaches are supported by sport psychologists in order to enhance athletes' competences to support their psycho-social network, to mobilize their coping resources, and to learn to buffer the impact of stressful aspects related to the transitions.

Finally, coaches can adopt an intervention approach. Acknowledging the multilevel challenges faced by transitional athletes, coaches can look towards career support services and career transition programs to support their athletes' personal growth, balance their lifestyles, and optimize post-athletic career life (Lavallee, Gorely, Lavallee, & Wylleman, 2001). These programs usually combine workshops with seminars and face-to-face counselling, and provide multidisciplinary support services to athletes with regard to their athletic involvement, developmental and lifestyle issues, and academic and vocational development. Support service provision generally includes career planning, goal setting, mentoring, and life development interventions. Target groups for career programs generally include prospective junior athletes, student athletes, elite senior athletes, and retiring/retired athletes (Stambulova et al., 2009). Provision of support services to elite athletes with regard to transitional challenges is not only growing worldwide but is actually becoming more and more an integrated part of this support provision to elite athletes (Reints & Wylleman, 2009).

As prevention may not be sufficient, some transitional challenges can result in developmental conflicts that affect athletes' mental function and lead to a psychological, interpersonal, social, or financial crisis or traumatic experience (Stambulova, 2010), thus requiring crisis-coping interventions such as counselling or therapy. While research among career assistance providers revealed that transition support is generally crisis-preventive in nature (Wylleman & Reints,

2014), experiential knowledge at Olympic level (Wylleman, 2015; Wylleman & Hendriks, 2015; Wylleman, Harwood, Elbe, Reints, & de Caluwé, 2009) also confirmed a significant need for crisis interventions. This may lead coaches to ensure interdisciplinary support, for example from health psychologists, clinical psychologists, or psychiatrists, in order to provide athletes in transition with behavioural, cognitive, and emotional interventions, or counselling and thera-peutic interventions, such as cognitive therapy, rational–emotional behaviour therapy, or cognitive restructuring, aimed not only at reducing anxiety, distress, maladaptive cognitions, and possible depression, but also at developing coping and problem solving skills, self-instructional training, and re-ordering life prior-ities (Lavallee, Sunghee, & Tod, 2010).

In conclusion

As their athletic careers can span 15 to 25 years (Sosniak, 2006; Wylleman et al., 1993), it is a given that athletes will face a series of multilevel transitions. Within an athlete-centred – coach-driven – expert-supported system, it is also clear that coaches are vital in order to optimize athletes' development and thus enable them to perform consistently at their maximum level. Coaches should therefore not only have the competences but also be able to solicit the interdisci-plinary support with which to ensure that these transitions are possible turning points at which talent may actually flourish rather than derail (Dweck, 2009).

Notes

1 Faculty of Physical Education and Physiotherapy, Vrije Universiteit Brussel, Belgium
2 Faculty of Psychology and Educational Sciences, Vrije Universiteit Brussel, Belgium

References

Alfermann, D. (2000). Causes and consequences of sport career termination. In D. Lavallee, & P. Wylleman (Eds.), *Career transitions in sport: International perspec-tives* (pp. 45–58). Morgantown, WV: Fitness International Technology.

Alfermann, D., & Gross, A. (1997). Coping with career termination: It all depends on freedom of choice. In R. Lidor, & M. Bar-Eli (Eds.), *Proceedings of the ninth world congress on sport psychology* (pp. 65–67). Netanya, Israel: Wingate Institute for Phys-ical Education and Sport.

Alfermann, D., & Stambulova, N. (2007). Career transitions and career termination. In G. Tenenbaum, & R. C. Eklund (Eds.), *Handbook of sport psychology* (3rd ed.). (pp. 712–733). New York: Wiley.

Australian Sports Commission. (2003). *How do elite athletes develop? A look through the "rear-view mirror." A preliminary report from the National Athlete Development Survey (NADS)*. Canberra, Australia: Australian Sports Commission.

Blinde, E. M., & Stratta, T. (1992). The "sport career death" of college athletes: Involun-tary and unanticipated sports exit. *Journal of Sport Behavior, 15*, 3–20.

Bouchetal Pellegri, F., Leseur, V., & Debois, N. (2006). *Carrière sportive. Projet de vie.* Paris: INSEP-Publications.

Brewer, B. W., Van Raalte, J. L., & Petitpas, A. J. (2000). Self-identity issues in sport career transitions. In D. Lavallee, & P. Wylleman (Eds.), *Career transitions in sport: International perspectives* (pp. 29–43). Morgantown, WV: Fitness International Technology.

Bruner, M. W., Munroe-Chandler, K. J., & Spink, K. S. (2008). Entry into elite sport: A preliminary investigation into the transition experiences of rookie athletes [Electronic version]. *Journal of Applied Sport Psychology, 20*(2), 236–252.

Bussmann, G., & Alfermann, D. (1994). Drop-out and the female athlete: A study with track-and-field athletes. In D. Hackfort (Ed.), *Psycho-social issues and interventions in elite sport* (pp. 89–128). Frankfurt: Lang.

Charner, I., & Schlossberg, N. K. (1986). Variations by theme: The life transitions of clerical workers. *The Vocational Guidance Quarterly, 34*(4), 212–224.

Cresswell, S. L., & Eklund, R. C. (2007). Athlete burnout: A longitudinal qualitative study. *The Sport Psychologist, 21*(1), 1–20.

Danish, S. J., Petitpas, A. J., & Hale, B. D. (1995). Psychological interventions: A life developmental model. In S. M. Murphy (Ed.), *Sport psychology interventions* (pp. 19–38). Champaign, IL: Human Kinetics.

De Brandt, K., Wylleman, P., & Van Rossem, N. (2015). The dual career of elite student-athletes: A competency profile. *During the 14th FEPSAC European Congress of Sport Psychology*. Bern, Switzerland: FEPSAC – University of Bern.

De Knop, P., Wylleman, P., Van Hoecke, J., & Bollaert, L. (1999). Sports management – A European approach to the management of the combination of academics and elite-level sport. In S. Bailey (Ed.), *Perspectives – The interdisciplinary series of physical education and sport science. Vol. 1. School sport and competition* (pp. 49–62). Oxford: Meyer & Meyer Sport.

Debois, N., Ledon, A., & Wylleman, P. (2015). A lifespan perspective on the dual career of elite male athletes. *Psychology of Sport and Exercise, 21*, 15–26.

Dweck, C. S. (2009). Foreword. In F. D. Horowitz, R. F. Subotnik, & D. J. Matthews (Eds.), *The development of giftedness and talent across the life span* (pp. xi–xiv). Washington DC: American Psychological Association.

EU guidelines on dual careers of athletes: Recommended policy actions in support of dual careers in high-performance sport. (2012). Retrieved from http://ec.europa.eu/sport/news/20130123-eu-guidelines-dualcareers_en.htm

Haerle, R. K. (1975). Career patterns and career contingencies of professional baseball players: An occupational analysis. In D. W. Ball, & J. W. Loy (Eds.), *Sport and social order* (pp. 461–519). Reading, MA: Addison-Wesley.

Lavallee, D. (2000). Theoretical perspectives on career transitions in sport. In D. Lavallee, & P. Wylleman (Eds.), *Career transitions in sport: International perspectives* (pp. 1–27). Morgantown, WV: Fitness International Technology.

Lavallee, D., Gorely, T., Lavallee, R. M., & Wylleman, P. (2001). Career development programs for athletes. In W. Patton, & M. McMahon (Eds.), *Career development programs: Preparation for life long career decision making* (pp. 125–133). Camberwell, VIC: Australian Council for Educational Research Press.

Lavallee, D., Sunghee, P., & Tod, D. (2010). Career termination. In S. J. Hanrahan, & M. B. Andersen (Eds.), *Routledge handbook of applied sport psychology. A comprehensive guide for students and practitioners* (pp. 242–249). New York: Routledge.

Lefkowitz, E. S. (2005). "Things have gotten better": Developmental changes among emerging adults after the transition to university. *Journal of Adolescent Research, 20*(1), 40–63.

Lorenzo, A., Borrás, P. J., Sánchez, J. M., Jiménez, S., & Sampedro, J. (2009). Career transition from junior to senior in basketball players. *Revista de Psicologia Del Deporte*, *18*, 309–312.

MacNamara, Á., & Collins, D. (2010). The role of psychological characteristics in managing the transition to university. *Psychology of Sport & Exercise*, *11*(5), 353–362.

Mihovilovic, M. (1968). The status of former sportsmen. *International Review of Sport Sociology*, *3*, 73–93.

Newman, B. M., & Newman, P. R. (2006). *Development through life: A psychosocial approach* (9th ed.). Belmont, CA: Thomson Wadsworth.

Orchard, J., & Seward, H. (2002). Epidemiology of injuries in the Australian Football League, seasons 1997–2000. *Sports Medicine*, *36*, 39–45.

Pummell, B., Harwood, C., & Lavallee, D. (2008). Jumping to the next level: A qualitative examination of within-career transition in adolescent event riders. *Psychology of Sport and Exercise*, *9*(4), 427–447.

Raedeke, T. D., & Smith, A. L. (2001). Development and preliminary validation of an athlete burnout measure. *Journal of Sport & Exercise Psychology*, *23*, 281–306.

Redgrave, S., & Townsend, N. (2001). *A golden age*. London: BBC Worldwide Ltd.

Reints, A. (2011). *Validation of the holistic athletic career model and the identification of variables related to athletic retirement* (Doctoral dissertation). Brussel, Belgium: Vrije Universiteit Brussel.

Reints, A., & Wylleman, P. (2009). *Career development and transitions of elite athletes.* Paper presented at the Symposium Managing elite sports: A multidisciplinary perspective on the management of elite sports in Flanders. Barcelona, Spain: Centre d'Alt Rendiment (C.A.R.)

Rosier, N., Wylleman, P., De Bosscher, V., & Van Hoecke, J. (2015). Four perceptions on the changes elite athletes experience during the junior-senior transition. *Manuscript submitted for publication.*

Salmela, J. H. (1994). Phases and transitions across sports career. In D. Hackfort (Ed.), *Psychosocial issues and interventions in elite sport* (pp. 11–28). Frankfurt: Lang.

Schinke, R. (2014). Adaptation. In R. C. Eklund, & G. Tenenbaum (Eds.), *Encyclopedia of sport and exercise psychology* (pp. 10–11). Thousand Oaks, CA: SAGE Publications.

Schlossberg, N. (1981). A model for analyzing human adaptation to transition. *The Counseling Psychologist*, *9*, 2–18.

Schlossberg, N. (1984). *Counseling adults in transition: Linking practice with theory.* New York: Springer.

Sinclair, D. A., & Orlick, T. (1993). Positive transitions from high-performance sport. *The Sport Psychologist*, *7*(2), 138–150.

Sosniak, A. (2006). Retrospective interviews in the study of expertise and expert performance. In K. A. Ericsson, N. Charness, P. J. Feltovich, & R. R. Hoffman (Eds.), *The Cambridge handbook of expertise and expert performance* (pp. 287–302). New York: Cambridge University Press.

Stambulova, N. (1994). Developmental sport career investigations in Russia: A post-perestroika analysis. *The Sport Psychologist*, *8*, 221–237.

Stambulova, N. (2000). Athletes' crises : A developmental perspective. *International Journal of Sport Psychology*, *31*, 584–601.

Stambulova, N. (2003). Symptoms of a crisis-transition: A grounded theory study. In N. Hassemen (Ed.), *SIPF yearbook 2003* (pp. 97–109). Örebro, Sweden: Örebro University Press.

Stambulova, N. (2010). Professional culture of career assistance to athletes: A look through contrasting lenses of career metaphors. In T. V. Ryba, R. J. Schinke, & G. Tenenbaum (Eds.), *Cultural turn in sport psychology* (pp. 285–314). Morgantown, WV: Fitness International Technology.

Stambulova, N., & Ryba, T. (2014). A critical review of career research and assistance through the cultural lens: Towards cultural praxis of athletes' careers. *International Review of Sport and Exercise Psychology, 7,* 1–17.

Stambulova, N., & Wylleman, P. (2015). Dual career development and transitions. *Psychology of Sport and Exercise, 21,* 1–3.

Stambulova, N., Alfermann, D., Statler, T., & Côté, J. (2009). ISSP Position Stand: Career development and transitions of athletes. *International Journal of Sport and Exercise Psychology, 7,* 395–412.

Stambulova, N., Franck, A., & Weibull, F. (2012). Assessment of the transition from junior-to-senior sports in Swedish athletes. *International Journal of Sport and Exercise Psychology, 10*(2), 79–95.

Taylor, J., & Ogilvie, B. C. (1998). Career transition among elite athletes: Is there life after sports? In J. M. Williams (Ed.), *Applied sport psychology: Personal growth to peak performance* (pp. 429–444). Mountain View, CA: Mayfield.

Tekavc, J., Wylleman, P., & Cecić Erpič, S. (2015). Perceptions of dual career development among elite level swimmers and basketball players. *Psychology of Sport and Exercise, 21,* 27–41.

Vanden Auweele, Y., De Martelaer, K., Rzewnicki, R., De Knop, P., & Wylleman, P. (2004). Parents and coaches: A help or harm? Affective outcomes for children in sport. In Y. Vanden Auweele (Ed.), *Ethics in youth sport.* Leuven, Belgium: Lannoocampus.

Webb, W. M., Nasco, S. A., Riley, S., & Headrick, B. (1998). Athlete identity and reactions to retirement from sports. *Journal of Sport Behavior, 21,* 338–362.

Wilkinson, J. (2006). *Jonny Wilkinson. My world.* London: Headline.

Wylleman, P. (1999). *A career assistance program for elite and student-athletes.* Workshop on Career Transitions, Copenhagen, Denmark: Olympic Team Denmark, December 8.

Wylleman, P. (2000). Interpersonal relationships in sport: Uncharted territory in sport psychology research. *International Journal of Sport Psychology, 31,* 1–18.

Wylleman, P. (2008). *Developmental aspects of sport psychology support.* Presentation at the International Sport Psychology Conference, Beijing, China.

Wylleman, P. (2010). *A holistic lifespan approach to the use of career transition skills with talented, elite and retired athletes.* Presentation at the 2010 Association of Applied Sport Psychology Annual Conference. Providence, RI.

Wylleman, P. (2015). *Perspectives on psychological interventions in elite and Olympic sport.* Presentation at the 50th Anniversary International Society of Sport Psychology International Seminar 'A bridge from the past to the future', Rome, Italy.

Wylleman, P., & Hendriks, M. (2015). *The organisation and provision of performance behaviour support to Dutch Olympic athletes.* Presentation at the 2015 European Congress of Psychology, Milano, Italy.

Wylleman, P., & Lavallee, D. (2004). A developmental perspective on transitions faced by athletes. In M. Weis (Ed.), *Developmental sport and exercise psychology: A lifespan perspective* (pp. 507–527). Morgantown, WV: Fitness International Technology.

Wylleman, P., & Reints, A. (2014). Career assistance programs. In R. Eklund, & G. Tenenbaum (Eds.), *Encyclopedia of sport and exercise psychology* (pp. 105–108). Los Angeles: Sage.

Wylleman, P., De Knop, P., Menkehorst, H., Theeboom, M., & Annerel, J. (1993). Van topsporter naar ex-topsporter. De noodzaak tot het optimaliseren van het beëindigen van de topsportcarrière. In K. Rijsdorp (Ed.), *Handboek voor lichamelijke opvoeding en sportbegeleiding*. Deventer: Van Loghum Slaterus.

Wylleman, P., De Knop, P., Verdet, M.-C., & Cecić Erpič, S. (2007). Parenting and career transitions of elite athletes. In S. Jowett, & D. E. Lavallee (Eds.), *Social psychology of sport* (pp. 233–248). Champaign, IL: Human Kinetics.

Wylleman, P., Harwood, C. G., Elbe, A. M., Reints, A., & de Caluwé, D. (2009). A perspective on education and professional development in applied sport psychology. *Psychology of Sport and Exercise*, *10*(4), 435–446.

Wylleman, P., Lavallee, D., & Theeboom, M. (2004). Successful athletic careers. In C. Spielberger (Ed.), *Encyclopedia of applied psychology* (Vol. 3, pp. 511–517). New York: Elsevier.

Wylleman, P., Reints, A., & De Knop, P. (2013a). A developmental and holistic perspective on athletic career development. In P. Sotiriadou, & V. De Bosscher (Eds.), *Managing high performance sport* (pp. 159–182). New York: Routledge.

Wylleman, P., Reints, A., & De Knop, P. (2013b). Athletes' careers in Belgium. A holistic perspective to understand and alleviate challenges occurring throughout the athletic and post- athletic career. In N. Stambulova, & T. Ryba (Eds.), *Athletes' careers across cultures* (pp. 31–42). New York: Routledge.

Wylleman, P., Reints, A., & Van Aken, S. (2012). Athletes' perceptions of multilevel changes related to competing at the 2008 Beijing Olympic Games. *Psychology of Sport and Exercise*, *13*(5), 687–692.

Wylleman, P., Verdet, M.-C., Lévêque, M., De Knop, P., & Huts, K. (2004). Athlètes de haut niveau, transitions scolaires et rôle des parents. *STAPS*, *64*, 71–87.

Zidane (2002). *Zinedine Zidane. The dream*. Canalsatelite/Kiosque/Studiocanal video.

2 Creating effective development environments for the adolescent athlete

Andrew Mills[1] and Matthew Pain[2]

Introduction

It has been remarked that all human accomplishment can be ascribed to "two crucial rolls of the dice over which no individual exerts any personal control. These are the accidents of birth and background. One roll of the dice determines an individual's heredity; the other, his formative environment" (Atkinson, 1978 p. 221). This quote eloquently serves to highlight the fundamentally important role that the environment plays in achieving success.

Within sport contexts, while the development and eventual success of a young athlete is considered to be influenced by a complex choreography of interrelated factors (e.g. innate, psychological, behavioural), the provision of an appropriate environment is thought to be a centrally important catalyst that enables athletes to translate their potential into excellence. Indeed, successful progression is considered to be largely contingent on the environment athletes find themselves in and, importantly, the way they interact with it (Mills, Butt, Maynard, & Harwood, 2012).

Supporting this notion, Gagné (2009) contends that exceptional natural abilities can remain solely as 'gifts' if not effectively nurtured via the developmental process into systematically developed 'talents'. Thus, while outstanding natural abilities are an indisputably essential element, successful athletes would appear to be largely 'built' not 'born'. This points towards the development environment as one of the most important and, crucially, directly controllable factors in the life of a young athlete (Martindale, Collins, & Abraham, 2007). Indeed, as Durand-Bush and Salmela (2001) note, "we cannot change our genetic make-up, but we can change our environment to make it as conducive as possible to improving performance" (p. 285).

Accordingly, the purpose of this chapter is to provide insight into an emerging area of the sport literature that explicitly focuses on the mechanisms, systems, processes, and behaviours that are considered to underpin effective development environments for young athletes. In addition to discussing several future research directions that might take the field forward, a number of applied implications will also be presented with a view to bridging the gap between research and practice.

Key terms

Before embarking on a review of the existing literature, it would seem important to first elucidate what is meant by the term 'development environment'. While it has been remarked that the development environment encompasses, "all aspects of the coaching situation" (Martindale, Collins, & Daubney, 2005, p. 354), its scope as an emerging research area extends well beyond the traditional focus on the coach–athlete dyad to accentuate the fundamental role of the holistic environment within which athletes develop. Accordingly, Henriksen, Stambulova, and Roessler (2010a) have conceptualised the development environment as being a dynamic interrelated system comprising the athletes' immediate surroundings at a micro-level (e.g. sports club, familial); the interrelations between these surroundings; and the larger context at a macro-level in which these surroundings are embedded (e.g. community, socio-cultural). While a variety of environmental factors that reside at a macro-level (e.g. political, socio-cultural, geographical) have the potential to exert an influence on the athletic environment, the thrust of this chapter will focus on the key features associated with effective development environments at a micro-level (i.e. organisational, familial) including, importantly, the interrelationships and dynamics both within and between these contexts.

Review of the literature

Traditionally, the lens of sport psychology research has largely been focused on the development of the individual athlete with comparatively less attention being placed on the broader environment in which they are nurtured. As a result, while contemporary research has generated a great deal of insight into the characteristics of those who achieve success in sport (e.g. Baker & Horton, 2004; Gould, Dieffenbach, & Moffett, 2002; MacNamara, Button, & Collins, 2010a, 2010b; Williams & Krane, 2001), considerably less is known about the broader higher-order goals and systems of the actual development environments that largely engender these characteristics and ultimately drive the talent development process (Martindale et al., 2007). To this end, sport and performance researchers are beginning to shift their attention from the individual to the holistic environments that are created to nurture the next generation of elite performers. Accordingly, the aim of this section is to provide an overview of this evolving line of talent development research.

The importance placed on studying the broader athletic context is becoming increasingly apparent in the sport literature. Examples of contemporary investigations that have focused on the wider sport environment include examinations of organisational stress (e.g. Fletcher & Wagstaff, 2009; Woodman & Hardy, 2001), and the impact of the environment on performance (e.g. Douglas & Carless, 2006; Gould, Greenleaf, Chung, & Guinan, 2002; Pain & Harwood, 2007, 2008). Although under-represented at present, research that has focused specifically on the factors that underpin effective athletic development environments is also slowly beginning to emerge. In one of the preliminary investigations in this area, Martindale et al. (2005) conducted a review of the extant talent development literature to identify factors that were considered pertinent to the creation of effective development environments. The key features that emerged were subsequently coalesced into a framework comprising five key themes. These were: (a) long-term aims and methods; (b) wide ranging coherent messages and support; (c) emphasis on appropriate development rather than early selection; (d) individualised and on-going development; and (e) integrated, holistic and systematic development.

With these key themes forming the impetus, Martindale et al. (2007) subsequently examined 16 elite UK coaches' perceptions of the goals, systems, and strategies required to implement effective development environments across a wide range of sports. Strategies that emerged included: long-term development versus early success, setting clear expectations and goals, having individualised programmes, role modelling and peer mentoring, athlete responsibility and autonomy, informal coach–athlete interactions, and a whole-person development focus. Taken together, the methods identified offered support for the five key themes outlined in Martindale et al.'s (2005) original framework and, in doing so, generated some much needed sport-generic information regarding the broader composition of effective development environments for athletes at all levels of the participation spectrum. Based on this research, Martindale and colleagues (2010) subsequently developed the Talent Development Environment Questionnaire (TDEQ) as a multidimensional self-report scale that assesses developing athletes' environmental experiences. Recently revised into the TDEQ-5 in an effort to make its psychometric properties more robust (see Li, Wang, Pyun, & Martindale, 2015), the questionnaire aims to better understand the five factors that Martindale and colleagues consider central to an effective athletic development environment.

In a parallel line of research, Pain and Harwood (2007) examined the environment around the England youth football teams. Taking a qualitative approach, the first study revealed eight overall dimensions of the environment: social, tactical, psychological, physical, planning and organisation, development and performance philosophy, the physical environment, and coaching interactions. The main positives centred on developing strong relationships and team cohesion, with the majority of negatives captured by over coaching, player boredom, limited player free time, player anxiety and fatigue. Using a conceptually grounded questionnaire developed from these themes, Pain and Harwood (2008) again revealed that team and social factors were perceived as critical to the overall success of the environment. Team leadership and strong team cohesion were identified by coaches and players as especially important. The main negatives common to both groups were player boredom and a lack of autonomy and ownership, with limited free time.

An ecological systems approach to understanding athletic development environments has also emerged in the sport literature. Developed by Henriksen et al. (2010a) and theoretically underpinned by the work of Bronfenbrenner

(1999), this ecologically grounded approach views talent development as a process of systematic and successive change arising from dynamic interrelationships between the developing athlete and the contexts in which they engage. To this end, Henriksen et al.'s (2010a) approach extends beyond the conventional focus on the athlete by also placing emphasis on the whole environment that young athletes develop within.

Specifically, this approach is characterised by two models known as the Athlete Talent Development Environment (ATDE) model and the Environment Success Factors (ESF) model. The ATDE model is essentially a framework for describing a particular athletic environment and for clarifying the roles and functions of the different components and relations within the environment. In this model, the athletes' environment is viewed holistically, consisting of micro (e.g. sports club, family environment) and macro levels (e.g. society), athletic and non-athletic domains, related cultural contexts and a time frame.

Equally, the ESF model proposes a set of factors, such as preconditions (e.g. material, financial), the process (e.g. practices, competitions), the organisational culture (e.g. core values, basic assumptions), and the individual/team development and achievements. For Henriksen et al. (2010a), it is the interaction of these ESFs that create the ATDE's effectiveness in nurturing athletes to the elite senior level in their respective sports. Thus, the two models complement each other in such a way that the ATDE provides a framework to describe the environment and the ESF helps to summarise the factors influencing the environments' effectiveness.

To develop the holistic ecological approach to examining athletic environments, Henriksen et al. (2010a, 2010b, 2011) have investigated ATDEs in three distinct sports – sailing, track and field, and kayaking – across different Scandinavian countries, each with a history of successfully producing elite-level senior athletes from their junior ranks. Taking the form of case studies, data collected to examine the respective sports clubs' environments was generated from multiple perspectives (e.g. in-depth interviews with administrators, coaches, and athletes) and from multiple situations (observation of training, competitions and meetings). Based on these data, empirical versions of the working models were created for each of the athletic environments that captured the unique features of each sports club. While the composition of factors characterising each athletic environment's success were largely idiosyncratic, cross-analysis also revealed a number of common features that the environments shared. These included: importance of role models; development of psychosocial competencies and life skills; a strong and cohesive group culture; and the environment's embeddedness in the wider cultural context (e.g. local community).

Based on the ecological approach and with the aim of positively shaping the development environment, Larsen, Henriksen, Alferman, and Christensen (2014) implemented an ecological-inspired intervention programme within a professional Danish football academy. Comprising four key systematic steps (assessment, feedback of objectives, delivery, evaluation), the programme was geared towards (i) reinforcing the culture of psychosocial development in everyday practice,

(ii) providing the requisite skills to be successful at the professional level such as overcoming adversity and (iii) establishing stronger relationships between youth and professional departments. The intervention programme was deemed a success because it allowed the youth players the opportunity to exchange experiences with the professional players and coaches which, in turn, created a stronger sense of clarity regarding the demands and expectations inherent in the development environment when attempting to progress to the professional level.

In another line of inquiry, Mills, Butt, Maynard, and Harwood (2014a) have examined the development environments of professional football academies in England. Specifically, highly successful elite coaches from a range of professional English football clubs were interviewed about the strategies and mechanisms they deployed to create effective development environments for adolescent players. The findings resulted in a conceptual framework (see Figure 2.1) that

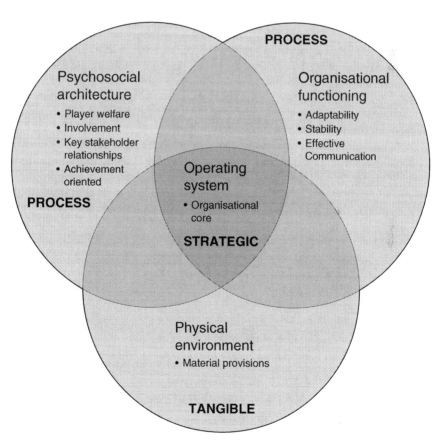

Figure 2.1 Towards an understanding of optimal development environments within elite English football academies: a conceptual framework of the interrelationships between key factors (Mills, Butt, Maynard, & Harwood, 2014a).

explained the dynamic interrelationships between the key factors at the organisational level of the club/academy. As displayed in this framework, it is suggested that optimal development environments are driven by the favourable interaction of four key strategic and process-oriented domains. These are: operating system (strategic); psychosocial architecture (process); organisational functioning (process); and physical environment (tangible).

In this model, at the heart of the development environment lies the operating system. Fundamentally, this represents the club's organisational core and relates to the mechanisms that collectively provide the strategic foundation for an effective development environment (e.g. philosophy, vision, values). With the organisational core acting as the catalyst, the psychosocial architecture domain comprises the processes that ultimately foster a supportive, engaged, and motivational developmental climate. In this regard, it largely represents both the psychological and social environments that are constructed within the club. Essentially, a strong psychosocial architecture is built through positive and empowering interpersonal relationships between all key stakeholders involved in the development process (i.e. player, coach, parent). Examples of sub-components and strategies within this key domain include player welfare (e.g. understanding the player's world-view), key stakeholder relationships (e.g. building trust with parents), involvement (e.g. encouraging players' ideas/feedback), and being achievement oriented (e.g. establishing an explicit pathway to the senior level).

Within this conceptual framework, the organisational functioning domain relates to the specific processes and behaviours that underpin the smooth daily operation of the club. Essentially, this process-oriented component is considered to act as a conduit between strategy and performance outcome. More precisely, via a favourable interaction with a coherent operating system and strong psychosocial architecture, this domain helps bring the philosophy, values, and vision to life, thereby facilitating the optimal functioning of the development environment. Lastly, the fourth key domain (i.e. physical environment) represents the tangible, material aspects of the development environment, such as training facilities and accommodation, and demonstrates the interlinking contextual role that these material provisions play in enabling young players to develop optimally.

By assembling these key factors into a conceptual model, this research advanced our understanding of development environments by determining how these factors interact to create the optimal conditions for development. Importantly, when viewing the framework as a whole, the findings point towards the importance of having a strong, dynamic, organisational culture as a keystone for the creation of an effective development environment.

Following on from this coach-focused research, Mills, Butt, Maynard, and Harwood (2014b) sought to examine the developing athletes' perspective of the environment. Specifically, 50 elite youth football academy players (15–18 years) from a range of English Premier League and Championship clubs were surveyed to capture perceptions about the quality of the development environment. In this study, the major strengths of the environment as seen through the eyes of the players largely related to coaching practice (e.g. technical instruction, training plans). Additional strengths related to a focus on improvement rather than winning, the promotion of self-responsibility, accessibility to sport science support, and the availability of coaches and support staff, all of which are considered key features of effective development environments (Martindale et al., 2007).

However, while it was found that the development environments of elite English academies were generally viewed favourably in areas related to coaching, organisation, and sport-related support, it was revealed that they were viewed less favourably in areas related to player welfare (e.g. understanding the athlete as a person), links to the senior level (e.g. opportunities to train with senior team), and key stakeholder relationships (e.g. discussing development with parents).

This latter finding reiterates the importance of creating positive working relationships with parents as a key feature of an effective development environment. Indeed, it is well documented that parents play a key role in transforming a developing athlete's potential into achievement (see Côté, 1999; Côté & Fraser-Thomas, 2007; Côté & Hay, 2002; Durand-Bush & Salmela, 2002; Gould et al., 2002; Wolfenden & Holt, 2005). At the most utilitarian level, parents provide two vital resources: money and time. From financial support for coaching and equipment to driving to practice, while continually adapting their routines to further their child's sport development, tangible support is undoubtedly a central feature of the parental role. For example, in a study examining talent development in elite junior tennis, Wolfenden and Holt (2005) found that parents played a vital role in an athlete's success in terms of the tangible support they provided and their readiness to make sacrifices for their child.

Aside from tangible support, a number of important values, attitudes, and characteristics associated with achievement are also considered to be engendered within the familial setting. For example, parents of committed individuals across a range of domains have been found to espouse constructive values related to the importance of hard work, success, and persistence (Csikszentmihalyi, Rathunde, & Whalen, 1993). Parents, whether consciously or unconsciously, have also been shown to help their child discover their natural abilities and aspire to the highest levels of achievement (Bloom, 1985; Côté, 1999). Research has also highlighted how parents play an instrumental role in bolstering a developing athlete's psychological strengths. For example, in their study of successful US Olympians, Gould et al. (2002) found that parents helped promote an optimistic belief (i.e. a 'can do' attitude) in their child's ability to succeed and also instilled adaptive characteristics via modelling values such as hard work and discipline.

While parental behaviours clearly have the potential to positively shape a young athlete's development, parents can, at times, also have a detrimental influence on youth sport experiences (see Côté & Fraser-Thomas, 2007; Fraser-Thomas & Côté, 2006). For example, research (e.g. Baker & Robertson-Wilson, 2003; Wiersma, 2000) has linked parents' criticisms and overly high expectations to burnout in young athletes. Furthermore, in their study of talent development within elite tennis, Wolfenden and Holt (2005) revealed that parents who get over-involved can, at times, place undue pressure on the child to achieve, thus interfering with their subsequent participation. Similarly, in a study identifying coaches' perceptions of the factors considered to influence the development of elite adolescent football players, Mills et al. (2012) found that parents were, on occasion, considered to exert a negative influence on development through a variety of unhelpful behaviours (e.g. conflicting coaching advice, pressure to succeed).

As a key stakeholder in the development process, the parents' perspective of the development environment has also started to receive attention. For example, Harwood, Drew, and Knight (2010) have studied the perceived stressors of youth football academy parents during their child's development. In this investigation, parents identified academy processes and quality of communication (e.g. limited information, feedback, and communication from coaches) as key stressors. Irrespective of the directional influence (i.e. positive or negative), it is evident that the familial context with particular emphasis on the role of parents is clearly an instrumental feature within the development environment.

Alongside parents, athletes' peers are another key social agent that appear to play an important role within the development environment. For example, Wylleman, Alfermann, and Lavallee (2004) suggest that peer relationships play a key function in an athlete's psychosocial development during adolescence. Moreover, in a study that investigated how coaches, parents, and peers might influence motivation, Keegan, Spray, Harwood, and Lavallee (2010) revealed that developing athletes perceived a multitude of motivationally relevant social cues from their peers. Of particular interest in this study was the differential nature of the influence that stemmed from peers. More precisely, it was found that while coaches' and parents' influences were related to their specific roles (e.g. instruction/assessment for coaches, support-and-facilitation for parents), peers were found to influence motivation through competitive behaviours, collaborative behaviours, evaluative communications, and via their social relationships. These findings provide a useful insight into the ways that peers can influence the psychosocial architecture that is constructed within the athletic development environment.

Collectively, the research reviewed herein has generated some valuable information about the factors considered to underpin effective development environments for adolescent athletes. While these studies have unearthed insights that have enhanced our understanding, our knowledge is far from complete within this emerging research area. Accordingly, the aim of the next section is to elucidate a number of potentially fruitful research avenues that might add to the existing knowledge base.

Implications for future research

A key implication of the extant research in this area points towards the need for sports clubs and organisations to promote an integrated approach to talent development that optimises the important role of each key stakeholder in the development process. In this regard, while research has sought to reveal coaches' and athletes' views of the development environment, additional investigations aimed at capturing parental perceptions across a range of sports and participation levels would help to build a clearer picture. Indeed, although the parental viewpoint has started to receive some attention (e.g. Harwood et al., 2010), research specifically geared toward identifying the positive and negative aspects associated with the parental experience during the developmental journey would certainly represent a worthy addition to the literature base. Along similar lines, given the delineated role that peers appear to play within the developmental process (Keegan et al., 2010, Wylemann et al., 2004), additional investigations that attempt to further elucidate the potentially unique positive and negative influences that peers exert on the athletic development environment would offer an equally fruitful line of future enquiry.

The value of continuing to examine the efficacy of athletic development environments based on the holistic ecological perspective would also appear to hold promise. Indeed, this research suggests that, while similarities between development environments can exist at their core (e.g. philosophy, espoused values), each sports club and/or organisation is likely to exhibit a variety of idiosyncratic features that are largely context specific in nature. To this end, further ecologically grounded investigations geared toward determining the features that underpin development environments across sports and participation levels would further examine the veracity of this approach. Certainly, and as suggested by the authors (see Henriksen et al., 2010a), additional investigations of athletic development environments in other countries (e.g. outside Scandinavia), across different sports, and of less successful environments would all offer potential to further advance the framework.

Another important area for future research is to provide guidelines for the environments that should be created to nurture adolescents through each stage of athletic development. While research (e.g. Mills et al., 2012, 2014a, 2014b) has begun to focus on the environments that are created for adolescent athletes at key stages along the developmental pathway, in general scant information exists about the environments that are established to support adolescent athletes at different temporal points along the developmental journey. Based on Côté's (1999) framework of sport development, the key athletic stages during adolescence are known as the specialising years (13–15 years) and the investment years (>15 years). Essentially, the specialising years are where young athletes select one or two sports and concentrate their efforts with more structured practice. Conversely, the investment years are personified by the dedicated pursuit of elite level performance involving a substantial investment (hence the term) in time, effort, and practice whereby training and competition become the major foci of the athlete's life. Elite athletes have frequently described this latter transition as the most difficult stage they encountered (Stambulova, Alfermann, Statler, & Côté, 2009). Despite this, little is known about the environments that are created to support adolescent athletes during these periods. Given the suggestion that athletes' needs vary at different stages in development and, as a result, require different coaching environments as they progress (Côté & Hay, 2002); the

scarcity of stage-specific investigations represents a gap in the existing knowledge base that warrants attention.

Another potentially fruitful avenue for future research relates to the importance of creating a strong organisational culture within athletic development
environments (e.g. Henriksen et al., 2010; Mills et al., 2014a). Cruickshank and
Collins (2012, p. 340) define culture as "a dynamic process characterised by the
shared values, beliefs, expectations and practices across the members and gener-
ations of a defined group". Fundamentally, organisational culture can be viewed
as "the way we do things around here", which, in turn, is considered a determining feature in the relationship between strategy, process, and performance (Reid
& Hubbell, 2005). When reflecting on England's World Cup rugby triumph in
2003, head coach Sir Clive Woodward spoke of the importance of having a
strong, dynamic, organisational culture that fully supported their vision for
success. As Woodward stated (2005, p. 6), "without it, our systems would have
been built on a foundation of sand and wouldn't have weathered the mildest of
storms". Certainly, for Woodward, it was the off-pitch systems and processes
that were viewed as crucial in order to create the environment for success
(Woodward, 2005). However, our understanding in sport and coaching psychology about how to create and regulate high-performing cultures within elite sport
settings is presently lacking (Cruickshank & Collins, 2012).

One area related to culture change that has received considerable empirical
support in the sport literature is transformational leadership. Indeed, its value for
creating team environments conducive to success is clear (e.g. Callow, Smith,
Hardy, Arthur, & Hardy, 2009; Vallee & Bloom, 2005; Zacharatos, Barling, &
Kelloway, 2000). By empowering athletes to reach their full potential through
"personal, emotional, and inspirational exchanges" (Callow et al., 2009, p. 396)
the approach holds much promise for creating a cohesive team that is highly
motivated to maximise their potential. However, while providing a set of principles (e.g. individual consideration, intellectual stimulation) that the 'leader'
may be wise to engender in their teams and/or personnel, it is suggested that this
body of work is limited in its failure to provide extensive guidance on the
situation-specific employment, deployment, and monitoring of such behaviours
(see Cruickshank & Collins, 2012). Moreover, the focus for the transformation
is still largely orientated around team success with scant information on how it
can be used to create meaningful change to the holistic development environment. To this end, understanding more precisely the strategies and processes that
can be deployed to create and maintain strong, dynamic organisational cultures
within youth sport contexts would appear to represent an important and stimulating area of future research that would advance the field.

From a more general applied research perspective, it is also apparent that substantiated, evidence-based practice to inform the creation of effective development environments is currently lacking. Certainly, what is needed are validated
'mechanisms of change' that help to drive the development environment optimisation process with practical and actionable insights. In this regard, additional
case studies that evaluate the efficacy of interventions along the lines of Larsen

et al.'s (2014) 'within-career transition' programme would help to bridge the theory–practice gap. Similarly, it would also seem important that researchers continue to utilise empirical findings to develop reliable measurement tools geared toward evaluating the efficacy of the development environment. Indeed, as a mechanism of change it is felt that such diagnostic tools would provide sports clubs and organisations with a clear understanding of the strengths of their current development environment and, importantly, generate awareness about areas that might require optimisation.

Lastly, it is important to consider that the extant development environment research is largely drawn from sports contexts within a western culture (e.g. Scandinavia, UK). As suggested by Martindale et al. (2010), not all environmental factors may be applicable in other sporting cultures, for example Asia. To this end, cross-cultural investigations of the factors considered to drive successful athletic development environments would appear to represent another worthwhile addition to the emerging literature in this area.

Implications for applied practice

Although underrepresented in the sport literature, the body of work reviewed in this chapter offers a number of salient applied implications for creating effective development environments in which to nurture adolescent athletes. A central overarching implication of the research to date is that many of the determinants of effective development environments are both controllable and malleable (e.g. key stakeholder relationships, organisational functioning). Given that the application of research into practice is a fundamental component of coach development (Williams & Kendall, 2007), the question remains how best this information can be utilised and put into practice in real world settings. Thus, in the interests of bridging the gap between research and practice, this section aims to offer a variety of practical recommendations for those responsible for the design, implementation, and maintenance of athletic development environments.

A cross-analysis of the reviewed literature reveals a number of consistent themes that appear pertinent to the creation of effective development environments. Specifically, the need to base the sport environment on a robust organisational core (e.g. espoused values, beliefs, goals) including a clear philosophy and vision for what the sports club or organisation wants to achieve appears crucial. Equally, and offering support for mainstream coaching literature (e.g. Cronin & Allen, 2015; Miller & Kerr, 2002), the importance of promoting whole-person development that caters for adolescent athletes' holistic well-being is clear. Along these lines, the need to equip adolescent athletes with appropriate psychosocial competencies and life skills is paramount. Thus, for a truly balanced approach to athletic development, sports clubs and organisations should strive to base their practice around athlete-centred philosophies. In this way, the sport environment acts as an incubator for both athletic and personal development. When applied, this approach to athletic development is considered a powerful tool in empowering young athletes to learn and take more responsibility for their own development, which, ultimately, results in a thriving, supportive environment and greater positive outcomes (Kidman, 2005).

While advocating whole-person development is not a particularly remarkable recommendation, given it features heavily in the extant coaching literature, it would seem important to note in reference to elite development environments. Indeed, research (e.g. Mills et al., 2014a) suggests that highly competitive, pressurised, extrinsically driven development environments might engender athletic-identities and potential athletic-foreclosure in young athletes. If adolescents develop a strong athletic identity, education and the acquisition of life skills might be neglected (see Grove, Lavallee, & Gordon, 1997). Indeed, such is the strength of a young athlete's desire to 'make it' to the elite level, it is somewhat understandable why some adolescents might be predisposed to prioritising their sport education over their academic and/or general life skill education. Accordingly, from an ethical standpoint it would appear vital that sports clubs and organisations should not only be cognisant of young athletes' psychosocial and emotional needs, but also make a genuine, concerted effort to prepare them for all eventualities.

Another important applied implication centres on the need for sports clubs and organisations to actively encourage an integrated approach when working toward establishing the environmental conditions conducive for successful development. Such an approach ensures that strong links and an aligned focus exist between all key stakeholders in the developmental process. Athletes, coaches, support staff and parents all need the confidence of a stable and cohesive social system underpinned by a clear organisational core (i.e. philosophy, values, vision) that is effectively communicated to all stakeholders.

In working towards a fully integrated approach, the need to build positive working relationships with parents is a particularly salient theme. Indeed, forming positive key stakeholder relationships and empowering parents to create a sense of ownership and relatedness are considered key factors underpinning the creation of optimal development environments (Mills et al., 2014b). To this end, it would be remiss of sports clubs and organisations to gloss over the significant role that parents play in the development process, even through the investment years (>15 years) where the coach is considered to exert a greater influence (Côté, 1999).

Rather than ostracising parents as a control measure, it would seem imperative for sports clubs and organisations to invest time in attempting to harness the positive potential of parental involvement. As a means to accomplish this, it is suggested that parent forums with an educational strand geared towards optimising their influential role as a 'sport parent' might prove beneficial. Indeed, effective sport parenting is considered to require parents to develop knowledge and deploy a variety of intrapersonal, interpersonal, and organisational skills in order to support their child, manage themselves, and function effectively as part of the wider youth sport environment (see Harwood & Knight, 2015).

Using Harwood and Knight's (2015) sport parenting expertise framework as the impetus, the educational strand of the parent forums could aim to generate awareness around key aspects of the parental role such as: understanding and applying appropriate parenting styles; managing the emotional demands of competitions; fostering healthy relationships with key stakeholders; managing organisational and developmental demands associated with sport participation; and adapting their involvement to different stages of their child's athletic development. Given the suggestion that the intensive journey of an adolescent athlete is mirrored by an equally demanding journey for their parents (Harwood et al. 2010), it is envisaged that these forums could play a key function in parental development not only by helping parents acquire the knowledge and awareness to give their child the positive push they require, but also by acting as an organised round-table per se for parents to share their experiences of the development process.

A further key implication – especially for elite sport – relates to the importance of ensuring that a clearly defined pathway to progression exists for young athletes. Such pathways, in part, appear to rest upon the need for strong and cohesive links between youth and senior levels. Certainly, from a developmental perspective, opportunities for young athletes to experience the advanced standard and increased pressure of higher levels (e.g. senior adult, professional) is considered crucial for effective development (Martindale et al., 2007; Mills et al., 2012). Allied to this, the need for positive role models for young athletes is also considered an important feature of an effective development environment (Henriksen et al., 2010a; Martindale et al., 2007; Mills et al., 2014). In addition to providing opportunities for developing athletes to experience advanced playing standards, it is felt that stronger links to senior levels and exposure to positive role models could be embedded into the environment in the form of mentoring schemes. Certainly, inviting established and well-respected senior and/or professional athletes to pass down their knowledge, share their experiences of the development process, and provide insights into how they met the challenges they now face might play a crucially important function in the development of adolescent athletes.

A final consideration for practice relates to the importance of stability and adaptability, both of which are considered vital elements in an optimally functioning development environment (see Mills et al., 2014a). To this end, when attempting to make changes to the development environment, it is crucial that any positive adaptations in the short term are entrenched in the environment for sustained and meaningful change. Indeed, according to change management theory (e.g. Kotter, 1996), for noteworthy long-term culture change to occur, it is vitally important that all stakeholders authentically embrace the changes and genuinely believe in the new way of doing things. Equally, any successes arising from the adaptations to the environment should be perceptible and well communicated so that all key stakeholders are made aware. Furthermore, to maintain the vitality and sustainability of the development environment over the long term, it would seem essential that the organisational core (i.e. philosophy, values, vision) be clearly and consistently communicated to all key stakeholders, both old and new. In doing so, sports clubs and organisations can attempt to ensure that their organisational culture is a powerful and enduring source of competitive advantage by being an enabler to their performance objectives rather than a hindrance.

Concluding remarks

The aim of this chapter was to elucidate ideas and concepts that it is hoped will encourage athletic directors, heads of sport, coaches, and all those involved in youth sport to look beyond the individual athlete to consider the wider framework in which they develop. While not disregarding the fundamental importance of the coach–athlete relationship as a central catalyst in successful development, it would be remiss of sports clubs and organisations to overlook the broader development environment that athletes are nurtured within and, crucially, how it can be positively shaped to their advantage.

What is demonstrably clear – not only from the development environment research presented here but also the wider talent development literature in general – is that even the presence of outstanding natural ability combined with a highly structured programme of training (i.e. deliberate practice) is not a guarantee of success. Rather, the successful development of young athletes is influenced by an intricate choreography of dynamic environmental factors which, crucially, have the capacity to either facilitate or impede the developmental process. To this end, what it is hoped is apparent from this chapter is that young athletes will only be afforded the opportunity to fully transform their potential into achievement when provided with appropriately stimulating, engaging, and supportive environmental conditions. Certainly, when philosophies, strategies, relationships, and processes are framed together and implemented in a cohesive and precise manner, the development environment becomes a fertile ground for young athletes to acquire the requisite competencies and skills to effectively translate their 'gifts' into systematically developed 'talents' and realise their potential both athletically and personally.

Notes

1 Catalyst3, Melbourne, Australia
2 The Football Association, England

References

Atkinson, J. W. (1978). Motivational determinants of intellective performance and cumulative achievement. In J. W. Atkinson, & J. O. Raynor (Eds.), *Personality, motivation, and achievement* (pp. 221–242). New York: Wiley.
Baker, J., & Horton, S. (2004) A review of primary and secondary influences on sport expertise, *High Ability Studies, 15* (2), 211–228.
Baker, J., & Robertson-Wilson, J. (2003). On the risks of early specialization in sport. *Physical and Health Education Journal, 69*, 4–8.
Bloom, B. S. (1985). Developing talent in young people. New York: Ballantine.

Bronfenbrenner, U. (1999). Environments in developmental perspective: Theoretical and operational models. In S. L. Friedman, & T. D. Wachs (Eds.), *Measuring environment across the life span. Emerging methods and concepts* (pp. 2–28). Washington, DC: American Psychological Press.

Callow, N., Smith, M. J., Hardy, L., Arthur, C. A., & Hardy, J. (2009). Measurement of transformational leadership and its relationship with team cohesion and performance level. *Journal of Applied Sport Psychology, 21*, 395–412.

Côté, J. (1999). The influence of the family in the development of talent in sports. *The Sport Psychologist, 13*, 395–417.

Côté, J, & Fraser-Thomas, J. (2007). Youth involvement in sport. In P. R. E. Crocker (Ed.), *Introduction to sport psychology: A Canadian perspective* (pp. 266–294). Toronto: Pearson Prentice Hall.

Côté, J., & Hay, J. (2002). Children's involvement in sport: A developmental perspective. In J. M. Silva & D. Stevens (Eds.), *Psychological foundations of sport* (pp. 484–502). Boston: Merrill.

Cronin, L., & Allen, J. (2015). Developmental experiences and well-being in sport: The importance of the coaching climate. *The Sport Psychologist, 29*, 62–71.

Cruickshank, A., & Collins, D. (2012). Culture change in elite sport performance teams: Examining and advancing effectiveness in the new era. *Journal of Applied Sport Psychology, 24*, 338–355.

Csikszentmihalyi, M., Rathunde, K., & Whalen, S. (1993). Talented teenagers: The roots of success and failure. New York: Cambridge University Press.

Douglas, K., & Carless, D. (2006). *The performance environment: A study of the personal, lifestyle, and environmental factors that affect sporting performance.* London: UK Sport.

Durand-Bush, N., & Salmela, J. H. (2001). The development of talent in sport. In R. N. Singer, H. A. Hausenblas, & C. M. Janelle (Eds.), *Handbook of sport psychology* (pp. 269–289). New York: Wiley.

Durand-Bush, N. & Salmela, J. H. (2002). The development and maintenance of expert athletic performance: Perceptions of World and Olympic Champions. *Journal of Applied Sport Psychology, 14*, 154–171.

Fletcher, D., & Wagstaff, C. R. D. (2009). Organizational psychology in elite sport: Its emergence, application and future. *Psychology of Sport and Exercise, 10*, 427–434.

Fraser-Thomas, J., & Côté, J. (2006). Understanding adolescents' positive and negative developmental experiences in sport. *The Sport Psychologist, 23*, 3–23.

Gagné, F. (2009). Building gifts into talents: Detailed overview of the DMGT 2.0. In B. MacFarlane, & T. Stambaugh, (Eds.), *Leading change in gifted education: The festschrift of Dr. Joyce VanTassel-Baska.* Waco, TX: Prufrock Press.

Gould, D., Dieffenbach, K., & Moffett, A. (2002). Psychological characteristics and their development in Olympic champions. *Journal of Applied Sport Psychology, 14*, 172–204.

Gould, D., Greenleaf, C., Chung, Y. C., & Guinan, D. (2002). A survey of US Atlanta and Nagano Olympians: Variables perceived to influence performance. *Research Quarterly for Exercise and Sport, 73*, 375.

Grove, A. R., Lavallee, D., & Gordon, S. (1997). Coping with retirement from sport: The influence of athletic identity. *Journal of Applied Sport Psychology, 9*, 191–203.

Harwood, C., & Knight, C. (2015). Parenting in youth sport: A position paper on parenting expertise. *Psychology of Sport & Exercise. 15*, (1), 24–35.

Harwood, C., Drew, A., & Knight, C. (2010). Parental stressors in professional youth football academies: A qualitative investigation of specializing stage parents. *Qualitative Research in Sport & Exercise, 2*, 39–55.

Henriksen, K., Stambulova, N., & Roessler, K. K. (2010a). Successful talent development in track and field: Considering the role of environment. *Scandinavian Journal of Medicine and Science in Sports, 20* (2), 122–132.

Henriksen, K., Stambulova, N., & Roessler, K. K. (2010b). A holistic approach to athletic talent development environments: A successful sailing milieu. *Psychology of Sport and Exercise, 11*, 212–222.

Henriksen, K., Stambulova, N., & Roessler, K. K. (2011). Riding the wave of an expert: A successful talent development environment in kayaking. *The Sport Psychologist, 25*, 341–362.

Keegan, R. J., Spray, C. M., Harwood, C. G., & Lavallee, D. E. (2010). The motivational atmosphere in youth sport: coach, parent, and peer influences on motivation in specializing sport participants. *Journal of Applied Sport Psychology, 22*, 87–105.

Kidman, L. (2005). *Athlete-centred coaching: Developing inspired and inspiring people.* Christchurch, NZ: Innovative Print Communications Ltd.

Kotter, J. P. (1996). *Leading change.* Boston MA: Harvard Business School Press.

Larsen, C. H., Henriksen, K., Alfermann, D., & Christensen, M. K. (2014). Preparing footballers for the next step: An intervention program from an ecological perspective. *The Sport Psychologist, 28*, 91–102.

Li, C., Wang, C. K. J., Pyun, D. Y., & Martindale, R. J. J. (2015). Further development of the talent development environment questionnaire for sport. *Journal of Sports Sciences, 33*, 1831–1843.

MacNamara, A., Button, A., & Collins, D. (2010a). The role of psychological characteristics in facilitating the pathway to elite performance. Part one: Identifying mental skills and behaviours. *The Sport Psychologist, 24*, 52–72.

MacNamara, A., Button, A., & Collins, D. (2010b). The role of psychological characteristics in facilitating the pathway to elite performance. Part two: Examining environmental and stage-related differences in skills and behaviours. *The Sport Psychologist, 24*, 74–96.

Martindale, R. J. J., Collins, D., & Abraham, A. (2007). Effective talent development: The elite coach perspective in UK sport. *Journal of Applied Sport Psychology, 19*, 187–206.

Martindale, R. J. J., Collins, D., & Daubney, J. (2005). Talent development: A guide for practice and research within sport. *Quest, 57*, 353–375.

Martindale, R. J. J., Collins, D., Wang, J., McNeill, M., Lee, S. K., Sproule, J., & Westbury T. (2010). Development of the talent development environment questionnaire for sports. *Journal of Sport Sciences, 28*, 1209–1221.

Miller, P. S., & Kerr, G. A. (2002). Conceptualising excellence: Past, present, and future. *Journal of Applied Sport Psychology, 14*, 140–153.

Mills, A., Butt, J., Maynard, I., & Harwood, C. (2012). Identifying factors perceived to influence the development of elite football academy players in England. *Journal of Sport Sciences, 30*, 1593–1604.

Mills, A., Butt, J., Maynard, I., & Harwood, C. (2014a). Toward an understanding of optimal development environments within elite English soccer academies. *The Sport Psychologist, 28*, 137–150.

Mills, A., Butt, J., Maynard, I., & Harwood, C. (2014b). Examining the development environments of elite English football academies: The players' perspective. *International Journal of Sports Science and Coaching, 9*, 1457–1472.

Pain, M., & Harwood, C. (2007). The performance environment of the England youth soccer teams. *Journal of Sport Sciences*, *25*, 1307–1324.

Pain, M., & Harwood, C. (2008). The performance environment of the England youth soccer teams: A quantitative study. *Journal of Sport Sciences*, *26*, 1157–1169.

Reid, J., & Hubbell, V. (2005). Creating a performance culture. *Ivey Business Journal*. Retrieved September 13, 2015 from www.iveybusinessjournal.com

Stambulova, N., Alfermann, D., Statler, T., & Côté, J. (2009). Career development and transitions of athletes: The ISSP position stand. *International Journal of Sport and Exercise Psychology*, *7*, 395–412.

Vallée, C. N., & Bloom, G. A. (2005). Building a successful university sport program: Key and common elements of expert coaches. *Journal of Applied Sport Psychology*, *17*, 179–196.

Weirsma, L. D. (2000). Risks and benefits of youth sport specialization. *Pediatric Exercise Science*, *12*, 13–22.

Williams, J. M., & Krane, V. (2001). Psychological characteristics of peak performance. In J. M. Williams (Eds.), Applied sport psychology: Personal growth to peak performance (pp. 137–147). Mountain View, CA: Mayfield.

Williams, S. J., & Kendall, L. (2007). Perceptions of elite coaches and sports scientists of the research needs for elite coaching practice. *Journal of Sport Sciences*, *25*(14), 1577–1586.

Woodman, T., & Hardy, L. (2001). A case study of organizational stress in elite sport. *Journal of Applied Sport Psychology*, *13*, 207–238.

Woodward, C. (2005). *Winning!* London: Hodder & Stoughton Ltd.

Wolfenden, L. E., & Holt, N. L. (2005). Talent development in elite junior tennis: Perceptions of players, parents, and coaches. *Journal of Applied Sport Psychology*, *17*, 108–126.

Wylleman, P., Alfermann, D., & Lavallee, D. (2004). Career transitions in sport: European perspectives. *Psychology of Sport and Exercise*, *5*, 7–20.

Zacharatos, A., Barling, J., & Kelloway, E. K. (2000). Development and effects of transformational leadership in adolescents. *Leadership Quarterly*, *11*, 211–226.

3 The theory (SDT) behind effective coaching

Megan Gilchrist[1] and Clifford J. Mallett[1]

Introduction

Sport coaching is a complex social practice (Amorose & Anderson-Butcher, 2007) that is influenced by a multitude of internal and external factors. However, the complexities of this occupation are not well understood (Potrac & Jones, 2009; Potrac, Jones, Gilbourne, & Nelson, 2013). With the rise of professional/ elite sport worldwide, an increased interest has been placed on understanding why coaches coach the way they do. One theoretical lens that can help coaches, athletes, scholars, and practitioners understand coaches' behaviours is Self-Determination Theory (SDT) (Deci & Ryan, 1985, 2000; Ryan & Deci, 2000). Within this theoretical framework, Mageau and Vallerand (2003) proposed two contrasting interpersonal (coaching) styles: autonomy-supportive and controlling. While SDT research has indicated that these contrasting interpersonal styles can have very different outcomes for athletes, little is known about the complexities associated with coaching in these ways and the difficulties of translating theory to practice in elite sport.

The aim of this chapter is to present research on sports coaching from an SDT perspective and highlight some of the potential challenges and barriers coaches may experience when trying to adopt a more autonomy-supportive coaching style. First, we will overview SDT and some of the mini-theories, as well as drawing on Mageau and Vallerand's (2003) motivational model of the coach–athlete relationship. Second, we will review relevant literature and make a case for moving beyond the oft simplistic and 'recipe' approach to autonomy-supportive coaching, especially in high performance sport. Finally, we present our thoughts about potential research to build the evidence base around autonomy-supportive coaching and then discuss some applied implications for coaches.

Key terms

Motivation is considered important because the quality of an athlete's (or coach's) motivation can contribute significantly to his/her performance. One of the central theories within the study of human motivation is Self-Determination

Theory (Deci & Ryan, 1985, 2000; Ryan & Deci, 2000). SDT is an organismic dialectic macro-theory that positions humans as innately proactive beings, naturally inclined to be drawn to activities that are inherently interesting and performed in the absence of separable outcomes (Deci & Ryan, 1985; Ryan & Deci, 2000). However, this does not occur in isolation or automatically. Certain sociocontextual conditions are required to support and nurture this development (Ryan & Deci, 2002). If these supportive conditions are not present, individuals' psychological growth and development may be hampered. Thus, SDT considers both the individual and the context when explaining motivational processes and associated outcomes.

As previously stated, SDT is a macro-theory. Within SDT are five separate, but inter-related mini-theories: basic needs theory, cognitive evaluation theory, organismic integration theory, causality orientation theory, and goal content theory. As a reflection of the focus of research within sport, only three of the mini-theories (basic psychological needs theory, cognitive evaluation theory, and organismic integration theory) will be discussed in this chapter.

Basic Needs Theory (Deci & Ryan, 1985) highlights that individuals all have innate, basic psychological needs that are necessary for optimal psychological growth and well-being. In order for these psychological needs to be satisfied, certain environmental conditions are necessary (Ryan & Deci, 2002). Individuals may not consciously place themselves in situations that satisfy their psychological needs; however, according to Ryan and Deci (2002), they will gravitate towards them if possible. It is important to recognise that psychological needs are universal and, as such, individuals of all ages, genders, and cultures have the same psychological needs (Deci & Ryan, 2000; Ryan & Deci, 2002). We will revisit this point later in the chapter with regards to youth sport coaching. However, needs may be satisfied or expressed differently depending on the interplay between person and context. That is, it is possible that a particular behaviour may satisfy the psychological needs of one individual and thwart the needs of another. For example, feedback given to one athlete may be interpreted as providing positive information about how effective they are at a particular task; whereas, the same feedback to another athlete in a different context may be interpreted as a way to control their behaviour.

Individuals are motivated to seek out situations and contexts that provide them with a sense of control over their behaviour (autonomy), the ability to effectively interact with their environment (competence) and the sense of connectedness and belonging to others (relatedness). When an individual's need for autonomy, competence, and relatedness is satisfied, they are likely to experience effective psychological functioning and growth (Deci & Ryan, 2000). Research has been inconsistent when it comes to reporting the relative importance of the three basic psychological needs. According to Amorose and Anderson-Butcher (2007), the importance of individual needs may vary depending on the context and activity. While it may be the case that different needs are more prominent than others at a particular time; it is important to recognise that in order for psychological well-being and optimal growth, all three psychological needs must be satisfied.

The perception that an individual is in control of their actions (i.e. internal perceived locus of causality; deCharms, 1968) is central to the definition of autonomy; however, there is more to consider. It is also important that individuals feel they are freely engaging in an activity and that the activity/behaviour aligns with their own personal values, needs, and preferences rather than feeling forced. Deci and Ryan (1985) position these concepts of locus of causality and psychological freedom on a continuum from pawn to origin and from forced to free, respectively. For an individual to shift from 'pawn' or 'forced' to 'origin' or 'free', perceived choice is an important construct to consider. Thus, autonomy can be considered multidimensional and, as such, individuals must feel they are the origin of their behaviour, and that their actions align with their own interests, preferences, and needs.

A distinction between autonomy and independence needs to be highlighted as the two are often mistaken as interchangeable constructs (Ryan, 1993). Independent behaviour is characterised as behaviour completed without external influence (Ryan & Deci, 2002), whereas autonomous behaviour is self-governed and congruent with an individual's values, needs, and preferences. According to Ryan and Deci (2000), autonomy is not restricted to "independent" initiatives but also applies to acts reflecting wholehearted consent to external inputs or inducements (p. 1560). Thus, individuals can be autonomously independent/ dependent (e.g. an athlete who engages in independent training because they value improving as an athlete/an athlete who willingly allows their coach to make important decisions for them); or forced into independence/dependence (e.g. an athlete who engages in independent training because they are not receiving the required training from their coach/an athlete who is being coerced into relying on their coach for important decisions).

People often participate in sport voluntarily and for fun; however, external events (e.g. rewards, feedback, social factors) have the ability to undermine or support intrinsic reasons for engaging in sport; this is the basic premise of Cognitive Evaluation Theory (Deci & Ryan, 1985). Activities performed for intrinsic reasons are "those that individuals find interesting and would do in the absence of operationally separable consequences" (Deci & Ryan, 2000, p. 233). It is important to acknowledge that it is not the external event per se that impacts on an individual's intrinsic motivation, but rather how they perceive it, as informational, controlling, or neutral (Deci, Koestner, & Ryan, 1999). Feedback and rewards, for example, can communicate to an individual that they are competent; conversely, a different athlete may perceive the same feedback or reward as communicating how they should think, feel, or behave and as such interpret it as controlling (Amorose & Horn, 2001; Hollembeak & Amorose, 2005). It is an individual's perception of the external event as controlling, informational, or neutral that is central to determining its influence on basic psychological need satisfaction and, in turn, intrinsic motivation.

Engaging in behaviours that are inherently enjoyable and interesting is desirable, but not always possible (this may be the case especially in elite sport). People may, at times, have to engage in activities that they do not find intrinsically motivating. When this is the case, CET becomes less relevant when trying to explain the reasons behind these behaviours. Organismic Integration Theory (OIT) (Deci & Ryan, 1985) suggests that, when this is the case, behaviours require some form of non-intrinsic regulation in order for them to be accomplished (Vansteenkiste, Niemiec, & Soenens, 2010).

An important distinction made by OIT is that behaviour can be underpinned by an internal or external locus of causality (whether behaviours are the result of internal and/or external forces) and, as such, be self-determined (internal locus of causality) or non-self-determined (external locus of causality) (Deci & Ryan, 2000). It is more important to consider this distinction in preference to the intrinsic/extrinsic motivation differentiation, as OIT recognises there can be some forms of extrinsic motivation that have an internal locus of causality (i.e. self-determined extrinsic motivation) and therefore can be associated with some of the positive outcomes linked to intrinsic motivation (Deci & Ryan, 2000).

To illustrate the different types of motivation, Deci and Ryan (2000) proposed a continuum of motivation varying in the degree of self-determination. Anchored by intrinsic motivation and amotivation (no motivation at all), the rest of the continuum is comprised of varying forms of extrinsic motivation. Extrinsic motivation can be divided into two forms: self-determined and non-self-determined. Individuals who are engaging in an activity for an external reward, such as money or recognition (external regulation) and/or to avoid feelings of guilt or shame (introjected regulation) are said to be motivated by non-self-determined (or controlled) motivation; that is, the activity is performed for reasons external to the self. Whereas individuals who engage in an activity because it is important to them (identified regulation) and/or they see it as forming a part of their identity and that it aligns with their other values (integrated regulation) are performing a behaviour for reasons they have internalised and/or integrated into their sense of self and, thus, are motivated by self-determined extrinsic motivation. This distinction is important because self-determined and non-self-determined motivation have different outcomes for an individual. For example, non-self-determined motivation has been associated with antisocial behaviour, burnout, and exhaustion (Bartholomew, Ntoumanis, Ryan, & Thøgersen-Ntoumani, 2011; Hodge & Lonsdale, 2011; Lonsdale, Hodge, & Rose, 2009). Self-determined motivation, on the other hand, is linked with persistence, well-being, and performance (Blanchard, Amiot, Perreault, Vallerand, & Provencher, 2009; Cheon, Reeve, Lee, & Lee, 2015; Gillet, Vallerand, Amoura, & Baldes, 2010; Pelletier, Fortier, Vallerand, & Briere, 2001).

Autonomy-supportive and controlling behaviours

Mageau and Vallerand's (2003) seminal paper presents SDT in a coherent manner within the sporting context. They draw on SDT literature to propose a motivational model of the coach–athlete relationship (see Figure 3.1). Specifically, they contend that a coach's behaviour (degree of autonomy-support,

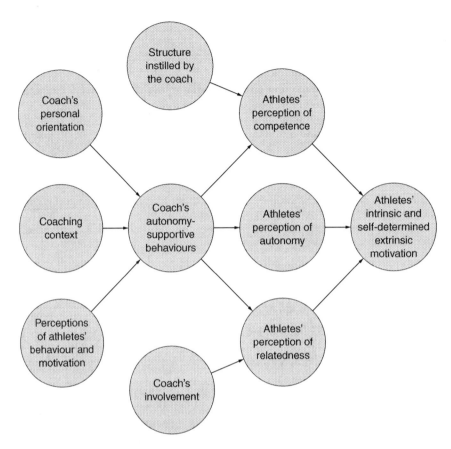

Figure 3.1 The motivational model of the coach–athlete relationship (Mageau & Vallerand, 2003).

structure, and involvement) influences an athlete's basic psychological need satisfaction and, in turn, their motivation. Their model also suggests that there are three factors that can determine the degree to which a coach is autonomy-supportive: the coach's personal orientation, the coaching context, and the coach's perceptions of an athlete's behaviour and motivation.

According to Mageau and Vallerand (2003), an autonomy-supportive interpersonal style revolves around seven strategies/behaviours that are drawn from the extant literature from both youth and adult sport: providing choice to athletes within specific limits and rules; providing a rationale for the tasks and limits that the coach sets; avoiding ego-involvement (i.e. not focusing on the comparison of athletes to each other to judge skill/ability) and controlling behaviours (e.g. overt control, criticizing and controlling statements, the use of tangible rewards); acknowledging athletes' feelings and perspectives; providing athletes with the opportunity to show initiative and complete individual work/tasks; and providing non-controlling feedback. When an athlete is part of an autonomy-supportive environment, he/she experiences psychological need satisfaction and, in turn, self-determined motivation that is associated with adaptive psychosocial outcomes (e.g. Adie, Duda, & Ntoumanis, 2008; Amorose & Anderson-Butcher, 2007).

Bartholomew, Ntoumanis, and Thøgersen-Ntoumani (2009) reviewed the literature and identified six controlling coaching behaviours: the use of tangible rewards, controlling feedback, excessive personal control, intimidation behaviours, conditional regard and the promotion of ego involvement. Controlling coaching behaviours are associated with psychological need thwarting (active frustration of needs) and, in turn, non-self-determined motivation and maladaptive outcomes (Bartholomew, Ntoumanis, Ryan, & Thøgersen-Ntoumani, 2011). For example, disordered eating, burnout (Bartholomew, Ntoumanis, Ryan, Bosch, & Thøgersen-Ntoumani, 2011) and exhaustion (Bartholomew, Ntoumanis, Ryan, & Thøgersen-Ntoumani, 2011).

The link between autonomy-supportive behaviours, psychological need satisfaction, and positive outcomes and between controlling behaviours, psychological need thwarting, and negative outcomes is well established. What is less well known is why coaches behave in autonomy-supportive/controlling ways. As previously mentioned, Mageau and Vallerand (2003) identify three factors (the coach's personal orientation and perception of the athlete's behaviours and motivation, and the coaching context) that may influence a coach's ability to be autonomy-supportive; however, research has largely focused on the outcomes for athletes, rather than the antecedents of coaching behaviour. If the goal is to improve the quality of the coach–athlete relationship, adaptive coaching behaviours should be promoted. However, changing coaching behaviours may be somewhat problematic (Occhino, Mallett, Rynne, & Carlisle, 2014). Furthermore, little is known about potential oscillations between autonomy-supportive and controlling coaching styles and the effect this might have on the athletes at particular moments. These will be explored in the next section.

Review of the literature

Research indicates autonomy-supportive interpersonal behaviours have positive consequences for people, yet the question remains: if autonomy-supportive behaviours are so beneficial, why aren't more coaches autonomy-supportive? This is not an easy question to answer, but we can draw on Reeve and colleagues' educational literature as well recent work by Mallett and colleagues for some insight. Common reasons for coaches not adopting autonomy-supportive behaviours are: they do not understand these behaviours; they feel pressured by others to coach a 'certain way'; their coaching style is built heavily on how they were coached; they do not think autonomy-supportive behaviours will be effective, especially in terms of successful performance outcomes (Cushion & Jones, 2006; Occhino et al., 2014; Reeve, 2009). These reasons/assumptions will be challenged in this section.

Research has shown unequivocally that coaches' autonomy-support and basic psychological need satisfaction has positive outcomes for athletes. Studies also show that when coaches experience psychological need satisfaction, they themselves experience positive outcomes as well as having a flow-on effect for the athletes (Allen & Shaw, 2009; Cheon et al., 2015; Stebbings, Taylor, & Spray, 2011). Therefore, while the coaches provide an environment conducive to psychological need satisfaction to ensure positive outcomes for athletes, it is also important for coaches to operate in a need supportive environment as well. For example, the behaviours of governing bodies and boards can influence the psychological need satisfaction of coaches and their subsequent motivation.

Autonomy-supportive coaching might be misunderstood as a laissez-faire approach to coaching (Occhino et al., 2014; Reeve, 2009). However, this is not the case. Laissez-faire coaching is typically characterised by a coach who provides little organisation or structure and is permissive towards the athlete (or student) (Mageau & Vallerand, 2003; Reeve, 2009). Autonomy-supportive coaching on the other hand provides structure, limits, and rules in a way that is non-controlling. For example, coaches provide athletes with a rationale for rules and limits that are in place that allows athletes to internalise them. Athletes are also provided choice within specific bounds (e.g., Mallett, 2005), which are identified by the coach (and/or athletes). Thus, while autonomy-supportive coaching may not be the dominant, coach-centred style some people are used to, it is also not a laissez-faire approach either.

Further problems may arise when coaches adopt an autonomy-supportive approach that may not 'look' like effective coaching according to relevant stakeholders (e.g., managers, athletes, other coaches, parents). One of the central reasons people use controlling behaviours is because they believe them to be accepted ways of coaching (Reeve, 2009: Occhino et al., 2014). These views of what coaching 'should look like' are heavily influenced by social and cultural values. English soccer coaches reported that using threatening behaviours when coaching professional youth academy players (Cushion & Jones, 2006), and limiting player input (Potrac, Jones, & Armour, 2002), were appropriate and accepted ways to coach. Research has also shown that coaches were hesitant to pose questions to athletes for fear that athletes would interpret questioning as coach incompetence, rather than the coach trying to develop the athletes' understanding (Cushion & Jones, 2006). Similarly, managers of elite/professional sports teams and organisations believed 'dark behaviours' (e.g., manipulation, deceit, influence over players outside of sport) were a key component of their success (Cruickshank & Collins, 2015). What these managers emphasised however, was that the key to using these 'dark behaviours' was knowing when, where, and how to use them. They also acknowledged that excessive use could be detrimental. While this research was not based on SDT, it is logical to draw comparisons between the behaviours of English soccer coaches/'dark behaviours' and controlling behaviours (and therefore, subsequent negative outcomes).

The idea of using controlling behaviours sporadically also warrants further investigation within SDT. Research has shown that autonomy-supportive and controlling behaviours are two distinct constructs, rather than opposite ends of the same continuum (Amoura et al., 2015; Barber, Bean, & Erickson, 2002; Silk, Morris, Kanaya, & Steinberg, 2003). This distinction is important because it indicates that a coach can be both autonomy-supportive and controlling. Further, if a coach is not autonomy-supportive, they are also not necessarily controlling (and vice versa). Given quantitative research (e.g. Amoura et al., 2015; Bartholomew, Ntoumanis, Ryan, Bosch, et al., 2011; Silk et al., 2003) has established the independence between the two interpersonal styles, it is necessary for research to examine why, when, and how coaches adopt certain coaching strategies and the consequences. Mageau and Vallerand (2003) suggest that when coaches are under pressure, or perceive athletes to be disengaged they tend to adopt controlling strategies. However, what particular strategies they use and how the athlete in that moment interprets these behaviours is unknown. For example, it is possible that athletes at certain times (e.g. during a match) may prefer controlling strategies. If this is the case, coaches and researchers need to understand what underlying factors encourage the use of that interpersonal style at that moment in order to understand how coaching behaviours influence athletes' motivational processes.

A perceived barrier to adopting an autonomy-supportive coaching interpersonal style is that individuals believe it is not conducive to successful athletic performance; however, this is not necessarily the case. In qualitative case studies, both Mallett (2005) and Hodge, Henry, and Smith (2014) made the case that autonomy-supportive coaching strategies were employed with the men's relay teams for the 2000 Sydney Olympics and the New Zealand All Blacks 2011 Rugby World Cup victory, respectively; and were reported as contributing to the success of these teams. Specifically, their autonomy-supportive motivational climates were characterised by treating athletes as individuals, involving athletes in the decision-making processes, and providing rationales for activities.

Recently, Cheon et al. (2015) added further weight to the use of autonomy-supportive strategies in elite sport by conducting an autonomy-supportive intervention with London 2012 Paralympic Games coaches. Results indicated that coaches who were part of the intervention delivered more medals, had greater job satisfaction and were perceived by athletes as more autonomy-supportive compared to the control group coaches. While it would be inappropriate to attribute success of these coaches entirely to an autonomy-supportive coaching style, it nevertheless provides evidence that autonomy-supportive coaching in an elite context can be beneficial for successful athletic performance.

While this body of research presents autonomy-supportive coaching in a positive light at an elite level, it fails to acknowledge issues or barriers associated with implementing these types of behaviours in an elite context. This problematic view of implementing a more autonomy-supportive coaching style was recently acknowledged by Occhino et al. (2014) in their attempt to move beyond the view of autonomy-supportive coaching as an unproblematic set of 'rules'. Behaviour change is not a straightforward task. This is particularly so in an elite context where people are likely to have a (strong) view on what coaching should look like and what the most effective way is to get the best out of athletes. These culturally entrenched views might be counterproductive to coaches, who are trying to adopt an autonomy-supportive style, and provide potential barriers to behaviour change. These coaches might be viewed as 'soft' and most likely ineffective, which may be due to the lack of understanding of what autonomy-supportive coaching 'should' look like. This education is not only necessary to inform managers and those individuals who are in positions to recruit elite coaches, but the athletes themselves. For some athletes it may be the case that the bulk of their playing career has been guided (dominated) by 'controlling' coaches. If this is the case, these athletes may need to be educated on how to operate in an autonomous manner where they are in a position to make decisions.

One way to foster adult elite athletes' awareness of autonomy-supportive coaching is to introduce it to them while they are young (i.e. in both recreational and elite youth sport contexts). The previously mentioned benefits of autonomy-supportive coaching (e.g. effort, persistence, performance, psychological well-being) are not confined to adult athletes. Research on youth sport participants has indicated that well-being among young female gymnasts ($M=13$ years old) increased from pre- to post-training based on psychological need satisfaction experienced by the gymnasts during training (Gagne, 2003). Further, perceptions of autonomy-supportive coaching amongst elite youth soccer players ($M=13.82$ years old) resulted in greater levels of subjective vitality over two seasons (Adie, Duda, & Ntoumanis, 2011). Psychological need satisfaction has also been linked with athletes showing leadership and responsibility, and with emotional regulation in youth elite soccer players ($M=14.23$ years) (Taylor & Bruner, 2012). Taylor and Bruner concluded that it is worthwhile to challenge the controlling coaching style often found in the professional football academy context as "approachable and trustworthy coaches who demonstrate concern for their players may satisfy the psychological needs of young players, thus creating a foundation for positive youth development" (p. 394).

Implementing autonomy-supportive strategies in youth sport may pose different barriers compared with coaches of elite adult athletes. Specifically, there may be a view that children and adolescents may not be able to make autonomous decisions about their sport engagement. In part, this could be the case. However, basic psychological need satisfaction is necessary for optimal psychological growth regardless of age (Deci & Ryan, 2000; Ryan & Deci, 2002). What is important for coaches of young athletes to recognise is that their autonomy-supportive behaviours should be tailored to suit the context (i.e. the age and skill level of the athletes). It would be unrealistic to expect a young athlete to design their week's training schedule or provide answers to sophisticated tactical questions posed by coaches. Further, research has also shown that too much choice can be detrimental (Iyengar & Lepper, 2000). However, providing choice within boundaries during training, listening to athletes' comments/concerns, and allowing athletes to show initiative relative to their skill and tactical levels are all possible with young athletes, and aspects of an autonomy-supportive environment.

Thus, it is not a question of whether young athletes are capable of being autonomous within a sporting environment; rather, it is whether the autonomy-supportive strategies employed by the coach are appropriate for the athlete(s) involved.

In sport (and education), both coaches and teachers perceived controlling strategies to be effective (e.g. Cushion & Jones, 2006; Reeve, 2009). While controlling strategies may elicit desired behaviours/outcomes in the short term, over time they can be detrimental to the athletes or students (e.g. Bartholomew, Ntoumanis, Ryan, & Thøgersen-Ntoumani, 2011; Pelletier et al., 2001). It is worthwhile noting that, while coaches may employ controlling strategies for a variety of reasons, they are likely to do so because coaches believe they are beneficial; that is, they are not controlling for the sake of being controlling, they are controlling because they believe it is an effective way to get the best out of people. This is in contrast to the key tenets of SDT; thus it is necessary to educate coaches and athletes of the benefits of autonomy-supportive coaching in order to promote a shift away from predominantly controlling coaching behaviours.

Where youth sport is concerned, it is also pertinent to educate parents with respect to autonomy-supportive strategies. Parents are a key socialising agent for young athletes; they provide financial (e.g. paying for equipment, lessons), logistical (e.g. transport to and from trainings/competitions), and emotional support to the athlete (e.g. Keegan, Spray, Harwood & Lavelle, 2010; Wolfenden & Holt, 2005). There is also a danger parents may be counterproductive to a young athlete's development (both within and outside of sport). We acknowledge that is it likely that parents want the best for their children; however, parents might not know the best approach to supporting their child's sporting engagement. Controlling and negative parental involvement such as trying to influence coaching decisions, shouting at players, and conditional regard (e.g. altering behaviour towards their child based on the outcome of the game/event) may all be detrimental to the child. Thus, educating parents on the benefits of autonomy-supportive coaching and what it looks like as well as positive parenting behaviours are vital to ensuring their child has a positive sporting experience.

As identified above, education is a necessary step in order to alter individuals' cognitive understanding of what autonomy-supportive strategies are, and how they can benefit athletes and coaches. However, it is likely that a disconnect remains between cognitive understanding and subsequent behaviour change. As Mageau and Vallerand (2003) identified, when under pressure, coaches may revert back to controlling strategies. If controlling strategies are implicitly learned over time (socialised), increased self-awareness of the effects of controlling behaviours and additional time may be required to allow for change.

There may be situations when athletes 'hand over' their decision making/choice to their coach. That is, an athlete may consciously decide his/her coach knows what is best for their performance and place the control with the coach (Mallett & Lara-Bercial, in press). This may appear, on some level at least, as controlling; however, if it was the athlete's decision to do this (i.e. the decision emanates from within the athlete) they are still exerting their autonomy (i.e. internal locus of causality/autonomous dependence). What may be important in these instances is that a coach provides structure and demonstrates they care about the athlete beyond how the athlete performs (other aspects of Mageau and Vallerand's 2003 model; see Figure 3.1). These other aspects may 'buffer' against potential controlling coaching behaviours and thus not have a detrimental effect on the athlete's basic psychological need satisfaction. Mallett and Lara-Bercial (in press) recently investigated a multi-layered understanding of some of the world's most successful coaches and reported that these highly successful coaches used both controlling and autonomy-supportive interpersonal styles. Successful (gold-medal winning) athletes trained by these coaches were happy for them to make the hard decisions on their behalf, because they trusted and respected them. These athletes were autonomous in their regulations because they chose when to allow coaches to make decisions on their behalf and in their best interests. While this research is not framed within SDT, it suggests that if athletes voluntarily give their coaches power over certain decisions, the outcomes are unlikely to be detrimental. If it was a case in which the coach demanded control over the athlete's decisions, it is likely that the athlete would interpret the coach's behaviour as controlling and that would subsequently lead to psychological need thwarting.

Mageau and Vallerand's (2003) model of the coach–athlete relationship presents antecedents (i.e. the coach's personal orientation, coaching context, and coaches' perceptions of athlete behaviour and motivation) and need supportive behaviours (i.e. structure, autonomy-support, and involvement) as independent dimensions. However, the complexities of the coach–athlete context suggest these relationships do not operate in isolation. That is, there is an interaction between the three types of behaviours: autonomy-support, structure, and involvement. For example, teachers who were perceived by students as uninvolved were also perceived as inconsistent (i.e. lacking structure) and coercive (i.e. controlling) (Skinner & Belmont, 1993). As well as having implications for research, there are also implications for coaches and practitioners, which will be addressed in more detail in final section of the chapter. Specifically, a coach's behaviour, while intended to influence a particular aspect of the environment, may have unexpected/unintended effects on other aspects of the psychosocial context.

Implications for future research

Research has established that autonomy-supportive coaching is associated with a host of benefits not only for the athletes, but for coaches as well. The research base is largely positivist (e.g. Adie et al., 2008; Amorose & Anderson-Butcher, 2007; Hodge & Lonsdale, 2011; Mallett & Hanrahan, 2004), with some exceptions examined within the interpretivist paradigm (e.g. Ahlberg, Mallett, & Tinning, 2007; Hodge et al., 2014; Mallett, 2005). While this provides sound data for strengthening the link between autonomy-supportive coaching and adaptive outcomes, post-positivist and phenomenological research is still needed to explore some of the complexities and issues in implementing autonomy-supportive coaching.

Furthermore, Bartholomew, Ntoumanis, and Thøgersen-Ntoumani (2009) identified six controlling strategies that coaches may use. However, it is important to acknowledge these are not the only types of controlling strategies. Cruickshank and Collins (2015) examined the 'dark behaviours' of elite sporting managers that included behaviours such as scepticism, Machiavellian behaviours, social dominance, performance-focused ruthlessness, and socio-political awareness and engineering. Naturally, there is some overlap between these behaviours and the controlling behaviours identified by Bartholomew and colleagues. However, it would be short sighted of researchers to assume there were only six types of controlling behaviours. Thus, further work is needed not only to identify what these behaviours are, but also who uses them (i.e. coaches, teammates, parents), and how they are received.

In addition, more understanding is necessary of the barriers and issues that high performance (youth and adult) coaches have when implementing autonomy-supportive behaviours. Coaches have already identified some barriers, (e.g. lack of time: Iachini, Amorose, & Anderson-Butcher, 2010); however, at an elite level these may be different depending on the context, and this context will further differ depending on the age of the athlete. For example, a coach's job in an elite context is heavily dependent on performance results. If the coach is having trouble implementing autonomy-supportive strategies, they may prematurely revert to implicitly learned controlling behaviours. It is also important to acknowledge that there is no 'right' way to be autonomy-supportive. The coach needs to consider their personality characteristics and causality orientation, their understanding of the athletes they are coaching, and the context within which they coach when deciding the most appropriate approach to coaching. It is also important to educate the wider stakeholders on the benefits of autonomy-support and what it looks like. Without this knowledge, players, managers, support staff, and parents may not be aware of the coach's approach. For example, athletes might not be accustomed to be given a choice; therefore, they need to be gradually educated (scaffolded) into how to do this within the bounds of the training program/team strategy.

Implications for applied practice

Based on the strong evidence that autonomy-supportive coaching is beneficial for all involved, a shift away from a predominantly controlling interpersonal coaching style to a more autonomy-supportive style is encouraged in order for athletes and coaches to experience psychological growth, well-being, and superior performance. Self-awareness of one's interpersonal style seems necessary before considering other styles. For example, coach educators/developers working with coaches and other key stakeholders should be aware of their own interpersonal style before advocating for an autonomy-supportive interpersonal style. Ensuring that any coach education is delivered in an autonomy-supportive manner enhances the likelihood of coaches internalising the value of this approach (internal motivation) and, in turn, adopting it as their interpersonal style. In other words, coach educators/developers who deliver in a controlling way do little to demonstrate or model what an autonomy-supportive interpersonal style might look like.

Autonomy-supportive coaching strategies are a guide, rather than a 'one size fits all'/recipe approach. Shifting a coach's style to align with autonomy-supportive strategies can involve a number of small manageable changes that can still have a positive effect on motivational processes (e.g. providing athletes with opportunities to make decisions, a meaningful rationale for an uninteresting task, clearly defined goals, or taking an interest in their lives outside of sport). Coach education in this case is about developing coaches' understanding of motivation and its associated outcomes, rather than providing a list of behaviours (Duda, 2013). As a consequence of coaches' enhanced understanding, they can apply autonomy-supportive strategies in a way that is conducive to their own personality, the context, and the athletes they are coaching. For example, autonomy-supportive strategies may need to be tailored to the age and skill level of the athletes.

As well as educating coaches about effective (i.e. autonomy-supportive) coaching, it is also necessary to challenge peoples' conceptions of what quality coaching looks like. Often coaches coach in a particular way because they think that is how they should do it, or it is how they were coached, rather than coaching in a manner that is best for the athlete(s). Challenging this culturally embedded view of quality coaching is not an easy task, but it is a necessary one to ensure that athletes are exposed to adaptive coaching styles and thus have a positive sporting experience.

Note

1 School of Human Movement and Nutrition Sciences, the University of Queensland, St Lucia, Australia

References

Adie, J. W., Duda, J. L., & Ntoumanis, N. (2008). Autonomy support, basic need satisfaction and the optimal functioning of adult male and female sport participants: A test of basic needs theory. *Motivation and Emotion, 32*(3), 189–199.

Adie, J. W., Duda, J. L., & Ntoumanis, N. (2011). Perceived coach-autonomy support, basic need satisfaction and the well- and ill-being of elite youth soccer players: A longitudinal investigation. *Psychology of Sport and Exercise, 13*, 51–59.

Ahlberg, M., Mallett, C. J., & Tinning, R. (2007). Developing autonomy supportive coaching behaviours: An action research approach to coach development. *International Journal of Coaching Science, 2*(2), 1–20.

Allen, J., & Shaw, S. (2009). Women coaches' perceptions of their sport organizations' social environment: Supporting coaches' psychological needs? *The Sport Psychologist, 23*, 346–366.

Amorose, A. J., & Anderson-Butcher, D. (2007). Autonomy-supportive coaching and self-determined motivation in high school and college athletes: A test of self-determination theory. *Psychology of Sport and Exercise, 8*, 654–670.

Amorose, A. J., & Horn, T. S. (2001). Pre- to post-season changes in the intrinsic motivation of first year college athletes: Relationships with coaching behavior and scholarship status. *Journal of Applied Sport Psychology, 13*(4), 355–373.

Amoura, C., Berjot, S., Gillet, N., Caruana, S., Cohen, J., & Finex, L. (2015). Autonomy-supportive and controlling styles of teaching: Opposite or distinct teaching styles? *Swiss Journal of Psychology, 74*(3), 141–158.

Barber, B. K., Bean, R. L., & Erickson, L. D. (2002). Expanding the study and understanding of psychological control. In B. K. Barber (Ed.), *Intrusive parenting: How psychological control affects children and adolescents* (pp. 263–289). Washington, DC: American Psychological Association.

Bartholomew, K. J., Ntoumanis, N., Ryan, R. M., Bosch, J. A., & Thøgersen-Ntoumani, C. (2011). Self-determination theory and diminished functioning: The role of interpersonal control and psychological need thwarting. *Personality and Social Psychology Bulletin, 37*(11), 1459–1473.

Bartholomew, K. J., Ntoumanis, N., Ryan, R. M., & Thøgersen-Ntoumani, C. (2011). Psychological need thwarting in the sport context: Assessing the darker side of athletic experience. *Journal of Sport & Exercise Psychology, 33*(1), 75–102.

Bartholomew, K. J., Ntoumanis, N., & Thøgersen-Ntoumani, C. (2009). A review of controlling motivational strategies from a self-determination theory perspective: Implications for sports coaches. *International Review of Sport & Exercise Psychology, 2*(2), 215–233.

Bartholomew, K. J., Ntoumanis, N., & Thøgersen-Ntoumani, C. (2010). The controlling interpersonal style in a coaching context: Development and initial validation of a psychometric scale. *Journal of Sport & Exercise Psychology, 32*(2).

Blanchard, C. M., Amiot, C. E., Perreault, S., Vallerand, R. J., & Provencher, P. (2009). Cohesiveness, coach's interpersonal style and psychological needs: Their effects on self-determination and athletes' subjective well-being. *Psychology of Sport and Exercise, 10*(5), 545–551.

Cheon, S. H., Reeve, J., Lee, J., & Lee, Y. (2015). Giving and receiving autonomy support in a high-stakes sport context: A field-based experiment during the 2012 London Paralympic Games. *Psychology of Sport and Exercise, 19*, 59–69.

Cruickshank, A., & Collins, D. (2015). Illuminating and applying "the dark side": Insights from elite team leaders. *Journal of Applied Sport Psychology, 27*(3), 249–267.

Cushion, C. J., & Jones, R. L. (2006). Power, discourse, and symbolic violence in professional youth soccer: The case of Albion Football Club. *Sociology of Sport Journal, 23*(2), 142–161.

deCharms, R. (1968). *Personal causation: The interal affective determinants of behavior.* New York: Irvington.

Deci, E. L., & Ryan, R. M. (1985). *Intrinsic motivation and self-determination in human behavior.* New York: Plenum Press.

Deci, E. L., & Ryan, R. M. (2000). The "what" and "why" of goal pursuits: Human needs and the self-determination of behavior. *Psychological Inquiry, 11*(4), 227–268.

Deci, E. L., Koestner, R., & Ryan, R. M. (1999). A meta-analytic review of experiments examining the effects of extrinsic rewards on intrinsic motivation. *Psychological Bulletin, 125*(6), 627–668.

Duda, J. L. (2013). The conceptual and empirical foundations of Empowering Coaching™: Setting the stage for the PAPA project. *International Journal of Sport and Exercise Psychology, 11*(4), 311–318.

Gagne, M. (2003). Autonomy support and need satisfaction in the motivation and well-being of gymnasts. *Journal of Applied Sport Psychology, 15*(4), 372–390.

Gillet, N., Vallerand, R. J., Amoura, S., & Baldes, B. (2010). Influence of coaches' autonomy support on athletes' motivation and sport performance: A test of the hierarchical model of intrinsic and extrinsic motivation. *Psychology of Sport & Exercise, 11*(2), 155–161.

Hodge, K., & Lonsdale, C. (2011). Prosocial and antisocial behavior in sport: The role of coaching style, autonomous vs controlled motivation, and moral disengagement. *Journal of Sport & Exercise Psychology, 33*(4), 527–547.

Hodge, K., Henry, G., & Smith, W. (2014). A case study of excellence in elite sport: Motivational climate in a world champion team. *The Sport Psychologist, 28*(1), 60–74.

Hollembeak, J., & Amorose, A. J. (2005). Perceived coaching behaviors and college athletes' intrinsic motivation: A test of self-determination theory. *Journal of Applied Sport Psychology, 17*(1), 20–36.

Iachini, A., Amorose, A., & Anderson-Butcher, D. (2010). Exploring high school coaches' implicit theories of motivation from a Self-Determination Theory perspective. *International Journal of Sports Science & Coaching, 5*(2), 291–308.

Iyengar, S. S., & Lepper, M. R. (2000). When choice is demotivating: Can one desire too much of a good thing? *Journal of Personality and Social Psychology, 79*(6), 995–1006.

Keegan, R., Spray, C., Harwood, C., & Lavallee, D. (2010). The motivational atmosphere in youth sport: Coach, parent, and peer influences on motivation in specialising sport participants. *Journal of Applied Sport Psychology, 22*(1) 870–105.

Lonsdale, C., Hodge, K., & Rose, E. (2009). Athlete burnout in elite sport: A self-determination perspective. *Journal of Sports Science, 27*(8), 785–795.

Mageau, G. A., & Vallerand, R. J. (2003). The coach–athlete relationship: A motivational model. *Journal of Sports Science, 21*(11), 883–904.

Mallett, C. J. (2005). Self-determination theory: A case study of evidence-based coaching. *The Sport Psychologist, 19*(4), 417–429.

Mallett, C. J., & Hanrahan, S. J. (2004). Elite athletes: Why does the "fire" burn so brightly? *Psychology of Sport & Exercise, 5*(2), 183–200.

Mallett, C. J., & Lara-Bercial, S. (in press). Serial winning coaches: People, vision and environment. In M. Raab, P. Wylleman, R. Seiler, A. Elbe, & A. Hatzigeorgiadis (Eds.), *Sport and exercise psychology research*. Amsterdam: Elsevier.

Occhino, J. L., Mallett, C. J., Rynne, S. B., & Carlisle, K. N. (2014). Autonomy-supportive pedagogical approach to sports coaching: Research, challenges and opportunities. *International Journal of Sports Science & Coaching, 9*(2), 401–416.

Pelletier, L. G., Fortier, M. S., Vallerand, R. J., & Briere, N. M. (2001). Associations among perceived autonomy support, forms of self-regulation, and persistence: A prospective study. *Motivation and Emotion, 25*(4), 279–306.

Potrac, P., & Jones, R. L. (2009). Micro-political workings in semi-professional football coaching. *Sociology of Sport Journal, 26,* 557–577.

Potrac, P., Jones, R. L., & Armour, K. (2002). "It's all about getting respect": The coaching behaviors of an expert English soccer coach. *Sport, Education and Society, 7*(2), 182–202.

Potrac, P., Jones, R. L., Gilbourne, D., & Nelson, L. (2013). Handshakes, BBQs, and bullets: A tale of self-interest and regret in football coaching. *Sport Coaching Review, 1*(2), 79–92.

Reeve, J. (2009). Why teachers adopt a controlling motivating style toward students and how they can become more autonomy supportive. *Educational Psychologist, 44*(3), 159–175.

Ryan, R. M. (1993). Agency and organization: Intrinsic motivation, autonomy and the self in psychological development. In J. E. Jacobs (Ed.), *Nebraska symposium on motivation: Developmental perspectives on motivation* (Vol. 40, pp. 1–56). Lincoln: University of Nebraska Press.

Ryan, R. M., & Deci, E. L. (2000). Self-determination theory and the facilitation of intrinsic motivation, social development, and well-being. *American Psychologist, 55*(1), 68–78.

Ryan, R. M., & Deci, E. L. (2002). An overview of self-determination theory. In E. L. Deci, & R. M. Ryan (Eds.), *Handbook of self-determination research* (pp. 3–33). Rochester, NY: University of Rochester.

Silk, J. S., Morris, A. S., Kanaya, T., & Steinberg, L. (2003). Psychological control and autonomy granting: Opposite ends of a continuum or distinct constructs? *Journal of Research on Adolescence, 13*(1), 113–128.

Skinner, E. A., & Belmont, M. J. (1993). Motivation in the classroom: Reciprocal effects of teacher-behavior and student engagement across the school year. *Journal of Educational Psychology, 85*(4), 571–581.

Stebbings, J., Taylor, I. M., & Spray, C. M. (2011). Antecedents of perceived coach autonomy supportive and controlling behaviors: Coach psychological need satisfaction and well-being. *Journal of Sport & Exercise Psychology, 33*(2), 255–272.

Taylor, I. M., & Bruner, M. A. (2012). The social environment and developmental experiences in elite youth soccer. *Psychology of Sport and Exercise, 13,* 390–396.

Vansteenkiste, M., Niemiec, C. P., & Soenens, B. (2010). The development of the five mini-theories of self-determination theory: An historical overivew, emerging trends, and future directions. In T. C. Urdan, & S. A. Karabenick (Eds.), *Advances in motivation and achievement – The decade ahead: Theoretical perspectives on motivation and achievement* (Vol. 16A, pp. 105–165). Bingley, West Yorkshire: Emerald Group Publishing Ltd.

Wolfenden, L. E., & Holt, N. L. (2005). Talent development in elite junior tennis: Perceptions of players, parents, and coaches. *Journal of Applied Sport Psychology, 17,* 108–126.

4 Understanding and enhancing coach–athlete relationships through the 3 + 1Cs model

Sophie X. Yang[1] and Sophia Jowett[2]

Introduction

There are so many high profile coach–athlete dyads (e.g. Toni Minichiello–Jessica Ennis Hill; Bob Bowman–Michael Phelps; Alex Ferguson–Christiano Ronaldo) that demonstrate the key role and practical significance of a good working relationship for performance accomplishment and psychological well-being. However, how much do we know about (a) the factors that make the coach–athlete relationship matter and (b) the consequences (costs and rewards or benefits) of this relationship for coaches and athletes? The aim of this chapter is to help readers develop a sound understanding of the predictive and explanatory functions of the coach–athlete relationship. More specifically, an overview of the key determinants and outcomes of the coach–athlete relationship that have emerged from the most recent empirical research will be offered. The chapter will also briefly highlight measurement issues in the operationalisation of the coach–athlete relationship. Finally, critical issues and implications surrounding research, theory and practice will be discussed.

Key terms

The history of studying coach–athlete interpersonal dynamics originally developed from a leadership approach during the 1970s and 1980s, in which theories and research primarily focused on the characteristics of the coach in terms of communicative acts or leadership behaviours towards their athletes in training and competition (e.g. Chelladurai & Saleh, 1980). However, the coach–athlete relationship is a two-way process, which needs to be considered from a dyadic perspective rather than as a single channel of communication. The past two decades have witnessed a growing number of researchers who have acknowledged the importance of investigating the unit relationship coaches and athletes develop over the course of the sporting partnership from an interpersonal relationship perspective (Jowett, 2007; Jowett & Shanmugam, in press; Wylleman, 2000). While over the past decade or so, numerous researchers acknowledged the importance of the coach–athlete relationship and proposed theoretical perspectives to study it (Jowett & Wylleman, 2006), there has been very limited concerted effort to carry out research in this area. The exception is the work conducted by Jowett and colleagues. In particular, Jowett and colleagues have conducted a significant amount of research to conceptualise or define, operationalise and measure the coach–athlete relationship. They started by conceptualising or defining the coach–athlete relationship as a social situation created by a coach and an athlete's interconnected interpersonal feelings, thoughts and behaviours (Jowett & Meek, 2000). This conceptualisation has provided the boundary conditions of the phenomenon under study and allowed progress in a number of ways in terms of assisting with operationalising and measuring coach–athlete relationships.

The conceptualisation of 3 + 1Cs model of the coach–athlete relationship

The coach–athlete relationship is defined or conceptualised as a social situation that coaches and athletes create by the ways in which feelings, thoughts and behaviours are mutually and causally interdependent (Jowett, 2005a; Jowett & Meek, 2000). Based on their definition, Jowett and Ntoumanis (2004) highlighted three psychological constructs – closeness, commitment and complementarity – that operationalise and measure the feelings, thoughts and behaviours of the coach and the athlete within a relationship.

Closeness refers to the affective aspect of the coach–athlete relationship, and it is reflected in mutual feelings of trust and appreciation, emotional caring and interpersonal liking that result from positive appraisals of coaches' and athletes' relationship experiences.

Commitment represents the cognitive aspect of the coach–athlete relationship, and is reflected in coaches' and athletes' long-term orientation towards the relationship as well as their intention or thoughts to maintain a close relationship with each other over time.

Complementarity indicates the behavioural aspect of the coach–athlete relationship, and is reflected in coaches' and athletes' levels of cooperation. There are two sets of co-operative acts of interaction: (a) corresponding behaviours highlight the degree to which both the coach and the athlete are friendly, responsive, ready (prepared or organised or eager) and comfortable in each other's presence (Jowett & Ntoumanis, 2004); and (b) reciprocal behaviours highlight the degree to which the coach and the athlete assume their unique relationship roles, on one hand being able to direct and on the other hand being able to execute (Yang & Jowett, 2013a).

While the 3Cs outline the social situation coaches and athletes create, the complex nature of this social situation and ultimately the quality of the relationship can be reflected in the degree of interdependence between the 3Cs. Co-orientation is the +1C of the coach–athlete relationship model, and captures the interdependence of the 3Cs (Jowett & Felton, 2014). Interdependence is an inherent element that connects relationship members and is also a platform from which other social psychological processes take place (Jowett & Poczwardowski,

2007). For example, a coach–athlete dyad which experiences a higher level of interdependence generally has mutual respect and trust for each other, both members have a long-term intention to maintain the relationship and the behavioural interaction in both training and competition is co-operative. In contrast, a less interdependent coach–athlete dyad will tend to have weaker emotional ties to each other, be less likely to have a long-term commitment to each other and will exhibit less cooperative behaviour in training and competition.

Jowett and colleagues (Jowett, 2007; Jowett & Clark-Carter, 2006) explained that coaches and athletes, like any people in a dyadic relationship (Laing, Phillipson, & Lee, 1966), consider at least two perceptual angles to assess the quality of their relationships: (a) direct/self-perception and (b) meta-perception. The direct perspective captures one's own perceptions about the 3Cs. For instance, an athlete's direct perception of closeness to his/her coach is, "I trust my coach" and a coach's direct perceptions of commitment to his/her athlete "I am committed to my athlete". The meta-perspective captures the degree to which one relationship member can infer the other member's closeness, commitment, and complementarity. For instance, the athlete's meta-perception of closeness for his/her coach is, "My coach trusts me", and the coach's meta-perception of commitment for his/her athlete is, "My athlete is committed to me". The combination of the coach's and the athlete's direct and meta-perceptions of the 3Cs can yield three dimensions of co-orientation (assumed similarity, actual similarity and empathic understanding) which uncover the content and quality of the coach–athlete relationship from a dyadic perspective (Jowett & Clark-Carter, 2006). In brief, *assumed similarity* reflects the degree to which a relationship member assumes similarity with the other member in terms of the 3Cs (e.g. not only I like my coach but I know my coach likes me), *actual similarity* reflects the degree to which the two relationship members are actually similar in terms of the 3Cs (e.g. both the coach and athlete report that they like one another a great deal) and *empathic understanding* reflects the degree to which a relationship member understands the other member in terms of the 3Cs (e.g. the coach understand exactly how much I like him/her).

Measurement of the 3 + 1Cs model of the coach–athlete relationships

A number of psychometric instruments have been developed and validated based on the conceptualisation of the 3 + 1Cs model. The 11-item Coach–Athlete Relationship Questionnaire (CART-Q) is the most utilised instrument to assess the quality of this relationship from a direct perspective (Jowett & Ntoumanis, 2004). More recently, Jowett (2009) validated the meta-perspective version of the CART-Q. The direct perspective of the CART-Q has been translated and validated in China (Yang & Jowett, 2010), Greece (Jowett & Ntoumanis, 2003), the Netherlands (Balduck & Jowett, 2010), Spain, America and Sweden (Yang & Jowett, 2012).

In an attempt to capture athletes' and coaches' perceptions of closeness, commitment and complementarity in a more detailed fashion, Rhind and Jowett (2010) developed and validated a 29-item Long Version of Coach–Athlete Relationship Questionnaire (Lv-CART-Q). Most recently, Yang and Jowett (2013a) have further expanded the construct of complementarity by developing the Coaches' Dominant Behavior Scale (CDB-S) and Athletes' Submissive Behavior Scale (ASB-S) to capture coaches' and athletes' reciprocal interactions during training and competition in both Chinese and British sporting contexts. This scale can be used as an individual instrument in assessing coaches' and athletes' behaviours, but can also be used in conjunction with the 11-item CART-Q. All these scales have demonstrated sound psychometric properties of validity and reliability.

Review of the literature

The antecedents of coach–athlete relationships

Due to the significant practical role that the coach–athlete relationship plays within sport, Jowett and Poczwardowski (2007) explained that this area of

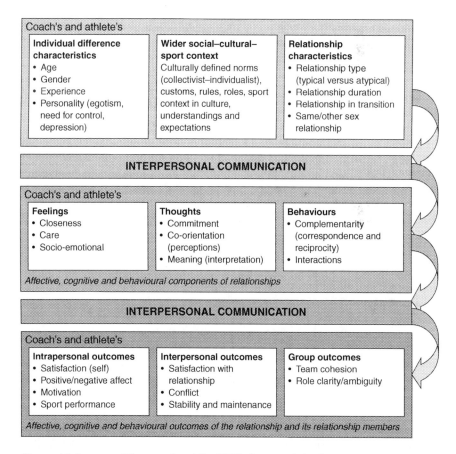

Figure 4.1 Jowett and Poczwardowski's (2007) framework for future research.

research requires a consistent body of knowledge that can be readily accessed by practitioners. Therefore, they presented a research model to map future research in the coach–athlete relationship.

In this research framework of coach–athlete relationships, individual differences (e.g. gender), the wider social context (e.g. social norms) and relationship characteristics (e.g. relationship duration) are theorised to have the potential to affect the quality of the coach–athlete relationship. In response to this proposition, empirical research has been conducted to examine the impact of coach leadership (Jowett & Chaundy, 2004), motivational climate (Olympiou, Jowett, & Duda, 2008), attachment orientations (Davis & Jowett, 2010, 2014; Davis, Jowett, & Lafreniere, 2013; Felton & Jowett, 2013a, 2013b), Big-five personality traits (Jowett, Yang, & Lorimer, 2012; Yang, Jowett, & Chan, 2014), social network (Jowett & Timson-Katchis, 2005), passion (Lafreniere, Jowett, Vallerand, & Carbonneau, 2011; Lafreniere, Jowett, Vallerand, Donahue, & Lorimer, 2008), culture (Jowett & Frost, 2007; Yang & Jowett, 2012, 2013a) and relationship type (Jowett & Meek, 2000; Jowett, Timson-Katchis, & Adams, 2007) on the content of the coach–athlete relationship, as well as the factors that mediate or moderate the relations between antecedents and coach–athlete relationships (Jowett, 2008; Jowett, Shanmugam, & Caccoulis, 2012).

Individual difference characteristics

Bowlby's Attachment Theory (1969/1982) has been used as a construct to capture coaches' and athletes' personality orientations which are responsible for regularities in the interaction patterns within the coach–athlete relational context. Research findings (Davis & Jowett, 2014; Davis et al., 2013) suggested that coaches' and athletes' attachment styles directly impact on their own perception of relationship quality. Moreover, athletes' avoidant attachment styles not only determined their own perceptions of relationship quality, but also their coaches' perceptions of relationship quality. Subsequently, Yang, Jowett and Chan's (2014) research employing the Big Five theory showed that athletes' and coaches' personality traits of extroversion, neuroticisim and conscientiousness significantly influenced their self-perceptions of relationship quality, but only athletes' personality traits of extroversion, neuroticisim and conciousentiousness were found to also influence their coaches' perception of relationship quality. The findings from both studies highlighted that coaches considered their athletes' personality orientations and traits to make judgements about the quality of their coach–athlete relationship. However, the findings also raise the question of why athletes do not consider their coaches' personalities when they make judgements about the quality of the relationship with them. This might imply that the personality of the coach may be less important in comparison to his/her ability to provide techinical and instrumental support for athletes' performance accomplishment when it comes to evaluating the quality of the relationship (Davis et al., 2013; Yang et al., 2014). Thus, what may matter most to athletes is their coaches' experience, qualification, coaching approach or style and previous record of success and failure among others. Further research is warranted to explore the relative contributions of personality factors to the quality of the coach–athlete relationship and to explore the way in which personality influences relationship quality.

Another individual difference that has been examined systematically within coach–athlete relationships is passion. Previous research adapted the dualistic model of passion (Vallerand et al., 2003) to assess the link between passion and relationship quality. The dualistic model of passion posits two distinct types of passion: harmonious and obsessive passion. Harmonious passion refers to a strong desire to engage freely in the activity (e.g. sport for the athlete and coaching for the coach) and results from an autonomous internalisation of the activity into the person's identity whilst obsessive passion refers to feeling compelled to engage in the activity and results from a controlled internalisation of the activity into one's identity (Vallerand et al., 2003). Vallerand et al. (2003) found that harmonious passion positively related to more satisfying relationships and negatively associated with interpersonal conflicts (Jowett, Lafreniere, & Vallerand, 2012; Lafreniere et al., 2008). In constrast, obsessive passion was positively related to interpersonal conflicts, but negatively associated with relationship satisfaction (Jowett, Lafreniere, et al., 2012). In further research, Lafreniere et al. (2011) found that coaches' harmonious passion positively predicted athletes' perception of relationship quality via the mediation effects of coaches' autonomy support, but coaches' controlling behaviour did not mediate the effects of obsessive passion on athletes' perception of relationship quality. In sum, the current literature supports the role of coaches' and athletes' attachment styles, personality traits and passion as determinants of the quality of coach–athlete relationships.

Wider social–cultural–sport context

Culturally defined norms, roles, rules, customs, expectations and values are the main antecedents identified this category by Jowett and Poczwardowski (2007). To date, empirical research has mainly focused on the impacts of motivational climate (Olympiou et al., 2008), culture (Yang & Jowett, 2010, 2012, 2013a) and social network characteristics (Jowett & Timson-Katchis, 2005) on the quality and function of coach–athlete relationships.

Culture is generally recognised as a social context which primarily defines and transmitts the norms, roles, rules, customs, understandings and expectations of the interpersonal relationships (Berscheid, 1995). Therefore, it is a key social-psychological factor that needs to be considered in the research of coach–athlete relationships. Over the last decade, a series of research studies has been conducted across the world, such as in Greece (Jowett & Ntoumanis, 2003; Trzaskoma-Bicserdy, Bognar, Revesz, & Geczi, 2007), Britain (Jowett & Frost, 2007), Switzerland (Philippe & Seiler, 2006), Hungary (Trzaskoma-Bicserdy et al., 2007), Cyprus (Jowett & Timson-Katchis, 2005), China (Yang & Jowett, 2010, 2013a), America, Spain, Sweden and Belgium (Balduck & Jowett, 2010; Yang & Jowett, 2012) to explore whether the current conceptualization of coach–athlete relationships can be applied effectively across different cultures. Overall, while the current cross-cultural research in coach–athlete relationships generally supports the 3Cs conceptualisation of coach–athlete relationships (Balduck & Jowett, 2010; Jowett & Ntoumanis, 2004), cultural variations have been found at a more specific level which need to be considered by researchers and practitioners.

As individual athletes and coaches are not islands, neither is the coach–athlete relationship. The relationship is surrounded by a number of individuals and other relationships creating a social network that can impact on the quality and outcomes of the coach–athlete relationship. Jowett and Timson-Katchis (2005) explored the nature of the influence that parents exert on the quality of the coach–athlete relationship through five in-depth interviews with coach–athlete–parent triads. Results indicated that athletes' parents form a "psychologically significant" network member, providing a range of information, opportunities, and extensive emotional support to their children, which significantly impacts on their childrens' relationship with their coach. This finding highlights the importance of social networks in influencing the dyadic coach–athlete relationship in youth sport. More research is warranted to explore how the entire entourage of an athlete and coach (not just the parents) influences coach–athlete relationship quality.

Motivational climate is another potential antecedent determining the quality of coach–athlete relationships. Olympiou et al. (2008) investigated the motivational significance of coach–athlete relationships with 591 team sports athletes. The findings indicated that athletes' perceptions of the task-involving features of the coaching climate were associated with higher quality coach–athlete relationships, whereas athletes' perceptions of ego-involving features linked to a relatively poor quality of coach–athlete relationship. This research implies coaches who focus on developing skills and teaching new techniques and improving individual performance are more likely to be viewed by their athletes as more respected, likeable and approachable. Hence coaches who nurture task-motivational climates also nurture high quality coach–athlete relationships.

Relationship characteristics

Every coach–athlete dyad can be categorised as either a typical or an atypical relationship. In a typical coach–athlete relationship, the relationship members (i.e. coach and athlete) only have a working partnership towards each other, whereas the relationship members in an atypical coach–athlete relationship could perform dual roles in their relationship including parent/coach, child/athlete husband/coach, wife/athlete (Jowett & Meek, 2000). The current research indicates that parents who assume the role of a coach tend to have difficulties in separating the two roles, which can lead to potential interpersonal or role conflicts in the dual role parent/coach–child/athlete relationship (Weiss & Fretwell, 2005). Another type of atypical coach–athlete relationship refers to the coach and the athlete who have a romantic relationship alongside their working or sporting partnership. Jowett and Meek (2000) examined coach–athlete relationships in married couples, and findings revealed that mutual trust, respect, appreciation and interpersonal liking between the relationship members can facilitate the formulation of co-oriented views towards training and competition. However, athletes and coaches also reported difficulties in role separation between the romantic and working partnership, causing interpersonal conflicts (e.g. misunderstanding and disagreement). Overall, research surrounding atypical coach–athlete relationships suggest that the atypical coach–athlete relationship is complex, challenging and difficult to manage. In addition, relationship duration, and same or other sex relationship are other antecedents that have been found to impact on the quality of coach–athlete relationships (Jowett, 2008; Jowett & Nezlek, 2012).

The outcomes of coach–athlete relationships

Jowett and Poczwardowski (2007) identified three categories of outcomes: intrapersonal variables, interpersonal variables, and group-outcome variables. In response to this, a substantial amount of empirical research has been conducted to unearth the consequences of the coach–athlete relationship.

In terms of intrapersonal outcomes, there is accumulated research to demonstrate the links between coach–athlete relationships and satisfaction with training and performance (Jowett, 2009; Lorimer & Jowett, 2009; Nezlek & Jowett, 2011; Rhind & Jowett, 2010; Yang et al., 2014), life satisfaction (Lorimer & Jowett, 2009), subjective well-being (Lafreniere et al., 2008), positive and negative affect (Felton & Jowett, 2013a), depression (Felton & Jowett, 2014), motivation (Adie & Jowett, 2010), self-esteem (Felton & Jowett, 2013b), physical self (Cramer & Jowett, 2010; Jowett, 2008), subjective vitality (Felton & Jowett, 2013a) and eating disorders (Shanmugam, Jowett, & Meyer, 2013).

The empirical research on interpersonal outcomes primarily focuses on interpersonal satisfaction and conflict. Findings consistently support the view that athletes' and coaches' perception of relationship satisfaction is a sound outcome of the coach–athlete relationship (Davis et al., 2013; Jowett, Lafreniere, et al., 2012; Yang & Jowett, 2013b). Research also reveals that athletes who perceive that they have a good quality relationship with their coaches are more likely to be satisfied with their coaches' treatment of them in terms of the coaches recognising and appreciating their effort and contribution (Jowett, 2009). Relationship conflict is considered as a negative outcome of coach–athlete relationships and the empirical research has shown that relationships that lack closeness, commitment and complementarity are more likely to experience conflict, disagreements and misunderstandings (Jowett, 2009; Jowett & Cockerill, 2002, 2003; Jowett, Lafreniere, et al., 2012). Interpersonal conflict in sport is an area that warrants more research especially within the context of the coach–athlete relationship.

The third category of outcome identified by Jowett and Poczwardowski (2007) is group outcomes such as perceptions of team cohesion, collective efficacy, role clarity/ambiguity, and social acceptance/popularity. This area of research is relatively limited in comparison to intrapersonal and interpersonal outcomes. However, researchers have attempted to understand the links between coach–athlete relationships and team cohesion (Jowett & Chaundy, 2004) and collective efficacy (Hampson & Jowett, 2014; Jowett, Shanmugam, et al., 2012), both fundamental components of creating a sense of togetherness in sport teams. The findings of this research support the central role of coach–athlete relationships (i.e. closenees, commitment and complementarity) within group dynamics (e.g. building social harmony, task purpose, collective behaviour, social identity) and their functions within group processes (e.g. how groups get things done, how groups influence their members, how members take their place in their groups). More research is warranted.

Guided by the research framework put forward by Jowett and Poczwardowski (2007), this section has briefly described the literature in an attempt to outline the current state of research on the coach–athlete relationship, its antecedents and consequences. This area has afforded theoretical, empirical and measurement advancements over the past decade or so; however, there is still scope for more and better research.

Implications for future research

Overall, the current research has primarily focused on correlational studies, but there is a need for more experimental (intervention-based) and longitudinal research to support the existing correlational data. In addition, the research highlights that building good quality relationships is paramount, as neither the coach nor the athlete can achieve performance success and experience a sense of satisfaction alone (Jowett, 2005b). It has recently been suggested that the quality of coach–athlete relationships may be a measure of coaching effectiveness and success (Jowett & Shanmugam, in press). Thus, when refering to coaching approaches as athlete-centred or coach-centred, the dyadic coach–athlete relationship is undermined as the emphasis is placed on either the athlete or the coach (Kidman & Davis, 2006). In this chapter, we supplied empirical evidence to demonstrate that it is the unique interrelating between the coach and the athlete that is likely to bring about positive benefits (e.g. success, satisfaction, motivation, confidence, team cohesion). With this evidence in mind, the notion of coach–athlete centred coaching or relational coaching (Jowett & Shanmugam, in press) has recently been introduced where the focus is on the unit relationship coaches and athletes develop over the course of their partnership. It is the power of relationship that can propel its members to continued sport participation and through the ups and downs of competitive sport.

While a sound theoretical foundation has been laid through the $3+1Cs$ model of the coach–athlete relationship, we propose that researchers should continue to examine the validity and application of the developed conceptualisation, employing a thoughtful selection of inquiry methods (both qualitative and quantitative, cross-sectional and longitudinal, intervention and experiment) to further expand our understanding. What is unique about the $3+1Cs$ model is that it has proposed valid psychometric measurements. Measurements have in turn allowed researchers to carry out research generating knowledge and understanding of coach–athlete relationships. There are a number of other conceptualisations in coach–athlete relationships that have been put forward over the last decade; however, they lack measurement suggestions, and without measurements empirical advancement is impossible (Jowett & Poczwardowski, 2007).

In addition, the adaption of diverse approaches from other disciplines such as social psychology, sociology, personal and social relationships is essential to the advancement of this line of inquiry. Moreover, disciplines such as sociology as well as teaching and pedagogy within sports sciences would help further develop knowledge in a manner that is well integrated and informed (Jowett & Poczwardowski, 2007; Poczwardowski, Barott, & Jowett, 2006). Jowett and Poczwardowski (2007) also argued that stronger inferences can be achieved through replicating findings. Replication is important because it can confirm or reject postulated association among theoretical variables (Pearn & Bareinboim, 2014). This review has shown that there is an impressive body of literature supporting the relationships between hypothesised antecedent and outcome variables and coach–athlete relationship quality. However, further research is needed to support and explain such relationships.

Implications for applied practice

Research conducted to date not only sheds light on the predictive and explanatory functions of the coach–athlete relationship, but also provides a greater insight into developing effective coach–athlete relationships. An effective coach–athlete relationship is underlined by stability, harmony, trustworthiness and dependability, and enables athletes and coaches to achieve performance goals and experience a great sense of psychological well-being. Interventions have already been implemented based on the 3Cs conceptualisation to help develop and maintain effective coach–athlete relationships. The COMPASS model (Rhind & Jowett, 2008) and its psychometric tool (Rhind & Jowett, 2007) offers consultants a method to support coaches and athletes *C*ommunicate effectively through being *O*pen, *M*otivating, *P*reventative, *A*ssuring, *S*upportive, as well as managing conflict and having the capacity to network with significant others efficiently (*S*ocial network includes: parents, teammates, other coaches, sport science providers). It is a model that can guide practitioners to enhance the positive effect on the quality of the coach–athlete relationship, and correspondingly, the absence of these aspects (i.e. COMPASS) was theorised to have a negative effect on relationship quality (Canary, Stafford, & Semic, 2002).

It has been argued that the heart of sports and exercise psychology research lies in its implications for practice (Lyle, 1999), and until recently it was argued that there is a gap between scientific knowledge regarding coach–athlete relationships and the practical benefits of this information for coaches, athletes and sport psychology consultants (Coppel, 1995; Poczwardowski,

1997; Rhind & Jowett, 2008). In 2015, Jowett launched a software tool (www. tandemperformance.com) to package the theory and research around relationships and communication in such ways that coaches and athletes can readily use it to improve the quality of experience, ensuring that everyone has the potential to succeed in sport.

To summarise, it is important for both researchers and practitioners to recognise that the coach–athlete relationship is at the heart of coaching, and thus the ultimate aim of studying coach–athlete relationships is to help improve and enhance coaches' and athletes' performance and their psychological well-being. We hope this chapter offers adequate breadth and depth that helps readers to build a better understanding about the nature of the coach–athlete relationship in competitive sports.

Notes

1 Business School, Sichuan University, China
2 School of Sport, Exercise and Health Sciences, Loughborough University, UK

References

Adie, J. W., & Jowett, S. (2010). Meta-Perceptions of the coach–athlete, achievement goals, and intrinsic motivation, sport participants. *Journal of Applied Social Psychology, 40*, 2750–2773.

Balduck, A. L., & Jowett, S. (2010). Psychometric properties of the Belgian coach version of the coach–athlete relationship questionnaire (CART-Q). *Scandinavian Journal of Medicine and Science in Sports, 20*(5), 779–786.

Berscheid, E. (1995). Help wanted – a grand theorist of interpersonal relationships, sociologist or anthropologist preferred. *Journal of Social and Personal Relationships, 12*(4), 529–533.

Bowlby, J. (1969/1982). *Attachment and loss: Vol. 1. Attachment* (2nd edn). New York: Basic Books.

Canary, D. J., Stafford, L., & Semic, B. A. (2002). A panel study of the associations between maintenance strategies and relational characteristics. *Journal of Marriage and the Family, 64*, 395–406.

Chelladurai, P., & Saleh, S. D. (1980). Dimension of leader behavior in sports: Development of a leadership scale. *Journal of Sport Psychology, 2*(1), 34–45.

Coppel, D. B. (1995). Relationship issues in sport: A marital therapy model. In S. M. Murphy (Ed.), *Sport psychology interventions* (pp. 193–204). Champaign, IL: Human Kinetics.

Cramer, D., & Jowett, S. (2010). Perceived empathy, accurate empathy and relationship satisfaction in heterosexual couples. *Journal of Social and Personal Relationships, 27*(3), 327–349.

Davis, L., & Jowett, S. (2010). Investigating the interpersonal dynamics between coaches and athletes based on fundamental principles of attachment. *Journal of Clinical Sport Psychology, 4*, 112–132.

Davis, L., & Jowett, S. (2014). Coach–athlete attachment and the quality of the coach–athlete relationship: implications for athlete's well-being. *Journal of Sports Sciences, 32*(15).

Davis, L., Jowett, S., & Lafreniere, M. A. (2013). An attachment theory perspective in the examination of relational processes associated with coach–athlete dyads. *Journal of Sport and Exercise Psychology*, *35*(2), 156–167.

Felton, L., & Jowett, S. (2013a). Attachment and well-being: The mediating effects of psychological needs satisfaction within the coach–athlete and parent–athlete relational contexts. *Psychology of Sport and Exercise*, *14*(1), 57–65.

Felton, L., & Jowett, S. (2013b). The mediating role of social environmental factors in the associations between attachment styles and basic needs satisfaction. *Journal of Sports Sciences*, *31*, 618–628.

Felton, L., & Jowett, S. (2014). On understanding the role of need thwarting in the association between athlete attachment and well/ill-being. *Scandinavian Journal of Medicine and Science in Sports*, *25*(2).

Hampson, R., & Jowett, S. (2014). Effects of coach leadership and coach–athlete relationship on collective efficacy. *Scandinavian Journal of Medicine and Science in Sports*, *24*(2), 454–460.

Jowett, S. (2005a). The coach–athlete partnership. *Psychologist*, *18*(7), 412–415.

Jowett, S. (2005b). On repairing and enhancing the coach–athlete relationship. In S. Jowett, & M. Jones (Eds.), *The psychology of coaching*. Leicester: The British Psychological Society.

Jowett, S. (2007). Interdependence analysis and the 3 + 1Cs in the coach–athlete relationship. In S. Jowett, & D. Lavalle (Eds.), *Social Psychology in Sport* (pp. 15–28). Champaign: IL: Human Kinetics.

Jowett, S. (2008). Moderators and mediators of the association between the coach–athlete relationship and physical self-concept. *International Journal of Coaching Science*, *2*, 43–62.

Jowett, S. (2009). Validating coach–athlete relationship measures with the nomological network. *Measurement in Physical Education and Exercise Science*, *13*(1), 34–51.

Jowett, S., & Chaundy, V. (2004). An investigation into the impact of coach leadership and coach–athlete relationship on group cohesion. *Group Dynamics – Theory Research and Practice*, *8*(4), 302–311.

Jowett, S., & Clark-Carter, D. (2006). Perceptions of empathic accuracy and assumed similarity in the coach–athlete relationship. *British Journal of Social Psychology*, *45*, 617–637.

Jowett, S., & Cockerill, I. M. (2002). Incompatibility in the coach–athlete relationship. In I. M. Cockerill (Ed.), *Solutions in Sport Psychology* (pp. 16–31). London: Thomson Learning.

Jowett, S., & Cockerill, I. M. (2003). Olympic medallists' perspective of the athlete–coach relationship. *Psychology of Sport and Exercise*, *4*(4), 313–331.

Jowett, S., & Felton, L. (2014). Coach–athlete relationships and attachments. In M. Beauchamp, & M. Eys (Eds.), *Group Dynamics Advances in Sport and Exercise Psychology* (2nd ed.). New York: Routledge.

Jowett, S., & Frost, T. C. (2007). Race/ethnicity in the all male coach–athlete relationship: Black footballers' naratives. *Journal of International Sport and Exercise Psychology*, *3*, 255–269.

Jowett, S., & Meek, G. A. (2000). The coach–athlete relationship in married couples: An exploratory content analysis. *Sport Psychologist*, *14*(2), 157–175.

Jowett, S., & Nezlek, J. (2012). Relationship interdependence and satisfaction with important outcomes in coach–athlete dyads. *Journal of Social and Personal Relationships*, *29*, 287–301.

Jowett, S., & Ntoumanis, N. (2003). The Greek coach–athlete relationship questionnaire (GrCART-Q): Scale construction and validation. *International Journal of Sport Psychology, 34*(2), 101–124.

Jowett, S., & Ntoumanis, N. (2004). The coach–athlete relationship questionnaire (CART-Q): Development and initial validation. *Scandinavian Journal of Medicine and Science in Sports, 14*(4), 245–257.

Jowett, S., & Poczwardowski, A. (2007). Understanding the coach–athlete relationship. In S. Jowett, & D. Lavalle (Eds.), *Social Psychology in Sport* (pp. 3–14). Champaign IL: Human Kinetics.

Jowett, S., & Shanmugam, V. (in press). Relational Coaching in Sports: Its psychological underpinnings and practical effectiveness. In R. Schinke, K. R. McGannon, & B. Smith (Eds.), *International Handbook of Sport Psychology*. Routledge.

Jowett, S., & Timson-Katchis, M. (2005). Social networks in sport: Parental influence on the coach–athlete relationship. *Sport Psychologist, 19*(3), 267–287.

Jowett, S., & Wylleman, P. (2006). Interpersonal relationships in sport and exercise settings: Crossing the chasm. *Psychology of Sport and Exercise, 7*(2), 119–123.

Jowett, S., Lafreniere, M. A., & Vallerand, R. J. (2012). Passion for activities and relationship quality: a dyadic approach. *Journal of Social and Personal Relationships*, 1–16.

Jowett, S., Shanmugam, V., & Caccoulis, S. (2012). Collective efficacy as a mediator of the link between interpersonal relationships and athlete satisfaction in team sports. *International Journal of Sport and Exercise Psychology, 10*, 66–78.

Jowett, S., Timson-Katchis, M., & Adams, R. (2007). Too close for comfort? Dependence in the dual role of parent/coach–child/athlete relationship. *International Journal of Coaching Science, 1*, 59–78.

Jowett, S., Yang, S. X., & Lorimer, R. (2012). The role of personality, empathy, and satisfaction with instruction within the context of the coach–athlete relationship. *International Journal of Coaching Science, 6*, 3–20.

Kidman, L., & Davis, W. (2006). Empowerment in oaching. In J. Broadhead, & W. Davis (Eds.), *Ecological task analysis perspectives on movement*. Champaign, IL: Human Kinetics.

Lafreniere, M. A. K., Jowett, S., Vallerand, R. J., & Carbonneau, N. (2011). Passion for coaching and the quality of the coach–athlete relationship: The mediating role of coaching behaviors. *Psychology of Sport and Exercise, 12*(2), 144–152.

Lafreniere, M. A. K., Jowett, S., Vallerand, R. J., Donahue, E. G., & Lorimer, R. (2008). Passion in sport: On the quality of the coach–athlete relationship. *Journal of Sport and Exercise Psychology, 30*(5), 541–560.

Laing, R. D., Phillipson, H., & Lee, A. R. (1966). *Interpersonal perception: A theory and a method of research*. New York: Springer.

Lorimer, R., & Jowett, S. (2009). Empathic accuracy, meta-perspective, and satisfaction in the coach–athlete relationship. *Journal of Applied Sport Psychology, 21*(2), 201–212.

Lyle, J. (1999). Coaching philosophy and coaching behaviour. In N. Cross, & J. Lyle (Eds.), *The coaching process: Principles and practice for sport* (pp. 25–46). Oxford: Butterworth-Heineman.

Nezlek, J., & Jowett, S. (2011). Relationship interdependenc and satisfaction with important outcomes in coach–athlete dyads. *Journal of Social and Personal Relationships, 29*(3), 287–301.

Olympiou, A., Jowett, S., & Duda, J. L. (2008). The psychological interface between the coach-created motivational climate and the coach–athlete relationship in team sports. *Sport Psychologist, 22*(4), 423–438.

Pearn, J., & Bareinboim, E. (2014). External validity: From do calculus to transportability across populations. *Statistical Science, 29*(4), 579–595.

Philippe, R. A., & Seiler, R. (2006). Closeness, co-orientation and complementarity in coach–athlete relationships: What male swimmers say about their male coaches. *Psychology of Sport and Exercise, 7*(2), 159–171.

Poczwardowski, A. (1997). Athletes and coaches: An exploration of their relationship and its meaning. Unpublished doctoral dissertation. University of Utah, Salt Lake City.

Poczwardowski, A., Barott, J. E., & Jowett, S. (2006). Diversifying approaches to research on athlete–coach relationships. *Psychology of Sport and Exercise, 7*(2), 125–142.

Rhind, D. J. A., & Jowett, S. (2007). Validation of the long versions of the direct and meta-perspectives of the coach–athlete relationship questionnaire. Under second review.

Rhind, D. J. A., & Jowett, S. (2008). Relationship maintenance strategies in the coach–athlete relationship. *International Journal of Psychology, 43*(3–4), 235–235.

Rhind, D. J. A., & Jowett, S. (2010). Initial evidence for the criterion-related and structural validity of the long versions of the direct and meta-perspectives of the coach–athlete relationship questionnaire. *European Journal of Sport Science, 10*(6), 359–370.

Shanmugam, V., Jowett, S., & Meyer, C. (2013). Interpersonal difficulties as a risk factor for athletes' eating psychopathology. *Scandinavian Journal of Medicine and Science in Sports, 24*(2).

Trzaskoma-Bicserdy, G. T., Bognar, J., Revesz., L., & Geczi, G. (2007). The coach–athlete relationship in successful Hungarian individual sports. *International Journal of Sport Science and Coaching, 2.*

Vallerand, R. J., Blanchard, C. M., Mageau, G. A., Koestner, R., Ratelle, C., & Leonard, M. (2003). Les passions de l'âme: on obsessive and harmonious passion. *Journal of Personality and Social Psychology, 85,* 756–767.

Weiss, M. R., & Fretwell, S. D. (2005). The parent-coach/child-athlete relationship in youth sport: Cordial contentious, or conundrum? *Research Quarterly for Exercise and Sport, 76,* 286–305.

Wylleman, P. (2000). Interpersonal relationships in sport: Uncharted territory in sport psychology research. *International Journal of Sport Psychology, 31*(4), 555–572.

Yang, S. X., & Jowett, S. (2010). An examination of the psychometric properties of the Chinese coach–athlete relationship questionnaire (CART-Q). *International Journal of Coaching Science, 4*(2), 73–89.

Yang, S. X., & Jowett, S. (2012). Psychometric properties of the coach–athlete relationship questionnaire (CART-Q) in seven countries. *Psychology of Sport and Exercise, 13*(1), 36–43.

Yang, S. X., & Jowett, S. (2013a). Conceptual and measurement issues of the complementarity dimension of the coach–athlete relationship across cultures. *Psychology of Sport and Exercise, 14*(6), 830–841.

Yang, S. X., & Jowett, S. (2013b). The psychometric properties of the short and long versions of the coach–athlete relationship questionnaire. *Measurement in Physical Education and Exercise Science, 17*(4), 281–294.

Yang, S. X., Jowett, S., & Chan, D. K. (2014). Effects of big-five personality traits on the quality of relationship and satisfaction in coach–athlete dyads. *Scandinavian Journal of Medicine and Science in Sports, 25,* 568–580.

5 Coaching through organizational change

The influence of leadership succession events

Christopher R. D. Wagstaff[1]

Introduction

The majority of sport organizations will encounter leadership change often, leading some scholars to argue that there is a natural time for a change in sport (see Tena & Forrest, 2007). For example, in elite sport, there are logical annual (e.g., the end of a season) or quadrennial (e.g., the end of an Olympiad) times for leadership change, just as in politics, where a party may change their leader following an unsuccessful election campaign, or in business, where leadership might be changed due to the expiration of a Chief Executive Officer's contract. Yet, while there might be a logical time for leadership change in elite sport, many organizations change leaders at unconventional and, in some cases, illogical times. In a commentary on such practices, Dobson and Goddard (2011) noted that a growing trend has emerged of dismissing sport leaders in-season in an attempt to improve performance and concluded that the role of the professional sport manager is one of chronic insecurity. Moreover, leadership succession events are often volatile and leave those remaining in the organization vulnerable to changes of climate, culture, and working practices. In this chapter, the research on the prevalence and influence of managerial change is reviewed, given that such dynamics present important challenges for coaches seeking to develop and maintain effective athletic performance.

Key terms

Delineating leader roles in sport organizations

Within elite sport organizations, a number of leadership positions exist, for which the roles are often blurred, mislabeled, and interchangeably used. Therefore, it is important to define and distinguish the roles of coach, head coach, manager, and performance director. This is not easy to do, given the roles associated with these positions vary by nation and sport. Nevertheless, for the purposes of this chapter, a coach is viewed as responsible for the development of a performance skill or component (e.g., attack, defense, or kicking coach in rugby), or group (e.g., forwards or backs coach), but not necessarily the whole team. Coaches typically direct training drills, skill development and exercise regimens, and oversee diet, injury and rehabilitation planning for athletes. Some organizations have a head coach who has similar responsibilities but also has substantial input on selection, and is collectively responsible for improving *team* performance, often with the support of other coaches. Thus, the head coach typically benefits from being able to concentrate solely on the on-field performance of the team, but does not necessarily have complete autonomy regarding the athletes or the support staff they work with.

Head coaches and managers are perhaps the most interchangeably used roles in sport. A manager's responsibilities typically include directing overall training and competition preparation, negotiating athlete transfers, team formation and strategy, competition tactics and selection, enforcing discipline, reinforcing the organization's image, building media relations, and organizing travel to and accommodation at competitions. A manager typically has substantial control over coaching and playing employees, transfers and contracts unless, of course, they are working under an owner or CEO who takes a more active role. In this role, the manager is supported by sport science and medicine staff, on whose appointments they have input along with the head of sport science and medicine (see Wagstaff, Gilmore, & Thelwell, 2015; Wagstaff, Thelwell, & Gilmore, 2016). The manager coordinates their team's general operational aspects and often has more "front of house" responsibilities than a coach. Hence, a manager's role is typically broader in scope than that of the coach in terms of their place in an organizational hierarchy. For example, in association football, the manager is the bridge between the club management (i.e., chairperson, board of directors, CEO), the performance department (i.e., players and support staff), and various other stakeholders (e.g., sponsors and other commercial entities, financial analysts, lawyers, agents). Confusion often arises where individuals fulfill the roles of coach (or head coach) and manager, or in sports or countries where head coaches have traditionally been labeled managers and visa versa (e.g., association football in the UK). A relatively recent development in UK sport organizations is the trend towards delineating the responsibilities of a manager (who handles operational responsibilities) and a Performance Director or Director of [Sport] (who handles commercial responsibilities, including athlete transfers and contract negotiations).

Importantly, in the UK at least, it is head coaches, managers, and Performance Directors who are deemed ultimately accountable for performance rather than coaches per se. In practice, however, the roles of these various positions remain blurred, leaving sport leaders open to role conflict and ambiguity. For example, some top-level coaches are given substantial voice in the sale and purchase of athletes to augment the strengths of their teams, while others must negotiate with the manager or Performance Director, CEO and owner to decide on athlete transfers. Others still prefer one job title to another but undertake the responsibilities aligned with another role.

The focus of this chapter is the influence of managerial change on coaches. That is, the chapter will consider how a change of manager influences those responsible for the hands-on skill development and preparation of athletes for performance.

Leadership succession events

Leadership change is commonly referred to in general management literature as a "succession event." (Karg, McDonald, & Schoenberg, 2015, p. 31) and the term is adopted here for consistency across academic literatures. While many succession events are "owned" by executive boards, a succession event refers to the departure and replacement of a leader regardless of whether the leader was dismissed or resigned and whether the successor was internal or external to the organization. Therefore, succession is a process of changing leaders that involves at least two distinct succession actions within a cycle – the removal of one leader and the appointment of another. These two actions can happen simultaneously, with a new leader immediately replacing the outgoing leader, or separately where there is a gap between the departure of one leader and the appointment of another (see Karg et al., 2015).

As alluded to above, although succession can be a natural, logical process, this is uncommon in elite sport. Such processes are often volatile and have direct and indirect performance effects for individuals throughout the sport organization (see Wagstaff et al., 2015; Wagstaff et al., 2016). For this reason, leadership succession events are viewed here as a form of organizational change (see Wagstaff et al., 2015; Wagstaff et al., 2016), which is defined normatively as "a deliberately planned change in an organization's formal structure, systems, processes, or product-market domain intended to improve the attainment of one or more organizational objectives" (Lines, 2005, pp. 9–10), reflecting the ownership of change by those occupying senior management positions in the organization. When change is initiated by executive boards, owners or CEOs (hereafter, referred to collectively as senior management), it is employees located at multiple levels of the organization's hierarchy who are tasked with implementing and coping with the change (Porras & Robertson, 1992). Unsurprisingly, the emotional and attitudinal responses of those change recipients are likely to influence their behavior during that process, and thus, play a significant role in determining the effectiveness of the overall outcome of change (e.g., Liu & Perrewe, 2005; Paterson & Hartel, 2002). One pivotal agent within sport organizations, who must develop and maintain effective working relationships with individuals across multiple organizational levels at the time of a leadership succession event (e.g., senior management, support staff, and players), is the coach.

Review of the literature

The contemporary sport organization: a changing landscape

In the latter part of the twentieth century, elite sport was host to substantial commercialization and globalization (see Fletcher & Wagstaff, 2009; Wagstaff & Larner, 2015; Wagstaff et al., 2015). Thus far, during the twenty-first century, there has been little indication that these complex, turbulent, and volatile changes will slow or desist. One implication of these changes has been a growing demand for organizational systems that facilitate and sustain competitive edge. Due to this changing landscape, sport managers and coaches must instantly and consistently deliver success in an environment that imposes numerous pressures on them. These pressures typically intensify in a results-orientated culture that characterizes elite sport (e.g., Fletcher & Scott, 2010).

The rationale for considering coaches during change can be argued on several fronts. First, undoubtedly, coaches are required to develop and maintain a broad network of relationships within their organization in order to promote effectiveness and deliver on performance indicators. In turn, the effective functioning of a coach's "sea of relationships" with peers (i.e., other coaches), as well as those with followers (i.e., athletes) and superiors (i.e., senior management) is influenced by personnel change as well as other organizational dynamics (see Wagstaff, Fletcher, & Hanton 2012). Indeed, researchers have argued that sport organizations' practices and culture influence coaches' experiences and effectiveness (Gould, Guinan, Greenleaf, & Chung, 2002; Wagstaff et al., 2012; West, Green, Brackenridge, & Woodward, 2001), to the extent that coaches should be perceived as performers in their own right (e.g., Gould et al., 2002), and their psychological needs must be considered (Giges, Petitpas, & Vernacchia, 2004).

Second, coaching is a tough job and coaches must navigate complex professional, intrapersonal, and interpersonal factors in order to enhance and sustain the performance of their athletes. To do so under benign environmental conditions would be a challenge, but, due to the inherent turnover of managers in sport, the typical environment in which coaches perform is far from benign. As a result, it is perhaps not surprising that coaches encounter organizational stressors associated with leadership succession (see Wagstaff et al., 2016). Researchers have noted that coaches are required to deal with daily organizational demands such as selection, media, tactics, financial matters, and transfers (see Fletcher & Scott, 2010; Thelwell, Weston, Greenlees, & Hutchings, 2008) that might be exacerbated during leadership succession events. For instance, the roles and responsibilities of the coach can often be ambiguous at times of change. They might perceive low job security, and may have to fulfil obligations usually handled by the manager (see Olusoga, Butt, Hays, & Maynard, 2009).

Third, the lack of research pertaining to the influence of the organization on coaches has been deemed unfortunate (e.g., Giges et al., 2004). While considerable research attention has been dedicated to enhancing the quality of athletes' experience of coaching, comparatively little research has been conducted into the social contexts in which coaches operate (see Allen & Shaw, 2009), or the environmental conditions in which coaches achieve optimal performance. Hence, as coaches play a pivotal role in the success or failure of elite sport organizations, it is critical to better understand their emotional and motivational experiences of organizational life. The study of organizational psychology in sport (see, for reviews, Fletcher & Wagstaff, 2009; Wagstaff et al., 2012; Wagstaff & Larner, 2015) refers to an umbrella research agenda focussed on examining topics such as attitudes, fairness, motivation, stress, leadership, teams, and broader aspects of organizational and work design in sport. In line with this collective emphasis on the reactions of people to work and their resultant action tendencies and responses, both organizations and the people within their sphere of influence are of importance. Recently, Wagstaff and Larner (2015) argued that organizational psychology principles can advance sport performance through two means: the development of optimally functioning sport organizations and the enhancement of the quality of worklife for employees. These means are perceived here to be particularly relevant for sport coaches. In the next section of this chapter, a review of leadership succession event research is presented before giving consideration to the potential influence of such change on coaches.

Coaching during leadership succession in sport organizations

Organizational change in the form of leadership succession has recently received attention as a salient theme within sport psychology literature (see Wagstaff et al., 2015; Wagstaff et al., 2016); however, the foundations of this work lie in sports management and economics, where the focus has been on the prevalence of succession events and their influence on performance.

Leadership succession prevalence

The hiring and firing of elite sport leaders is a commonplace occurrence. Karg et al. (2015) recently reported that less than 5 percent of coaches across the four major US professional leagues (Major League Baseball (MLB); the National Basketball Association (NBA); the National Football League (NFL); and the National Hockey League (NHL)) had tenures longer than a decade, while less than 10 percent of coaches in the entire English football league had a tenure of longer than four years. There have been a number of previous studies that relate to leader succession in the sporting context dating back as far as the 1960s. Some of these have focussed on the major American sports industries such as the NBA (e.g., Giambatista, 2004), NHL (e.g., Rowe, Cannella, Rankin, & Gorman, 2005), MLB (e.g., Grusky, 1963; McTeer, White, & Persad, 1995) and the NFL (e.g., Brown, 1982). Others have focussed on football in European leagues such as the English Premier League (EPL), Dutch Eredivisie, German Bundesliga, Spanish La Liga and Italian Serie A (Audas, Dobson, & Goddard, 2002; Bell, Brooks, & Markham, 2013; Bruinshoofd & ter Weel, 2003; De Paola & Scoppa, 2011; Frick & Simmons, 2008; Gonzalez-Gomez, Picazo-Tadeo, & García-Rubio, 2011; Koning, 2003; Tena & Forrest, 2007; ter Weel, 2011). For example, Audas et al. examined data for all English Football League and EPL fixtures completed during the 28 seasons between 1972–1973 and 1999–2000. During this period 1,138 separate managerial spells occurred, of which 1,058 spells terminated during the observation period. While Audas et al. did not distinguish between manager and head coach roles, an increasing trend of leader turnover was clear, driven mainly by a rise in involuntary departures. While voluntary departures have remained roughly constant, 736 (69.6 percent) of the 1,058 departures took place within-season, and only 322 (30.4 percent) during the close season. Only 12.9 percent of the 736 within-season departures were voluntary, while 27.3 percent of the 322 close season departures were voluntary. Both the number of involuntary departures and the total departures vary inversely with divisional status. The high degree of leader turnover observed by Audas et al. has been mirrored in other countries. For instance, based on 22 years of data Frick et al. (2010) reported that, on average, 35 percent of managers in Germany's Bundesliga are fired each year. In Argentina, based on a similar period of 20 years, the incidence of sackings is more than one per season per club (Flores, Forrest, & Tena, 2012).

Leadership succession and performance

The research examining the influence of leadership succession events on performance in the USA has produced mixed findings. To elaborate, in the MLB, Grusky (1963) found a negative relationship between managerial change and performance that created a vicious circle of continual decline, whereby poor performance triggered a succession event that intensified poor performance. This spiral led to a perpetual cycle of decline driven by increased organizational instability brought on by a leadership change. Brown (1982) drew similar conclusions in the NFL, and proposed that organizational effectiveness and performance do not increase following managerial change. McTeer et al. (1995) concluded that there was no improvement in performance in the full season after a leadership succession event, but did notice a fleeting minor increase in performance immediately after the change. More recently, Rowe et al. (2005) suggested that giving managers more time leads to better performance in the NHL. Rowe et al. added that this improvement occurs because new managers need time to lead organizational reconstruction and implement the right initiatives to achieve their goals.

Beyond the North American context, research from Dutch football (e.g., Bruinshoofd & ter Weel, 2003; Koning, 2003; ter Weel, 2011) has found that club performance did not improve when a manager was fired and that new managers performed worse than their fired predecessors in several instances. Also using data from Dutch football, Koning (2003) found that team performance decreased following 11 of the 28 manager changes made by Dutch Eredivisie clubs during the seasons 1993–1994 to 1997–1998. De Paola and Scoppa (2011) drew similar conclusions in relation to data from Italian football, where the results of a four-year study indicated that changing a manager does not improve club performance.

Researchers have recently examined the influence of mid-season managerial change, also noting disruptions to performance rather than improvements (Giambatista, 2004). Nevertheless, converse findings were reported by Gonzalez-Gomez et al. (2011), who reviewed the influence of mid-season succession events on sporting performance in Spanish first division football clubs. They found that a mid-season managerial change improved clubs' end-of-season league standing, but their final league position was worse than comparable teams that had not changed managers during the season. Gonzalez-Gomez et al. concluded that changing managers mid-season can be effective when the team is not performing well, but recommended that club executives should plan the season well beforehand to avoid the necessity for such change (Gonzalez-Gomez et al., 2011). Unfortunately, it is evident that the majority of club executives do not subscribe to this advice and more often than not a change of manager mid-season is a short-term decision made in reaction to a poor run of results, rather than anything that has stemmed from poor planning in the first instance.

In one of the most rigorous examinations to date, ter Weel (2011) used difference-in-difference estimates and a two-stage least squares (2SLS) regression analysis strategy to model the influence of leadership succession on team performance using information from the Dutch soccer league in the period 1986–2004. Ter Weel's analyses indicated that the strongest determinants of forced manager turnover include manager investments (measured by the number of players bought) and remaining contract length at the time of a performance dip. That is, when managers have invested more money on player resources, they are more likely to be sacked during performance dips, but less likely to be fired when they have a longer period left on their current contract. This is likely to be due, in part, to the substantial compensation required when manager contracts are terminated or boards still having trust in the manager. Ter Weel (2011) also highlighted that tenure had a small effect on forced managerial turnover, with more experienced managers having a lower probability to be fired. Ter Weel (2011) also observed a brief period (i.e., one game) of performance increase following managerial turnover. Ter Weel proposed that this effect was a "shock effect" influenced by popular media and expectation of the team members to perform better in order to justify the release of the previous manager. However, this effect did not last long and those teams with new managers performed worse compared to control groups for the next three periods (i.e., games). The medium- and long-term effects indicated an unclear, but largely negative, picture. Moreover, manager quality (measured by the manager's previous achievements as a player, years of managerial experience and number of spells) did not significantly matter for predicting turnover and did not explain performance variation after departure. In interpreting these findings, ter Weel argued, "manager quality does not matter in predicting manager turnover and success … [and is] generally not able to influence firm outcomes and only play a role in the process of mean reversion after a performance dip" (p. 291). These findings largely support those using data from other countries (Audas et al., 2002; Frick & Simmons, 2008).

Leadership succession and coaching practice

In addition to the research that has examined the performance outcomes associated with leadership succession events, there has been a growing body of research examining the psychosocial consequences of such change for other stakeholders within sport organizations. For example, in a study of an EPL football club, Gilmore and Sillince (2014) illustrated how science and medicine practices that were previously embedded within coaching were deinstitutionalised within a six-month period following managerial change. Further, the authors noted that leadership change disrupted working practices and routines, and challenged coach philosophy.

Recently, Wagstaff et al. (2015) presented findings from a programme of research exploring the change experiences of individuals employed within elite sport organization performance departments. Specifically, using a two-year longitudinal design, data were collected in three temporally defined phases via 49 semi-structured interviews with 20 sport medics and scientists employed by three organizations competing in the top tiers of English football and cricket. Findings highlighted four distinct stages of change (see Figure 5.1): anticipation and uncertainty, upheaval and realization, integration and experimentation, normalization and learning. Anticipation and uncertainty was defined as the process of attempting to gather information to understand the change and was characterized by a climate of sensitivity, rumour, speculation, and gossip. Upheaval and realization was defined as the process of confirming assumptions and gaining perspective regarding the implications of change for extant practice and was characterized by a focus on past practices, varyingly resulted in resistance to new practices, opportunism, and

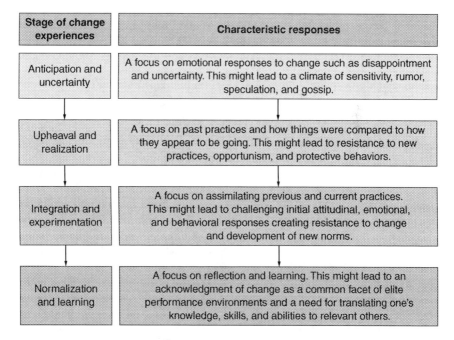

Figure 5.1 A stage-based process model of organization change experiences in professional sport medicine and science departments.

protective behaviors. Integration and experimentation was defined as the process by which assumptions regarding change were challenged and new practices developed, and was characterized by a focus on assimilating previous and current practices. Normalization and learning was defined as the process of establishing norms that align with emerging practices and reflecting on the change as a past event and was characterized by a focus on translating one's knowledge, skills, and abilities to relevant others. In their conclusion, Wagstaff et al. drew attention to salient emotional, behavioral, and attitudinal employee experiences, the existence of poor employment practices, and direct and indirect implications for on-field performance associated with organizational change.

Wagstaff et al. (2016) recently extended the psychosocial research on leadership succession by exploring employees' responses to *recurrent* change events as opposed to a single event. Given the infancy of repeated change research, the authors adopted an exploratory approach to investigate employees' responses to repeated leadership succession events. Data were gathered via 20 semi-structured interviews with employees from two organizations competing in the EPL. Ten employees from each organization were sampled. All of the participants were paid employees of their respective organization and fulfilled roles as medical practitioners (e.g., doctor, physiotherapist), sport scientists (e.g., psychologist, performance analyst), coaches whose work was densely infused by sport science activities (e.g., strength and conditioning) or training practices (e.g., technical coaches), and athletes (e.g., players). At the time of data collection, the organizations from which the participants were sampled had both made five managerial changes within the preceding four year period ($M^{tenure} = 12.28$ months, $SD = 9.27$). These figures were comparable to the English football league average managerial tenure of 1.4 years (i.e., 1.58 years; see LMA, 2016). The participants had encountered an average of 4.2 ($SD = 0.89$) managerial changes in their current position. The results indicated that employees responded to recurrent leadership succession events in positive (namely resilience, learning, performance, challenge appraisals, and autonomy) and negative (namely trust, cynicism, organizational development, motivation, turnover, engagement, and commitment) emotional, behavioral and attitudinal ways. Specifically, the data indicated increasingly deteriorating employee attitudes across succession events, but also highlighted the important role of cognitive appraisal in influencing responses to each succession event.

Karg et al. (2015) recently examined the immediate influence of leadership succession on organizational stakeholders located *outside* of the performance department, in a study of season ticket holder (STH) attitudes (i.e., satisfaction and renewal intentions). The data showed that appointing a new coach (used interchangeably with manager) was met with increases in positive attitudes towards almost every aspect of the STH experience, whereas removing a coach had no meaningful influence on attitudes. The authors argued that their findings support the view that leadership succession is a multiple-phase process including distinct stages of removal and replacement. While it is the desire for improved performance that often motivates leader succession, Karg et al.'s data indicate that the influence of succession activities on fans is more wide ranging.

In reflecting on the emerging responses to leadership succession research, Gilmore, Wagstaff, and Reeves (in press) voiced their concern regarding the emotional impact of employment volatility on the well-being of those working in sport performance departments. In doing so, they drew attention to the high turnover, satisfaction, and effectiveness of performance department staff (i.e., players, coaches, sport science and medical staff), suggesting that precariousness of employment is not simply experienced by traditional "players" (i.e., athletes and managers) but is now witnessed across the performance department.

These findings provide an insight into the employment realities within sport organizations' performance departments during change. Coaches must be aware that leadership succession is unlikely to positively influence performance, and will likely negatively affect support staff, athlete, and coach effectiveness, and influence fan attitudes, for a short period of time, nominally between 16 matches and six months (see Audas et al., 2002; ter Weel, 2011; Wagstaff et al., 2015), regardless of any short-term honeymoon spike in performance. Nevertheless, this literature remains nascent and it is important to consider avenues for the future of this line of enquiry.

Implications for future research

In order to advance research in this area, and, in doing so, better understand the succession phenomena in sport and the associated consequences, researchers might seek to further integrate theoretical models of succession and change from other domains of study. There is much excellent work conducted across diverse domains of academia, and a more holistic conceptual approach would benefit all. For instance, the recent psychological research might offer insights for sport economists attempting to explain honeymoon and long-term slump effects following leadership succession. Yet, in order to facilitate a bidirectional transference of knowledge, it is important for sport psychology researchers to be cognizant of, and where possible test, extant theoretical models from other domains to better understand why leaders are fired and why these changes often have undesirable consequences.

The majority of the research examining leadership succession in the sport management and economics domains is based on a fairly straightforward premise that the outgoing leader was performing poorly and change should be related to performance improvements (Kesner & Sebora, 1994; Soebbing & Washington, 2011). As is clear from the review above, this "common sense" theory has received limited and much contradictory empirical support. Alternative theories include the "vicious circle" theory (Grusky, 1963), which suggests that the problems that led to one leader being removed are rarely addressed by action of removing the leader alone, and therefore the new leader will continue to get negative results, at least in the short term (see Rowe et al., 2005). Ritual scapegoating theory (Gamson & Scotch, 1964; Flores, Forrest, & Tena, 2012) has also been used to suggest that the role of a manager is not relevant when explaining sporting performance and is often "simply a strategy employed by club executives to appease members and fans following a series of bad sporting results" (Gonzalez-Gomez et al., 2011, p. 29). Proponents of this theory argue that results are not related to leadership change, and that variation in competitive environment, culture, time of succession, leader background, and team inputs (i.e., playing talent) limit the effectiveness of attempts to generalize performance using winning as the dominant outcome variable. Further, it is clear boards and owners of sport organizations are regularly faced with a decision on whether to fire the manager when results are going badly. Scapegoating theory would posit that decisions might be based on fan, media, or stakeholder pressure to "do something." That is, the decision to terminate the contract of the manager is without material benefit to the organization, but is to appease these critics. Such leader succession will often be irrational from the perspective of the organization (even if it serves the immediate interests of the decision-taker) and will therefore fail to achieve the supposed objectives. Moreover, the body of sport psychology research reviewed above indicates that changing manager actually has perverse consequences such as deinstitutionalisation of practices or long-term disruption to working relationships and practices, as well as added complexity where new management might be lacking knowledge of idiosyncrasies particular to the organization and its personnel. Further research examining these potential consequences is important because, even in the short-term, repeated failure in competition may quickly lead to relegation (or failure to qualify for international competitions) and thus catastrophic revenue loss (not to mention more leader succession). It would appear that the latter two theories introduced above to explain leader succession (i.e., vicious circle and scapegoating) offer an interesting avenue due to their acknowledgment of the inherent complexity of social and political factors that can affect decision-making and succession decisions and, more importantly, the implications of this change for other organizational employees, not least coaches and performance department staff.

Research is also required to better understand why teams perform worse on average following managerial change and to understand the role of the coach in this process. If a manager has a preference for a particular style of play, then it would seem reasonable that they assemble coaches and players with attributes consistent with this tactical choice. An incoming manager will often alter tactics, yet the coaches and players in place may take time to adapt to a new style of play, or may simply be unsuited to it, in which case some turnover of coaching or playing staff is also common. Hence, one might assume that, until the manager has assembled a squad of players, coaches and support staff, consistent with their preferred style the team will not perform to its potential (Audas et al., 2002). The empirical results from Audas et al.'s (2002) analysis suggest that on average it takes up to 16 matches (around three months) for a team experiencing a within- season change of manager to adapt to any subsequent changes in tactics and playing style. Further support for this adaptation comes from Wagstaff and colleagues (Wagstaff et al., 2015, 2016) who found employees to experience a range of positive and negative responses and effectiveness to be disrupted for a period of six months following leadership succession. It is likely that these timelines will be influenced by numerous variables, but future research might explore ameliorating factors that might reduce or eradicate this slump period. Such research would contribute to the wider organizational psychology in sport literature and advance practitioner understanding of organizational issues.

Implications for applied practice

In this review, findings from sports management, economics, sociology, and psychology have been integrated. The collective findings are quite alarming, given the prevalence of leader succession events. It would appear logical for organizations to retain a performance department *system* that integrates coaching, sport science, and medicine expertise, and then hire individuals with outstanding managerial capabilities to the position of manager or performance director to coordinate commercial and operational needs. The working practices of this system should then remain intact regardless of managerial change. This system approach could be developed in alignment with the culture, goals, and practices of the organization, providing stability during change and reducing the upheaval currently observed following managerial change. Nevertheless, two things appear evident from the preceding review. First, managers get fired at an alarming rate at unpredictable times. Second, sport psychologists might assist organizations during times of leadership succession. Taking the first point, employees in performance departments (i.e., coaches, sport science and medicine staff, athletes) become increasingly frustrated and disenchanted with their work when exposed to repeated leadership succession events (see Wagstaff et al., 2015; Wagstaff et al., 2016). At such times, these individuals – who have both direct and indirect influences on performance – also look for opportunities for self-expression, self-fulfilment, and self-progression, and therefore, respond to succession event circumstances in various ways. These responses occur in tandem with reduced effectiveness and performance for an extended period of time until working practices, culture, and responsibilities are routinized. Further, the research indicates that these decrements are associated with a weakening psychological contract and increasing cynicism toward the employing organizations that must be addressed by the incoming manager and any remaining personnel (see Wagstaff et al., 2015; Wagstaff et al., 2016).

Taking the second conclusion alluded to, sport psychologists can assist organizations during times of leadership succession. To better assist coaches to understand the typical responses of those around them, sport psychologists might consider the use of Wagstaff et al.'s (2015) stage-based process model of organization-change experiences. It is likely that progress across each stage can be expedited with appropriate interventions that might be developed in collaboration between sport psychologists and incoming managers. Such interventions might also assist remaining coaches to better understand the experiences of their "sea of relationships" to promote effective practice during the change process and foster psychosocial capital (see Wagstaff et al., 2012).

A second model that practitioners might use in conjunction with Wagstaff et al.'s stage-based general response model is the exit, voice, loyalty, and neglect

(EVLN) model (Farrell, 1983; Hirschman, 1970; Rusbult, Farrell, Rogers, & Mainous, 1988). EVLN offers a typology of four specific behavioral responses that employees might exhibit during adversity: to leave the organization, speak up, patiently and confidently hope for a better future, or be lax and disregardful. Hirschman originally conceived of his seminal exit, voice, and loyalty model to explain customers' and employees' responses to "lapses from efficient, rational, law-abiding, virtuous, or otherwise functional organizational behaviour" (1970, p. 1). Hirschman's account has made its way into various research areas, such as comparative politics, labor economics, marketing, political sciences, and social and even intimate relationships, to capture and structure the various ways in which individuals might respond to adverse circumstances. In the organizational literature, it has acquired a position as a model that allows for and differentiates a variety of employees' responses to adverse conditions in the workplace (Farrell, 1983; Rusbult et al., 1988; Turnley & Feldman, 1999).

Commonly, in the case of the EPL, coaches either leave with immediate effect on the sacking of a manager, or remain *in situ*, sometimes acting as a "caretaker manager," until a replacement manager can be found. At this point, the continuance of their services is dependent on the incoming manager, or a combination of manager and CEO. Nevertheless, in those circumstances where coaches are retained, they must quickly mobilize working relationships to promote effectiveness. In order to support them through this process, sport psychologists could encourage coaches to reflect on individual responses to change according to the stage-based and EVLN models presented above. They might then use these reflections to communicate in an emotionally intelligent manner (see Wagstaff, Hanton, & Fletcher, 2013) and "steady the ship" where there is upheaval and uncertainty. Such models are also likely to also provide a guide for both sport psychologists and coaches when supporting athletes and support staff through leadership succession. For instance, both Wagstaff et al.'s stage-based and the EVLN model offer an insight into the possible emotional, attitudinal, and behavioral responses of sport performers or those they rely on for optimal performance and how they might change over time. In turn, practitioners and coaches might use such information to develop tailored culture change (see Cruickshank, Collins, & Minten, 2013) or emotion ability and regulation strategy interventions (see Wagstaff et al., 2012) to promote organizational functioning during periods of change.

To conclude, the acquisition of the right manager is likely to be integral to a sport organization's success as they are responsible for selecting the players and the style in which they play, ultimately leading to success or failure. If failure persists, the club owners might feel they have little option but to dismiss the manager in a "scapegoat" reaction. However, the appointment and subsequent dismissal of the wrong manager can be extremely costly against performance (see ter Weel, 2011), financial (see Bell et al., 2013), and employee well-being (see Wagstaff et al., 2015, 2016) metrics. Although further research is required to further illuminate these organizational dynamics, it would appear that there is a role for sport psychologists in ameliorating the current volatile employment affairs in elite sport.

Note

1 University of Portsmouth, UK

References

Allen, J. B., & Shaw, S. (2009). Women coaches' perceptions of their sport organizations' social environment: Supporting coaches' psychological needs? *Sport Psychologist, 23,* 346–366.

Audas, R., Dobson, S., & Goddard, J. (2002). The impact of managerial change on team performance in professional sports. *Journal of Economics and Business, 54*(6), 633–650.

Bell, A., Brooks, C., & Markham, T. (2013). The performance of football club managers: skill or luck? *Economics and Finance Research, 1*(1), 19–30.

Brown, M. C. (1982). Administrative succession and organizational performance: The succession effect. *Administrative Science Quarterly,* 1–16.

Bruinshoofd, A., & ter Weel, B. (2003). Manager to go? Performance dips reconsidered with evidence from Dutch football. *European Journal of Operational Research, 148*(2), 233–246.

Cruickshank, A., Collins, D., & Minten, S. (2013). Culture change in a professional sports team: Shaping environmental contexts and regulating power. *International Journal of Sports Science and Coaching, 8,* 271–290.

De Paola, M., & Scoppa, V. (2011). The effects of managerial turnover: evidence from coach dismissals in Italian soccer teams. *Journal of Sports Economics, 13,* 152–268.

Dobson, S., & Goddard, J. (2011). *The economics of football.* Cambridge: Cambridge University Press.

Farrell, D. (1983). Exit, voice, loyalty, and neglect as responses to job dissatisfaction: A multidimensional scaling study. *Academy of Management Journal, 26*(4), 596–607.

Fletcher, D., & Scott, M. (2010). Psychological stress in sports coaches: A review of concepts, research, and practice. *Journal of Sports Sciences, 28*(2), 127–137.

Fletcher, D., & Wagstaff, C. R. (2009). Organizational psychology in elite sport: Its emergence, application and future. *Psychology of sport and exercise, 10*(4), 427–434.

Flores, R., Forrest, D., & Tena, J. D. D. (2012). Decision taking under pressure: Evidence on football manager dismissals in Argentina and their consequences. *European Journal of Operational Research, 222*(3), 653–662.

Frick, B., & Simmons, R. (2008). The impact of managerial quality on organizational performance: Evidence from German soccer. *Managerial and Decision Economics, 29*(7), 593–600.

Frick, B., Barros, C. P., & Prinz, J. (2010). Analysing head coach dismissals in the German "Bundesliga" with a mixed logit approach. *European Journal of Operational Research, 200,* 151–159.

Gamson, W. A., & Scotch, N. A. (1964). Scapegoating in baseball. *American Journal of Sociology, 70,* 69–72

Giambatista, R. C. (2004). Jumping through hoops: A longitudinal study of leader life cycles in the NBA. *The Leadership Quarterly, 15*(5), 607–624.

Giges, B., Petitpas, A. J., & Vernacchia, R. A. (2004). Helping coaches meet their own needs: Challenges for the sport psychology consultant. *The Sport Psychologist, 18*(4), 430–444.

Gilmore, S., & Sillince, J. (2014). Institutional theory and change: the deinstitutionalisation of sports science at Club X. *Journal of Organizational Change Management, 27*(2), 314–330.

Gilmore, S., Wagstaff, C. R. D., & Reeves, C. (in press). Sports psychology in the English Premier League: 'You live and breathe what happens to the team'. *Work, Employment & Society*.

González-Gómez, F., Picazo-Tadeo, A. J., & García-Rubio, M. Á. (2011). The impact of a mid-season change of manager on sporting performance. *Sport, Business and Management: An International Journal, 1*(1), 28–42.

Gould, D., Guinan, D., Greenleaf, C., & Chung, Y. (2002). A survey of US Olympic coaches: Variables perceived to have influenced athlete performances and coach effectiveness. *The Sport Psychologist, 16*(3), 229–250.

Grusky, O. (1963). Managerial succession and organizational effectiveness. *American Journal of Sociology, 69*, 21–31.

Hirschman, A. O. (1970). The search for paradigms as a hindrance to understanding. *World Politics, 22*, 329–343.

Karg, A., McDonald, H., & Schoenberg, G. (2015). The immediate impact of coach succession events on season ticket holder attitudes. *Sport Marketing Quarterly, 24*(1), 30.

Kesner, I. F., & Sebora, T. C. (1994). Executive succession: Past, present and future. *Journal of Management, 20*(2), 327–372.

Koning, R. H. (2003). An econometric evaluation of the effect of firing a coach on team performance. *Applied Economics, 35*(5), 555–564.

League Managers Association (2016). LMA Report: Mid-season manager statistics, January, 2016.

Lines, R. (2005). The structure and function of attitudes toward organizational change. *Human Resource Development Review, 4*(1), 8–32.

Liu, Y., & Perrewe, P. L. (2005). Another look at the role of emotion in the organizational change: A process model. *Human Resource Management Review, 15*(4), 263–280.

McTeer, W., White, P. G., & Persad, S. (1995). Manager/coach mid-season replacement and team performance in professional team sport. *Journal of Sport Behavior, 18*(1), 58.

Olusoga, P., Butt, J., Hays, K., & Maynard, I. (2009). Stress in elite sports coaching: Identifying stressors. *Journal of Applied Sport Psychology, 21*(4), 442–459.

Porras, J. I., & Robertson, P. J. (1992). *Organizational development: Theory, practice, and research*. Palo Alto, CA: Consulting Psychologists Press.

Paterson, J. M., & Härtel, C. E. (2002). An integrated affective and cognitive model to explain employees' responses to downsizing. In N. M. Ashkanasy, C. E. J. Härtel, & W. J. Zerbe (Eds.), *Managing emotions in a changing workplace* (pp. 25–44). Armonk, NY: Sharpe.

Rowe, W. G., Cannella, A. A., Rankin, D., & Gorman, D. (2005). Leader succession and organizational performance: Integrating the common-sense, ritual scapegoating, and vicious-circle succession theories. *The Leadership Quarterly, 16*(2), 197–219.

Rusbult, C. E., Farrell, D., Rogers, G., & Mainous, A. G. (1988). Impact of exchange variables on exit, voice, loyalty, and neglect: An integrative model of responses to declining job satisfaction. *Academy of Management Journal, 31*(3), 599–627.

Soebbing, B. P., & Washington, M. (2011). Leadership succession and organizational performance: Football coaches and organizational issues. *Journal of Sport Management, 25*(6), 550–561.

Tena, J. de Dios, & Forrest, D. (2007). Within-season dismissal of football coaches: Statistical analysis of causes and consequences. *European Journal of Operational Research, 181*(1), 362–373.

Thelwell, R. C., Weston, N. J., Greenlees, I. A., & Hutchings, N. V. (2008). Stressors in elite sport: A coach perspective. *Journal of Sports Sciences, 26*(9), 905–918.

Turnley, W. H., & Feldman, D. C. (1999). The impact of psychological contract violations on exit, voice, loyalty, and neglect. *Human Relations, 52*(7), 895–922.

Wagstaff, C. R. D., & Larner, R. J. (2015). A review of organizational psychology in elite performance domains: Recent developments and future directions. In S. D. Mellalieu, & S. Hanton (Eds.), *Contemporary reviews in sport psychology* (pp. 91–110). London: Routledge.

Wagstaff, C. R. D., Fletcher, D., & Hanton, S. (2012). Positive organizational psychology in sport: An ethnography of organizational functioning in a national sport organization. *Journal of Applied Sport Psychology, 24*(1), 26–47.

Wagstaff, C. R. D., Gilmore, S., & Thelwell, R. C. (2015). Sport medicine and sport science practitioners' experiences of organizational change. *Scandinavian Journal of Medicine and Science in Sports, 25*(5), 685–698.

Wagstaff, C. R. D., Gilmore, S., & Thelwell, R. C. (2016). When the show must go on: Investigating repeated organizational change in elite sport. *Journal of Change Management, 16*(1), 1–7.

Wagstaff, C. R., Hanton, S., & Fletcher, D. (2013). Developing emotion abilities and regulation strategies in a sport organization: An action research intervention. *Psychology of Sport and Exercise, 14*(4), 476–487.

ter Weel, B. (2011). Does manager turnover improve firm performance? Evidence from Dutch soccer, 1986–2004. *De Economist, 159*(3), 279–303.

West, A., Green, E., Brackenridge, C. H., & Woodward, D. (2001). Leading the way: Women's experiences as sports coaches. *Women in Management Review, 16*(2), 85–92.

6   The coach–parent interaction

Support or distraction?

Camilla J. Knight[1,2] and Daniel G. Gould[3]

Introduction

As researchers and practitioners working within the field of youth sport, we are both motivated to help aspiring young athletes enjoy their participation and achieve their potential. Such outcomes will only occur if children receive the appropriate encouragement, guidance, and support from their parents and coach(es) (Holt & Knight, 2014). As such, we both spend much time trying to understand how parents and coaches can best support children's involvement in sport (e.g., Gould, Lauer, Rolo, Pennisi, & Jannes, 2006, 2008; Knight, Boden, & Holt, 2010; Knight, Neely, & Holt, 2011). Through such work, we have learnt that facilitating positive and appropriate engagement between parents and coaches is extremely important. When parents and coaches "get it right" – with both parties successfully fulfilling their individual roles and responsibilities, as well as supporting, trusting, and communicating with each other – the consequences are invariably positive.

Unfortunately, positive parent–coach relationships are not always present in youth sport; the popular press is seemingly littered with stories of violence between parents and coaches. Although not encountering physical violence, we have both been confronted with situations where the relationship between parents and coaches could be described as nothing less than toxic. Such extreme negative relationships are, thankfully, not the norm. However, there does appear to be an acceptance that parents and coaches will be critical, negative, and, in some instances, derogatory about each other. Given the negative perceptions parents and coaches often have of each other, it is perhaps not surprising that we have both worked with parents and coaches who seek to avoid any communication or interaction with each other. However, based on our experiences and the research in this area, our contention is that avoidance is *not* the best policy! In fact, our suggestion is quite the opposite and through this chapter we hope to illustrate why. Based on the available literature, along with our professional experience, the intent of this chapter is to highlight why we think interactions between parents and coaches are so important within youth and elite sport, why interactions might "go wrong," and how to enhance parent–coach interactions.

Key terms

When discussing parental involvement in sport and the interactions between parents and coaches, two terms are consistently used: support and pressure. These terms are often used as a "catch all" to explain good or bad sport parenting (or coaching) behavior. However, they do have specific meanings in relation to parental involvement in sport, and understanding such meanings is critical for ensuring that literature is appropriately interpreted. In 1995, Leff and Hoyle provided definitions of these terms that continue to be used by researchers today. Leff and Hoyle described pressure as "behavior exhibited by parents that is perceived by their children as indicating high, unlikely, or possibly even unattainable expectations" (p. 190). In contrast, they explained that support is "an athlete's perception of his or her parents' behavior aimed at facilitating his or her involvement and participation" (p. 190). These definitions highlight an important consideration when discussing parents (and coaches') behaviors, which are that behaviors labeled as pressuring or supportive are dependent upon individual athletes' perceptions. Thus, as practitioners and researchers we must remember that athletes can react differently to different types of parental and coach involvement. Similarly, parents and coaches will have differing perceptions of behaviors, and not all coaches and parents will want or like the same types of interaction.

Review of literature

The influence of parents and coaches

The opportunities for children to participate in sport, enjoy their involvement, and achieve their potential are largely influenced by the support they receive from those around them (Wylleman & Lavallee, 2004), with parents and coaches having arguably the greatest influence throughout an athlete's life (Martin, Ewing, & Gould, 2014). Through their engagement and behaviors, coaches and parents can influence young athletes' enjoyment, motivation, perceptions of competence, self-confidence, feelings of anxiety and pressure, and continued participation (e.g., Bois, Lalanne, & Delforge, 2009; Chan, Lonsdale, & Fung, 2012; Jones, Armour & Potrac, 2003).

Parents and coaches, however, do not only exert their individual influence in sport. Rather, together they help create the background climate of youth sports (e.g. Atkins, Johnson, Force, & Petrie, 2015; O'Rourke, Smith, Smoll, & Cumming, 2014). The climate or nature of the interactions that exist between parents and coaches can have a substantial impact on the psychological development of a child (Davis & Jowett, 2010). For example, a study of athletes, parents, and coaches identified that moderately frequent angry interactions occurred, often between adults, during youth sport events (Omli & LaVoi, 2009). Anger such as this has been shown to lead to feelings of sadness, anger, and distress for children (see Omli & LaVoi, 2009). Further, through their behaviors and engagement, parents and coaches can influence each other's experiences within youth sport (e.g., Dorsch, Smith, Wilson, & McDonough, 2015; Hellstedt, 1987) and also the quality of the relationship the athlete has with each party (e.g., Balish & Côté, 2013; Jowett & Timson-Katchis, 2005). Consequently, the creation and preservation of positive parent–coach interactions and climates is vital (Smoll, Cumming, & Smith, 2011).

Parent and coach engagement throughout athletes' careers

When considering the interactions between parents and coaches, it is first important to understand how parent and coach relationships differ depending upon an athlete's stage of development (Martin et al., 2014). When children first engage in sport, the support and encouragement they receive from their parents is the most influential; parents are responsible for introducing their children to sports and providing them with opportunities, equipment, and time to engage in training (Bloom, 1985; Côté, 1999; Wylleman & Lavallee, 2004). Further, parents provide the emotional support required by children at this early stage (Bloom, 1985; Côté, 1999). Coaches are important in so far as they teach children fundamental sporting skills and influence the quality of children's experiences through the praise and feedback they provide (Wylleman & Lavallee, 2004), but compared to parents their influence is limited (Bloom, 1985). As such, interactions between parents and coaches are often minimal during children's initial stages of involvement in sport. Nevertheless, coaches may play an important role in influencing parents' socialization into the youth sport environment at this stage (Dorsch, Smith, & McDonough, 2009).

As children develop and increase their commitment to sport, the roles of parents and coaches begin to shift. Parents continue to play an important role in providing tangible, informational, and emotional support to children (Wolfenden & Holt, 2005; Wylleman & Lavallee, 2004), and make a commitment to be supporters of the young athlete (Côté, 1999). However, as children spend more time in training and at competitions, coaches take on a more prominent position (Bloom, 1985; Côté, 1999; Wuerth, Lee, & Alfermann, 2004). Given the increasing amount of time children spend in the sports environment, the opportunities and need for parents and coaches to interact also increases (Knight & Harwood, 2009; Lauer, Gould, Roman, & Pierce, 2010a, 2010b). Thus, the potential for parents and coaches to clash, particularly in the emotionally charged environment of sports competitions, can increase (see Knight & Harwood, 2009; Wolfenden & Holt, 2005; Wiersma & Fifer, 2008). The shifting roles and influences of parents and coaches can also be a cause for concern, particularly for parents who have to learn to "share" their child with the coach (Jowett & Timson-Katchis, 2005; Wylleman & Lavallee, 2004).

As athletes continue to progress and make a commitment to one sport, their support network may well expand to include team managers, sport scientists, agents, and sponsors. Nevertheless, athletes continue to depend heavily upon the support and involvement of their parents and their coach(es) (Bloom, 1985; Côté, 1999; Wuerth et al., 2004; Wylleman & Lavallee, 2004). But again, this support is changing; coaches often take the lead with regards to athletes' sporting experiences, dictating training and competition schedules and interacting with athletes on a daily basis, while parents take more of a back seat providing support as and when it is required (Côté, 1999; Wylleman & Lavallee, 2004). Once again, such a shift in roles, combined with the increasing number of individuals involved in the athletes' lives, requires parents and coaches to re-negotiate their relationship and interactions. Unfortunately, this can become a source of challenge or conflict for both parties (Lauer et al., 2010a).

Positive parent–coach interactions in sport

Positive relationships between parents and coaches are associated with better experiences for athletes (Wolfenden & Holt, 2005), demonstrated through higher enjoyment levels and reduced perceptions of pressure and anxiety (see Strean, 1995; Jowett & Timson-Katchis, 2005). Positive parent–coach interactions are also associated with smoother transitions and successful talent development (e.g., Knight & Holt, 2014; Lauer et al., 2010a; Wolfenden & Holt, 2005). Finally, positive parent–coach interactions and relationships are deemed to be beneficial in helping parents to be involved in their children's sport in the best possible ways (Knight & Holt, 2013a, 2014) and also facilitating coaches' work with athletes (Gould et al., 2008).

Given the influence parents and coaches have on each other and children's lives, it is important to understand the factors that contribute to positive parent–coach relationships (Holt & Knight, 2014). Unfortunately, we have more information pertaining to those factors that lead to negative relationships than positive ones. Nevertheless, some insights about positive influences can be gained from the talent development and youth sport literature. With regards to parents' behaviors, it appears that parents respecting and trusting the coach is important (Jowett & Timson-Katchis, 2005; Wolfenden & Holt, 2005), as is open, honest, and regular communication (Gould et al., 2008; Knight & Holt, 2014; Lauer et al., 2010a; Wolfenden & Holt, 2005). Parents' expressing support for coaches and ensuring they do not undermine coaches in front of athletes is also pertinent (Jowett & Timson-Katchis, 2005). Finally, parents understanding their role and adapting their involvement as their children progress also appears necessary to facilitate positive parent–coach interactions (Côté, 1999; Lauer et al., 2010a; Wolfenden & Holt, 2005).

In addition, the behavior of coaches is also important in facilitating positive parent–coach relationships. Knight and Holt (2013a) examined how parents of elite junior tennis players were able to support their children in tennis, and one key strategy was through selecting an appropriate coach. An appropriate coach was deemed to be someone who provided a holistic training programme to help children develop as players and people as well as supporting parents themselves. Specifically, parents indicated that they sought coaches who were able to provide them with guidance and support, particularly emotional support. Similarly, Knight and Holt (2014) identified that a strong parent–coach relationship was critical to enhancing parents' understanding of tennis and thus influencing their involvement. Such a relationship was characterized by frequent communication and coaches' taking the time to educate parents regarding what they should be doing to support their children and the consequences of their behaviors. Our practical experiences working with coaches and sport parents has also taught us that coaches should initiate structured processes for parents to come to them with problems or concerns and, most importantly, not be afraid of doing so.

Challenges associated with parent–coach interactions

Given the numerous benefits that parents, coaches, and athletes gain from positive parent–coach interactions, we find it disappointing that the parent–coach relationship is often perceived so poorly, particularly by coaches. Unfortunately, coaches have identified working with parents as one of the main sources of stress in their work (Reade & Rodgers, 2009). Further, difficulties working with parents have been identified as one of the main reasons coaches would leave a position or stop coaching entirely (Gilbert, Gilbert, & Trudel, 2001; Strean, 1995).

The issues coaches associate with parents are extensive, including parents' interfering with tactics, techniques, and training schedules, and placing excessive demands on coaches' time, as well as a lack of parental understanding of sport, an overemphasis on winning, scrutinizing coaches when teams are losing, and conflict (Gould et al., 2006, 2008; Strean, 1995). Parents have been identified as a major source of conflict for child athletes, coaches, and other parents (Elliott & Drummond, 2015). Conflict between parents and coaches is often due to communication issues, such as a lack of opportunities for parents and coaches to share concerns, the way in which parents raise issues with coaches (e.g., argumentative, derogatory), and when issues are raised (e.g., during training sessions or late at night) (Knight & Harwood, 2009; Lauer et al., 2010a, 2010b). Conflict is further attributed to coaches' perceiving that parents are either too involved or not sufficiently involved in their child's sport, parents' challenging coaches decisions regarding squad or team selections, and power struggles between parents and coaches when, for example, both believe they are giving the child-athlete the most important information (Knight & Harwood, 2009; Harwood & Knight, 2009a, 2009b).

In addition to the direct effect of parents' behaviors on coaches, parents can also negatively influence the parent–coach relationship through their interactions with their own child. For example, in a series of studies exploring parental influence on the development of junior tennis players, coaches highlighted numerous issues with parents (Gould et al., 2006, 2008; Lauer et al., 2010a, 2010b). Some of these issues were directly experienced by the coaches, such as parents interfering in coach–player interactions or undermining coaches (e.g., parents telling their children to use tactics or skills that are in opposition to the coaches' suggestions) whereas other issues indirectly affected coaches (e.g., criticizing their child). A study specifically examining parent-induced stressors among tennis coaches similarly identified direct and indirect stressors coaches associate with parents (Knight & Harwood, 2009). Direct coaching stressors included parents' negative perceptions of coaches, viewing them as babysitters or not trusting or respecting their knowledge and experience, and placing excessive demands upon coaches' time. Stressors coaches encountered indirectly from parents arose due to the negative influence coaches perceived parents had upon their child. For example, coaches recalled the challenges of watching parents shout at or punish children for losing, encouraging children to engage in inappropriate training programs, and encouraging poor sportspersonship. When reviewing the player-related stressors, it was apparent that many of the stressors coaches experienced arose as a result of parents' inability to detach themselves from their child's results.

Although many of the issues between parents and coaches are often attributed to parents, negative relationships and interactions can also arise due to the behavior of coaches (see Harwood, Drew, & Knight, 2010; Harwood & Knight, 2009a, 2009b). For example, parents of youth tennis players explained that a lack of feedback, respect, and commitment from coaches were some of the main stressors they experienced when supporting their children in the sport (Harwood & Knight, 2009a, 2009b). Further, concerns regarding coaches' behaviors at training and competitions have been identified as stressors for tennis and football parents (Harwood et al., 2010; Harwood & Knight, 2009a, 2009b). Such concerns include the quality of their children's training programs, the scheduling of training, favoritism shown to particular players, as well as a lack of attendance at matches, and poor planning and scheduling. A lack of regular communication and information from coaches to parents about their child, as well as a perception that parents should not approach coaches to ask questions, are also major issues for parents (Harwood et al., 2010). Finally, stressors related to coaches' lack of knowledge and empathy, particularly relating to a limited understanding of child development and the demands parents experience in youth sport, have also been noted (Harwood & Knight, 2009b; Wiersma & Fifer, 2008).

Although the findings of the aforementioned studies are concerning, it is important to remember that the majority of these studies specifically sought to uncover stressors or challenges (e.g., Harwood & Knight, 2009a, 2009b; Reade & Rodgers, 2009) and were not looking at positive parent–coach interactions. Further, these results should also be considered in light of the fact that coaches often indicate that "negative" or "bad" parents usually overshadow the positive, supportive or helpful parents (Holt & Knight, 2014). Many parents and coaches do manage their interactions successfully, and many parents are involved in youth sport in appropriate manners (Gould et al., 2006; Knight & Harwood, 2009; Strean, 1995). In fact, in a survey of American junior tennis coaches, Gould and colleagues (2006) found that approximately six out of ten parents were not viewed as problems or engaging in behaviors that interfered with their child's development. Rather, they were perceived as positively influencing their child's development. Thus, perhaps the first step in helping to facilitate positive parent–coach interactions is to present a more balanced approach to understanding parent–coach interactions. Second, it is important to understand why such issues might arise when/if they do.

Factors influencing the interactions between parents and coaches

Relationships and interactions do not occur in a vacuum. Rather they are woven into the broader social context (Harwood & Knight, 2009a). As such, before we can seek to enhance parent–coach interactions, it is necessary to consider how contextual factors, particularly the culture of sport, might influence the interactions that occur between parents and coaches (Cushion, Armour, & Jones, 2003). Much has been written about the changing landscape of youth sport over the last few decades (Coakley, 2006; Horn, 2011). Specifically, it has been acknowledged that youth sport is increasingly following a professional model, in which winning and achievement is more highly valued than physical, psychological, and social development (Horn, 2011; Knight & Holt, 2014). Further, as Bergeron et al., (2015) explained, children are increasingly specializing in sports at a younger age. Thus, children, and as a consequence parents and coaches, are increasingly encountering a highly competitive and professionalized environment, which increases the demands parents and coaches experience (Brustad, 2011). Such demands may well be influencing the quality of the interactions between parents and coaches (Horn, 2011).

It has been suggested that many of the negative types of behaviors displayed by parents that result in negative outcomes for children and also cause conflict between parents and coaches might, at least to some extent, be a result of this professionalized, pressured environment (e.g., Horn 2011; O'Connor, 2011; Smoll et al., 2011). In fact, in a recent review of the influence of youth sport engagement on the family, Bean, Fortiner, Post, and Chima (2014) highlighted that the increasing demands arising from the shift towards early specialization and a professionalized model have impacts not only on athletes but also on parents. One such impact is upon parents' finances and time. Financial, time, and emotional demands on parents from youth sport have been identified as stressors for parents (Harwood & Knight, 2009a, 2009b) and such stressors may ultimately influence parents' emotional reactions at competitions or the expectations they place on their children in youth sport settings (Harwood & Knight, 2009b).

Such a professionalized, outcome-oriented environment can also influence the behaviors of coaches and consequently affect the relationship they have with parents. In such a professionalized model, coaches are often judged or measured against the success of their athletes. Working in such a performance-related environment that is open to public evaluation can increase the stress coaches' experiences (Frey, 2007), which could lead to an increase in the pressure they place on athletes to succeed and subsequently affect the parent–coach relationship (see Wiersma & Fifer, 2008). Moreover, if coaches are under pressure to achieve outcomes and they perceive that parental behaviors will limit athletes' development, parents will clearly be perceived negatively (Knight & Harwood, 2009).

Societal expectations and organization of the sport could also influence the interactions that exist between parents and coaches. For example, in Knight and Harwood's (2009) study of parent-induced stressors, coaches perceived that many of the stressors they experienced related to parents were due to societal and organizational issues. Two broad categories of influence were identified. The first influence were socio-cultural considerations such as attitudes towards success, safety concerns in society, and even the British economy. The second consideration was factors within the Lawn Tennis Association. Specifically, a lack of trust in the system to produce successful athletes, the continually changing tennis structure, and the rating structure were all deemed to increase parents' emphasis and pressure on outcomes, and lead to them questioning coaches. Similarly, a lack of communication from leagues and organizations to coaches has also been identified as leading to coaches' encountering criticism from parents (Rundle-Thiele & Auld, 2009).

The specific culture within a sport could also influence the interactions between parents and coaches (see Clarke & Harwood, 2014; McMahon & Penney, 2014). For example, a study by Lally and Kerr (2008) examining parents' experiences of their children's retirement from elite gymnastics highlighted a number of concerns regarding coach behavior within the gymnastic environment. For example, parents explained that, when their children retired, they were left with lingering doubts regarding coaching behaviors and their own failure to intervene. Unfortunately, although all parents have a right to take an interest in and inquire into their children's activities (Lininskienė & Šukys, 2014), in this study, parents indicated that they felt uncertain regarding how they could approach coaches and that they often felt powerless and distressed because they were not in control of the situation. Similar thoughts have also been expressed by youth soccer parents (Clarke & Harwood, 2014) and in relation to the parents of swimmers in Australia (McMahon & Penney, 2014). Such a perceived lack of approachability speaks to a communication-poor climate (i.e., a climate where communication is not encouraged or facilitated) in which coaches actively avoid parents or limit conversations with then. Such an environment is concerning both from a child-protection perspective and also for facilitating the engagement and enjoyment of athletes, parents, and coaches in youth sport settings.

Finally, parents' experiences at competitions could also influence their behaviors and consequently their interactions with coaches. For example, it is frequently recognized that watching children compete in youth sport is an emotional experience for parents (Dorsch et al., 2009; Holt, Tamminen, Black, Sehn, & Wall, 2008). When parents witness their children appearing distressed, underperforming, or not succeeding, they empathize with their children, which can lead to (often negative) emotional reactions (e.g., Holt et al., 2008; Knight & Holt, 2013b; Wiersma & Fifer, 2008). Such a reaction is not surprising as the parent–child bond is one of the strongest relationships people encounter during their lifetimes and parents have an innate desire to protect their children. However, negative emotional reactions at competitions are a contributing factor to poor interactions between parents and coaches and thus, although it is perhaps an understandable reaction, it is still one that needs considering when studying or seeking to improve parent–coach relationships.

Implications for future research

Although numerous researchers and practitioners have discussed the importance of positive parent–coach interactions and provided suggestions to increase the success of such interactions occurring (e.g., Brustad, 2011; Harwood, 2011; Knight & Holt, 2014; Smoll et al., 2011; Vergas, 2011), the amount of research explicitly examining parent–coach interactions is relatively limited. As such, there are numerous areas that require further examination. Five areas that are noticeably absent in the current literature base are: examples of best practice; research considering different youth sport contexts; studies combining multiple perspectives; evaluations of strategies for enhancing interactions; and interventions to enhance parent–coach relationships.

A fundamental principle in sport psychology research has been to examine elite athletes and identify the defining characteristics that make these athletes great. However, to date, little attention has been given to examining successful parent–coach interactions (Holt & Knight, 2014). To improve knowledge of this area, and ultimately enhance the interactions between parents and coaches, studies of successful coach–parent relationships would be extremely beneficial. Even more powerful would be comparisons of both successful and unsuccessful coach–parent relationships.

Research across different sport contexts, with different parents and coaches, would also be beneficial (Holt & Knight, 2014). For example, almost all the current sport parent research has occurred with white middle-class families. We know little about sport parenting with underserved children, where parents have fewer resources to support their child's sport involvement and where a lack of parent involvement may be an issue. Similarly, the influence of being a parent from a single versus dual parent family or from different cultural backgrounds on the coach–parent relationship needs to be explored. As Gilbert and Hamel (2011) explained, youth sport occurs across a diverse range of settings, and strategies that work to enhance parent–coach interactions in one setting might not necessary apply to other settings. To date, many of the strategies that have been suggested to improve parent–coach interactions have not explicitly accounted for such variations.

To further expand this research area, more studies combining multiple perspectives are also needed. Although much research is conducted that relates to and is applied to the athletic triangle (e.g., parents, coaches, and athletes), little attention has been given to incorporating all these individuals within one study. To gain the greatest insights into parent–coach interactions, particularly the impact on parents, coaches, and athletes, research incorporating all these individuals would be useful. Although there are exceptions, much of the research to date has included only one or two of the three members within the triad and more often than not only one parent in two-parent households. To further this area we need to understand the inter-related influences of all the different parties involved.

Finally, based on sound theory and professional practice, a number of suggestions regarding how to improve parent–coach relationships and interactions have been provided. However, while most of these ideas make conceptual sense, there is a lack of systematic research demonstrating the success of different techniques and strategies. Furthermore, no interventions have been developed or tested that are specifically aimed at enhancing parent–coach interactions. Given that both coaches' and parents' time is often limited, the importance of maximizing the time and effort that is put into enhancing parent–coach relationships cannot be overestimated. For instance, it is often suggested that coaches schedule parent orientation meetings. However, an increasing number of coaches have told us that it is very difficult to get parents to attend such meetings and/or that the parents who, in their opinion, most need to attend do not. For this reason other communication formats need to be examined. Developing an intervention specifically aiming at enhancing parent–coach interactions (particularly communication) and assessing child, coach, and parent outcomes as a result of the intervention would help identify the strategies and communication vehicles that are most effective in different settings.

Implications for applied practice

Given the importance of parents and coaches within youth sport and the range of positive outcomes that arise when parents and coaches have a good relationship, a number of researchers have provided suggestions regarding how to enhance parent–coach interactions (see *International Journal of Coaching Science*, 2011, Issue 1 for a full review). A consistent view throughout the parent and coach literature is the need for coaches to be proactive in their interactions with parents (Brustad, 2011; Vargas, 2011), that parents should be recognized as positive supporters of coaches (Harwood, 2011), and that parents and coaches should seek to work in partnership (Horn, 2011). Specifically, in being proactive in their interactions with parents, it has generally been suggested that coaches seek to educate parents (e.g., Smoll et al., 2011). Such an approach has been advocated because it is perceived that many of the issues that exist within the parent–coach relationship are due to parents' lack of knowledge and understanding (Smoll et al., 2011).

With regards to education, Smoll and colleagues (2011) advocated for the importance of educating parents regarding the purpose of developmental sport and how it differs to professional sport, the objectives of youth sport, and the roles and responsibilities of parents. By educating parents regarding these aspects, Smoll and colleagues perceive that you would overcome many of the issues that parents cause for coaches because they do not understand what they are doing or the consequences of their behaviors (Lisinskienė & Šukys, 2014). Moreover, educating parents on these aspects will ensure that parents and coaches are viewing youth sport from a similar platform (Brustad, 2011), which might reduce the conflict that arises from parents and coaches misunderstanding each other's expectations and roles (Knight & Harwood, 2009).

It has also been suggested that coaches would benefit from education (Bergeron et al., 2015; Vergas, 2011). Some of this education might be targeted at the same areas as for parents – for example, ensuring that coaches appreciate the difference between professional and developmental sport (Holt & Knight, 2014) and that they realize that early specialization is not beneficial (O'Connor,

2011). Additionally, education for coaches could be targeted at providing coaches with the skills to manage their interactions with parents, for example improving their communication skills (Bergeron et al., 2015; O'Connor, 2011; Vergas, 2011). Such education for coaches regarding communication skills ties in closely with the suggestion that parents and coaches need to engage in two-way communication (Hellstedt, 1987; Smoll et al., 2011) and that coaches particularly need to work to create an environment in which communication from parents is welcomed and encouraged, rather than dismissed or avoided.

The most common cause of coach–parent conflict is a difference of opinions about the young athletes' abilities (Smoll et al., 2011), thus developing strategies to facilitate and encourage structured and open two-way communication is critical. Moreover, such communication can help to empower coaches (and parents) and help them to feel that they are able to air concerns when/if they arise (Brustad, 2011). Communication could occur through pre-season and during-season team meetings (Smoll et al., 2011; Strean, 1995). However, such meetings might not be feasible for all teams or within all parent–coach relationships (Gilbert & Hamel, 2011) and other strategies to enhance communication might also be required (Gilbert & Hamel, 2011)

Another strategy that has been advocated for enhancing parent–coach relationships is for both parties to commit time to understanding the demands and challenges that the other party encounters (Harwood, 2011; Knight & Harwood, 2009). As highlighted, coaches experience a range of demands and stressors in sport (Harwood & Knight, 2009a, 2009b; Knight & Harwood, 2009). Sharing these with parents early and also ensuring that expectations, rules of engagement, and coaching philosophy are communicated should help to ensure parents know what is happening from the outset (Harwood, 2011). Similarly, if opportunities are provided for parents to share their experiences with coaches, coaches might approach their interactions with parents with more empathy (Harwood, 2011), which would reduce some of the stressors parents experience in their sport parenting role (Harwood & Knight, 2009a).

Finally, in seeking to understand parents' experience, it is important for coaches to recognize that most parents are just really enthusiastic and are simply concerned for their children's well-being and development. Such parents might not understand the issues they are creating for coaches and thus coaches need to work with parents to help them understand the consequences of their behaviors (Holt & Knight, 2014; Smoll et al., 2011). Additionally, it is important for coaches to recognize how the sports environment might be influencing the behaviors of parents and account for the demands and contextual influences when establishing expectations and relationships (Horn, 2011).

Notes

1 Applied Sport, Technology, Exercise, and Medicine Research Centre, Swansea University, UK
2 Welsh Institute of Performance Science, UK
3 Institute for the Study of Youth Sport, Michigan State University, USA

References

Atkins, M. R., Johnson, D. F., Force, E. C., & Petrie, T. A. (2015). Peers, parents, and coaches, oh my! The relation of the motivational climate to boys' intention to continue to sport. *Psychology of Sport and Exercise, 16*, 170–180.

Balish, S., & Côté, J. (2003). The influence of community on athletic development: an integrated case study. *Qualitative Research in Sport, Exercise and Health, 6*, 98–120.

Bean, C. N., Fortiner, M., Post, C., & Chima, K. (2014). Understanding how organized youth sport may be harming individual players within the family unit: A literature review. *International Journal of Environmental Research and Public Health, 11*, 10226–10268.

Bergeron, M. F., Mountjoy, M., Armstrong, N., Chia, M., Côté, J., & Engebretsen, L. (2015). International Olympic Committee consensus statement on youth athletic development. *British Journal of Sports Medicine, 49*, 843–851.

Bloom, B. (1985). *Developing talent in young people.* New York: Ballantine.

Bois, J. E., Lalanne, J., & Delforge C. (2009). The influence of parenting practices and parental presence on children's and adolescents' pre-competitive anxiety. *Journal of Sports Sciences, 27*, 995–1005.

Brustad, R. J. (2011). Enhancing coach–parent relationships in youth sport: Increasing harmony and minimizing hassle. A commentary. *International Journal of Sport Science and Coaching, 6*, 33–36.

Chan, D. K., Lonsdale, C., & Fung, H. H. (2012). Influences of coaches, parents, and peers on the motivational patterns of child and adolescent athletes. *Scandinavian Journal of Medicine and Science in Sports, 22*, 558–568

Clarke, N. J., & Harwood, C. G. (2014). Parenting experiences in elite youth football: A phenomenological study. *Psychology of Sport and Exercise, 15*, 528–537.

Coakley, J. (2006). The good father: Parental expectations and youth sports. *Leisure studies, 25*, 153–163.

Côté, J. (1999). The influence of the family in the development of talent in sport. *The Sport Psychologist, 13*, 395–417.

Cushion, C. J., Armour, K. M., & Jones, R. L. (2003). Coach education and continuing professional development: Experience and learning to coach. *Quest, 55*, 215–230.

Davis, L., & Jowett, S. (2010). Investigating the interpersonal dynamics between coaches and athletes based on fundamental principles of attachment. *Journal of Clinical Sport Psychology, 4*, 112–132.

Dorsch, T. E., Smith, A. L., & McDonough, M. H. (2009). Parents' perceptions of child-to-parent socialization in organized youth sport. *Journal of Sport and Exercise Psychology, 31*, 444–468.

Dorsch, T. E., Smith, A. L., Wilson, S. R., & McDonough, H. (2015). Parent goals and verbal sideline behavior in organized youth sport. *Sport, Exercise, and Performance Psychology, 4*, 19–35.

Elliott, S. K., & Drummond, M. J. N., (2015). Parents in youth sport: what happens after the game? *Sport, Education and Society*, pre-print online version retrieved from doi:10.1080/13573322/2015/1036233.

Frey, M. (2007). College coaches' experiences with stress – "problem solvers" have problems, too. *The Sport Psychologist, 21*, 38–57.

Gilbert, W., & Hamel, T. (2011). Enhancing coach–parent relationships in youth sport: Increasing harmony and minimizing hassle. A commentary. *International Journal of Sport Science and Coaching, 6*, 37–42.

Gilbert, W. D., Gilbert, J. N., & Trudel, P. (2001). Part 2: Personal characteristics, parental influence, and team organization. *Journal of Physical Education, Recreation, and Dance, 72*(5), 41–46.

Gould, D., Lauer, L., Rolo, C., Jannes, C., & Pennisi, N. (2006). Understanding the role parents play in tennis success: A national survey of youth tennis coaches. *British Journal of Sports Medicine, 40*, 632–636.

Gould, D., Lauer, L., Rolo, C., Jannes, C., & Pennisi, N. (2008). The role of parents in tennis success: Focus group interviews with youth coaches. *The Sport Psychologist, 22*, 18–37.

Harwood, C. (2011). Enhancing coach–parent relationships in youth sports: Increasing harmony and minimizing hassle: A commentary. *International Journal of Sports Science and Coaching, 6*, 61–64.

Harwood, C. G., & Knight, C. J. (2009a). Stress in youth sport: A developmental investigation of tennis parents. *Psychology of Sport and Exercise, 10*, 447–456.

Harwood, C. G, & Knight, C. J. (2009b). Understanding parental stressors: An investigation of British tennis-parents. *Journal of Sports Sciences, 27*, 339–351.

Harwood, C., Drew, A., & Knight, C. J. (2010). Parental stressors in professional youth football academies: A qualitative investigation of specializing stage parents. *Qualitative Research in Sport and Exercise, 2*, 39–55.

Hellstedt, J. C. (1987). The coach/parent/athlete relationship. *The Sport Psychologist, 1*, 151–160.

Holt, N. L., & Knight, C. J. (2014). Parenting in youth sport: From research to practice. Abingdon, Oxon: Routledge.

Holt, N. L., Tamminen, K. A., Black, D. E., Sehn, Z. L., & Wall, M. P. (2008). Parental involvement in competition youth sport settings. *Psychology of Sport and Exercise, 9*, 663–685.

Horn, T. S. (2011). Enhancing coach–parent relationships in youth sports: Increasing harmony and minimizing hassle. A commentary. *International Journal of Sports Science and Coaching, 6*, 27–32.

Jones, R. L., Armour, K. M., & Potrac, P. (2003). Constructing expert knowledge: A case study of a top-level professional soccer coach. *Sport, Education and Society, 8*, 213–229.

Jowett, S., & Timson-Katchis, M. (2005). Social networks in sport: Parental influence on the coach–athlete relationship. *The Sport Psychologist, 19*, 267–287.

Knight, C. J., & Harwood, C. G. (2009). Parent-initiated coaching stress: A developmental study. *International Journal of Sports Science and Coaching, 4*, 545–565.

Knight, C. J., & Holt, N. L. (2013a). Strategies used and assistance required to facilitate children's involvement in tennis: Parents' perspectives. *The Sport Psychologist, 27*, 281–291.

Knight, C. J., & Holt, N. L. (2013b). Factors that influence parents' experiences at junior tennis tournaments and suggestions for improvement. *Sport, Exercise, and Performance Psychology, 2*, 173–189.

Knight, C. J., & Holt, N. L. (2014). Parenting in youth tennis: Understanding and enhancing children's experiences. *Psychology of Sport and Exercise, 15*, 155–164.

Knight, C. J., Boden, C. M., & Holt, N. L. (2010). Junior tennis players' preferences for parental behaviors at tournaments. *Journal of Applied Sport Psychology, 22*, 377–391.

Knight, C. J., Neely, K. C., & Holt, N. L. (2011). Parental behaviors in team sports: How do female athletes want parents to behave? *Journal of Applied Sport Psychology, 23*, 76–92

Lally, P., & Kerr, G. (2008). The effects of athlete retirement on parents. *Journal of Applied Sport Psychology, 20*, 42–56.

Lauer, L., Gould, D., Roman, N., & Pierce, M. (2010a). Parental behaviors that affect youth tennis player development. *Psychology of Sport and Exercise, 11*, 487–496.

Lauer, L., Gould, D., Roman, N., & Pierce, M. (2010b). How parents influence youth tennis players' development: Qualitative narratives. *Journal of Clinical Sport Psychology, 4*, 69–92.

Leff, S. S., & Hoyle, R. H. (1995). Young athlete's perceptions of parental support and pressure. *Journal of Youth and Adolescence, 24*, 187–203.

Lisinskienė, A., & Šukys, S. (2014). The athlete triangle: Coach, athlete and parents as an educational system. *Global Journal of Sociology, 4*, 46–51.

Martin, E. M., Ewing, M. E., & Gould, D. (2014). Social agents' influence on self-perceived good and bad behavior of American youth involved in sport: Developmental level, gender, and competitive level effects. *The Sport Psychologist, 28*, 111–123.

McMahon, J. A., & Penney, D. (2014). Sporting parents on the pool deck: Living out a sporting culture? *Qualitative Research in Sport, Exercise and Health, 7*, 153–169.

O'Connor, D. (2011). Enhancing coach–parent relationships in youth sports: Increasing harmony and minimizing hassle: A commentary. *International Journal of Sports Science and Coaching, 6*, 49–52.

O'Rourke, D. J., Smith, R. E., Smoll, F. L., & Cumming, S. P. (2014). Relations of parent- and coach-initiated motivational climates to young athletes' self-esteem, performance anxiety, and autonomous motivation: Who is more influential? *Journal of Applied Sport Psychology, 26*, 395–408.

Omli, J., & LaVoi, N. M. (2009). Background anger in youth sport: A perfect storm? *Journal of Sport Behavior, 32*, 242–260.

Reade, I. L., & Rodgers, W. M. (2009). Common coaching challenges and their association with coach and contextual characteristics. *Journal of Coaching Education, 2*(2), 1–24.

Rundle-Thiele, S., & Auld, C. (2009). Should I stay or should I go? Retention of junior sport coaches. *Annals of Leisure Research, 12*, 1–21.

Smoll, F. L., Cumming, S. P., & Smith, R. E., (2011). Enhancing coach–parent relationships in youth sports: Increasing harmony and minimizing hassle. *International Journal of Sports Science and Coaching, 6*, 13–26.

Strean, W. B. (1995). Youth sport contexts: Coaches perceptions and implications for intervention. *Journal of Applied Sport Psychology, 7*, 23–27.

Vargas, T. M. (2011). Enhancing coach–parent relationships in youth sports: Increasing harmony and minimizing hassle: A commentary. *International Journal of Sports Science and Coaching, 6*, 43–44.

Wiersma, L. D., & Fifer, A. M. (2008). "The schedule has been tough but we think it's worth it": The joys, challenges, and recommendations of youth sport parents. *Journal of Leisure Research, 40*, 505–530.

Wolfenden, L. E., & Holt, N. L. (2005). Talent development in elite youth tennis: Perceptions of players, parents, and coaches. *Journal of Applied Sport Psychology, 17*, 108–126.

Wuerth, S., Lee, M. J., & Alfermann, D. (2004). Parental involvement and athletes' career in youth sport. *Psychology of Sport and Exercise, 5*, 21–33.

Wylleman, P., & Lavallee, D. (2004). A developmental perspective on transitions faced by athletes. In M. Weiss (Ed.) *Developmental sport and exercise psychology: A life-span perspective* (pp. 507–527). Champaign, IL: Human Kinetics.

Part II
Enhancing coach performance

7 Helping coaches meet their psychological needs

Paul McCarthy[1] and Burt Giges[2]

Introduction

For those who learn about the role of a sports coach from television and radio reports, it might appear that the coach's performance correlates directly with the outcome of each sporting contest. In victory, the coach's inimitable faculties guided the athlete to the podium; but in failure, the coach spoiled what was obvious to all ex post facto. This representation of the coach, propagated by the media, hints at a one-dimensional entity: the coach as a performer. Underneath this abridged portrayal, however, lies a multifaceted job description that reveals what a coach does, but does not disclose the coach's complex amalgamation of other skills (e.g. duties, relationships) needed to fulfil the coaching role or the coach's psychological needs.

Even within the peer-reviewed research, under greatest scrutiny are the coach's actions such as coaching style and relationships (Smith & Smoll, 1997) but not the coach as a person with psychological, emotional and social needs. Almost twenty years ago, Vernacchia and McGuire (1998) explained that "Coaches had needs from the sport psychology profession that were not currently being addressed in a practical manner" (p. xi). A point that was further emphasised by Gould, Greenleaf, Guinan, and Chung (2002) who revealed that although "coaches and their practices have always been of interest to sport psychology researchers, seldom has the coach been viewed as a performer in his or her own right" (p. 231).

One only needs to read the manifold duties subsumed within a coaching role (i.e. teacher, organizer, administrator, leader, performer, competitor, learner, friend and mentor (Giges, Petitpas, & Vernacchia, 2004; Short & Short, 2005) to appreciate its burdens. The responsibility for success, however one defines it, sits squarely with the coach. From the outside looking in, society creates a performance narrative (Douglas & Carless, 2006) where the coach's story is told through performance outcomes, with all other roles (e.g. life roles and identities) subsumed under this contract. The coach's story, therefore, emerges through the cultural perspective on values, expectations and accepted behaviour in sport (from recreational to elite) without ever asking the coach: "What's going on for you?" With the accruing success of the coach, however, popular cultural interest extends from the professional or performance script toward the personal script: Who is this person? What does she do when she is not coaching? In professional and elite sport, through media interviews, biographies and autobiographies, we are afforded a chance to see the person whom the athletes call 'coach'. We argue that the personal script and all it entails deserves its place alongside the performance script for the psychological health and well-being of the coach as well as the pursuit of athletic excellence.

Key terms

Within this chapter we depict the 'coach' as a person with basic psychological needs. Modern use of the word 'coach' has broadened to include life coach, executive coach, business coach, wellness coach, or health coach. Although the discussion of coaches' psychological needs may well apply to these other types of coaches, the focus of this chapter is on coaches in sport. We examine the 'coach' as an entity in itself, rather than on the effect the coach has upon others, while acknowledging the effect that others have upon the coach.

Though most perplexing within the literature is how few articles are devoted to the psychological needs of the coach and related features such as self-awareness and self-care (Allen & Shaw, 2009; Pope & Hall, 2015), yet psychological needs are the base upon which we construct psychological well-being. Common psychological needs include security, autonomy, identity, self-worth, mastery, intimacy, belonging and a sense of meaning in one's life (Deci, 2002; Frankl, 1992; Maslow, 1987). When circumstances permit, coaches may satisfy particular psychological needs through the coaching process; yet many psychological needs remain concealed and unsatisfied, in part because coaches are not aware of these needs or the connection between these needs and behaviour. Maslow's (1987) hierarchy of human needs proposes that each person has a hierarchy of human needs that must be satisfied. This hierarchy of needs includes biological and physiological needs, safety needs, belongingness and love needs, esteem needs and, finally, self-actualization. Biological and physiological needs include food, water, shelter, warmth, clothing, sex, sleep and stimulation. Safety needs comprise protection, stability, structure, order, predictability, boundaries and law. With belongingness and love needs, we meet these through family, friends, relationships, love, affection, acceptance and a sense of belonging to a group. Esteem needs include self-respect, respect from others, status, prestige, independence and recognition. Finally, self-actualization encompasses achieving full potential, self-fulfilment, peak experiences, spirituality and seeking personal growth. According to Maslow's theory, only when each need is satisfied are we motivated to reach the next higher level. For instance, a person who lacks food or shelter cannot concentrate on higher needs until these needs are satisfied. This hierarchy changes depending upon one's situation; so while a professional football coach might be high on self-actualization today, losing her job tomorrow means that she plunges back to satisfying a basic psychological need for security before beginning that climb again. In our everyday lives, we are meeting our basic needs, so rather than considering these needs as steps of a ladder, we view them concurrently.

If we examine these five levels of the hierarchy with coach-specific examples in mind, first, we see that, without a secure job or enough money to live, a youth sport coach would struggle to fulfil these unmet biological and physiological needs. Second, an environment without stability, predictability and firm boundaries promotes feelings of insecurity and such environments abound in sport. For instance, some owners and directors of high performance sport teams (e.g. professional football and rugby) demand immediate and sustained success beyond what might reasonably be expected from a coach and squad adjusting to the caprices of a sport season. Third, each human being harbours a deep psychological need to belong. Growing up with a sense of being loved, accepted, valued and chosen by others for valuable social roles makes one's world safer and happier. This sense flourishes for a coach when an athlete achieves success but diminishes during lengthy failure. Fourth, esteem needs are many and varied; however, a low sense of one's esteem sways us toward perceived weaknesses, dwelling upon our mistakes and an unforgiving drive toward perfectionism. In professional sport, the media seize upon a coach's perceived weaknesses and mistakes which intensify these concerns about esteem. Finally, to be all we can be, we focus upon achieving our potential. We stride forward in pursuit of our potential through a process of becoming (Sutton & Stewart, 2012). A sensible plan for professional coaches, youth coaches, and coaches of team/individual sport athletes would be to find dependable footholds or firmly anchored stones to grasp as they ascend and descend this hierarchy of needs. We begin with one foothold – self-awareness.

Review of literature

Self-awareness represents knowledge of one's thoughts, feelings, behaviour, needs and wants (Giges et al., 2004; Goleman, 1998; Ravizza, 1998). It can lead to a fuller knowledge of oneself, and a greater appreciation of one's complexity and wholeness. But this knowledge alone, without understanding and action, prevents one from developing enough openness and self-acceptance to learn from within and from others. In sport, an often demanding and unrelenting competitive environment that emphasizes strength and success, it can be unsettling to acknowledge weakness and failure. Yet the extent to which one accepts others depends upon the extent to which one is self-aware and self-accepting. Learning to accept ourselves as we are and others as they are liberates us from many binds that enslave us. In an attempt to accept ourselves and others, we ought to recognize the roadblocks that prevent it, such as stereotyping, a limited knowledge of human behaviour, hidden agendas, biases, prejudices, values, beliefs or losing respect for the athlete (Sutton & Stewart, 2012). The process of overcoming such roadblocks, which is analogous to removing psychological barriers, involves identifying them, exploring their meaning, and initiating a change that will decrease their influence (Giges, 2000).

Psychological well-being grows when one's psychological needs are met. Several steps follow one another to achieve this aim. The psychological growth afforded to the coach lies within the coach's grasp when she begins a process of self-awareness. This process invites the sport psychologist, for example, and the coach to see whom they see without judgment. Self-awareness, according to Burnard (1997), involves the "continuous and evolving process of getting to know who you are" (p. 25). A corollary of this definition suggests that, not 'feeling at home with ourselves', we restrict our capacity to grow, as well as to understand and accept others as they are. When we understand ourselves, we open a window to understand what other people experience, and to accept them as we find them without judgment.

Concepts related to self-awareness such as self-observation and self-reflection play a role in helping the person to see him or herself. But to corral one's derivations of the self, we ought to frame an understanding of the self before proceeding. The 'self' encapsulates "the mental apparatus that allows people (and a few other species of animals) to think consciously about themselves" (Leary & Tangney, 2003, p. 5). The capacity to think about oneself, the notion of 'me-ness' or 'I-ness', a self-identity with feelings about who we are and how we would like others to see and relate to us presents us with a firm and frightening realization – inside our heads, we are alone. The world we have created resides only within our heads (Gilbert, 2009). Humans, therefore, connect with others grow, prosper and survive.

After a quick glance at a professional coach's duties you might tacitly conclude that the coach primarily prepares athletes for competition. Yet this restricted view neglects the coach's time spent organizing, administrating and managing numerous people to achieve this primary aim, which draws us to the heart of their work: developing and managing interpersonal relationships. Relationships, therefore, are the base upon which success grows. But if one's relationship with another demands an overhaul, how does one recognize that an overhaul is required? This enlightenment might lie within the organization in which the coach operates that places professional development as an indicator of success; if it does not exist, the coach might engage in reflective practice. Douglas and Carless (2008) suggested that reflective practice allows the coach to learn from coaching experiences by changing and adapting in response to these learning experiences. What is unknown, however, is whether these thought processes (e.g. evaluation, pondering) represent reflective practice (Cropley & Hanton, 2011), and also how effective reflective practice might be compromised in the process because coaches do not know how to reflect. It might also be true that coaches do not participate in self-awareness because they do not know how to conduct the process.

If his notion of the self allows us to think about ourselves consciously, we bring to mind our memories of ourselves, our values and our behaviours today, yesterday and the possibility of ourselves tomorrow (McGregor & Marigold, 2003). Penetrating introspection also dredges up thoughts and feelings that we might not exist tomorrow. Through this sifting process, we can recognize others and it prompts us to consider the self among others – a social awareness. How do I relate to others? How do I compare with others? How do others see me?

Coaches, then, in relation to other coaches present a challenge to see themselves favourably or unfavourably and judge how they think others see them. The key decision makers in many sports are often coaches. They decide who plays and who does not; they decide the content of each training session; they decide about the competence of the athlete. But within this decision-making process, the judgment that falls on the coach or athlete is often arbitrary, with little room for negotiation or understanding. The coach's own judgment of himself or the athlete could be an evaluation and rejection of one's self-worth.

Coaches, therefore, can form notions and images about themselves (i.e. self-concept), judgments about themselves (i.e. self-evaluations) but also manage their own behaviour (i.e. self-control) to reach a conscious goal. Strangely, few of us ever ruminate about how we might function as humans if this capacity to think about ourselves were not possible. We distinguish ourselves from most other animals in this capacity because we can plan, make decisions and control our behaviour, create mental representations and evaluations of the self, think about thinking, feeling and behaving and finally, take perspective (Leary, 2004). These five abilities offer many prospects but are burdened with shortcomings. We shall probe these abilities from the coach's perspective.

Planning affords the coach a ticket to mental time-travel. A coach might manipulate a thought or image of the future, perhaps success in a national championship, and the possible and probable steps to secure that goal. Such planning enables the coach to prepare for seen and unforeseen challenges along the way. The coach's ability to mental time travel allows her to decide and control behaviour to some extent. If she were to alter her coaching style she could play out the possible consequences of such actions, choosing which option to adopt. Former Liverpool manager Bill Shankly used such clever strategies when he needed to drop a player for a game. As former player Alex McIntosh explained: "if you were dropped, he would tell you why. You didn't feel that you were being dropped. It was simply that the pitch wasn't suitable for you" (Kelly, 1997). Information processing and decision-making fall into two distinct mental systems; one is conscious and controlled while the other is non-conscious and automatic. Each system dovetails to grant the coach a resource that yields appropriate solutions to everyday challenges, yet limitations arise when we invoke the wrong mental system. Thinking in a conscious and controlled fashion might enhance team selection but would likely hamper braking in an emergency stop. Self-conceptualization and evaluation offer the coach a chance to think about himself and his actions and such a self-concept influences his decisions (Epstein, 1973; Markus & Wurf, 1987). For instance, a coach's beliefs about his characteristics might encourage him do certain things in a certain way because that is how he views himself. Similarly, his views about his abilities persuade him to tackle certain tasks but to avoid others.

Having a self-concept, therefore, suggests that our behaviour is influenced by our beliefs about our personal characteristics. If a coach were to consider whether her coaching behaviour fits the 'good coaching' model, she might feel that some characteristics and actions help while others require an overhaul to meet this valuation. Coaches, it would seem, can decide upon a course of action that best meets their needs. Fourth, introspection – or taking perspective – allows us to think about thinking, feeling and behaving. A coach might be about to lose his temper again with a tardy athlete, yet can think about his own thoughts and feelings before acting. Finally, and appropriately for coaches, self-awareness allows the coach to think about the behaviour and mental lives of others. This perspective-taking, for instance, presents the coach with an imagination of what it might like to be an athlete and how she is perceived and evaluated by others. Putting ourselves in the minds of others then leads to several advantages for forming strong social bonds (e.g. showing empathy, helping others). Former Olympic swimmer and gold medallist Matt Biondi offered this advice to coaches:

> The duality of admitting your weaknesses and knowing your strengths will help you in the long run. Every athlete should keep in mind when thinking about his or her athletic career to do what it takes to be good for ten years, not by age ten.
>
> (Morin, 2013)

In conclusion, living in one's internal (e.g. thinking about a sore tooth) and external (e.g. watching players at training) world challenges our attentional capacity to attend appropriately to the task at hand to achieve an anticipated goal. A fine balance between these two worlds prevents the coach from self-preoccupation when others' needs unfold, yet allows him to engage self-analysis when the time is right. A coach worried about her appearance might be lost in self-thought and relay perfunctory guidance to an athlete before competition without assessing the athlete's genuine reasons for speaking with her. When we arrange these capacities afforded to us through self-awareness, we can recognize clearly how we learn to live harmoniously with each other, and support and develop education and governance for the benefit of all. Yet, in the same instance, we can also imagine the possible dark side of our capacity to plan, make decisions and control behaviour, self-evaluate, introspect, and adopt another's perspective to meet our devastating ends. Evidence to illustrate both sides abounds in sport.

Of course, the notion of self-awareness and psychological needs among coaches is only beginning to emerge within the research literature (Allen & Shaw, 2009; Pope & Hall, 2015) so we tentatively suggest how researchers and applied practitioners might advance.

Implications for future research

One of the most obvious findings from the literature on sport coaching is the conspicuous dearth of research on the psychological needs of the coach. Lyle (2002) reflected that research on sport coaching within the UK hitherto focused mainly on the science of performance and much less on coaching behaviour and practice. While the latter issues have been addressed more thoroughly in the literature since 2002, the 'act' of coaching still overshadows the 'person' doing the coaching (Allen & Shaw, 2009). We encourage researchers to place the 'person' doing the coaching as the focus of their research attention to augment our understanding about the psychological health and well-being of all coaches.

To begin this process, we have two fundamental and related questions to address from our literature review. First, do coaches engage in a process of self-awareness? And second, what are the psychological needs of sport coaches emerging from this self-examination. These research questions can be differentiated by age, gender, sport, coaching level and coaching style. By answering these elementary questions we could begin to explore the levels of coach self-awareness, the structures used to understand the self and the benefits or drawbacks of such introspection. We could also realise the prominence of the different psychological needs of coaches, and how these psychological needs are met functionally or dysfunctionally in professional and personal settings. This preliminary information could be aligned with constructs already well established such as burnout, stress and mental health. The first study of burnout in sport examined burnout among coaches (Caccese & Mayerberg, 1984) and over time research began to examine burnout among athletes. Goodger, Gorely, Lavallee and Harwood (2007) reported that perceived stress (100 per cent) was positively associated with burnout whereas commitment (100 per cent) and social support (75 per cent) were negatively associated with it. Other correlates of coach burnout included timetabling, budgets, role conflict and perceived success. Studies of coach burnout mostly used self-report measures, especially the Maslach Burnout Inventory (MBI) by Maslach and Jackson (1984); however, comparisons among studies are difficult because different versions of scales (especially the MBI) were used as well as different methods of calculating and reporting burnout scores. The nature, causes and consequences of coach burnout need to be better understood for the betterment of coach welfare (Goodger et al., 2007). Like other issues that affect coaches and athletes in sport, theoretical frameworks and suitable measurement strategies are necessary to understand burnout more thoroughly, especially how it manifests itself, affects individuals and in the short- and long-term can be prevented and treatment provided for those already affected.

One arm of the burnout literature relates to stressors experienced by coaches in sport. Thelwell, Weston, Greenlees and Hutchings' (2008) examination of stressors in elite sport from a coach's perspective identified various performance and organizational stressors. From a performance perspective, the coaches not only identified their athletes' performances but also their own, which they suggested added further evidence to support the notion that coaches should be labelled 'performers' in their own right. We encourage researchers to continue this line of research and explore how psychological, emotional and social support is best offered to, and used by, coaches.

In keeping with this theme, Olusoga, Butt, Hays and Maynard (2009) identified various stressors (e.g. conflict, pressure and expectation, isolation, athlete concerns) among six male and six female elite sport coaches within the UK. One key theme – conflict within the organization – highlighted the centrality of communication skills to manage relations in organizational teams. The need for communications skills suggests that other skills (e.g. time management) and broader psychological skills training form an arsenal from which the coach can draw when necessary. At a macro level, the concern among professional clubs, governing bodies of sport and national coach education agencies should be to clearly acknowledge the coaching experience and the likely challenges coaches will experience as they progress in sport. But awareness of stressors alone will not address the education provision necessary to help coaches cope effectively with stressors and sources of strain in sport (Thelwell et al., 2008). Regrettably, we have a limited knowledge base to understand the coping mechanisms to overcome stressors and sources of strain among coaches and this gap ought to be addressed more comprehensively. In an attempt to address this gap in the literature, Thelwell, Weston and Greenlees (2010), through interviews with three elite-level coaches, revealed strategies such as problem-, emotion-, avoidance-, appraisal-, and approach-focused dimensions to handle performance and organizational stressors. This is a fruitful line of research to follow that can ultimately feedback into the preparation, development and ongoing support of coaches from grassroots to elite and professional levels. Researchers are encouraged to design studies to evaluate the effectiveness of stress management interventions with sport coaches and this addition to our canon would allow sport psychology consultants to best support coaches to manage their effectiveness in work, whilst balancing professional and personal needs.

One of the reasons why coaches choose to coach is to contribute towards the development (i.e. physical, psychological, emotional, social) of others; but this development occurs within an erratic environment beset with loss, setbacks and failure. To bear with the suffering of others, one requires compassion. Compassion derives from the Latin words 'pati' and 'cum' which together represent 'to suffer with' (McNeill, Morrison & Nouven, 1982). But such compassion offered to so many comes at a cost and compassion fatigue ensues (Figley, 1995). Compassion fatigue accumulates through bearing the suffering of others and reflects the cost of caring (Figley, 2002). Coaches need an empathic ability to notice the pain of others, yet this ability makes one susceptive to compassion fatigue. When we turn toward self-compassion – "a basic kindness with a deep awareness of suffering of oneself and others" (Gilbert, 2009, p. xiii), we encounter a resource with several benefits such as resilience against depression and anxiety, as well as an increase in optimism and social connectedness. In psychotherapy, self-critical therapists with limited self-compassion are also critical of patients and show poorer patient outcomes (Henry, Schacht & Strupp, 1990). Without self-compassion, therefore, the person and those whom the person supports, suffer. Coming to terms with one's shortcomings is a prerequisite for compassionate care. It would be immensely enriching to know how levels of self-compassion affect the psychological health of the coach and the nature of his or her relations with others. Finally, research on the psychology of coaching in sport overwhelmingly favours the act of coaching over the person who does the coaching. In seems sensible that, for the betterment of coaching in all sports, the research emphasis should begin with the person who does the coaching and recognize how the person can be best supported to coach and from there enrich their own lives and the many thousands who pass before them from playground to podium.

Implications for applied practice

When Gould, Greenleaf, Chung and Guinan, (2002) explored US Olympic athletes and their coaches' judgments about coach–athlete relationship factors that influence performance, it appeared as though the balance of responsibility for sound relationships and successful performance tilted irrevocably toward the coach. For example, the factors included the athlete's trust in the wisdom and experience of the coach; the coach's ability to keep things simple, to deal with crisis situations, to be decisive but fair; the coach's ability to establish trust with the athlete; and the coach's ability to stay calm under pressure. In short, the coach not only coaches but also performs; thus, just like athletes, coaches need support to manage stress and other distractions.

A balance between athletic and personal excellence seems a worthy pursuit that can be achieved through established coach education programmes and discussion forums. Sport psychology practitioners, through listening, emotional support and personal assistance, can also offer social support to coaches who may not receive it through other channels within their organisation (Giges et al., 2004). Although the competent sport psychologist can fulfil this role, it might not be a role willingly accepted by the coach because of present perceptions, beliefs, and attitudes toward sport psychology support. Even if the coach accepts sport psychology support for other professional concerns (e.g. to work with a diffident athlete), the coach's personal difficulties might remain off limits regardless of the effects of these personal difficulties in relations with others (e.g. athletes, sport science team, administrators). The challenge with such psychological barriers places the onus on the sport psychology consultant to find ways to build trust with the coach through her professional competencies (perhaps working with athletes or assistant coaches) whilst remaining open and adapting cautiously to opportunities for more personal discussions with the coach.

Some coaches might be keen to engage in self-reflection, but, as we indicated earlier with reflective practice, might not have the skills and experience to do so. At this juncture, the sport psychology consultant can create appealing educations sessions that present strategies for assessing self-awareness such as the Johari window (Luft & Ingham, 1955), illustrate psychological needs apparent in everyday life and demonstrate how emotions (e.g. guilt, shame) might manifest themselves in personal and professional life (Giges et al., 2004).

More broadly, given the often overwhelming psychological demands placed upon coaches at all levels, it seems prudent to support coaches to manage those (Fletcher & Scott, 2010). We need evidence-based stress management strategies differentiated by the level of intervention: primary, secondary, and tertiary (see Fletcher, Hanton & Mellalieu, 2006). A sensible, rational and ethical first step ought to be primary intervention to reduce the quantity, frequency, and/or intensity of stressors (Fletcher & Scott, 2010). Interventions can help coaches to manage their duties, (e.g. workload, work patterns), relationships (e.g. reducing conflict and promoting positive relations), role (e.g. understand, accept and manage the role), and change (e.g. manage and communicate change fairly and transparently). Sensible procedures and practices such as skills assessment and development, time management and communication skills training, active management of the organisational environment, educational workshops and formal and informal group discussions can support the coach (Cassidy, Potrac & McKenzie, 2006; Giges et al., 2004). Secondary intervention involve helping coaches to modify their responses to stressors though self-awareness and enhancing resilience to external demands (see Giges et al., 2004). The sport psychologist can facilitate the coach's self-awareness through appropriate questioning and discussion as well as developing interventions and beginning change. One particular intervention emphasis would be on hardiness training, which intends to optimize the coaches' commitment and motivational profiles, and help coaches to focus on controllable aspects of the environment, viewing events as challenges rather than threats. At this juncture, psychological skills such as self-talk, imagery and relaxation are relevant to the coach. As mentioned earlier, social support represents a vital, sustaining element of coaches' resilience.

Finally, for those coaches who require support to recover from the damaging consequences of stress, we engage tertiary interventions. These interventions are a rehabilitative approach to stress management after coaches have suffered illness or burnout from the strain of their work. No research to date has examined how effective counselling of distressed coaches or rehabilitation techniques for coaches suffering burnout are. These three levels of intervention persuade us that organizational change offers the most benefit to coaches but is pragmatically difficult to implement. We can, however, focus on managing coach behaviours and help coaches to manage their own stress.

Recently, Pope and Hall (2015) examined the relationship between coaches' basic psychological needs, identity prominence and their commitment, positive affect and intentions to persist. They found initial support for the links from coaches' basic psychological needs and identity prominence to their positive affect and commitment. Coaches' autonomy need satisfaction is positively related to their psychological well-being (Stebbings, Taylor & Spray, 2011). In other words, coaches who experience a sense of volition and feel that they are the instigator of their behaviour are likely to flourish psychologically within their coaching role. Similar to athlete-based research, Stebbings et al. (2011) reported competence as the strongest predictor of psychological well-being. One's perceived competence, therefore, ought to be facilitated through the workplace via coach education, supportive structures to allow each coach to develop coaching techniques and any other facet of the coaching role that would raise perceptions of competence. Autonomy and competence form a central pillar of psychological well-being for the coach but one's relatedness need satisfactions cannot be overestimated (Bartholomew, Ntoumanis, Ryan, Bosch & Thogersen-Ntoumani, 2011; Mageau & Vallerand, 2003).

If we consider formal sport as a mechanism that houses many cogs intentioned to cooperate by design to achieve a desired outcome (e.g. help athletes to gain enjoyment, competence, confidence, success) we see that coaches form a dominant function within that mechanism. The mesh between this cog and the others depends significantly upon the interpersonal skills of the coach as well as technical, tactical, pedagogical and organisational skills; but, fundamentally, coaches are people too whose psychological needs, growth and well-being deserve our empirical attention and support in professional practice.

Notes

1 Glasgow Caledonian University, Glasgow, UK
2 Springfield College, USA

References

Allen, J. B., & Shaw, S. (2009). Women coaches' perceptions of their sport organiza-tions' social environment supporting coaches' psychological needs? *The Sport Psychologist, 23*, 346–366.

Bartholomew, K. J., Ntoumanis, N., Ryan, R. M., Bosch, J. A. & Thogersen-Ntoumani, C. (2011). Self-determination theory and diminished functioning: The role of interpersonal control and psychological need thwarting. *Personality and Social Psychology Bulletin, 37*, 1459–1473.

Burnard, P. (1997). *Know yourself! Self-awareness activities for nurses and other health professionals.* London: Wiley-Blackwell.

Caccese, T. M., & Mayerberg, C. K. (1984). Gender differences in perceived burnout of college coaches. *Journal of Sport and Exercise Psychology, 6*, 279–288.

Cassidy, T., Potrac, P. & McKenzie, A. (2006). Evaluating and reflecting upon a coach education initiative: The CoDe of rugby. *The Sport Psychologist, 20*, 145–161.

Deci, E. L. (2002). Facilitating autonomous self-regulation through support of basic psychological needs. *Journal of Sport and Exercise Psychology, 24* (Suppl.), S50.

Douglas, K., & Carless, D. (2006). Performance, discovery and relational narratives among women professional tournament golfers. *Women in Sport and Physical Activity Journal, 15*(2), 14–27.

Douglas, K., & Carless, D. (2008). Using stories in coach education. *International Journal of Sports Science and Coaching, 3(1)*, 33–49.

Epstein, S. (1973). The self-concept revisited: Or a theory of a theory. *American Psychologist, 28*, 404–16.

Figley, C. R. (1995). Compassion fatigue as secondary trauma stress disorder: An overview. In C. R. Figley (Ed.), *Compassion fatigue: Coping with secondary trauma stress disorder in those who treat the traumatized* (pp. 1–20). New York: Routledge.

Figley, C. R. (2002). Compassion fatigue: Psychotherapists chronic lack of self-care. *Journal of Clinical Psychology, 58*, 1433–1441.

Fletcher, D., & Scott, M. (2010). Psychological stress in sports coaches: A review of concepts, research and practice. *Journal of Sports Sciences, 28*(2), 127–137.

Fletcher, D., Hanton, S. & Mellalieu, S. D. (2006). An organizational stress review: Conceptual and theoretical issues in competitive sport. In S. Hanton, & S. D. Mellalieu (Eds.), *Literature reviews in sport psychology* (pp. 321–373). Hauppauge, NY: Nova Science.

Frankl, V. (1992). *Man's search for meaning: An introduction to logotherapy.* Boston: Beacon Press.

Giges, B. (2000). Removing psychological barriers: Clearing the way. In M. B. Andersen, (Ed.), *Doing sport psychology* (pp. 17–31), Champaign, IL: Human Kinetics.

Giges, B., Petitpas, A. J. & Vernacchia, R. A. (2004). Helping coaches meet their own needs: Challenges for the sport psychology consultant. *The Sport Psychologist, 18*, 430–444.

Gilbert, P. (2009). *The compassionate mind.* London: Constable & Robinson Ltd.

Goleman, D. (1998). *Working with emotional intelligence.* New York: Bantam Books.

Goodger, K., Gorely, T., Lavallee, D. & Harwood, C. (2007). Burnout in sport: A systematic review. *The Sport Psychologist, 21*, 127–151.

Gould, D., Greenleaf, C., Chung, Y. & Guinan, D. (2002). A survey of US Atlanta and Nagano Olympians: Factors influencing performance. *Research Quarterly for Exercise and Sport, 73*, 175–186.

Gould, D., Greenleaf, C., Guinan, D. & Chung, Y. (2002). A survey of US Olympic coaches: Variables perceived to have influenced athlete performances and coach effectiveness. *The Sport Psychologist, 16*, 229–250.

Henry, W. P., Schacht, T. E. & Strupp, H. H. (1990). Patient and therapist introject interpersonal process, and differential psychotherapy outcome. *Journal of Consulting and Clinical Psychology, 58*, 768–774.

Kelly, S. F. (1997). *Bill Shankly: It's much more important than that: The biography.* London: Ebury Publishing.

Leary, M. R. (2004). *The curse of the self: Self-awareness, egotism, and the quality of human life.* New York: Oxford University Press.

Leary, M. R., & Tangney, J. P. (2003). The self as an organizing construct in the behavioural sciences. In M. R. Leary, & J. P. Tangney, *Handbook of self and identity* (pp. 3–14). New York: Guilford.

Luft J., & Ingham H. (1955). *The Johari window: A graphic model for interpersonal relations.* University of California: Western Training Lab.

Lyle, J. (2002). *Sports coaching concepts: A framework for coaches' behaviour.* London: Routledge.

Mageau, G. A., & Vallerand, R. J. (2003). The coach–athlete relationship: A motivational model. *Journal of Sports Sciences, 21*, 883–904

Markus, H., & Wurf, E. (1987), The dynamic self-concept: A social psychological perspective. *Annual Review of Psychology, 38*, 299–337.

Maslow, A. (1987). *Motivation and personality* (3rd edn). New York: Harper & Row.

Maslach, C., & Jackson, S. E. (1984). Burnout in organizational settings. In S. Oskamp (Ed.), *Applied social psychology annual: Applications in organizational settings* (Vol. 5, pp. 133–153). Beverly Hills, CA: Sage.

McGregor, I., and Marigold, D. C. (2003). Defensive zeal and the uncertain self: What makes you so sure? *Journal of Personality and Social Psychology, 85*, 838–852.

McNeill, D. P., Morrison, D. A., & Nouwen, H. (1982). *Compassion: A reflection on the Christian life.* Garden City, NJ: Doubleday.

Morin, T. (2013). *No more broken eggs: A guide to optimizing the sports experience for athletes, coaches, parents, and clinicians.* Inkwater Press: Kindle Edition.

Olusoga, P., Butt, J., Hays, K., & Maynard, I. W. (2009). Stress in elite sports coaching: Identifying stressors. *Journal of Applied Sport Psychology, 21*(4), 442–459.

Pope, J. P., & Hall, C. (2015). Understanding the relationship between coaches' basic psychological needs and identity prominence and their commitment, positive affect, and intentions to persist. *The Sport Psychologist, 29*, 134–142.

Ravizza, K. (1998). Increasing awareness for sport performance. In J. M. Williams (Ed.), *Applied sport psychology: Personal growth to peak performance* (3rd edn, pp. 171–181). Mountain View, CA: Mayfield.

Short, S. E., & Short, M. W. (2005). Role of the coach in the coach–athlete relationship. *Lancet, 366*: s29–s30.

Smith, R. E., & Smoll, F. L. (1997). Coaching the coaches: Youth sports as a scientific and applied behavioural setting. *Current Directions in Psychological Science, 6,* 16–21.

Stebbings, J., Taylor, I. M. & Spray, C. M. (2011). Antecedents of perceived coach autonomy supportive and controlling behaviours: Coach psychological need satisfaction and well-being. *Journal of Sport and Exercise Psychology, 33*(2), 255–272.

Sutton, J., & Stewart, W. (2012). *Learning to counsel: Develop the skills, insight and knowledge to counsel others.* Oxford, UK: How To Books Ltd.

Thelwell, R. C., Weston, N. J. V. & Greenlees, I. (2010). Coping with stressors in elite sport: A coach perspective. *European Journal of Sport Science, 10*(4), 243–253.

Thelwell, R. C., Weston, N. J. V., Greenlees, I. A. & Hutchings, N. V. (2008). Stressors in elite sport: A coach perspective. *Journal of Sports Sciences, 26*(9), 905–918.

Vernacchia, R. A., & McGuire, R. T. (1998). What coaches want from sport psychology. *Journal of Applied Sport Psychology, 10,* (Suppl), 129–130.

8 High performance coaching

Demands and development

*Steven B. Rynne,[1] Clifford J. Mallett,[1]
and Martin W. O. Rabjohns[1]*

Introduction

Despite its predominately volunteer workforce, the professionalisation agenda in sports coaching has been promoted in a variety of forums. This drive has most notably taken place within high performance coaching realms (Lyle, 2002; Rynne & Mallett, 2012; Trudel & Gilbert, 2006). Foundational to this notion of professionalisation is a greater acknowledgement of coaches as performers in their own right. That is, if coaches are viewed as performers in the sporting environment, we might better consider and develop the associated knowledge bases informing their practice, establish and refine the organisational structures that support them, and continue to develop, refine, and enforce the ethical practices of performance coaches.

Once coaches are more accurately positioned as performers in their own right, it becomes more obvious that there is a need to support their performance. For too long it has been assumed that coaches are appointed to roles because they have all of the answers. In this chapter we seek to continue the repositioning of coaches as performers who should be expected to continually develop their craft and who are deserving of ongoing support. For high performance coaches, this includes the need to demonstrate significant personal agency in continually evolving their practices. For the employers of high performance coaches, this includes the need to continue to invest in those deemed suitable for appointment to coaching roles.

Key terms

To fully understand the notion of performance coaching, it is imperative for the notion to be contextualised with respect to the literature to date, and in relation to suggestions for moving forward. With this in mind, 'performance coaching' is understood to involve intensive commitment to the preparation of programs with obvious attempts to influence and control performance variables (Lyle, 2002). This work requires high levels of coach and athlete commitment and interaction, the development of systematic and evidence-based performance programs, and engagement in highly formalised competition structures, and takes place with respect to specific contextual constraints. The result is a highly complex collection of practices that has variously been described as chaotic and ever evolving (Bowes & Jones, 2006; Cushion, 2007; Lyle, 2002; Rynne, Mallett, & Tinning, 2006). Supporting the notion of performance coaching is that of 'quality coaching' that involves context-specific appraisals of what the coach intends to do and how able they are to achieve that. In this sense, quality coaching is associated with goal achievement. It is, however, bounded by time and place so there is a need to consider the quality of players, available resources, and prevailing climate (Mallett, 2011). Learning is central to quality coaching in that it should be facilitated for coaches, athletes and their support staff (Armour, 2004; Mallett, 2011).

Review of the literature

Coach as performer

In advancing the case that the coach is a performer, a variety of scholars have sought to better understand what tasks coaches actually undertake in performing their work. A related line of inquiry examines the knowledge and skills that coaches must possess if they are to successfully carry out their craft. There have also been a variety of studies that focus on the practices used to evaluate the performance of coaches. With these approaches in mind, the section that follows first includes some consideration of the key aspects that comprise performance coaching work, the role of contexts in carrying out these tasks, and the inherent complexity involved. We then offer some commentary regarding the ways in which performance coaches inform their practice, and conclude the section with some discussion of how performance may be judged in sports coaching.

What tasks are coaches performing?

One starting point in our appraisal of coach performance is through an examination of the great number of tasks that coaches are responsible for in undertaking their work. Indeed, behavioural accounts have historically been popular in examinations of performance coaching (Côté & Salmela, 1996; Douge & Hastie, 1993; Gilbert & Trudel, 2004a; Smith, Smoll, & Christianson, 1996). Early work revealed much about performance coaching related to observable behaviours such as feedback, instruction, and questioning (Côté, Yardley, Hay, Sedgwick, & Baker, 1999; Cushion, 2010). However, insights were often limited to training and competition environments, with much of the coach's work remaining largely unaccounted for. More recent behavioural accounts have sought to build on previous endeavours while expanding in scope so as to capture the variety of tasks required of modern professional and Olympic sport coaches (Bloom, 2002; Côté & Sedgwick, 2003; Cushion, Armour, & Jones, 2006; Gilbert & Trudel, 2004b; Lyle, 2002). For example, Rynne and colleagues (Rynne et al., 2006, Rynne, Mallett, & Tinning, 2010) found that high performance coaches were responsible for a variety of direct task behaviours (e.g. hands on coaching, pastoral care), indirect task behaviours (e.g. programming, managing a program/squad, managing support staff, research involvement, talent identification and selection), administrative maintenance behaviours (administration – budgeting, reporting and generic paperwork) and public relations behaviours (liaising with stakeholders, representing the organisation, sharing with other coaches).

Having established some of the tasks that performance coaches may be held responsible for, an interrelated area is the context in which the coach operates. Highlighting the importance of context and its relationship with appraisals of coach performance, Côté and Gilbert (2009) make the point that "in order to be effective, coaches must be aware of the over-riding sport context in which they work" (p. 315). Some of the most destructive examples of coaching have come from the inappropriate adoption of coaching practices from one context (e.g. elite, professional sport) to another (e.g. junior sport) (Mallett & Rynne, 2012). Indeed, the most fundamental differences between coaching contexts relate to competitive level and desired outcomes (Erickson, Bruner, MacDonald, & Côté, 2008). The implication is that any consideration of coach performance must take into account the prevailing context.

Underpinning the work of coaches across a variety of contexts is the requisite knowledge. Côté and Gilbert (2009) proposed that we might better understand the performance of coaches through a consideration of three types of requisite knowledge: professional knowledge, interpersonal knowledge, and intrapersonal knowledge. Even among the general sporting public, there would be widespread agreement that high quality coaches are recognisable through their extensive professional knowledge. While knowledge of the sport is important, Côté and Gilbert (2009) note that professional knowledge also relates to the relevant sport sciences (e.g. anatomy and biomechanics, exercise physiology), as well as the pedagogical knowledge that is foundational to coaching practice. Even so, professional knowledge alone is insufficient to wholly inform performance-coaching work. Coaches do not work in isolation. In short, to perform well coaches must interact with myriad individuals and groups. For this reason, the performance of coaches is underpinned by an interpersonal knowledge base that is appropriate regarding age, competitive level, and social circumstances, and that informs the performance coach's multifarious relationships with others. Finally, and advocated by many (e.g. Carson, 2008; Gilbert & Trudel, 2005; Knowles, Gilbourne, Borrie, & Nevill, 2001; Lyons, Rynne, & Mallett, 2012; Nelson & Cushion, 2006), performance coaches require comprehensive understandings of themselves – intrapersonal knowledge. This propensity for introspection and reflection is said to drive the learning of coaches, facilitating ongoing improvements in coach performance and subsequent athletic outcomes.

Making judgements about coaches and coaching practice is a crucial yet seemingly complex task. A major issue (as alluded to above) is that people often do not have a sound understanding of what coaches do (sometimes even coaches themselves) (Bloom, 2002; Mallett & Côté, 2006). Another issue is that many of the ways in which coaches are typically evaluated are premised on unexplained assumptions about what impact the coach can reasonably have and do not account for a range of confounds (e.g. contested nature of sport, physical maturation effects). The fact that evaluations occur is no bad thing. Evaluation has been promoted as being essential to ensure the effectiveness and optimisation of development systems (for coaches and athletes alike) (Erickson et al., 2008; Howe, 1990; Mallett & Côté, 2006). While there are many options, below we note three prominent methods of evaluating coach performance.

One frame for evaluating coaches relates to success. This frame has been by far the most popular form of evaluation (Côté & Gilbert, 2009; Dawson, Dobson, & Gerrard, 2000; Howe, 1990; Mallett & Côté, 2006). Success is tied to the achievement of an objective and is related to publicly recognisable accomplishments and, traditionally, coaching success has been marked by an association with successful performers. While this approach is easy and convenient to measure, the obvious issue is that the contribution of the coach to individual or team performance outcomes cannot be clearly judged (e.g. relative contribution, different circumstances, effective recruitment vs competition management, inheriting a successful team).

Many, generally under the auspices of coach certification/accreditation systems, have sought to evaluate coach performance with respect to their relative competence (Dickson, 2001a, 2001b; ICCE, 2013; Lyle, 2007; Myers, Wolfe, Maier, Feltz, & Reckase, 2006; Trudel & Gilbert, 2006). Competence may be thought of as some kind of threshold ability to fulfil a role. Evaluations of coach competence are generally considered to be useful insofar as they may assist in very basic gatekeeping/quality assurance for sports. Of issue is that competence might suggest some minimal ability, maybe 50 per cent pass, rather than some standard of excellence. In short, being told you are competent is not really a mark of high esteem!

In attempting to evaluate quality coaching, Mallett and Côté (2006) have previously proposed a three-step method of evaluating high performance coaches that involves data collected using an instrument such as the Coaching Behaviour Scale for Sport (Côté et al., 1999), the generation of a summary report inclusive of descriptive information regarding frequency of behaviours demonstrated by the coach, which can be compared to previous results or to a criterion measure, with a final stage whereby appropriate personnel view the combined report and provide guidance for individual coach development. The most interesting aspect to this proposed evaluation of coaching performance is the emphasis on gaining feedback about coach performance from multiple sources, including athletes. It is argued that any single account of coaches' work is problematic and, as such, Mallett and Côté (2006) argue that any assessment of coach performance could complement results from athlete evaluations with data from other sources such as objective indicators of performance (e.g. win/loss records, annual progression over the past three years, observation of coaches' behaviours in practices and competitions).

Summarising the coach as performer

- In elite sport, coaches are being positioned as performers in their own right, with scrutiny being given to the tasks that they are responsible for, the contexts they operated within, and the knowledge that is foundational to their practice.
- While we have attempted to provide an account of coaching performance that might appear rather simplistic in nature, the work of high performance coaches (tasks and contexts) is complex, and subsequently the examination of their work is problematic.
- Despite this, progressive researchers, coaching administrators and coaches themselves will continue to seek clarity regarding the work that high performance coaches undertake and what can reasonably be attributed to them regarding their performance.

Much of what underpins this desire for clarity is a drive for improvement, which is what we address in the following section – Coach as learner.

Coach as learner

Performance coaches should, by necessity, be learners (Armour, 2010; Cushion et al., 2010; Mallett, 2011; Rynne & Mallett, 2014). The regular turn-over of athletes and the ever-evolving nature of performance sport require that even the most proficient of coaches seek to develop and alter their practice. It might be said that coaches are not alone in this regard. Highly skilled workers in a variety of industries (e.g. educators, medical practitioners, business managers) carry out their roles in similarly dynamic and professionally challenging workplaces, requiring regular improvements to their practices. Coaching, however, is quite different to many other vocations. The most relevant example relates to the absence of firmly established educational pathways such as those that exist in Physical Education teaching. Of course this has the potential to make learning and development more of a challenge for coaches. There are also many other characteristics that are shared with other vocations/professions that make learning similarly challenging. For example, as in other workplaces, coach development is characterised by differential access and guidance based on cultural practices, competition, group affiliations, and hierarchies (Billett, 2001; Rynne & Mallett, 2012). The section that follows includes a consideration of how it is that performance coaches are able to develop their practice under such conditions.

Prior to examining coach learning it is worth noting that there are various conceptualisations of learning. While all offer valuable insights, none could be considered to be universal, nor universally compelling. Even within our relatively small field of sports coaching, numerous theories have been employed to varying effect (for a useful review see e.g. Cushion et al., 2010). The point is that the perspective adopted must be fit for purpose. In this section, we make use of the terms 'formal', 'non-formal', and 'informal' (Coombs & Ahmed, 1974;

Mallett, Trudel, Lyle, & Rynne, 2009; Nelson, Cushion, & Potrac, 2006) to categorise learning opportunities. We do so with the aim of providing conceptual clarity and ease of interpretation. These terms will be described later in this section.

Formal learning situations can be thought of as occurring in 'traditional' learning settings. They are institutionalised, hierarchically structured and part of a broader educational system (Coombs & Ahmed, 1974; Mallett et al., 2009; Nelson et al., 2006). The two areas that fit within formal learning that we will focus on are large-scale coach education (accreditation/certification) programs and tertiary (university/college) coaching programs.

Coaches engage frequently with formal learning. Indeed, coach accreditation (certification) programs are still the most widespread attempt to direct the learning of coaches in many western countries. These programs have experienced some success. For example, accreditation has fairly widespread recognition within sport and has served an important 'ticketing' function in many western countries (Dickson, 2001b). An issue, however, is that they have been shown to be relatively low impact when compared with the many hours spent in informal learning situations as an athlete and coach (Mallett et al., 2009; Nelson et al., 2006). Beyond this, programs have been criticised with respect to content (e.g. over-emphasis on biophysical and under representation of sociocultural aspects of coaching), delivery (e.g. artificially discrete topic presentation format, over-simplification of process, cramming too much information into very short courses), and assessment (e.g. lack of assessment and unsound practices) (Erickson et al., 2008; Lyle, 2007; Nelson et al., 2006; Sullivan & Gee, 2008). So it is clear that, for coaches who have continued to evolve and develop their craft, they have done so beyond such offerings.

Another formal learning situation is tertiary study in sports coaching. As opposed to formal offerings through accreditation pathways, there is some evidence to show that those coaches who complete tertiary study (in any field but especially for those who completed it in a coaching-related field) rate it as being extremely valuable (Araya, Bennie, & O'Connor, 2015; Demers, Woodburn, & Savard, 2006; Mallett & Dickens, 2009; Mallett, Rynne, & Billett, 2014; Rynne et al., 2010). For performance coaches, the value of tertiary programs relates to the foundational knowledge development (i.e. to inform practice and enhance interactions with paraprofessionals), emphasis on the development of critical thinking and reflective skills, and widespread (i.e. within and beyond sport) recognition of the qualifications. Beyond this, an area of even more recent attention is that of formal online learning. Under the right circumstances, formal learning opportunities (e.g. tertiary programs that make use of online educational platforms and/or shared online blogs) have the potential to increase levels of reflection and impact on coaching practice (Mallett & Dickens, 2009; Stoszkowski, Collins, & Olsson, 2015). It should be noted though, that formal tertiary study options for coaches are still a relatively recent phenomenon in western countries.

Non-formal learning situations are somewhat similar to formal learning situations in that they are organised and systematic. The primary difference is that they occur outside of overall educational frameworks or formal systems (Coombs & Ahmed, 1974; Mallett et al., 2009; Nelson et al., 2006). In high performance coaching, examples might include discrete coaching clinics or seminars, specialist conferences and workshops. Research on the contribution of non-formal learning is scarce in coaching. What we do know from related studies is that there is great variability with respect to the content and perceived benefit and that informal contributions (discussed next) are of far greater significance to performance coaches.

Informal learning has been universally recognised as the form of learning that has most informed the practices of current high performance coaches. Informal learning is the learning that occurs through daily experiences and exposure to the environment (Coombs & Ahmed, 1974; Mallett et al., 2009; Mallett, Rossi, Rynne, & Tinning, 2015; Nelson et al., 2006). The two areas of greatest interest in this regard for high performance coaches are experiences as an athlete and experiences as a coach (on the job learning).

With few exceptions, high performance coaches have been athletes in the sports they now coach (Erickson, Côté, & Fraser-Thomas, 2007; Gilbert, Côté, & Mallett, 2006; Occhino, Mallett, & Rynne, 2013; Trudel & Gilbert, 2006). It has previously been argued that, through their time as athletes, future coaches are actually undertaking a sort of 'apprenticeship of observation' whereby they are observers and recipients of coaching practice (Cushion, Armour, & Jones, 2003; Schempp & Graber, 1992; Sage, 1989). The implication is that they become familiar with many of the technical aspects of coaching as well as the coaching culture and 'what it means to be a coach'. This acculturation has both positive and negative implications. For example, it may help facilitate the easy transition into coaching roles through the individual's familiarity with the associated sport-specific language and practices; however, it may in fact inhibit innovation and stifle new ways of thinking if the culture is simply endorsed, unchallenged, and/or resistant to change.

It must be acknowledged that not all playing experience is equal. The social capital that comes with being an elite performer in your sport affords ex-players who now coach a variety of opportunities that those of less athletic prowess simply do not have access to (Rynne, 2014). For instance, ex-elite athletes are presumed to have instant credibility with players and their sporting communities more broadly (Côté & Gilbert, 2009; Occhino et al., 2013). As a result, those with elite athletic backgrounds in the sport tend to be offered high performance coaching positions earlier than and in preference to their non-elite athlete peers, and are able to access more experienced and knowledgeable coaches and/or former teammates when presented with problems early in their coaching careers (Occhino et al., 2013; Rynne, 2014). Their privileged position within their sports means they have access to significant learning opportunities that are inaccessible to other coaches.

A key question becomes of importance when considering the contributions that a playing background has on current coaching practice and future coaching potential: how much experience as an athlete is enough (e.g. how many seasons, at what level, with what outcomes)? A number of authors have noted large ranges in the previous athletic experiences of current coaches, suggesting that there may be a minimum threshold of experience necessary for competence (Côté, 2006; Erickson et al., 2007; Rynne et al., 2010). In addition, what we do know about experience is that it is a necessary but not sufficient criterion for expertise; that is, experience is crucial to becoming good at something but it does not guarantee that improvement will occur. With respect to experience as an athlete at the highest level, it is being increasingly recognised that having been an elite player does not necessarily ensure success as a coach (Hoch, 2004; Irwin, Hanton, & Kerwin, 2004; Rynne et al., 2010). It is possible that coaches who were better-than-average but less-than-outstanding athletes had opportunities to develop their coaching skills early in their personal histories. In a related way, there is no compelling evidence that most aspects of coaching could not be learned via other means in the absence of specific experience as an athlete at a comparable level. Finally, irrespective of level, it has also been argued that, while experience as an athlete is highly valued early in a coach's career, it becomes less important as that career progresses (Mallett et al., 2014) should they remain employed.

High performance coaches rate 'on the job experience' (that is, experiences while performing coaching work) as being of greatest value to their development (Abraham, Collins, & Martindale, 2006; Cushion et al., 2010; Gilbert et al., 2006; Mallett et al., 2014; Nelson et al., 2006; Trudel & Gilbert, 2006). However, Irwin and colleagues (2004) noted that, while learning in this way was a major source, it was not necessarily by choice. Like the athletic experiences of coaches, the previous coaching experiences of individual high performance coaches are variable and idiosyncratic. The implication is that, like athletic background, judgments regarding coaching ability cannot be based on the volume of coaching experience alone. The mere accumulation of coaching experience is not sufficient to facilitate meaningful learning (Eraut, 2004; Lynch & Mallett, 2006). In short, the quality of those experiences is going to be more important than the quantity of those experiences (Mallett et al., 2014).

It has been proposed that previous coaching experience (in combination with previous athletic experience) is the closest thing to having formal professional socialisation for coaching (Sage, 1989). More appropriately, the notion of 'coming to know' was a theme that has emerged more recently in coaching research, whereby no single incident is typically identified for the development of an aspect of coaching work. Rather, upon reflection, coaches report an overall process of becoming, in which they make incremental changes to their practices (Mallett et al., 2015). Coaches learn a variety of things while preparing for, or performing, their work. The ability to take shortcuts or at least make more educated decisions was something that has previously been identified by coaches as a contribution previous coaching experiences made to current coaching work. These skills are hallmarks of expertise (Collins & Collins, 2014; Côté & Gilbert, 2009; Nash, Sproule, & Horton, 2011).

A fundamental aspect of engaging in coaching work is interactions with athletes. While this is an aspect that is surprisingly absent in many accounts of coach learning, it has received some recognition as an important source for high performance coaches. Coaches have reported that previous experiences coaching athletes allowed them to be more efficient and effective by taking pre-emptive measures. Their previous experiences undoubtedly also gave them, and presumably their current athletes, some piece of mind regarding the outcomes of current training or treatment. The authenticity of this learning is said to make it most compelling for coaching. Learning in this way has, however, been somewhat likened by coaches and administrators to drowning, in that coaches either learned to perform the roles quickly or perished.

Coaching is a social activity (Lyle, 2002) and the significance of learning from and through others has been recognised in many studies (e.g. Occhino et al., 2013; Trudel & Gilbert, 2006). While learning coaching work has been found to be problematic largely because of the highly contested nature of the culture of sport (Mallett et al., 2014, 2015) nonetheless it is apparent that 'significant others' strongly influence the development of high performance coaches. The typical lack of constructive feedback available for coaches regarding their practice, coupled with the need to constantly update and improve their coaching, precipitates the need to develop a network of external confidantes and contacts that high performance coaches can draw upon. These 'people of influence' (Mallett et al., 2015) include assistant coaches, coaching peers, former coaches and high performance personnel, paraprofessionals (e.g. sport science staff), and administrators. Developing a social network assists coaches in affirming and challenging their coaching practices.

Summarising the coach as learner

- Positioning high performance coaches as learners is central to the professionalisation of coaching as a vocation; this is due to the evolving nature of high performance coaches' work and the lack of a formal educational pathway for entry into the vocation.
- High performance coaches are learners – and they learn from a variety of sources (idiosyncratic and serendipitous development).
- Formal contributions to learning have a mixed history with many people (scholars and practitioners) expecting too much of coach accreditation processes, and quality tertiary programs in sports coaching being a relatively new advent in many western countries.
- Non-formal learning opportunities differentially contribute to coach development.
- Informal contributions to learning continue to be dominant (as is the case with most vocations/professions). Questions are increasingly being raised about the contribution of athletic experience in coaching, but on-the-job experiences continue to be a primary source of learning for high performance coaches (as for most vocations/professions).

Implications for future research

While there have been excellent gains made regarding what we know about high performance coaching demands and development, there is still much to be advanced. Of primary concern regarding our understanding of coaching performance is the need to better inform processes such as identification, development, recruitment, appointment, deployment, and termination of coaches. Recent interest in the 'profiling' (i.e. assessment/evaluation) of coaches may help achieve this. An important caveat is that the scope of profiles must accurately reflect what it is that coaches can be held responsible for, and that they are conducted with a developmental focus (i.e. strengths based and with a view to foster and improve future coach performance).

Building on this developmental focus, there is a need to further investigate formal and non-formal learning opportunities available for high performance coaches such as accreditation, given its widespread and generally compulsory nature; tertiary study, given its recent emergence and financial costs; and Continuing Professional Development (CPD), given its prevalence in other fields. Studies could consider the integration of accreditation, tertiary programs and CPD offerings, connections with international frameworks, and the emergence of digital landscapes. Informal contributions to learning could also be explored further with more research required to examine the contribution of elite experience as an athlete and harnessing 'on-the-job' contributions so that they can be recognised and better shaped (including learning from athletes).

Implications for applied practice

There are a number of implications for those who are involved in the employment, support, and evaluations of coaches. The volatile and political nature (Potrac & Jones, 2009) of high performance coaching environments means that in any given year millions of dollars are wasted and numerous careers are ended through poor hire or early separation related to high performance coaches. Organisations that employ high performance coaches should be engaging in evidence-based appointments and evaluations that strongly consider the personal–organisational fit. Once judgements have been made, organisations should also seek to consider their social and physical environments with respect to learning opportunities and structure them accordingly to support the on-going development of their coaches. It makes sense to appropriately nurture a significant investment such as a high performance coach.

There are also implications for coaches themselves in advancing their practice and position. Fundamentally, high performance coaches should be aware of their practice. In reality this means engaging in systematic data collection regarding their own coaching and involving themselves in regular structured reflection. Related to this, high performance coaches should value the importance of life-long learning, investing in their own learning and prioritising it as part of the daily training environment. Just as they expect incremental improvements in their athletes' performances, they too should seek improvement and identify ways to evaluate the quality of their work, and from multiple sources, especially the athletes.

Note

1 The University of Queensland, Australia

References

Abraham, A., Collins, D., & Martindale, R. (2006). The coaching schematic: Validation through expert coach consensus. *Journal of Sports Sciences*, *24*(6), 549–564.

Araya, J., Bennie, A., & O'Connor, D. (2015). Understanding performance coach development: Perceptions about a postgraduate coach education program. *International Sport Coaching Journal*, *2*(1), 3–14.

Armour, K. (2010). The learning coach … the learning approach: Professional development for sports coach professionals. In J. Lyle, & C. Cushion (Eds.), Sports coaching: Professionalisation and practice (pp. 153–164). Edinburgh: Elsevier.

Armour, K. M. (2004). Coaching pedagogy. In R. Jones, K. Armour, & P. Potrac (Eds.), *Sports coaching cultures: From practice to theory* (pp. 94–115). London: Routledge.

Billett, S. (2001). Learning throughout working life: Interdependencies at work. *Studies in Continuing Education*, *23*(1), 19–35.

Bloom, G. (2002). Coaching demands and responsibilities of expert coaches. In J. M. Silva, & D. Stevens (Eds.), *Psychological foundations of sport* (pp. 438–465). Boston, MA: Allyn and Bacon.

Bowes, I., & Jones, R. L. (2006). Working at the edge of chaos: Understanding coaching as a complex, interpersonal system. *The Sport Psychologist*, *20*(2), 235–245.

Carson, F. (2008). Utilizing video to facilitate reflective practice: Developing sports coaches. *International Journal of Sports Science and Coaching*, *3*(3), 381–390.

Collins, L., & Collins, D. (2014). Integration of professional judgement and decision-making in high-level adventure sports coaching practice. *Journal of Sports Sciences*, 1–12.

Coombs, P. H., & Ahmed, M. (1974). *Attacking rural poverty: How nonformal education can help*. Baltimore, MD: Johns Hopkins University Press.

Côté, J. (2006). The development of coaching knowledge. *International Journal of Sports Science and Coaching*, *1*(3), 217–222.

Côté, J., & Gilbert, W. (2009). An integrative definition of coaching effectiveness and expertise. *International Journal of Sports Science and Coaching*, *4*(3), 307–323.

Côté, J., & Salmela, J. H. (1996). The organisational tasks of high-performance gymnastic coaches. *The Sport Psychologist*, *10*, 247–260.

Côté, J., & Sedgwick, W. A. (2003). Effective behaviours of expert rowing coaches: A qualitative investigation of Canadian athletes and coaches. *International Sports Journal*, *7*(1), 62.

Côté, J., Yardley, J., Hay, J., Sedgwick, W., & Baker, J. (1999). An exploratory examination of the coaching behaviour scale for sport. *Avante*, *5*, 82–92.

Cushion, C. (2007). Modelling the complexity of the coaching process. *International Journal of Sports Science and Coaching*, *2*(4), 395–401.

Cushion, C. J. (2010). Coach behaviour. In J. Lyle, & C. J. Cushion (Eds.), *Sports coaching: Professionalisation and practice* (pp. 43–62). Sydney: Elsevier.

Cushion, C. J., Armour, K. M., & Jones, R. L. (2003). Coach education and continuing professional development: Experience and learning to coach. *Quest, 55*, 215–230.

Cushion, C. J., Armour, K. M., & Jones, R. L. (2006). Locating the coaching process in practice: Models 'for' and 'of' coaching. *Physical Education and Sport Pedagogy, 11*(1), 83–99.

Cushion, C. J., Nelson, L., Armour, K., Lyle, J., Jones, R., Sandford, R., & O'Callaghan, C. (2010). Coach learning and development: A review of literature. Leeds: Sports Coach UK.

Dawson, P., Dobson, S., & Gerrard, B. (2000). Estimating coaching efficiency in professional team sports: Evidence from English association football. *Scottish Journal of Political Economy, 47*(4), 399–421.

Demers, G., Woodburn, A. J., & Savard, C. (2006). The development of an undergraduate competency-based coach education program. *The Sport Psychologist, 20*, 162–173.

Dickson, S. (2001a). Advancement in sport coaching and officiating accreditation. New South Wales: Australian Sports Commission.

Dickson, S. (2001b). A preliminary investigation into the effectiveness of the national coach accreditation scheme. New South Wales: Australian Sports Commission.

Douge, B. M., & Hastie, P. R. (1993). A review of coach effectiveness literature 1988–1992. *Sport Science Review, 2*(2), 14–29.

Eraut, M. (2004). Informal learning in the workplace. *Studies in Continuing Education, 26*(2), 247–273.

Erickson, K., Bruner, M. W., MacDonald, D. J., & Côté, J. (2008). Gaining insight into actual and preferred sources of coaching knowledge. *International Journal of Sports Science and Coaching, 3*(4), 527–538.

Erickson, K., Côté, J., & Fraser-Thomas, J. (2007). Sport experiences, milestones, and educational activities associated with high-performance coaches' development. *The Sport Psychologist, 21*, 302–316.

Gilbert, W., & Trudel, P. (2004a). Analysis of coaching science research published from 1970–2001. *Research Quarterly for Exercise and Sport, 75*(4), 388–402.

Gilbert, W., & Trudel, P. (2004b). Role of the coach: How model youth team sport coaches frame their roles. *The Sport Psychologist, 18*, 21–43.

Gilbert, W., & Trudel, P. (2005). Learning to coach through experience: Conditions that influence reflection. *Physical Educator, 62*(1), 32–43.

Gilbert, W., Côté, J., & Mallett, C. (2006). The talented coach: Developmental paths and activities of successful sport coaches. *International Journal of Sport Science and Coaching, 1*(1), 69–76.

Hoch, D. (2004). Coaching education and certification. *Coach and Athletic Director, 74*(2), 14.

Howe, B. (1990). Coaching effectiveness. *New Zealand Journal of Health, Physical Education and Recreation, 23*(3), 4–8.

International Council for Coaching Excellence, Association of Summer Olympic International Federations, & Leeds Metropolitan University. (2013). *International Sport Coaching Framework version 1.2*. Champaign, IL: Human Kinetics.

Irwin, G., Hanton, S., & Kerwin, D. G. (2004). Reflective practice and the origins of elite coaching knowledge. *Reflective Practice, 5*(3), 425–442.

Knowles, Z., Gilbourne, D., Borrie, A., & Nevill, A. (2001). Developing the reflective sports coach: A study exploring the processes of reflective practice within a higher education coaching programme. *Reflective Practice, 2*(2), 185–207.

Lyle, J. (2002). *Sports coaching concepts: A framework for coaches' behaviour*. London: Routledge.

Lyle, J. (2007). A review of the research evidence for the impact of coach education. *International Journal of Coaching Science, 1*(1), 19–36.

Lynch, M., & Mallett, C. (2006). Becoming a successful high performance track and field coach. *Modern Athlete and Coach, 22*(2), 15–20.

Lyons, M., Rynne, S. B., & Mallett, C. J. (2012). Reflection and the art of coaching: Fostering high performance in Olympic Ski Cross. *Reflective Practice, 13*(3), 359–372.

Mallett, C. J. (2011). Quality coaching, learning and coach development. *Japanese Journal of Sport Education Studies, 30*(2), 51–62.

Mallett, C., & Côté, J. (2006). Beyond winning and losing: Guidelines for evaluating high performance coaches. *The Sport Psychologist, 20*(2), 213–221.

Mallett, C. J., & Dickens, S. (2009). Authenticity in formal coach education: Online postgraduate studies in sports coaching at The University of Queensland. *International Journal of Coaching Science, 3*(2), 79–90.

Mallett, C. J., & Rynne, S. B. (2012). *Review of junior sport framework briefing paper: Role of adults in junior sport*. Queensland: The University of Queensland.

Mallett, C. J., Rossi, T., Rynne, S., & Tinning, R. (2015). In pursuit of becoming a senior coach: The learning culture for Australian Football League coaches. *Physical Education and Sport Pedagogy, 21*(1), 24–39.

Mallett, C. J., Rynne, S. B., & Billett, S. (2014). Valued learning experiences of early career and experienced high-performance coaches. *Physical Education and Sport Pedagogy*, 1–16.

Mallett, C. J., Trudel, P., Lyle, J., & Rynne, S. B. (2009). Formal vs informal coach education. *International Journal of Sports Science and Coaching, 4*(3), 325–334.

Myers, N. D., Wolfe, E. W., Maier, K. S., Feltz, D. L., & Reckase, M. D. (2006). Extending validity evidence for multidimensional measure of coaching competency. *Research Quarterly for Exercise and Sport, 77*(4), 451–463.

Nash, C. S., Sproule, J., & Horton, P. (2011). Excellence in coaching: The art and skill of elite practitioners. *Research Quarterly for Exercise and Sport, 82*(2), 229–238.

Nelson, L. J., & Cushion, C. J. (2006). Reflection in coach education: The case of the national governing body coaching certificate. *The Sport Psychologist, 20*, 174–183.

Nelson, L. J., Cushion, C. J., & Potrac, P. (2006). Formal, nonformal and informal coach learning: A holistic conceptualisation. *International Journal of Sport Science and Coaching, 1*(3), 247–253.

Occhino, J., Mallett, C. J., & Rynne, S. B. (2013). Dynamic social networks in high performance football coaching. *Physical Education and Sport Pedagogy, 18*(1), 90–102.

Potrac, P., & Jones, R. L. (2009). Power, conflict, and cooperation: Toward a micropolitics of coaching. *Quest, 61*, 223–236.

Rynne, S. B. (2014). 'Fast track' and 'traditional path' coaches: Affordances, agency and social capital. *Sport, Education and Society, 19*(3), 299–313.

Rynne, S. B., & Mallett, C. J. (2012). Understanding the work and learning of high performance coaches. *Physical Education and Sport Pedagogy, 17*(5), 507–523.

Rynne, S. B., & Mallett, C. J. (2014). Coaches' learning and sustainability in high performance sport. *Reflective Practice, 15*(1), 12–26.

Rynne, S. B., Mallett, C. J., & Tinning, R. (2006). High performance sport coaching: Institutes of sport as sites for learning. *International Journal of Sport Science and Coaching, 1*(3), 223–233.

Rynne, S. B., Mallett, C. J., & Tinning, R. (2010). Workplace learning of high performance sports coaches. *Sport, Education and Society, 15*(3), 315–330.

Sage, G. H. (1989). Becoming a high school coach: From playing sports to coaching. *Research Quarterly for Exercise and Sport, 60*(1), 81–92.

Schempp, P. G., & Graber, K. C. (1992). Teacher socialization from a dialectic perspective: Pretraining through induction. *Journal of Teaching in Physical Education, 11*, 329–348.

Smith, R. E., Smoll, F. L., & Christianson, D. S. (1996). Behavioural assessment and interventions in youth sport. *Behaviour Modification, 20*(1), 3–29.

Stoszkowski, J., Collins, D., & Olsson, C. (2015). Using shared online blogs to structure and support informal coach learning. Part 2: the participants' view and implications for coach education. *Sport, Education and Society*, 1–19.

Sullivan, P., & Gee, C. (2008). The effect of different coaching education content on the efficacy of coaches. *International Journal of Coaching Science, 2*(2), 59–66.

Trudel, P., & Gilbert, W. (2006). Coaching and coach education. In D. Kirk, D. Macdonald, & M. O'Sullivan (Eds.), *The handbook of physical education* (pp. 516–539). London: Sage.

9 Coach stress and associated impacts

Peter Olusoga[1] and Richard Thelwell[2]

Introduction

> The expectation of our coaches taking these athletes to the Olympics is to win medals. That's the expectation. It's not to *get* to the Olympics, it's to *perform* at the Olympics. There's a lot of pressure on the coaches.
>
> (Coach of double Olympic gold medal winner, Olusoga et al., 2009)

The ability to cope with stress is often cited as a significant factor in determining success in sport (Nicholls & Polman, 2007). Understanding the role that stress plays in sporting performance and the ways in which performers attempt to manage stress effectively have been popular topics within sport psychology literature (see Thomas, Mellalieu & Hanton, 2009). However, it is not just athlete performers who must be able to manage the various demands of competition and training in pursuit of their goals. Several researchers have argued that, given the multiple roles a coach must take on, sports coaches should be regarded as performers in their own right (e.g. Gould, Guinan, Greenleaf & Chung, 2002; Olusoga, Butt, Maynard & Hays, 2009; Thelwell, Weston, Greenlees & Hutchings, 2008a).

Coaching has been described as a "very consuming, demanding, and frustrating experience" (Raedeke, 2004, p. 333), and the impact of stress on sports coaches has been a fruitful topic of investigation. Coaches' stress responses can be positively toned, for example, heightened awareness, energising effects, or increased motivation (Frey, 2007; Olusoga, Butt, Hays & Maynard, 2010). Unfortunately, responses to stress can also have negative consequences, and coaches have reported experiencing anxiety, losing confidence, and a variety of symptoms often associated with burnout, such as emotional and physical exhaustion, and withdrawal from sport (Kelley, 1994; Kelley & Gill, 1993; Olusoga et al., 2010). Moreover, these negative impacts on coaches have also been linked to a host of potentially damaging athlete outcomes (Price & Weiss, 2000).

Being able to understand and manage stress is vital for sports coaches in a variety of domains, not only to optimise the satisfaction and performance of athletes, but also to ensure coach well-being. The purpose of this chapter is to discuss the stress process as applied to coaches and to review the literature that has attempted to uncover the complexity of the stress process in coaching at all levels, from teacher-coaches at high-school and collegiate level (e.g. Frey, 2007), through to international Olympic coaches (e.g. Knight, Reade, Selzler & Rodgers, 2013; Olusoga et al., 2009, 2010; Thelwell et al., 2008a). Practical implications for coaches and sport psychologists attempting to manage coaches' stress experiences will also be explored, and suggestions for future research within the area will be discussed.

Key terms

Virtually every chapter or research article written on stress in sport begins with a discussion of how a failure to consistently define stress has limited our theoretical understanding of the concept (Fletcher, Hanton & Mellalieu, 2006; Fletcher & Scott, 2010; Gould, Greenleaf & Krane, 2002). Moreover, it has been suggested that this lack of consistency and clarity in defining stress and its associated concepts has influenced recommendations for effectively applying stress management interventions (Thomas et al., 2009). Before discussing stress in relation to coaching, we feel it important to comment on this lack of consistency, albeit briefly, and to provide clear definitions of key terms, including 'stress', 'stressors', 'strain' and 'coping'.

Within the sport psychology literature, stress has been described as a stimulus variable (or environmental demand) and as a response to a specific situation (Gould & Petlichkoff, 1988). A comprehensive review and discussion can be found elsewhere (Fletcher et al., 2006), but, in short, to address issues of definitional and conceptual uncertainty, Lazarus's (Lazarus & Folkman, 1984; Lazarus & Launier 1978) transactional theory of stress has generally been adopted by sport psychology researchers. According to Lazarus (2000), stress is not a factor that lies within the individual or within the environment; rather, it is a *process*, involving a transaction between the individual and the environment. Put simply, stress is the process by which individuals weigh up the demands they face, against their ability to cope with those demands.

Based on previous reviews of the stress literature (e.g. Fletcher et al., 2006; Woodman & Hardy, 2001) and Lazarus's conceptualisations of stress as a transaction (Lazarus & Folkman 1984; Lazarus, 2000), we offer the following definitions:

- *Stress* – an ongoing process that involves individuals transacting with their environments, making appraisals of the situations they find themselves in, and endeavouring to cope with any issues that may arise;
- *Stressors* – environmental demands (stimuli) encountered by an individual;
- *Strain* – an individual's negative psychological, physical, and behavioural responses to stressors;
- *Competition/Organisational stress* – an ongoing transaction between an individual and the environmental demands associated primarily and directly with the competition/organisation within which he or she is operating;

- *Competition/Organisational stressors* – the environmental demands (i.e. stimuli) associated primarily and directly with the competition/organisation within which an individual is operating;
- *Competition/Organisational strain* – an individual's negative psychological, physical, and behavioural responses to competition/organisational stressors;
- *Coping* – constantly changing cognitive and behavioural efforts to manage specific external and/or internal demands that are appraised as taxing or exceeding the resources of the person.

Review of the literature

Coaching stress

Coaching is regarded as a potentially stressful occupation (e.g. Gould et al., 2002; Taylor, 1992) insofar that coach education programmes often describe the multiple roles that coaches should attempt to take on – educator, instructor, mentor, organiser, planner, counsellor, to name a few. Undeniably, the highly interpersonal nature of sports coaching is a major factor in the role having the potential for stress. In one early study of US high school coaches (Kroll & Gundersheim, 1982), all 93 of the coaches surveyed suggested that their roles were stressful and that interpersonal stressors (e.g. disrespect from athletes) were the "most significant".

The study of stress in relation to sports coaching has largely been guided by an attempt to gain a deeper understanding of the overall transactional stress *process* as applied to coaches. However, the majority of this research has been focused on selected elements of the process rather than on the transactional process itself. Hanton, Fletcher and Coughlan (2005) suggested that a more in-depth and broader understanding of the stressors that exist within elite sport would allow sport organisations, sport psychology practitioners and coaches themselves to design and implement more appropriate interventions to manage the demands placed on performers. Based largely on research in occupational settings and on his own applied practice experience, Taylor (1992) suggested that stressors in coaching fall into three broad categories: *personal stressors* (factors intrinsic to the individual, such as lack of experience, lack of skills, or self-doubts), *social stressors* (interactions with others both in and outside of the immediate working environment), and *organisational stressors* (factors originating "within the team's organisational superstructure", such as long hours, lack of organisational support, and budget/financial concerns). Coaching stress research that made the identification of stressors a priority will be reviewed in the following section.

Identifying coaching stressors

While coaching stress research is sparse in comparison with athlete research, it is certainly not a recent research topic. As far back as 1982, Walter Kroll and Julius Gundersheim used a combination of questionnaires and interviews to identify various "stress factors" involved in high school coaching. Almost 800 "stress items" were sorted into categories including disrespect from players (accounting for 42.8 per cent of total responses), not being able to reach athletes (20.7 per cent), and being underappreciated by athletes (3 per cent). In another study, Pastore (1991) found too much stress, intensity of recruitment, pressure to win, and difficulty in motivating athletes, to be factors associated with coaches' motivations to continue coaching. Using different terminology again, Wang and Ramsey (1998) developed the Inventory for New Coaches' Challenges and Barriers, and found communication skills, clearing a negative team atmosphere, recruiting, keeping non-starters motivated, and lack of financial aid to be the most important challenges/barriers for coaches transitioning into new coaching roles.

More recently, Frey (2007) investigated the stress experiences of 10 NCAA Division I coaches from a variety of different sports. Nine stressor themes emerged from the interviews (interpersonal/personal sources, other people, self-imposed stress, task-related sources, being the head coach, time demands, recruiting, outcome of competition, and sources that would lead to quitting), many of which could be considered similar to Kroll and Gundersheim's (1982) "stress factors" and Wang and Ramsey's (1998) "challenges/barriers". Terminology aside, it seems clear that collegiate coaches experience a wide range of stressors, which fall broadly into the three categories (personal, social, organisational) described by Taylor (1992).

Up to this point, the majority of research into coaching stress had sampled high school and collegiate, teacher-coaches in North American educational institutions, whose experiences of stress might be tempered by the 'dual-role' nature of their jobs (Capel, Sisley & Desertrain, 1987). In response to this, research began to recognise the importance of exploring stressors for coaches operating at the world-class level of competition (Thelwell et al., 2008a; Olusoga et al., 2009). Thelwell et al. interviewed eleven British coaches of elite athletes, who were employed by their respective National Governing Bodies, or by professional clubs. Compared to Frey's (2007) nine stressor themes, coaches in Thelwell et al.'s study reported 182 distinct stressors. Through content analysis procedures, these stressors were categorised into 34 lower order themes, related either to performance or organisational issues. Performance stressors were demands related to either the performances of the athletes (athlete coachability, training performance, competition preparation, competition performance, attitude, competition, schedule, injury and opponents), or coaches' own performances (training, competition preparation, competition issues, post-competition issues, pressure – general, opponents, and officials). Organisational stressors included demands related to the particular sport organisation within which the coach worked and were, consistently with previous athlete stress research, categorised into environmental (training environment, competition environment, finances, stability, selection, travel, safety, administration), leadership (organisation, other coaches, athletes), personal (private life, social life, contractual issues), and team (team atmosphere – athletes, team atmosphere – support staff, roles, communication) stressors. Although Frey did not specifically report the individual stressors that her collegiate coaches discussed, the sheer number of stressors reported by Thelwell et al. appears significantly higher (Fletcher & Scott, 2010).

Qualitative methods were also employed by Olusoga et al. (2009) to investigate the stressors experienced by 12 experienced, world-class coaches, again from a variety of individual and team sports. Using inductive analysis procedures, 130 distinct stressors were categorised into 10 stressor themes reflecting organisational, competitive, and personal issues: conflict, pressure and expectation, managing the competition environment, athlete concerns, coaching responsibilities to the athlete, consequences of the sport status, competition preparation, organisational management, sacrificing personal time, and isolation. Taken together, coaching stress research in various environments has provided a valuable insight into the range of organisation-related, competition-related, and personal stressors, often experienced in combination by sports coaches.

Limitations of stressor research

While understanding the stressors that coaches experience is certainly important, this is a good point at which to highlight a number of issues worthy of consideration. Specifically, in terms of their methods of investigation, Kroll and Gundersheim (1982) were no more specific than explaining that they used "questionnaires and personal interviews" (p. 47) to generate their data on coach stressors. Similarly, in developing the Inventory for New Coaches' Challenges and Barriers (INCCB), Wang and Ramsey (1998) provided no detail as to how the 26 questionnaire items were chosen, other than being based on consultations with "many coaches at the collegiate levels" (p. 6). To use the INCCB, coaches are asked to rate their agreement with a series of statements (e.g. "establishing a good relationship between returning players and new players has been a difficult challenge for me as a coach") using a 1–5 likert-type scale. However, a coach agreeing that something has been a challenge does not necessarily mean that it results in some sort of strain response. Similarly, while Olusoga et al. (2009) and Thelwell et al. (2008a) identified stressors, there was no indication from coaches as to whether or not these stressors elicited significant responses. Establishing the challenges, barriers, and stressors coaches experience is insufficient. To gain an overall understanding of coaches' experiences of stress, exploring the ways in which coaches respond to stressors is essential.

Stress responses

> We all know that coach doesn't handle pressure well. Basically, she freaks out! She starts pointing out problems and trying to change things at the last minute, so we try and avoid her the last week before nationals.
>
> Multiple national champion and Olympian (McCann, 1997, p. 12)

Four types of stress response have been proposed in the literature: behavioural (e.g. observable actions such as withdrawal or shouting), affective (e.g. emotional states like anxiety), cognitive (e.g. negative thinking and maladaptive attributions), and physiological (e.g. increased heart rate) (Fletcher & Scott, 2010; Frey, 2007). Distinctions have also been made between these more immediate responses to stress and longer-term effects of stress on well-being and performance (Olusoga et al., 2010).

The ways in which coaches at various levels respond to and are affected by stressors have been examined in detail. In line with the taxonomy outlined above, coaches have reported that experiencing stress could have an immediate negative effect on their behaviours (e.g. body language becoming agitated, tone of voice is sharper), emotions (e.g. becoming more 'moody', anger), and cognitions (e.g. losing the ability to focus, worry, more negative in decision making), and lead to physiological changes (e.g. tension, hands shaking, numbness) (Frey, 2007; Olusoga et al., 2010). Regarding stress effects, negative impacts on athlete performance, becoming too directive in coaching style and lower standards of work have also been reported (Olusoga et al., 2010). The UK coaches in Olusoga et al.'s study suggested that there were longer term effects of stress for the coaches themselves, with themes such as negative affect (e.g. emotional fatigue, depression), decreased motivation (e.g. reduced enjoyment), relationships with others (e.g. not happy at home), and withdrawal (becoming more introspective) emerging from the interviews.

While it is important to note that coaches in both Frey's (2007) and Olusoga et al.'s (2010) studies discussed positive stress responses (e.g. increase productivity, motivation, opportunities for learning), the majority of the reported responses were negative in tone, and, in many respects, similar to characteristics of burnout, "a syndrome of emotional exhaustion, depersonalisation, and reduced personal accomplishment" (Maslach & Jackson 1986, p. 1) typically associated with chronic stress (Smith, 1986). Indeed, these two studies aside, research into the effects of stress on coaches has largely focused on the potential relationship between stress and burnout (e.g. Caccese & Mayerberg, 1984; Capel et al., 1987; Vealey, Udry, Zimmerman & Soliday, 1992). Reported levels of burnout in the coaching literature have varied from low-moderate (e.g. Caccese & Mayerberg, 1984; Capel et al., 1987), to moderate-high (e.g. Kelley et al., 1999); however, in collegiate coaching in particular, stress appraisals (e.g. perceived stress, role conflict and 'coaching issues') have been significantly related to all three dimensions of burnout (Kelley, 1994; Kelley & Gill, 1993).

While burnout has implications for the coaches themselves (e.g. emotional exhaustion, withdrawal from sport), the consequences of coach burnout for athletes have also been examined, although the research is somewhat limited (see Goodger, Gorley, Lavallee & Harwood, 2007 for a review). Coaches reporting high levels of emotional exhaustion can be perceived by athletes as making more autocratic and fewer democratic decisions, providing less training instruction and less social support, and being less empathetic, with the athletes of these coaches reporting higher levels of anxiety and scoring higher on several burnout dimensions (Price & Weiss, 2000; Vealey, Armstrong, Comar & Greenleaf, 1998).

Based on the growing body of literature in this area, it would be fair to assume that coaches experience numerous stressors, and that the ways in which coaches respond might have important implications for their own well-being and for the performance and satisfaction of their athletes. There is, however, limited research into the processes of appraisal involved in the perception of stress (Knight et al., 2013). That is, while coaches experience a range of stressors, and the responses can be severe, the factors influencing whether or not coaches perceive stressors to be stressful remain less clear.

Factors influencing stress perceptions

The early burnout research discussed above has enhanced our understanding of personal and situational factors that might influence coaches' perceptions of stress. For instance trait anxiety has been found to predict burnout in collegiate and high school coaches (Vealey et al., 1992), perceived coaching issues have been found to increase during the course of a competitive season (Kelley, 1994), while gender (Kelley, 1994; Kelley & Gill, 1993), experience (Malinauskas, Malinauskiene & Dumciene, 2010), and a range of demographic and job role factors (e.g., Knight et al., 2013), have also been explored as a variables influencing perceptions of stress. In Vealey et al.'s study of over 800 coaches, perceived overload and lack of autonomy were factors associated with burnout for both sexes, yet lack of meaningful accomplishments, lack of professional support, and lack of perceived success, were associated with burnout in male coaches only. Other findings have suggested that female coaches experience higher levels of burnout than male coaches (e.g. Kelley et al., 1999), or that there is no difference between sexes (Malinauskas et al., 2010). Malinauskas et al. also found that coaches with over ten years of experience were six times more likely to experience burnout and suggested that less experienced coaches might be "less sensitive to the pressures of the people surrounding them and the stress of work" (p. 305). In a study of over 500 Canadian coaches (Knight et al., 2013), factors such as age, sex, annual and total household income, the type of athletes coached, employment type (self-employed or not), administrative tasks, contribution to the sport, athlete recruitment and athlete or team achievement were not significantly associated with stress. Factors that were related to coaching stress included having unclear expectations, working longer than 40 hours per week, lack of agreed criteria for evaluation, lack of social support and higher salaries.

Coping with stressors

The ability to cope with stressors is clearly an important factor in determining whether or not sport will be a satisfying experience for the performer (Nicholls & Polman, 2007). From an applied perspective, developing a greater understanding of how coaches cope with the demands of their sports is of clear benefit. Kosa (1990) for example, found that, for secondary school coaches, problem-focused coping was negatively related to two of the burnout dimensions (depersonalisation and personal accomplishment). However, tension-releasing coping (e.g. getting angry, crying, worrying) was positively related to higher frequency and intensity of emotional exhaustion and depersonalisation. Frey's (2007) study shed further light on the subject, with cognitive strategies (e.g. focusing on the processes rather than winning), emotional-control strategies (e.g. social support), and behavioural strategies (e.g. preparation), all being reported by NCAA Division I head coaches as important for managing stress.

In assessing coaches' coping strategies and styles, qualitative methods have provided an in-depth look at coaches' attempts to manage their stress experiences. For example, Levy, Nicholls, Marchant, and Polman (2009) carried out a longitudinal diary study, during which one UK-based elite coach recorded the organisational stressors he encountered, his coping responses, and the effectiveness of those responses over a 28-day period. Organisational stressors consistent with previous research were identified (e.g. administration, communicating with management, financial issues) and a total of 70 coping strategies were reported by the participating coach, with communication, planning, preparation, social support and self-talk cited most frequently.

While athletes might use different strategies to cope with organisational and performance-related stressors (Hanton et al., 2005), no such differences have been found with coaches. Frey (2007), for example, found similar coping strategies in her study of collegiate coaches' performance related stressors (e.g. preparation, social support), to those reported by Levy et al. (2009) in their study of organisational stress. Thelwell et al. (2008b), found elite UK-based coaches employed a variety of traditional mental skills (e.g. self-talk, imagery, relaxation) to control their emotions and to cope with "tough situations" in training and competition, and in a follow-up study, Thelwell, Weston, and Greenlees (2010), reported the dynamic nature of coaches' coping attempts. Three coaches (cricket, rugby union, soccer) not only reported using the same coping techniques (e.g. self-talk) to manage organisational and performance stressors, but also reported using a wide range of escape/avoidance (e.g. go to gym), appraisal (e.g. reflection), problem-focused (e.g. communicate with other coaches), and emotion-focused (e.g. positive reminders) strategies, in attempts to manage the same stressor (in this case, selection issues).

Olusoga et al. (2010) further highlighted the multiple coping strategies of elite UK-based coaches with problem-focused (e.g. structuring and planning, confrontation), and emotion-focused (e.g. support) strategies being reported. Importantly, distraction and avoidance were two other notable coping themes. Moreover, while ten of the 12 coaches in this study explained the importance of psychological skills to cope with stressors, fewer than half referred to self-talk or other emotional control methods (e.g. masking emotions from athletes), and only one coach reported using any kind of relaxation technique. In a follow up study (Olusoga, Maynard, Hays, & Butt, 2012), Olympic medal-winning British coaches highlighted the importance of psychological attributes (e.g. emotional control, confidence, communication) for working effectively in a highly pressurised environment. Furthermore, strategic preparation (e.g. contingency planning, team and athlete preparation), and having the specific skills required to cope with stress at the Olympics (e.g. team support, taking time out) were also reported as essential for successful coaching under pressure. Taken together, the research outlined highlights the inherent difficulty in suggesting that specific stressors might lead to specific responses. It seems clear that stressors are likely to be experienced in combination, rather than as isolated demands, and that having a range of coping strategies available is imperative if coaches are to effectively manage the stressors they encounter.

Implications for future research

The research to date provides a solid foundation for understanding coaches' experiences of stress. A clear limitation, however, is the noticeable absence of stress management intervention studies carried out with coaches. In the early 1990s, Taylor (1992) commented on the "growing concern" over stress in coaching and outlined a five-step process for developing coach-specific stress management interventions (SMIs). Taylor advocated the use of cognitive, behavioural and emotional/psychological coping skills, including relaxation training and cognitive restructuring. The 1990s and 2000s saw a surge in research devoted to evaluating the efficacy of reduction (reducing the intensity of responses) and restructuring (developing a more facilitative interpretation of responses) approaches to stress management for athletes (see Thomas et al., 2009, for a detailed review), but it seems coaches were somewhat neglected during this period.

As no such literature base exists for coaching populations, an obvious avenue for further research would be to develop and evaluate SMIs with coaching populations at various levels of competition. In one of the few studies that have tried to redress this balance, Olusoga, Maynard, Butt and Hays (2014) evaluated a Psychological Skills Training (PST) programme designed specifically to help coaches manage stress. Five university/national level, UK coaches (all men) underwent a six-week group-based PST programme, which included both reduction and restructuring approaches to managing stress responses, and opportunities for coaches to reflect on the stressors that affected them and their appraisals of those stressors. In their post intervention evaluations, coaches reported improvements in their confidence, their ability to relax, and perceived a variety of coping strategies (e.g. venting, active coping, planning) as more effective. Future research might look to compare the efficacy of SMIs between elite and sub/non-elite coaches and, perhaps, between genders, as female coaches are damningly underrepresented in the research literature.

Further research evaluating SMIs for coaches is important, yet it is also prudent to consider alternative approaches. While PST interventions generally focus on teaching methods for controlling cognitive and affective experiences (e.g. reducing or restructuring anxiety), Mindfulness–Acceptance–Commitment (MAC) (Gardner & Moore, 2004) approaches to performance development have gained traction within sport psychology over the last decade. Although a detailed discussion of this approach is not appropriate within the scope of this chapter (see Gardner & Moore, 2006, for a detailed review), mindfulness and acceptance based interventions focus on viewing internal events (such as thoughts and emotional experiences) as normal and transient, rather than as experiences that need to be brought under conscious control or eliminated altogether. Research has begun to explore MAC interventions for performance enhancement with some encouraging results (Wolanin, 2005). Adding to the extant literature by investigating the efficacy of MAC and PST approaches to enhance coaches' stress management abilities might be an interesting and worthwhile endeavour.

Adopting a focus on coaching burnout might also provide some direction for future research. Lundkvist, Gustafsson, Hjälm & Hassmén (2012), for example, developed two distinct burnout profiles based on interviews with eight elite soccer coaches, and suggested that recovery strategies might differ based on an individual's burnout profile. Specifically, energy saving/boosting strategies were reported by coaches whose burnout was linked to their overall life situations, whereas developing a broader identity, learning to live with, and letting go of the situation were strategies reported by coaches whose burnout was linked to the performance culture of elite sport. Developing a further understanding of how coaches effectively cope with stressors through different temporal phases (e.g. episodic daily coping; stages of a competitive season) might prove useful for the development of intervention protocols.

Researchers interested in these areas should, however, consider some of the constraints of carrying out research with coaching populations. Large sample sizes for group-based coaching intervention studies are not always practically available, so idiographic, case-study or single-subject research designs might be more appropriate than typical nomothetic, between-groups research. Moreover, the measures used to evaluate whether or not interventions are successful, and measure coaches experiences of stress in general, are also areas for further discussion given the questioning of whether the existing measures are appropriate for coaching populations.

Implications for applied practice

In this final section, we present a number of practical recommendations, based on the literature discussed throughout the chapter. The findings from the ever-expanding body of research into coaching stress have implications not only for sports coaches themselves, but also for sport organisations, and sport psychology consultants (SPCs) working with coaches. One of the most striking findings from the coaching stress research is the sheer number and variety of organisational, competition, and personal stressors that coaches at all levels appear to encounter as part of their coaching roles. Furthermore, research has suggested that the consequences of experiencing stress can be far reaching and potentially serious, with coaches' health, productivity, relationships with athletes, and performance all being affected. It would seem prudent, therefore, that coaches are equipped with the necessary skills and strategies to be able to cope effectively.

Only limited research has explored the impact of PST for sports coaches (Olusoga et al., 2014), but several studies have suggested that multiple coping strategies (including psychological skills such as self-talk and relaxation) might prove useful for coping with the varied demands of coaching (Frey, 2007; Olusoga et al., 2010, 2012; Thelwell et al., 2010). We suggest that coaches have a responsibility to consider themselves as performers in their own right and to "use all the performance skills that [they] encourage in [their] athletes" (Olusoga et al., 2014, p. 41). SPCs working with coaches should also encourage them to develop a performer's mind-set and the associated 'performance skills' that they can utilise in a variety of settings. In this regard, the sport organisation also has an important role to play. It has been argued that formal coach education programmes might not necessarily cater adequately for the needs of coaches (Trudel & Gilbert, 2006). There is, however, evidence to suggest that formal coach education is actually desired by coaches (Erickson, Bruner, MacDonald & Côté, 2008). We suggest that national governing bodies and other sports organisations should utilise coaches' thirst for relevant and useful coach education, ensuring that psychological development and support for their coaching staff is embedded within their coach education and training programmes.

Coaches, SPCs and sport organisations should also work hard to remove some of the barriers that appear to prevent coaches from accessing psychological support. In particular, there still exists a culture in which seeking support from a sport psychologist might be viewed as a sign of weakness, especially within the culture of high performance sport. Raedeke, Kentta and Olusoga (2014) found that coaches' fear of showing weakness or asking for help was a contributing factor to their burnout and eventual withdrawal from sport. The perception that experiencing strain or seeking support because of overwhelming job demands is a sign of weakness is a perception that must change.

It is widely acknowledged that interaction with other coaches, whether in a formal or an informal setting, is an important part of coach education and development (e.g. Cushion, Armour & Jones, 2003). Formal mentoring might prove a significant source of social support for coaches managing stressors. As such, organisations must foster a culture in which coaches are encouraged to share their experiences, their stories, and their best practice, thus providing a vital support network for coaches. Experienced coaches must also be aware of the significance of their contribution to the development of less experienced coaches, and be encouraged to take on a supportive role by the culture of the organisations they work within. Where mentoring systems are in place, assuming that they are productive is not enough, and periodic review of their effectiveness is critical.

Research into stress in sports coaching has been conducted across the broad spectrum of competitive standards. As such, SPCs working at all levels should develop an in-depth knowledge of, and have the ability to address, a range of stressors that spans beyond the competitive arena. Indeed, SPCs might have an important role to play in effecting some of the cultural change discussed above.

Moreover, while coaches certainly seem to recognise the importance of sport psychology for performance, another challenge for practitioners might be in encouraging coaches to be open and honest in discussing their own challenges, and in presenting options that will empower coaches to manage the stressful coaching environment.

Notes

1 Sheffield Hallam University, UK
2 University of Portsmouth, UK

References

Caccese, T. M., & Mayerberg, C. K. (1984). Gender differences in perceived burnout of college coaches. *Journal of Sport Psychology, 6,* 279–288.

Capel, S. A., Sisley, B. L. & Desertrain, G. S. (1987). The relationship of role conflict and role ambiguity to burnout in high school basketball coaches. *Journal of Sport Psychology, 9,* 106–117.

Cushion, C. J., Armour, K. M. & Jones, R. L. (2003). Coach education and continuing professional development: Experience and learning to coach. *Quest, 55,* 215–230.

Erickson, K., Bruner, M. W., MacDonald, D. J. & Côté, J. (2008). Gaining insight into actual and preferred sources of coaching knowledge. *International Journal of Sports Sciences and Coaching, 3,* 527–538.

Fletcher, D., & Scott, M. (2010). Psychological stress in sports coaches: A review of concepts, research, and practice. *Journal of Sports Sciences, 28,* 127–137.

Fletcher, D., Hanton, S., & Mellalieu, S. D. (2006). An organizational stress review: conceptual and theoretical issues in competitive sport. In S. Hanton, & S. D. Mellalieu (Eds.), *Literature reviews in sport psychology* (pp. 321–374). New York: Nova Science Publishers.

Frey, M. (2007). College coaches' experiences with stress – "problem solvers" have problems too. *The Sport Psychologist, 21,* 38–57.

Gardner, F. L., & Moore, Z. E. (2004). A mindfulness–acceptance–commitment (MAC) based approach to athletic performance enhancement: Theoretical considerations. *Behaviour Therapy, 35,* 707–723.

Gardner, F. L., & Moore, Z. E. (2006). *Clinical sport psychology.* Champaign, IL: Human Kinetics.

Goodger, K., Gorley, T., Lavallee, D., & Harwood, C. (2007). Burnout in sport: A systematic review. *The Sport Psychologist, 21,* 127–151.

Gould, D. & Petlichkoff, L. (1988). Psychological stress and the age-group wrestler. In E. W. Brown & C. F. Branta (Eds.), *Competitive sports for children and youth: An overview of research and issues* (pp. 63–73). Champaign, IL: Human Kinetics.

Gould, D., Guinan, D., Greenleaf, C. & Chung, Y. (2002). A survey of US Olympic coaches: Variables perceived to have influenced athlete performances and coach effectiveness. *The Sport Psychologist, 16,* 229–250.

Gould, D., Greenleaf, C. & Krane, V. (2002). Arousal-anxiety and sport behaviour. In T. S. Horn (Ed.), *Advances in sport psychology* (2nd edn), (pp. 207–241). Champaign IL: Human Kinetics.

Hanton, S., Fletcher, D. & Coughlan, G. (2005). Stress in elite sport performers: A comparative study of competitive and organizational stressors. *Journal of Sports Sciences*, *23*, 1129–1141.

Kelley, B. C. (1994). A model of stress and burnout in collegiate coaches: effects of gender and time of season. *Research Quarterly for Exercise and Sport*, *65*, 48–58.

Kelley, B. C., & Gill, D. L. (1993). An examination of personal/situational variables, stress appraisal, and burnout in collegiate teacher-coaches. *Research Quarterly for Exercise and Sport*, *64*, 94–102.

Kelley, B. C., Eklund, R. C. & Ritter-Taylor, M. (1999). Stress and burnout among collegiate tennis coaches. *Journal of Sport & Exercise Psychology*, *21*, 113–130.

Knight, C. J., Reade, I. L., Selzler, A. & Rodgers, W. M. (2013). Personal and situational factors influencing coaches' perceptions of stress. *Journal of Sports Sciences*, *31*, 1054–1063.

Kosa, B. (1990). Teacher–coach burnout and coping strategies. *Physical Educator*, *47*, 153–158.

Kroll, W., & Gundersheim, J. (1982). Stress factors in coaching. *Coaching Science Update*, *23*, 47–49.

Lazarus, R. S. (2000). How emotions influence performance in competitive sports. *The Sport Psychologist*, *14*, 229–252.

Lazarus, R. S., & Folkman, S. (1984). *Stress, appraisal, and coping*. New York: Springer.

Lazarus, R. S., & Launier, R. (1978). Stress-related transactions between person and environment. In L. A. Pervin, & M. Lewis (Eds.), *Perspectives in interactional Psychology* (pp. 287–327). New York: Plenum.

Levy, A., Nicholls, A., Marchant, D. & Polman, R. (2009). Organizational stressors, coping, and coping effectiveness: A longitudinal study with an elite coach. *International Journal of Sports Science and Coaching*, *4*, 31–45.

Lundkvist, E., Gustafsson, H., Hjälm, S. & Hassmén, P. (2012). An interpretive phenomenological analysis of burnout and recovery in elite soccer coaches. *Qualitative Research in Sport, Exercise, & Health*, 4(3), 400–419.

Malinauskas, R., Malinauskiene, V. & Dumciene, A. (2010). Burnout and perceived stress among university coaches in Lithuania. *Journal of Occupational Health*, *52*, 302–307.

Maslach, C., & Jackson, S. E. (1986). *MBI: Maslach Burnout Inventory; Manual research edition*. Palo Alto, CA: Consulting Psychologists Press.

McCann, S. (1997). Overcoaching and undercoaching: What pressure can do to coaches. *Olympic Coach*, *7*, 12.

Nicholls, A. R., & Polman, R. C. J. (2007). Coping in sport: A systematic review. *Journal of Sports Sciences*, *25*, 11–31.

Olusoga, P., Butt, J., Hays, K. & Maynard, I. W. (2009). Stress in elite sports coaching: Identifying stressors. *Journal of Applied Sport Psychology*, *21*, 442–459.

Olusoga, P., Butt, J., Maynard, I. W. & Hays, K. (2010). Stress and coping: A study of world class coaches. *Journal of Applied Sport Psychology*, *22*, 274–293.

Olusoga, P., Maynard, I., Hays, K. & Butt, J. (2012). Coaching under pressure: A study of Olympic coaches. *Journal of Sports Sciences*, *30*, 229–239.

Olusoga, P., Maynard, I. W., Butt, J. & Hays, K. (2014). Coaching under pressure: Mental skills training for sports coaches. *Sport and Exercise Psychology Review*, *10*, 31–43.

Pastore, D. L. (1991). Male and female coaches of women's athletic teams: Reasons for entering and leaving the profession. *Journal of Sport Management*, *5*, 128–143.

Price, M. S., & Weiss, M. R. (2000). Relationships among coach burnout, coach behaviours, and athletes' psychological responses. *The Sport Psychologist*, *14*, 391–409.

Raedeke. T. D. (2004). Coach commitment and burnout: A one-year follow-up. *Journal of Applied Sport Psychology, 16*, 333–349.

Raedeke, T. D., Kenttä, G. & Olusoga, P. (2014). *Calling 'time-out': A narrative analysis of burnout and recovery in sports coaching.* Research paper presented at the Association of Applied Sport Psychology (AASP) Annual Conference, Las Vegas, USA.

Smith, R. (1986). Toward a cognitive-affective model of athletic burnout. *Journal of Sport Psychology, 8*, 36–50.

Taylor, J. (1992). Coaches are people too: An applied model of stress management for sports coaches. *Journal of Applied Sport Psychology, 4*, 27–50.

Thelwell, R. C., Weston, N. J. V. & Greenlees, I. A. (2010). Coping with stressors in elite sport: A coach perspective. *European Journal of Sport Science, 10*, 243–253.

Thelwell, R. C., Weston, N. J. V., Greenlees, I. A. & Hutchings, N. V. (2008a). Stressors in elite sport: A coach perspective. *Journal of Sports Sciences, 26*, 905–918.

Thelwell, R. C., Weston, N. J. V., Greenlees, I. A. & Hutchings, N. V. (2008b). A qualitative exploration of psychological-skills use in coaches. *The Sport Psychologist, 22*, 38–53.

Thomas, O., Mellalieu, S. D. & Hanton, S. (2009). Stress management in applied sport psychology. In S. D. Mellalieu, & S. Hanton (Eds.), *Advances in applied sport psychology: A review* (pp. 124–161). London: Routledge

Trudel, P., & Gilbert, W. D. (2006). Coaching and coach education. In D. Kirk, M. O'Sullivan & M. McDonald (Eds.), *Handbook of physical education* (pp. 516–539). London: Sage.

Vealey, R. S., Armstrong, L., Comar, W. & Greenleaf, C. A. (1998). Influence of perceived coaching behaviours on burnout and competitive anxiety in female college athletes. *Journal of Applied Sport Psychology, 10*, 297–318.

Vealey, R. S., Udry, E. M., Zimmerman, V. & Soliday, J. (1992). Intrapersonal and situational predictors of coaching burnout. *Journal of Sport and Exercise Psychology, 14*, 40–58.

Wang, J., & Ramsey, J. (1998). The relationship of school type, coaching experience, gender and age to new coaches' challenges and barriers at the collegiate level. *Applied Research in Coaching and Athletics, 13*, 1–22.

Wolanin, A. T. (2005). Mindfulness–acceptance–commitment (MAC)-based performance enhancement for Division I collegiate athletes: A preliminary investigation. (Doctoral dissertation, La Salle University, 2003). *Dissertation Abstracts International-B, 65*, pp. 3735–3794.

Woodman, T., & Hardy, L. (2001). A case study of organizational stress in elite sport. *Journal of Applied Sport Psychology, 13*, 207–238.

10 Athlete expectancies of coaches and their consequences

Andrew Manley,[1] Iain Greenlees,[2] and Richard Thelwell[3]

Introduction

Over the last 15–20 years, a body of literature examining expectancies (or expectations) and their consequences in the context of sport has emerged. Examples of expectancy effects have been demonstrated in research involving judges (e.g. Findlay & Ste-Marie, 2004), officials (e.g. Souchon, Coulomb-Cabagno, Traclet, & Rascle, 2004), coaches (e.g. Horn, 2008), and athletes (e.g. Buscombe, Greenlees, Holder, Thelwell, & Rimmer, 2006). The coach–athlete relationship has received particular attention with regard to the potential for expectancy effects, although this has traditionally been investigated from the perspective of the coach (e.g. Horn, Lox, & Labrador, 2010; Solomon & Rhea, 2008). For example, Wilson, Cushion, and Stephens (2006) reported that coaches' expectancies of athletes have the potential to impact on the subsequent behaviour and performance of sports performers. Although such research emphasises the importance of expectancies regarding effective coach–athlete relations and subsequent performance outcomes, there remains a dearth of research that has examined expectancies and impressions that originate from athletes' impressions, beliefs, and predictions regarding coaches. Given suggestions that the coach–athlete relationship should be primarily athlete-centred (Jowett & Cockerill, 2003) and that a multitude of problems that occur within the coach–athlete relationship (e.g. conflict between coach and athlete, lack of support, dropout from sport) have been proposed to be interpersonal in nature (Becker, 2009; Jowett & Poczwardowski, 2007), it is surprising that the study of expectancies from the perspective of the athlete has been largely neglected.

The aim of this chapter is to provide a review of literature investigating expectancies and their consequences within the coach–athlete relationship from the athlete's point of view. Based on the summarised findings, the chapter will discuss some of the primary practical implications for coaches and athletes alike, while also suggesting directions for future research.

Key terms

Interpersonal perception has been defined as "the study of the ways people react and respond to others, in thought, feeling and action" (Cook, 1971, p. 14), and according to Higgins and Bargh (1987), "was founded on the idea that internal factors such as … expectancies influence the outcome of perception" (p. 370). Categorised as "beliefs about a future state of affairs" (Olson, Roese, & Zanna, 1996, p. 211), *expectancies* represent the process of utilising past experience and knowledge to predict the future and develop a set of rules about the world. At any one time, perceivers can develop and hold a variety of these rules and predictions, ranging from 'intrapersonal' expectancies about themselves, 'interpersonal' expectancies about other individuals or groups, and 'impersonal' expectancies about specific situations or events (Ditto & Hilton, 1990; Olson et al., 1996). In other words, expectancies in social interactions not only allow the perceiver to make sense of the target and themselves, but also help people to make predictions about ensuing interactions (Miller & Turnbull, 1986). Expectancies play a major role in everyday social interactions, and have the potential to influence the first impressions that are made during initial interpersonal evaluations (Darley & Fazio, 1980).

According to Jowett and Poczwardowski (2007), the affiliation between coach and athlete is highly interdependent, meaning that the quality of this relationship is shaped by the interactions that occur between the athlete and coach. This notion was reinforced by Becker (2009), who stated that a core attribute of great coaches is their ability to develop and maintain effective professional and personal relationships with their athletes. Thus, athletes' expectancies of coaches are likely to play a significant role in the development and outcomes of the coach–athlete relationship. This chapter will focus primarily on *interpersonal perception* within the coach–athlete relationship, providing an overview of how *interpersonal expectancies* are developed by athletes during initial interactions with coaches. In addition, the potential consequences that first impressions can have within the context of coach–athlete interactions will be discussed.

Review of the literature

An 'expectancy effect' is a response or outcome that has been determined in some way by the initial expectancy that was formed by the perceiver. Most of the expectancy effect literature has examined the 'self-fulfilling prophecy': "a false definition of the situation evoking a new behaviour which makes the originally false conception come true" (Merton, 1948, p. 195). In the decades which followed, the four-step expectancy cycle (e.g. Becker & Solomon, 2005; Horn et al., 2010; Solomon, 2016) was developed as a model of how self-fulfilling prophecies can occur. According to the four-step cycle, the process regarding interpersonal self-fulfilling prophecies is as follows: (i) beliefs and expectancies about a target person are formed by the perceiver; (ii) the perceiver behaves toward the target as if his or her expectancies are true; (iii) the target interprets the perceiver's behaviour towards them and behaves in accordance with this interpretation; (iv) the perceiver sees the target's behaviour as evidence for the accuracy of his or her initial impression. The key point to notice here is that the expectancy effect process begins at point (i) with the formation of an initial interpersonal expectancy, making it a crucial stage in the expectancy effect process. Therefore, to better understand and guard against expectancy effects that may be detrimental to the coach–athlete relationship, it is vital that we understand the types of informational cues that are utilised by athletes when forming their initial expectancies of coaches.

Although little research has examined athletes' perceptions, impressions, and expectancies of coaches, there are examples where the role of the athlete as 'perceiver' has been acknowledged as an important element of the coach–athlete relationship. For example, Smoll and Smith (1989) argued that "the ultimate effects that coaching behaviour exerts are mediated by the meaning that players attribute to them" (p. 1527). More recently, Horn (2008) agreed that the influence of coach behaviour on athletes' attitudes, self-perception, and performance is partly mediated by athletes' evaluations and expectancies of the coach, arguing that by understanding how athletes form impressions and expectancies, coaches will be in a position to utilise their own behaviour as a beneficial tool. Such advocates have instigated subsequent investigations (e.g. Boardley, Kavussanu, & Ring, 2008; Wang, Koh, & Chatzisarantis, 2009) regarding athletes' perceptions of coaching behaviour and the consequences they may have within the context of the coach-relationship. However, none of these studies has made a concerted effort to identify and understand the sources of information that athletes use as the basis of their initial expectancies of coaches. This realisation led to the conception of a series of exploratory yet experimental studies designed to address this specific gap in the literature.

Influential sources of interpersonal expectancies within the coach–athlete relationship

Horn et al. (2010) postulated that there are two main types of informational cue that coaches use to form expectancies of athletes. The first type, "person cues", reflects information that remains relatively stable across the interaction between coach and athlete (e.g. socio-economic status, race/ethnicity, gender). The second, labelled "performance information", encompasses cues that are more dynamic or changeable over the course of coach–athlete interactions and observations (e.g. athletes' scores on physical tests, direct observation of athletes' performance and behaviour). Supplementary to the work of Horn et al. (2010), Becker and Solomon (2005) proposed that "performance information" could be broken down into three further yet distinct categories: "personal cues" (e.g. body language, facial expressions), "performance cues" (e.g. physical test scores), and "psychological cues" (e.g. confidence, anxiety).

In their assessments of the extent to which each of these types of informational cue were deemed to influence coaches' expectancies of athletes, there was consensus between the researchers. Horn et al. (2010) stated that dynamic and changeable behavioural cues appeared to be the major determinant in the formation of coaches' expectancies of athletes, and are more likely to result in the development of accurate expectancies. Similarly, Becker and Solomon (2005) reported that coaches did not view static, stable, unchangeable cues (e.g. gender, nationality) as particularly salient sources of information when developing expectancies of athlete ability, and that athletes' psychological cues (considered a sub-category of performance information) were perceived by coaches to be the most influential sources during expectancy formation.

In conjunction with the framework provided by the four-step expectancy cycle (e.g. Becker & Solomon, 2005; Horn et al., 2010; Solomon, 2016), these initial studies from the perspective of the coach inspired a similar investigation from the athlete's point of view. Manley et al. (2008) asked a sample of 534 athletes from a range of sports, ages, and participation levels to rate the perceived influence of various informational cues on the development of their expectancies of a coach. Exploratory Factor Analysis extracted a three-factor model reflecting the types of cues athletes use as the primary basis for the formation of coach-referent expectancies. The three types of cue included within the model were defined as "static cues" (e.g. gender, age, race/ethnicity), "dynamic cues" (e.g. body language, facial expressions) and "third-party reports" (e.g. reputation, coaching experience).

The model demonstrated some overlap with the previous research conducted from the perspective of the coach, with athletes' mean ratings indicating that dynamic cues and third-party reports were considered to be more influential as a source of expectancy formation compared with static cues. However, the findings by Manley et al. suggested that "third-party reports" should be considered as a distinct category of informational cue available to athletes rather than a mere sub-component of "performance information", as was suggested in the work conducted with coaches. This finding reinforced initial evidence to support the notion that third-party reports such as reputation can impact on the expectancies formed by sports personnel including judges (Findlay & Ste-Marie, 2004) and referees (Jones, Paull, & Erskine, 2002). Yet, given the novelty and explorative nature of Manley et al.'s work, the reported findings were deemed worthy of further investigation. Furthermore, despite the apparent agreement with previous literature which had focused on the coach as the "perceiver" (e.g. Becker & Solomon, 2005; Horn et al., 2010; Solomon & Rhea, 2008), other experimental studies had demonstrated that static cues such as gender (Coulomb-Cabagno, Rascle, & Souchon, 2005), race/ethnicity (Jowett, Frost, & Timson-Katchis, 2006), and physique (Lubker, Watson, Visek, & Geer, 2005) could have a significant influence on perceivers' expectancies of a target within sport-specific settings. As a result, Manley et al. called for further experimental research. While there remains a need for investigations of this nature, the remainder of this section will provide a synopsis of the recent work that has been conducted.

Manley, Greenlees, Thelwell, and Smith (2010) recruited 304 male and female athletes from a range of sports and participation levels to examine their perceptions of coach competence based on specific sources of information (i.e. coach reputation and gender). Participants were presented with a coach profile which consisted of a photograph of either a male or female coach, as well as a brief vignette describing the coach as having a reputation for being 'successful' or 'unsuccessful'. Through the manipulation of these two independent variables, four experimental conditions were created (i.e. female–successful, male–successful, female–unsuccessful, male–unsuccessful) with participants randomly assigned to one of them as part of a between-groups experimental design. After viewing the coach profile, participants were asked to rate their perceptions of coach competence using an adapted version of the Coach Competency Questionnaire (CCQ) (Myers, Feltz, Maier, Wolfe, & Reckase, 2006).

Results revealed that, regardless of participant gender, participants expected 'successful' coaches to be significantly more competent than 'unsuccessful' coaches in terms of the character-building of their athletes, identifying and developing game-strategies, motivating athletes, and teaching relevant skills. Ultimately, these results indicated that coach reputation information is significantly more influential than the static cue of coach gender in terms of athletes' initial expectancies of coaches. The larger effect size for reputation ($\eta^2 = 0.43$) compared with that for coach gender ($\eta^2 = 0.04$), in conjunction with the fact that coach gender was only shown to impact on expectancies related to two of the four elements of coaching competency, provided additional support for Manley et al.'s (2008) three-factor model, which proposed that third-party reports such as reputation information exert greater influence over athletes' expectancies than do static cues such as the gender of the coach. Despite this discrepancy in the levels of influence that have been observed between types of informational cue, coaches should remain aware of the power that static cues can wield over athletes' initial expectancies of coaches.

Building on the work of Manley et al. (2010), Thelwell, Weston, Greenlees, Page, and Manley (2010) explored how athletes formulate their beliefs and expectancies of coaches using non-verbal cues that would be considered static or stable during the course of short-term interpersonal interactions. A series of four static photographs of coaches were developed and utilised as the experimental stimuli to depict variations in the combinations of clothing (sporting vs academic) and physique/build (lean vs large) exhibited by the target coach. Participants observed all four experimental photographs in random order prior to rating their perceptions of coaching competence in response to each photograph using the CCQ.

The findings revealed that coaches depicted as having a lean physique and wearing either sporting or academic clothing were perceived as most competent in terms of their ability to motivate athletes, while a lean physique combined with sporting attire was shown to enhance athletes' evaluations of a coach's technical and character-building competence. The authors explained that the target coaches wearing sporting attire may have given the impression that they were knowledgeable of sport and as such able to motivate their athletes, while the target coach wearing academic clothing but with a lean build may have portrayed themselves as possessing the appropriate characteristics (e.g. commitment to maintain physical fitness and conditioning) that would facilitate increased motivation in their athletes. In terms of the findings for technique competence, Thelwell et al. (2010) argued that the technical development of athletes tends to take place in the training environment, which in itself could be enough to explain the findings, especially given that it is unlikely to see coaches wearing non-sporting clothing in a training context. However, since the ability to help develop athletes' technical ability could feasibly be labelled as task competence, the findings are congruent with previous evidence (e.g. Lennon & Miller, 1984) that clothing has the potential to determine judgments of a person's levels of task competence. Additionally, Thelwell et al. (2010) revealed that a lean physique combined with academic clothing is most conducive for coaches aiming to enhance athletes' perceptions of their game strategy competence. In explaining these findings, the authors argued that the participants might have attributed certain traits (e.g. thoughtful, reflective, prepared) to the coach wearing the academic clothing, which in turn may have enhanced judgments relating to the coach's strategic competence.

Both Manley et al. (2010) and Thelwell et al. (2010) made tentative suggestions regarding the ways in which the findings of their respective studies could be used by coaches (e.g. emphasise positive aspects of their reputation when meeting athletes for the first time, basing clothing choice on the context within which they will be operating). However, they also suggested that alternative experimental techniques were warranted prior to drawing any firm conclusions. For example, although static photographs had been successfully employed in a range of previous studies examining expectancies and their effects within interpersonal interactions (e.g. Lubker et al., 2005; Naylor, 2007), the authors claimed that future research should adopt more dynamic experimental methods such as the use of video footage. The use of such methods and stimuli would not only ensure that participants were presented with more extensive and varied information prior to initial expectancy formation, but would also help to reflect the complex nature of coach–athlete interactions more closely.

With the above in mind, Thelwell, Page, Lush, Greenlees, and Manley (2012) utilised video footage of target coaches in conducting two studies to explore how coach reputation would influence athletes' expectancies of coaches. In study one, a sample of undergraduate Sport and Exercise Science students ($N = 326$) were presented with video footage of a male strength and conditioning coach leading a group of athletes through a series of four structured exercise drills. While there were no differences in the actual video footage presented, participants were randomly allocated to one of three experimental conditions (labelled as 'professional', 'in-training', and 'no reputation' conditions) where differing coach reputation information was provided to participants immediately prior to the footage being presented. Participants were then asked to evaluate the competence of the target coach by completing the CCQ immediately after viewing the video footage. In line with the findings of previous studies (e.g. Manley et al., 2010; Thelwell et al., 2010), coaches alleged to have a 'professional' reputation were rated as significantly more competent than those with either an 'in-training' reputation or 'no reputation'.

Thelwell et al.'s (2012) second study utilised exactly the same experimental procedure as study one, with the exception that a head-mounted eye-tracking system was also incorporated to facilitate examination of participants' visual search strategies that were employed when watching the video footage of the coach. The participants in study two were also undergraduate Sport and Exercise Science students ($N=22$). Visual search measurements analysed were total number of fixations (where a fixation was defined as when gaze remained within 1° of visual angle of a location or moving object for ≥ 120 ms), the average duration of fixations, and the total number of areas fixated (Williams, Ward, Knowles, & Smeeton, 2002). Significant differences across reputation conditions were only reported in relation to the total number of fixations. Specifically, those observing the 'in-training' coach had a greater number of fixations compared to the 'professional' and 'no reputation' conditions. Other than that, visual search strategies employed by participants across the three conditions were largely consistent. Although Thelwell et al. (2012) offered several tentative explanations as to how and why search patterns were consistent in the face of differing reputation information, the most robust explanation put forward was that the reputation information provided prior to the video was potent enough to determine and confirm participants' initial expectancy of the coach's competence. In other words, the influential strength of the reputation information provided meant that any perceptual strategy subsequently employed was used to merely confirm the initial impression created. Therefore, Thelwell et al. (2012) postulated that consistent search patterns might have been used across participants to attend to pre-defined indicators of coach competency, which might be similar regardless of whether they were confirming a 'professional' or 'in-training' coach.

Behavioural consequences of interpersonal expectancies within the coach–athlete relationship

Despite making a unique contribution to the literature, the studies reviewed so far all failed to implement experimental designs high in external validity (Smith, Mackie, & Claypool, 2014). Despite efforts to enhance levels of experimental realism (e.g. replacing static photographs with dynamic video footage as the experimental stimuli), participants in the above studies responded to stimuli in controlled, synthetic environments such as a classroom, without any direct personal interaction with the target coach. This does not adequately simulate the authentic surroundings in which athletes would be likely to form initial expectancies of coaches. Subsequently, Thelwell et al. (2012) argued that only when such approaches are utilised would a detailed understanding of such expectations and their consequences be established.

In an effort to build on existing findings and simultaneously address some of the methodological drawbacks of previous laboratory-based studies (e.g. Jones et al., 2002; Manley et al., 2010; Thelwell et al., 2010, 2012), Manley, Green-lees, Smith, Batten, and Birch (2014) developed a naturalistic experimental design to explore the behavioural consequences of athletes' expectancies of coaches. Specifically, the primary aim of this study was to examine the extent to which athletes' reputation-based expectancies can influence their behavioural responses towards a previously unknown coach, thus providing the first field-based examination of athlete-centred expectancy effects within the context of coach–athlete interactions. Thirty-five male soccer players (M age $= 18.2 \pm 2.2$) were recruited from three British college and university soccer teams. Participants were randomly assigned to one of three experimental conditions before engaging in a two-hour coaching session led by a previously unknown coach. During the warm-up period for each coaching session, a confederate research assistant who was familiar to participants provided them with reputation information about the unknown coach (i.e. experienced reputation, inexperienced reputation, or no reputation) prior to his arrival and introduction. In addition to the warm-up period, each two-hour session consisted of a set of passing and shooting drills, verbal summaries from the coach, and a ten-minute 'free practice' period. Each verbal summary served as a way of recapping on the previous drills, describing/demonstrating the content and relevance of the upcoming drill, and providing an opportunity to observe the specific behaviours exhibited by participants when directly addressed by the coach. Similarly, the 'free practice' period was included as a means of capturing participants' behaviours as part of the coaching session but in the absence of the coach. During the verbal summaries and 'free practice' period, participant behaviours deemed to be valid indicators of attention (i.e. longer periods of gaze in the direction of the coach – Langton, Watt, & Bruce, 2000), higher frequency of fixations on the coach – Jacob & Karn, 2003) and effort/persistence (i.e. high levels of engagement in the 'free practice' period – Wild, Enzle, & Hawkins, 1992) were observed and assessed using video recording procedures. To guard against confounding expectancy effects and demand characteristics, participants were told that the video capture was necessary to enable assessment of the coach's behaviour as part of a formal evaluation regarding his conduct and competence.

The findings obtained from the study indicated that reputation-based expectancies have the potential to influence athletes' behavioural responses to coaches within a field-based setting. Data obtained during the verbal summaries revealed significant differences in participants' gaze behaviour between reputation conditions. Specifically, the gaze behaviour of participants' in the experienced reputation condition (i.e. significantly longer/more frequent gaze in the direction of the coach) suggested that they paid more attention to coach instruction and demonstration during verbal summaries compared with participants in the inexperienced reputation condition (i.e. significantly shorter/less frequent gaze in the direction of the coach). Furthermore, participants in the no reputation condition exhibited less gaze in the direction of the coach, and thus appeared to pay less attention to the coach's verbal summaries than participants in the experienced reputation condition. However, there were no significant differences between the inexperienced reputation and no reputation groups regarding gaze direction during verbal summaries. Such results provide a contrast to the implication (e.g. Fiske & Taylor, 1991) that negative expectancy effects are more potent than expectancy effects based on positive information. Rather, the results seem to align more closely with claims (e.g. Jussim & Harber, 2005) that positive expectancy effects are often more powerful than negative ones. As a consequence, the findings for gaze behaviour suggest that, if coaches wish to maximise athletes' attention to instruction, they should harness the beneficial aspects of expectancies by placing greater emphasis on positive informational cues (e.g. experienced reputation) and/or accentuating positive qualities (e.g. autonomy-supportive behaviours) to help athletes maintain an optimal level of attention to instructions.

During the 'free practice' period, participants in the experienced reputation condition completed more drill-specific activities (e.g. shots, passes, tackles/blocks), spent less time standing still, and retrieved the ball from out of play on more occasions compared with participants in the inexperienced reputation condition. Such findings implied that participants in the experienced reputation condition exerted more effort and showed greater persistence during 'free practice' than did participants who were told that the coach was inexperienced. In addition, participants coached by a reportedly experienced coach exhibited significantly greater desire to continue with 'free practice' than participants in the no reputation condition, as indicated by the percentage of time they retrieved the ball from out of play. By voluntarily retrieving the ball from out of play more frequently than others, Manley et al. (2014) argued that the participants in the experienced coach condition were exhibiting a greater level of urgency to continue with the training session (and therefore greater effort) than those within the inexperienced and no reputation conditions. Thus, as with the findings related to participants' attentive gaze behaviour, the findings reported for 'free practice' behaviour in the absence of the previously unknown coach have added further credence to the suggestion (e.g. Jussim & Harber, 2005) that positive expectancy effects are more powerful than expectancy effects elicited by negative information.

Implications for future research

This chapter has reviewed studies that have explored the sources and consequences of athletes' expectancies of coaches, with specific foci on athletes' evaluations of coaching competence and athletes' naturalistic behavioural responses within the coaching context. Whilst the studies have made valuable contributions to relevant theoretical underpinnings and the empirical evidence base, they also reveal a number of implications for future research.

First, it is important that future research examines other sources of information in relation to athletes' expectancies of coaches and their consequences. For example, Manley et al. (2008) identified the category of 'dynamic' cues (e.g. body language, posture, eye contact, tone/clarity of voice) to be potentially influential sources of information for athletes when forming initial impressions and expectancies of coaches. Previous work by Greenlees and colleagues (Buscombe et al., 2006; Greenlees, Bradley, Holder, & Thelwell 2005; Greenlees, Buscombe, Thelwell, Holder, & Rimmer, 2005) demonstrates that dynamic cues such as body language can determine the impressions that athletes form of their opponents, as well as the athletes' subsequent thoughts and predictions regarding the outcomes of competitive encounters with that target opponent. With this in mind, a worthy avenue of future research would be to explore the influence of dynamic cues such as a coach's body language, facial expressions, or even verbal language on the expectancies and impressions formed by the coach's athletes.

Second, future research would do well to manipulate different levels of third-party reports, as the studies reviewed within this chapter have merely scratched the surface in terms of what is truly meant by 'coach reputation'. For example, in addition to 'success rate' and 'experience', the term 'coach reputation' could also be interpreted to represent a wide range of other qualities, characteristics, and/or achievements such as 'previous playing experience' or specific 'qualifications', both of which were reported by athletes to be highly influential sources of their initial expectancies of coaches (Manley et al., 2008). Exploration and analysis of such informational cues would provide a greater insight regarding the degree to which certain types of coach reputation information should be emphasised to athletes. Additionally, there are other modes or sub-categories of third-party report that warrant further scrutiny. For example, performance expectancies conveyed via the media have been recently identified as a specific type of third-party report which have the potential to shape athletes' thoughts, feelings and behaviours in relation to themselves, others, and upcoming events (e.g. Heaviside, Manley, Backhouse & Didymus, 2015). Thus, it would seem appropriate for future research to explore various media reports (e.g. printed press, online news items, social media posts) within the context of athlete-centred expectancies of coaches and their subsequent impact on coach–athlete interactions.

A limitation of the research reviewed in this chapter not yet highlighted is that participants' responses were only observed over the course of single, short-term exposures or interactions. In each of the studies reviewed, it is reasonable to assume that additional findings and implications might have been reported had the studies consisted of a greater number of occasions on which participants were exposed to experimental conditions and corresponding stimuli. This is especially true of the study conducted by Manley et al. (2014), where athlete behaviour in response to a previously unknown coach was evaluated over the course of a fleeting two-hour coaching session. According to Snyder and Stukas (1999), the greater the likelihood of future interactions (in this case between the athlete and the coach), then the greater is the likelihood of the occurrence of expectancy effects. Thus, participants' responses in this particular study may have been influenced by their knowledge that their interaction with the coach was a one-off event that they were unlikely to experience again. Consequently, researchers in this area should look to conduct similar investigations over the course of multiple viewings, exposures, and interactions, just as athletes often interact with coaches over the course of multiple coaching sessions/seasons. Such experimental designs would offer an appropriate opportunity to examine whether the previously reported consequences of athletes' expectancies of coaches have a subsequent impact on other observable behaviours or important outcome measures (e.g. fluctuations in athletes' adherence to training, changes in athletes' technical ability). Moreover, given that the effects of initial expectancies may dissipate over time (Jussim & Harber, 2005), longitudinal research designs, particularly those conducted in naturalistic settings, would enhance our understanding of the degree to which expectancies based on short-term interactions can determine the long-term nature of coach–athlete relationships.

Finally, the work of Jussim and colleagues (Jussim, 1991, 1993; Jussim & Harber, 2005) proposes that it is possible for expectancies to represent an accurate prediction of behaviour (i.e. expectancies reflect social reality) rather than being a moderator of behaviour (i.e. expectancies construct social reality). Therefore, it is vital that future research examining the impact of expectancies on the coach–athlete relationship is carefully designed so that the findings can be confidently identified as expectancy effects as opposed to accuracy in the perceiver's predictions.

Implications for applied practice

This chapter has highlighted some important implications for coaches, particularly in relation to the expectancies formed by athletes when evaluating a new coach. Most notably, the consensus from research findings reported to date indicates that coaches have a significant amount of control over the initial impressions and expectancies formed of them by their athletes. For example, the evidence consistently reflects that athletes' expectancies of coaches are influenced primarily by sources of information (e.g. dynamic cues, third-party reports) that are more malleable and open to adaptation than the less controllable 'static' cues. Furthermore, the general findings imply that positive information has a compelling effect on athletes' cognitive and behavioural responses to a coach they are expected to or have briefly worked with. Thus, it is suggested that coaches – and their employers/ support staff – utilise this evidence to their advantage (e.g. by placing emphasis on positive aspects of the coach's reputation prior to his/her first meeting with athletes, by dressing appropriately having considered the context in which interactions with athletes will take place). By maximising the positive information that athletes receive about a coach (even prior to their first direct interaction), the chances of developing positive coach–athlete relationships may be enhanced as a result of the initial positive expectancies that athletes are more likely to form about the coach in response to such information. By adopting such strategies and implementing them as part of their general planning and organisation ahead of interactions with their athletes, coaches will be better equipped to overcome the barriers to forging a good working relationship with their performers.

Notes

1 Leeds Beckett University, UK
2 University of Chichester, UK
3 University of Portsmouth, UK

References

Becker, A. J. (2009). It's not what they do, it's how they do it: Athlete experiences of great coaching. *International Journal of Sports Science and Coaching, 4*, 93–119.

Becker, A. J., & Solomon, G. B. (2005). Expectancy information and coach effectiveness in intercollegiate basketball. *The Sport Psychologist, 19*, 251–266.

Boardley, I. D., Kavussanu, M., & Ring, C (2008). Athletes' perceptions of coaching effectiveness and athlete-related outcomes in Rugby Union: An investigation based on the Coaching Efficacy Model. *The Sport Psychologist, 22*, 269–287.

Buscombe, R., Greenlees, I., Holder, T., Thelwell, R., & Rimmer, M. (2006). Expectancy effects in tennis: The impact of opponents' pre-match non-verbal behaviour on male tennis players. *Journal of Sports Sciences, 24*, 1265–1272.

Cook, M. (1971). *Interpersonal perception*. Harmondsworth, Middlesex: Penguin Education.

Coulomb-Cabagno, G., Rascle, O., & Souchon, N. (2005). Players' gender and male referees' decisions about aggression in French soccer: A preliminary study. *Sex Roles, 52*, 547–553.

Darley, J. M., & Fazio, R. H. (1980). Expectancy confirmation processes arising in the social interaction sequence. *American Psychologist, 35*, 867–881.

Ditto, P. H., & Hilton, J. L. (1990). Expectancy processes in the health care interaction sequence. *Journal of Social Issues, 46*, 97–124.

Findlay, L. C., & Ste-Marie, D. M. (2004). A reputation bias in figure skating. *Journal of Sport and Exercise Psychology, 26*, 154–166.

Fiske, S. T., & Taylor, S. E. (1991). *Social Cognition* (2nd edn). New York: McGraw-Hill.

Greenlees, I., Bradley, A., Holder, T., & Thelwell, R. (2005). The impact of opponents' non-verbal behaviour on the first impressions and outcome expectations of table-tennis players. *Psychology of Sport and Exercise, 6*, 103–115.

Greenlees, I., Buscombe, R., Thelwell, R., Holder, T., & Rimmer, M. (2005). Impact of opponents' clothing and body language on impression formation and outcome expectations. *Journal of Sport & Exercise Psychology, 27*, 39–52.

Heaviside, H. J., Manley, A. J., Backhouse, S. H., & Didymus, F. (2015). "Put up there on a pedestal and expected to be the star.... But nobody really knows how difficult it is": An in-depth analysis of media-constructed expectations within elite sport. *Paper presented at the British Psychological Society's Division of Sport & Exercise Psychology Conference*. Leeds, UK.

Higgins, E. T., & Bargh, J. A. (1987). Social cognition and social perception. *Annual Review of Psychology, 38*, 369–425.

Horn, T. S. (2008). Coaching effectiveness in the sports domain. In T. S. Horn (Ed.), *Advances in sport psychology* (3rd edn), 239–267. Champaign, IL: Human Kinetics.

Horn, T. S., Lox, C. L., & Labrador, F. (2010). The self-fulfilling prophecy theory: When coaches' expectations become reality. In J. Williams (Ed.), *Applied sport psychology: Personal growth to peak performance* (6th edn), 81–105. Boston, MA: McGraw-Hill.

Jacob, R. J. K., & Karn, K. S. (2003). Eye tracking in human–computer interaction and usability research: Ready to deliver the promises. In J. Hyönä, R. Radach, & H. Deubel (Eds.), *The mind's eye: Cognitive and applied aspects of eye movement research*, 573–605. Amsterdam: Elsevier.

Jones, M. V., Paull, G. C., & Erskine, J. (2002). The impact of a team's aggressive reputation on the decisions of association football referees. *Journal of Sports Sciences, 20*, 991–1000.

Jowett, S., & Cockerill, I. M. (2003). Olympic medallists' perspective of the athlete-coach relationship. *Psychology of Sport and Exercise, 4*, 313–331.

Jowett, S., Frost, T., & Timson-Katchis, M. (2006). Race/ethnicity in the all male coach–athlete relationship: Black footballers' narratives. *Paper presented at the British Psychological Society Annual Conference.* Cardiff, UK.

Jowett, S., & Poczwardowski, A. (2007). Understanding the coach–athlete relationship. In S. Jowett, & D. Lavallee (Eds.), *Social Psychology in Sport,* 3–14. Champaign, IL: Human Kinetics.

Jussim, L. (1993). Accuracy in interpersonal expectations: A reflection–construction analysis of current and classic research. *Journal of Personality, 61,* 637–668.

Jussim, L. (1991). Social perception and social reality: A reflection–construction model. *Psychological Review, 98,* 54–73.

Jussim, L., & Harber, K. D. (2005). Teacher expectations and self-fulfilling prophecies: Knowns and unknowns, resolved and unresolved controversies. *Personality and Social Psychology Review, 9,* 131–155.

Langton, S. R. H., Watt, R. J., & Bruce, V. (2000). Do the eyes have it? Cues to the direction of social attention. *Trends in Cognitive Science, 4,* 50–59.

Lennon, S. J., & Miller, F. G. (1984). Salience of physical appearance in impression formation. *Home Economics Journal, 13,* 95–104.

Lubker, J. R., Watson II, J. C., Visek, A. J., & Geer, J. R. (2005). Physical appearance and the perceived effectiveness of performance enhancement consultants. *The Sport Psychologist, 19,* 446–458.

Manley, A. J., Greenlees, I., Graydon, J., Thelwell, R., Filby, W. C. D., & Smith, M. J. (2008). Athletes' perceived use of information sources when forming initial impressions and expectancies of a coach: An exploratory study. *The Sport Psychologist, 22,* 73–89.

Manley, A. J., Greenlees, I. A., Smith, M. J., Batten, J., & Birch, P. D. J. (2014). The influence of coach reputation on the behavioral responses of male soccer players. *Scandinavian Journal of Medicine and Science in Sports, 24,* e111–e120.

Manley, A. J., Greenlees, I., Thelwell, R., & Smith, M. (2010). Athletes' use of reputation and gender information when forming initial expectancies of coaches. *International Journal of Sports Science and Coaching, 5,* 517–532.

Merton, R. K. (1948). The self-fulfilling prophecy. *Antioch Review, 8,* 193–210.

Miller, D. T. & Turnbull, W. (1986). Expectancies and interpersonal processes. *Annual Review of Psychology, 37,* 233–256.

Myers, N. D., Feltz, D. L., Maier, K. S., Wolfe, E. W., & Reckase, M. D. (2006). Athletes' evaluations of their head coach's coaching competency. *Research Quarterly for Exercise and Sport, 77,* 111–121.

Naylor, R. W. (2007). Nonverbal cues-based first impressions: Impression formation through exposure to static images. *Marketing Letters, 18,* 165–179.

Olson, J. M., Roese, N. J., & Zanna, M. P. (1996). Expectancies. In E. T. Higgins, & A. W. Kruglanski (Eds.), *Social psychology: Handbook of basic principles,* 211–238. New York: The Guildford Press.

Smith, E. R., Mackie, D. M., & Claypool, H. M. (2014). *Social psychology* (4th edn). New York: Psychology Press.

Smoll, F. L., & Smith, R. E. (1989). Leadership behaviours in sport: A theoretical model and research paradigm. *Journal of Applied Social Psychology, 19,* 1522–1551.

Snyder, M., & Stukas, Jr., A. A. (1999). Interpersonal processes: The interplay of cognitive, motivational, and behavioural activities in social interaction. *Annual Review of Psychology, 50,* 273–303.

Solomon, G. B. (2016). Improving performance by means of action-cognition coupling in athletes and coaches. In: M. Raab, B. Lobinger, S. Hoffmann, A. Pizzera, & S. Laborde

(Eds.), *Performance psychology: Perception, action, cognition, and emotion*, 88–101. London: Elsevier Academic Press.

Solomon, G. B., & Rhea, D. J. (2008). Sources of expectancy information among college coaches: A qualitative test of Expectancy Theory. *International Journal of Sports Science and Coaching, 3*, 251–268.

Souchon, N., Coulomb-Cabagno, G., Traclet, A., & Rascle, O. (2004). Referees' decision making in handball and transgressive behaviours: Influence of stereotypes about gender of players? *Sex Roles, 51*, 445–453.

Thelwell, R. C., Page, J. L., Lush, A., Greenlees, I. A., & Manley, A. J. (2012). Can reputation biases influence the outcome and process of making competence judgments of a coach? *Scandinavian Journal of Medicine and Science in Sports, 23*, 65–73.

Thelwell, R. C., Weston, N. J. V., Greenlees, I. A., Page, J. L., & Manley, A. J. (2010). Examining the impact of physical appearance on impressions of coaching competence. *International Journal of Sport Psychology, 41*, 277–292.

Wang, C. K. J., Koh, K. T., & Chatzisarantis, N. (2009). An intra-individual analysis of players' perceived coaching behaviours, psychological needs, and achievement goals. *International Journal of Sports Science and Coaching, 4*(2), 177–192.

Wild, T. C., Enzle, M. E., & Hawkins, W. (1992). Effects of perceived extrinsic versus intrinsic teacher motivation on student reactions to skill acquisition. *Personality and Social Psychology Bulletin, 18*, 245–251.

Williams, A. M., Ward, P., Knowles, J. M., & Smeeton, N. J. (2002). Anticipation skill in a real-world task: Measurement, training, and transfer in tennis. *Journal of Experimental Psychology: Applied, 8*, 259–270.

Wilson, M. A., Cushion, C. J., & Stephens, D. E. (2006). "Put me in coach … I'm better than you think I am!" Coaches' perceptions of their expectations in youth sport. *International Journal of Sports Science and Coaching, 1*, 149–161.

11 Understanding effective coaching

Antecedents and consequences

M. Ryan Flett,[1] Sarah Carson Sackett,[2] and
Martin Camiré[3]

Introduction

What actions can coaches take to promote effective outcomes, and what are the resulting benefits? This chapter describes actions coaches can take to promote positive outcomes for their athletes. Athlete-outcomes/consequences are discussed to justify the recommended coaching-actions and to provide a more complete literature review. We intentionally limited our review to empirical studies of coaching practices linked to successful outcomes that were published between 2000 and 2015. Though research was reviewed across three distinct sporting contexts (recreational, developmental, and elite), several common themes emerged that operationalize *effective coaching* across all contexts: skilful pedagogy, instruction, and communication; thoughtful, actionable philosophies; caring rapport that supports holistic athlete development; and a disciplined but intrinsically motivating, process/mastery-oriented, and autonomy-building climate.

Key terms

While many researchers agree that *coaching effectiveness* leads to positive outcomes such as sport skill development, psychosocial development, positive mental states, and performance success, explanations of the elements and mechanisms that help cultivate these results are diverse and often quite complex (Horn, 2008). Côté and Gilbert (2009) integrated information from coaching, athlete development, positive psychology, and teaching/instruction literatures to define coaching effectiveness as "the consistent application of integrated professional, interpersonal, and intrapersonal knowledge to improve athletes' competence, confidence, connection, and character in specific coaching contexts" (p. 316). The recognition that effective coaching is contingent on sport-contexts reminds us that the best practitioners adapt their methods to, for example, sport, level, objectives and culture.

Trudel and Gilbert (2006) classified coaching effectiveness within recreational, developmental, and elite sport contexts. Accordingly, this chapter reviews literature from: (a) early recreation sport contexts for children; (b) developmental (school and club) sport contexts for adolescents; and (c) elite sport focusing on adult populations. We recognise the use of this typology will elim-inate certain coaching populations (e.g., coaches of elite-youth and adult-recreational athletes). However, this delineation lends itself to a systematic review of the current literature based on the objectives of each sport context and the age of the populations studied. Within these three sections, our review of literature describes effective coaches' actions (antecedents) and outcomes (con-sequences) for athletes, teams, and/or coaches themselves. Finally, implications for future research and applied practice are provided in the concluding sections.

Review of the literature

Effective coaching in recreational child sport

Recreational youth sport emphasizes participation and basic skill development in a lightly organized and relatively low-intensity environment (Lyle, 2002). Inves-tigating the role frames (i.e., attitudes/philosophies that guide one's practice) of youth sport coaches, Gilbert and Trudel (2004) interviewed six model coaches who identified core coaching responsibilities that aligned nicely with the follow-ing basic objectives: coaching discipline; constructing a fun atmosphere; foster-ing personal development; developing sport-specific skills and competencies; emphasizing team; providing a positive, safe, and equitable team environment; and winning. Understanding that a coach's roles are influenced by situational factors, it was also suggested that the importance of each of these approaches would likely vary by the athlete's age, gender, and competitive level.

Côté and Gilbert (2009) suggested that the successful application of profes-sional, interpersonal, and intrapersonal knowledge at the recreational youth sport level is impacted by expectations such as: engaging all interested participants; fostering a mastery-oriented motivational climate; promoting fun and play; adopting an athlete-centered approach; focusing on fundamental skill develop-ment; and encouraging positive social interactions. These expectations can be viewed as antecedents of effective coaching, with direct consequences such as enhanced motivation, fun, skill development, and social skills. In combination, these guidelines uncover the reality that effective coaches at this level have a complex set of responsibilities that are the foundation for subsequent athlete development. It would seem, then, that much of the literature should be dedic-ated to assessing this diverse set of effective coaching practices at this particular level of sport. Unfortunately, the extant literature is quite narrow in scope – both in concepts examined and raw number – likely due, in part, to challenges with sampling this younger population and a largely voluntary coaching staff. That said, the bodies of work that do exist focus heavily on the topics of creating a mastery-oriented, autonomy-supportive, and caring sport climate.

Fostering a positive motivational climate has long been a subject of study because a significant responsibility for youth coaches is to make sport intrinsic-ally gratifying in order to promote outcomes such as effort, engagement, and maintenance of participation (see Harwood, Spray, & Keegan, 2008). While coaches are not the only individuals who influence team climate, they play a substantial role due to the feedback and incentives provided, rules/boundaries maintained, and interpersonal relationships fostered with and between athletes. Across many studies, a mastery-oriented climate has been shown to more effectively cultivate positive developmental outcomes and the psychological states that should lead to superior skill development and performances than a climate that is centrally focused on winning.

Investigating the efficacy of the mastery approach to coaching (MAC), Smith, Smoll, and Cumming (2007) demonstrated great utility in a sample of 37 coaches of 10–14-year-old recreational basketball athletes. MAC is an intervention that promotes the use of: positive reinforcement for personal improvement, effort, and adaptive behaviors; mistake-contingent encouragement; abundant technical instruction; encouraging corrective instruction; framing mistakes as learning opportunities; discipline-focused team rules; individualized attention; and supportive coach–athlete interactions. Compared to a control group who showed increased anxiety scores across the season, athletes with MAC-trained coaches reported lowered anxiety on all somatic and cognitive variables assessed, with those related to somatic anxiety, worry, and the composite anxiety scores reaching significance. Additionally, the dropout rate for athletes of MAC-trained coaches was lower than the control group (11 percent versus 26 percent, respectively). Coatsworth and Conroy (2006) also found positive results from a coaching-effectiveness training program (CET; Smith & Smoll, 1996) for impacting athlete self-esteem, but the relationship was only significant among athletes who were younger (i.e., 7–11 years) and females who had lower baseline self-esteem levels.

Looking at a younger sample, Keegan, Harwood, Spray, and Lavallee (2009) conducted focus groups to assess coaching behaviors that influence motivational climates and resulting athlete motivation. Participants were recreational athletes from 17 sports who were under the age of 12 and had less than 3 years of playing experience. Coaching behaviors deemed most influential included positive feedback and praise, rewarding normative success, effort-contingent reinforcement, more collaborative and less controlling leadership styles, positive affective responses, tolerance, and reinforcement for approaching challenges. Also, more efficacious pedagogical practices used equitable and individualized instruction, competition in a fun and developmentally appropriate manner, and mastery- and normative-based evaluations.

More recently, Saville et al. (2014) investigated how motivational climate factors influence youth athletes' self-efficacy and relation-inferred self-efficacy (RISE). RISE represents what an individual believes others think about his/her capabilities, which is believed to shape self-efficacy (Lent & Lopez, 2002). Focus groups with a sample of 28 community recreational athletes (ages 8–12) found self-efficacy was improved by coaches' use of such strategies as providing mastery experiences that relate to relationally and self-referenced situations, positive feedback, and modeling. RISE beliefs were also enhanced by encouragement, technical and corrective instruction, deemphasizing performance outcomes, positive and supportive interpersonal interactions, and providing athletes with challenging opportunities to stretch themselves in their roles on the team.

The previous theme highlights the importance of providing athletes with an autonomy-supportive climate (i.e., one that provides athletes with choice, ownership, and the ability to exercise initiative and self-determined behavior; Mageau & Vallerand, 2003). Reynolds and McDonough (2015) found positive correlations between coach autonomy-support and motivation of youth recreation soccer players, but only when measures of coach involvement/social support were high. In a slightly older recreational sample ($M = 13.4$ years), Cronin and Allen (2015) looked at the relationship between an autonomy-supportive climate and a cluster of psychological development and well-being variables. Athletes from 13 sports completed surveys, with analyses yielding positive relationships among autonomy-support, personal and social skills, cognitive skills, goal setting, and initiative. In particular, the development of personal and social skills was positively related to athletes' self-esteem, positive affect, and life satisfaction (and served as a mediator between the coach behaviors and well-being variables). In a recreational swimming sample of similar age ($M = 12.1$ years), Coatsworth and Conroy (2009) identified links between autonomy-supportive coaching and several positive outcomes (e.g., self-esteem, identity reflection, initiative) that were mediated by coaching behaviors such as process-focused praise that helped satisfy athletes' basic needs of competence and relatedness.

A final consistent theme in the literature (mentioned previously as it relates to positive interpersonal relationships) is the impact of a caring climate on positive outcomes for youth athletes. Fry and Gano-Overway (2010) define a caring climate as one in which "individuals perceive a particular setting to be interpersonally inviting, safe, supportive, and able to provide the experience of being valued and respected" (p. 296). While much of the research in this area has been conducted in the summer camp context with promising results related to mental well-being, empathetic concern, motivation for future participation, and valuing of participation (e.g., Fry et al., 2012; Gano-Overway et al., 2009), Fry and Gano-Overway examined the impact of a caring climate on youth soccer experiences. Although strength of the relationships ranged from moderately weak ($r = 0.33$) to moderate ($r = 0.64$), there were significant and positive correlations between a caring climate and attitudes toward the coach and one's teammates, caring behaviors, enjoyment, and commitment. Similarly, a study of 239 underserved urban-American youth found participants reported more positive developmental outcomes (e.g., initiative, team and social skills, adult networks/social capital, reduced social exclusion, and other outcomes) in more caring and mastery-oriented climates (Gould, Flett, & Lauer, 2012).

Effective coaching in developmental adolescent sport

Although providing athletes with opportunities to learn technical and tactical skills is a fundamental component of coaching (Gilbert & Trudel, 2004), several studies have indicated how developmental coaches believe their primary role ultimately rests in offering adolescent-aged athletes a sporting experience that is conducive to personal growth. Lesyk and Kornspan (2000) surveyed 109 American coaches to examine their expectations of youth sport participation. Results indicated that coaches prioritized having fun, learning life skills, being part of a team, and developing confidence as their most important objectives for youth. Similarly, Gould, Chung, Smith, and White (2006) surveyed 154 American high school coaches on their perceived role, with results indicating that these coaches ranked the psychosocial and physical development of students as their central objective. In Australia, Vella, Oades, and Crowe (2011) interviewed 22 coaches to investigate how they viewed their role. The results suggested again that coaches saw themselves as responsible for fostering adolescents' competence, confidence, connection, and character.

Research has identified that developmental coaches' abilities to enact their objectives is often tempered by the extent to which they can articulate a clear coaching philosophy. Nash, Sproule, and Horton (2008) interviewed 21 coaches from the United Kingdom and found differences in their approaches based on their career stage. The authors discussed how coaches often focus initially on coping with the more tangible aspects of coaching (e.g., improving their athletes' fitness level, developing drills) and see less value in considering their practice from a broader role frame. However, as coaches gain knowledge and experience in coaching and life, their ability to articulate a clear coaching philosophy and put it into practice is enhanced. Such findings were evidenced in a study of 10 highly experienced American high school coaches (Collins, Gould, Lauer, & Chung, 2009). The findings demonstrated how coaches developed their athletes as people above all and had well-developed philosophies emphasizing pleasure and psychosocial development. Camiré, Trudel, and Forneris (2012) interviewed nine model high school coaches from Canada, who discussed the importance of considering their athletes' internal and external assets and having athlete-centered philosophies consistent with their school's mandate.

In addition to well-developed philosophies, effective developmental coaches have also been shown to have a genuine openness to learning. Flett, Gould, Griffes, and Lauer (2013) interviewed and observed 12 American youth sport coaches, and discussed how effective coaches were open to coach training and revealed signs of being lifelong learners. Camiré, Trudel, and Forneris (2014) interviewed 16 model high school coaches from Canada and discussed how these coaches also identified themselves as reflective practitioners who actively sought out formal, non-formal, and informal learning situations to continuously improve their craft.

Having objectives focused on athletes' global development, a clear coaching philosophy, and an openness to learning are key factors in being an effective developmental coach. However, philosophies only fulfill their potential when enacted through concrete strategies deliberately built into coaching plans. McCallister, Blinde, and Weiss (2000) noted how inconsistencies often exist between coaching philosophies and actual implementation, which reinforces the need for an intentional approach to development.

In recent years, a number of studies have been conducted in different countries, examining the strategies employed by developmental coaches to foster adolescents' growth through sport. In Canada, Camiré and colleagues conducted several qualitative studies (Camiré & Trudel, 2013, 2014; Camiré, Trudel, & Bernard, 2013; Camiré et al., 2012) examining the developmental strategies employed by high school coaches. From these studies, the notion of creating quality coach–athlete relationships has been highlighted as a critical precursor to development in order to gain athletes' trust. To nurture relationships, caring climates were created whereby coaches constantly reiterated to those under their tutelage that they cared about them as people, not just as athletes. Moreover, to promote healthy coach–athlete interactions, the coaches used several relational strategies over the course of the season, such as having pre-game meals as a team and organising regular coach–athlete meetings. Through these strategies, athletes gathered that coaches genuinely had their best interests at heart, making them more receptive to the range of developmental strategies implemented. Volunteering in the community was deemed a particularly useful strategy to foster caring team climates in addition to providing athletes with tangible opportunities to transfer their life skills outside of sport. For instance, Camiré et al. (2013) conducted a case study of a high school ice hockey program to examine its approach to athlete development. In one activity, the coaches arranged for their athletes to volunteer at a rink to help underserved children learn how to skate. For an entire afternoon, each athlete was paired with one child and was responsible for implementing a lesson plan. Through this initiative, the athletes not only learned leadership and organisational skills, but also the importance of giving back.

In Australia, Vella and colleagues have conducted several studies with youth sport coaches, investigating their approach to development. Vella, Oades, and Crowe (2013) designed an intervention with two soccer clubs, examining how coaches' transformational leadership behaviors influenced adolescents' development. Transformational leadership was considered a strong predictor of developmental experiences, manifesting itself through behaviors such as individual consideration, intellectual stimulation, and appropriate role modeling. Based on their recent empirical findings, Vella, Cliff, Okely, Weintraub, and Robinson (2014) suggested six instructional strategies to promote adolescents' development: focusing on effort and persistence; facilitating challenge; promoting the value of failure; defining success as effort; promoting learning in a mastery climate; and providing high expectations. According to the authors, such strategies, when implemented appropriately, are conducive to positive motivational, behavioral, and affective outcomes for adolescent athletes.

In the United States, Collins et al. (2009) examined high school coaches' philosophies, but also their strategies to foster athletes' development. Winning and development were not viewed as incompatible outcomes, but rather as equal and inclusive pursuits of coaching that were achieved through strategies such as communicating openly with athletes and offering individualised feedback. Flett et al. (2013) discussed how the coaches in their sample who were deemed effective had many strategies for development. Specifically, these coaches worked to develop a positive team climate, challenged their athletes in a supportive manner, and discussed the transfer of life skills outside of sport.

In the United Kingdom, Felton and Jowett (2013) surveyed 300 athletes to examine their psychological need satisfaction and well-being in sport. Results were in line with self-determination theory and highlighted that what coaches do, and how they relate to athletes, are central to the satisfaction of athletes' psychological needs and the promotion of their well-being. Fenton, Duda, Quested, and Barrett (2014) conducted a study with 105 male youth footballers to examine perceptions of the social environment created by their coach. Findings highlighted how fostering autonomous reasons for sport engagement represented an effective strategy for coaches to increase their athletes' moderate-to-vigorous physical activity and reduce their sedentary time.

In Brazil, Flett and Huth (2014) explored the coaching of young athletes and found that effective coaches were enthusiastic, supportive, and professional in their approach. In their everyday coaching practice, they optimised training through excellent pedagogical skills (e.g., having diverse instructional techniques, and modifying drills based on athletes' needs).

Effective coaching in elite adult sport

Over the past 15 years, there has been a marked increase in coaching research involving elite adult athletes. For instance, Wang and Straub (2012) interviewed 21-time national champion (US College) and world champion women's soccer coach Anson Dorrance to study his coaching methodology. Dorrance's approach balanced developmental and competitive objectives, and included eight components: effective leadership; a positive, disciplined team environment; a competitive team environment; teaching key psychology principles; competing with strong opponents; talent development and recruiting; decorum in competition; and professional development as a coach. Supporting Dorrance's emphasis on professional development, 15 Canadian Olympic coaches interviewed by Werthner and Trudel (2009) were also described as life-long learners with otherwise idiosyncratic developmental paths.

In another case study of an exceptional American college coach, Becker and Wrisberg (2008) observed women's basketball coach Pat Summitt across six practices, finding that instructional actions represented nearly half of her behaviors (followed by praise, hustle, management, and scolding statements). The legendary coach provided equal attention to individuals and the team as a whole, and to "high- and low-value" players. Her behaviors fostered efficient practices, confidence, and the development of all players (not just the most talented ones). Consequently, Summitt achieved an 84 percent winning record with a strong developmental and instructional focus.

Gearity (2012) also concluded that instruction was fundamental to effective coaching, based on interviews with 16 collegiate, professional, and semi-pro athletes who described their lived experiences of "poor" coaching. From this opposing vantage point, Gearity described ineffective teaching as involving inadequate instruction on and off the field (e.g., lacking in amount, timing, clarity, rapport, life skills emphasis, or out-dated); not individualizing to athletes' distinct needs; and not being knowledgeable about skills, tactics, and pedagogy. Consequently, participants reported not learning from poor coaches.

In addition to effective pedagogy and similar to coaches of younger/novice levels, most studies emphasize that effective elite coaches have a developmental focus that goes beyond immediate competitive success. For example, Flett and Paule-Koba (2015) conducted interviews with 10 Canadian university coaches who had strong performance and championship records. These coaches believed coaching the whole athlete was more important than immediate wins, because the development of character and life skills facilitates long-term competitive goals. This holistic approach resulted in stronger teamwork and work ethic, long-term athletic development, and performance under pressure. Similarly, Martindale, Collins, and Abraham (2007) interviewed 16 elite UK coaches representing 13 sports and confirmed a model of talent development that included long-term development versus early success, clear expectations and goals, and individualized programs, as well as four humanistic qualities: role modeling and peer mentoring; athlete ownership, autonomy, and self-motivation; informal and regular coach–athlete interactions; and respecting athletes holistically by supporting sport and life.

Other examples of holistic coaching approaches come from Becker (2009) who conducted interviews with 18 collegiate, professional, and international athletes (aged 22–42) about their best coaching experiences. Participants described great coaches as having robust attributes (e.g., abilities, personality, more than just a coach); creating strong general, practice, and communication environments; developing deep and lasting personal and professional relationships; having a framework in which to implement their philosophy; and acting as teachers and motivators that prepared their athletes to perform under pressure. As a result of these five conditions, participants reported that coaches influenced their athletic development, performance, self-perceptions, and desire to be their best in sport and in life.

Corroborating many of the aforementioned strategies, Bennie and O'Connor (2012a, 2012b) examined the philosophies, coach–athlete relationships, and perceptions of effective coaches across three professional Australian teams, representing six coaches and 25 players. The coaches' philosophies emphasized education and player development, rather than winning alone, and players' on- and off-field development. Relationships were described as either family-oriented or professional (i.e., approachable but arms-length; Bennie & O'Connor, 2012a), with the ideal type of relationship depending on the coach's philosophy and athlete's personality preferences. Regardless of the relationship type, participants believed professional coaches must be approachable, honest, trustworthy, and respectful; show interest in the players; and maintain regular dialog. Players were more comfortable, relaxed, trusting, and responsive to coaches when the above relationship was established.

To be effective leaders, coaches must also personalize their approach and delegate responsibly (to empower athletes and utilize assistants efficiently), but make assertive and responsible decisions (Bennie & O'Connor, 2012b). This person/player-centered approach to professional coaching was described as one in which "the coaching staff became more like advisors, mentors and sources of information rather than strictly directing the coaching process" (p. 87). These coaches delegated purposefully to build rapport, motivate, and empower players, but did not decentralize decision-making to the point of destabilizing the team, creating conflict, or undermining their own authority. This style of leadership improved players' focus, commitment, and energy dedicated to team and personal goals.

Research has begun to provide more detail about the nature of effective coach–athlete relationships. Bennie and O'Connor (2012a, 2012b) found that professional coaches must consider players' preferences while remaining true to themselves to facilitate relationship fit. Expanding on this point, Jackson, Dimmock, Gucciardi, and Grove (2011) analysed 91 coach–athlete dyads, concluding that opposite personalities did not attract. Furthermore, similar personalities (particularly agreeableness, extraversion, and openness) were associated with positive relationship outcomes (i.e., a sense of commitment and relatedness) – especially if their partners were conscientious and agreeable. Likewise, Jowett and Cockerill (2003) interviewed twelve Olympic medallists across five sports and eight nationalities who described three key relationship factors: closeness, co-orientation, and complementary roles/tasks. The authors concluded that coach–athlete relationships were vital to athlete success and strong relationships benefit athletes' personal well-being and performance.

Beyond instruction and development, elite coaches must be able to manage the distinct demands of highly competitive sport. Coaches must effectively prepare athletes for intense competitions such as championships and rivalry games (Becker, 2009; Gearity, 2012; Wang & Straub, 2012). At the international and professional levels, coaches must effectively identify talented athletes (Bennie & O'Connor, 2012b; Wang & Straub, 2012); and at the university level, coaches must be strong recruiters so that they can coach the most talented athletes (Becker, 2009). Identifying/recruiting talent is increasingly difficult because early recruiting drives coaches to commit to younger athletes whose abilities as 15-year-olds may not forecast their ultimate potential (Paule & Flett, 2011). Effective coaches obtain as much information as possible about recruits' tangible and intangible assets, based on formal and informal assessment of the athlete and their support network (Flett & Paule-Koba, 2015).

Summary: consequences of effective coaching antecedents.

The review of research defined effective coaching across three sport contexts and described the characteristics of an effective coach for each – but why should a coach incorporate these recommendations? Why should educators and academics promote them? The simple answer is because of the positive outcomes associated with these antecedents. In summary, the identified effective coaching antecedents are associated with the following consequences for teams: better practices and learning; performing well under pressure; athlete confidence, focus, and motivation; lower anxiety and reduced dropout; attainment of team and individual goals; a positive and productive team climate; team commitment, support, trust, and stronger rapport; and reduced conflict. These antecedents have a positive effect on athletes' personal development, psychological need satisfaction, self-esteem, self-efficacy, empowerment, cognitive skills, initiative, identity reflection, enjoyment, life-satisfaction, psychological well-being, social skills, and empathy. Finally, effective coaches are more likely to work with the most talented athletes; have more authority, respect, commitment, trust, and responsiveness from athletes; and benefit from being life-long learners.

Implications for future research

When outlining this chapter, it was assumed that there would be stark contrasts across contexts; but as the chapter emerged, the similarities across contexts were glaring, and the differences subtler. Many of the studies reviewed support Lyle (2002) and Côté and Gilbert's (2009) holistic and humanistic approaches to effective coaching and athlete development. Research paradigms influence what is studied and how it is studied, and, as such, the results and conclusions from coaching research. Consequently, it may be that a trend in taking a humanistic approach to coaching research is partly responsible for humanistic findings and recommendations across sport contexts.

Gould and Carson (2008) provided several recommendations for coaching research that remain relevant. Longitudinal designs and intervention-based projects are required to identify causal relationships between coaching actions and athlete outcomes that are authentic and practitioner oriented. Deliberate transfer strategies are needed to foster holistic youth development in sport, but the exact role that "intentionality" plays in a coach's approach has rarely been explored empirically. Studies investigating whether and how psychosocial development is transferred outside of sport are also lacking. This gap undermines the significant role that coaches play in youth development, and may perpetuate the presumption that life skills are automatically learned and transferred from sport.

The role of transformational leadership in coaching effectiveness appears to be an important construct, yet we know little about how it is developed in coaches and how it affects athletes. Finally, of the three forms of knowledge in the Côté and Gilbert (2009) definition, research on the impact of coaches' intrapersonal knowledge on athlete outcomes is most scarce (e.g., exploring the associations between self-awareness, regulation and emotional intelligence, and the quality of coach–athlete relationships and role modeling).

Balancing competition and long-term/holistic development is especially germane to elite adult contexts, and is increasingly pertinent to adolescent sports (Côté & Gilbert, 2009). Evidence supporting a humanistic, developmental approach in elite coaching is robust and should be enthusiastically promoted among practitioners. Reciprocating this middle-way approach, positive competition should be emphasized in recreational and developmental contexts. Teaching children the value of positive competition and mentoring youth away from *decompetition* can teach practical life skills for a competitive society (Shields & Bredemeier, 2009). Applying a middle-way approach to the definition provided at the beginning of this chapter, researchers, and practitioners should consider adding a fifth 'C' in coaching effectiveness – positive *competitiveness* – to the existing competence, confidence, connection, and character outcomes.

Implications for applied practice

So, how can a coach become more effective? Our review of literature could justify curriculum recommendations for coaching educators, but these implications could also be framed as coaching "self-help." Accelerated early development and on-going professional development are critical for coaches. If we can help novice coaches appreciate a broader role frame sooner and give them the knowledge/tools they need, we can develop effective coaches more quickly. You cannot develop if you do not learn, and you cannot learn without leaving your comfort zone (e.g., coaching more than skills/tactics, and embracing relationship building, practice planning, etc.). If coaches want their athletes to be open-minded and constantly improving, so too must they be. Côté and Gilbert's (2009) definition of effective coaching may provide a useful framework for career-long professional development in terms of growing professional knowledge (e.g., instructional techniques), developing interpersonal skills (e.g., asking athletes questions), and enhancing intrapersonal awareness (e.g., mindfulness/self-reflection).

The literature across all sport contexts featured in this chapter shows there is much more to effective coaching than counting wins and sound pedagogy. Fostering rapport and trust is foundational for effective coaching, and facilitates coaches' efforts to build strong relationships with each athlete, individualize their approach, and maximize athletes' holistic development. Nurturing close relationships and utilizing teachable moments with athletes requires investing time and must be a deliberate component in a coach's annual and daily plans.

In conclusion, effective coaching involves a complex set of behaviors and characteristics that nurture technical, tactical, psychomotor, and psychosocial growth in athletes. In behaving in this way, effective coaches create opportunities for their athletes, and instill a level of self-belief that they might not reach on their own. While great coaches are made by the sum of many things done right, there are essential elements that appear to transcend contexts in sport. When philosophies, strategies, relationships, and climates are implemented in a precise manner, the context of sport becomes fruitful ground for athletes to learn psychological, social, and sport skills essential to thrive on and off the playing field. Demonstrating care for athletes' progress and well-being, and creating an environment that allows them to be active agents in their own sport experience are cornerstones of developing more capable and well-rounded athletes. From there, the reciprocal benefits to sport and its stakeholders are innumerable.

Notes

1 Department of Coaching and Teaching Studies, West Virginia University, USA
2 Department of Kinesiology, James Madison University, USA
3 School of Human Kinetics, University of Ottawa, Canada

References

Becker, A. (2009). It's not what they do, it's how they do it: Athlete experiences of great coaching. *International Journal of Sports Science and Coaching, 4*, 93–119.

Becker, A., & Wrisberg, C. (2008). Effective coaching in action: Observations of legendary collegiate basketball coach Pat Summitt. *The Sport Psychologist, 22*, 197–211.

Bennie, A., & O'Connor, D. (2012a). Coach–athlete relationships: A qualitative study of professional sport teams in Australia. *International Journal of Sport and Health Science, 10*, 58–64.

Bennie, A., & O'Connor, D. (2012b). Perceptions and strategies of effective coaching leadership: A qualitative investigation of professional coaches and players. *International Journal of Sport and Health Science, 10*, 82–89.

Camiré, M., & Trudel, P. (2013). Using high school football to promote life skills and student engagement: Perspectives from Canadian coaches and students. *World Journal of Education, 3*(3), 40–51.

Camiré, M., & Trudel, P. (2014). Helping youth sport coaches integrate psychological skills in their coaching practice. *Qualitative Research in Sport, Exercise and Health, 6*, 617–634.

Camiré, M., Trudel, P., & Bernard, D. (2013). A case study of a high school sport program designed to teach athletes life skills and values. *The Sport Psychologist, 27*, 188–200.

Camiré, M., Trudel, P., & Forneris, T. (2012). Coaching and transferring life skills: Philosophies and strategies used by model high school coaches. *The Sport Psychologist, 26*(2), 243–260.

Camiré, M., Trudel, P., & Forneris, T. (2014). Examining how model youth sport coaches learn to facilitate positive youth development. *Physical Education and Sport Pedagogy, 19*, 1–17.

Coatsworth, J. D., & Conroy, D. (2006). Enhancing the self-esteem of youth swimmers through coach training: Gender and age effects. *Psychology of Sport and Exercise, 7*, 173–192.

Coatsworth, J. D., & Conroy, D. (2009). The effects of autonomy-supportive coaching, need satisfaction and self-perceptions on initiative and identity in youth swimmers. *Developmental Psychology, 45*, 320–328.

Collins, K., Gould, D., Lauer, L., & Chung, Y. (2009). Coaching life skills through football: Philosophical beliefs of outstanding high school football coaches. *International Journal of Coaching Science, 3*, 29–54.

Côté, J., & Gilbert, W. (2009). An integrative definition of coaching effectiveness and expertise. *International Journal of Sports Science and Coaching, 4*, 307–323.

Cronin, L., & Allen, J. (2015). Developmental experiences and well-being in sport: The importance of the coaching climate. *The Sport Psychologist, 29*, 62–71.

Felton, L., & Jowett, S. (2013). "What do coaches do" and "how do they relate": Their effects on athletes' psychological needs and functioning. *Scandinavian Journal of Medicine and Science in Sport, 23*, 130–139.

Fenton, S., Duda, J., Quested, E., & Barrett, T. (2014). Coach autonomy support predicts autonomous motivation and daily moderate-to-vigorous physical activity and sedentary time in youth sport participants. *Psychology of Sport and Exercise, 15*, 453–463.

Flett, M. R., & Huth, M. (2014). Ethnographic descriptions of youth training environments and coaching in Brazil. *International Journal of Coaching Science, 8*, 3–25.

Flett, M. R., & Paule-Koba, A. (2015). Nice guys finish first: How instrumental character facilitates performance in competition. *Applied Research in Coaching and Athletics Annual, 30*(2), 83–112.

Flett, M. R., Gould, D., Griffes, K., & Lauer, L. (2013). Tough love for underserved youth: A comparison of more and less effective coaching. *The Sport Psychologist, 27*, 325–337.

Fry, M., & Gano-Overway, L. (2010). Exploring the contribution of the caring climate to the youth sport experience. *Journal of Applied Sport Psychology, 22*, 294–304.

Fry, M., Guivernau, M., Kim, M., Newton, M., Gano-Overway, L., & Magyar, T. M. (2012). Youth perceptions of a caring climate, emotional regulation, and psychological well-being. *Sport, Exercise, and Performance in Psychology, 1*, 44–57.

Gano-Overway, L., Newton, M., Magyar, T. M., Fry, M., Kim, M., & Guivernau, M. (2009). Influence of caring youth sport contexts on efficacy-related beliefs and social behaviors. *Developmental Psychobiology, 45*, 329–340.

Gearity, B. (2012). Poor teaching by the coach: A phenomenological description from athletes' experience of poor coaching. *Physical Education and Sport Pedagogy, 17*, 79–96.

Gilbert, W., & Trudel, P. (2004). Role of the coach: How model youth team sport coaches frame their roles. *The Sport Psychologist, 18*, 21–43.

Gould, D., & Carson, S. (2008). Life skills development through sport: Current status and future directions. *International Review of Sport and Exercise Psychology, 1*, 58–78.

Gould, D., Chung, Y., Smith, P., & White, J. (2006). Future directions in coaching life skills: Understanding high school coaches' views and needs. *Athletic Insight, 8*(3), 1–9.

Gould, D., Flett, M. R., & Lauer, L. (2012). The relationship between psychosocial developmental and the sports climate experienced in underserved settings. *Psychology of Sport and Exercise, 13*, 80–87.

Harwood, C., Spray, C., & Keegan, R. (2008). Achievement goal theories in sport. In T. Horn (Ed.), *Advances in sport psychology* (3rd ed.), pp. 157–185. Champaign, IL: Human Kinetics.

Horn, T. (2008). *Advances in sport psychology* (3rd ed.). Champaign, IL: Human Kinetics.

Jackson, B., Dimmock, J., Gucciardi, D., & Grove, J. R. (2011). Personality traits and relationship perceptions in coach–athlete dyads: Do opposites really attract? *Psychology of Sport and Exercise, 12*, 222–230.

Jowett, S., & Cockerill, I. (2003). Olympic medallists' perspective of the athlete–coach relationship. *Psychology of Sport and Exercise, 4*, 313–331.

Keegan, R., Harwood, C., Spray, C., & Lavallee, D. (2009). A qualitative investigation exploring the motivational climate in early career sports participants: Coach, parent and peer influences on sport motivation. *Psychology of Sport and Exercise, 10*, 361–372.

Lent, R., & Lopez, F. (2002). Cognitive ties that bind: A tripartite view of efficacy beliefs in growth-promoting relationships. *Journal of Social and Clinical Psychology, 21*, 256–286.

Lesyk, J., & Kornspan, A. (2000). Coaches' expectations and beliefs regarding benefits of youth sport participation. *Perceptual and Motor Skills, 90*, 399–402.

Lyle, J. (2002). *Sports coaching concepts: A framework for coaches' behaviour*. London: Routledge.

Mageau, G., & Vallerand, R. (2003). The coach–athlete relationship: A motivational model. *Journal of Sport Sciences, 21*, 883–904.

Martindale, R., Collins, D., & Abraham, A. (2007). Effective talent development: The elite coaching perspective in UK sport. *Journal of Applied Sport Psychology, 19*, 187–206.

McCallister, S., Blinde, E., & Weiss, W. (2000). Teaching values and implementing philosophies: Dilemmas of the youth sport coach. *Physical Educator, 57*, 35–57.

Nash, C., Sproule, J., & Horton, P. (2008). Sport coaches' perceived role frames and philosophies. *International Journal of Sports Science and Coaching, 3*, 539–554.

Paule, A., & Flett, M. R. (2011). What's the rush? Early recruiting in Division I NCAA athletics. *Applied Research in Coaching and Athletics Annual, 26*, 55–78.

Reynolds, A., & McDonough, M. (2015). Moderated and mediated effects of coach autonomy support, coach involvement, and psychological need satisfaction on motivation in youth soccer. *The Sport Psychologist, 29*, 51–61.

Saville, P., Bray, S., Martin Ginis, K., Cairney, J., Marinoff-Shupe, D., & Pettit, A. (2014). Sources of self-efficacy and coach/instructor behaviors underlying relation-inferred self-efficacy (RISE) in recreational youth sport. *Journal of Sport and Exercise Psychology, 36*, 146–156.

Shields, D. L., & Bredemeier, B. L. (2009). *True competition*. Champaign, IL: Human Kinetics

Smith, R., & Smoll, F. (1996). The coach as a focus of research and intervention in youth sports. In F. L. Smoll, & R. E. Smith (Eds.), *Children and youth in sport. A biopsychosocial perspective* (pp. 125–141). Dubuque, IA: Brown & Benchmark.

Smith, R., Smoll, F., & Cumming, S. (2007). Effects of a motivational climate intervention for coaches on children's sport performance anxiety. *Journal of Sport and Exercise Psychology, 29*, 39–59.

Trudel, P., & Gilbert, W. (2006). Coaching and coach education. In D. Kirk, M. O'Sullivan, & D. McDonald (Eds.), *Handbook of physical education* (pp. 516–539). London: Sage.

Vella, S., Cliff, D., Okely, A., Weintraub, D., & Robinson, T. (2014). Instructional strategies to promote incremental beliefs in youth sport. *Quest, 66*, 357–370. Vella, S., Oades, L., & Crowe, T. (2011). The role of the coach in facilitating positive youth development: Moving from theory to practice. *Journal of Applied Sport Psychology, 23*, 33–48.

Vella, S., Oades, L., & Crowe, T. (2013). A pilot test of transformational leadership training for sports coaches: Impact on the developmental experiences of adolescent athletes. *International Journal of Sports Science and Coaching, 8*, 513–530.

Wang, J., & Straub, W. (2012). An investigation into the coaching approach of a successful world class soccer coach: Anson Dorrance. *International Journal of Sports Science and Coaching, 7*, 431–477.

Werthner, P., & Trudel, P. (2009). Investigating the idiosyncratic learning paths of elite Canadian coaches. *International Journal of Sports Science and Coaching, 4*, 433–449.

12 Definitions and correlates of coach psychological well- and ill-being

Juliette Stebbings[1] *and Ian M. Taylor*[2]

Introduction

The aim of this chapter is to describe how coaches' psychological health can be developed or harmed, and to explore the potential consequences of such processes for coaches and athletes. The development of the well- and ill-being literature will be described in order to define important concepts and their measurement. We subsequently explain potential processes behind the development of well- and ill-being, and provide insight into how the coaching environment may influence coach psychological health. Research on the potential consequences of coaches' well- and ill-being for coaches and athletes will be presented with an emphasis on interpersonal processes, which leads into a description of the contagion of well- and ill-being between coaches and athletes. Finally, gaps in knowledge and the implications of this work will be presented with the intention of stimulating new research and effective applied practice.

Key terms

Understanding and attaining well-being has been an agenda for philosophers and scholars since Aristotle described happiness as the ultimate motivation for human action (Diener, 1994). The topic's importance is also reflected in the wealth of research attempting to define well-being and identify its components. However, this has led to the development of multiple perspectives and a lack of consensus on definitions, correlates, and measurement approaches.

Subjective well-being (SWB) was the first conceptualisation of well-being to be afforded systematic empirical attention (Diener, 1984). SWB refers to the appraisal of one's global life experience by evaluating cognitions and affective experiences according to personal criteria. The cognitive element is termed *life satisfaction* and represents the degree to which an individual judges the quality of his or her life in a favourable manner. The affective component refers to the experience of positive and negative moods and emotions. Well-being in this sense occurs when there is a dominance of *positive* over *negative affect* (Diener, 1984, 1994). Self-report measurement tools to assess these dimensions include the Satisfaction with Life Scale (Pavot & Diener, 1993) and the Positive and

Negative Affect Schedule (PANAS; Watson, Clark & Tellegen, 1988). Immunological and neural indicators of SWB have also been suggested as alternative methods of measurement (Diener, 2012). Despite the simplicity of this tripartite definition (life satisfaction, positive affect and negative affect), there is debate concerning the structure of SWB. Rather than conceptualising life satisfaction, positive affect and negative affect as independent indicators of SWB, some researchers argue that positive and negative affect have a causal effect on life satisfaction (see Busserri & Sadava, 2011). Nonetheless, SWB remains a popular and important paradigm to study well-being globally (e.g. Diener, 2012; Tay & Diener, 2013).

Researchers have also proposed that the SWB perspective does not consider self-realisation or eudaimonism as defining features of positive psychological functioning, and focuses too much on happiness and hedonism (Deci & Ryan, 2008; Ryff, 1989; Waterman, 1993). *Hedonia* refers to the momentary satisfaction of obtaining pleasure and enjoyment, regardless of its cause (Tatarkiewicz, 1976), and reflects the colloquial definition of happiness (Waterman, 1993). *Eudaimonia* is defined as living in accordance with one's true self and the realisation of one's potential through personally meaningful and expressive activities (e.g. Waterman, 1990). A eudaimonic state is accompanied by intense involvement, feelings of aliveness, fulfilment, and an impression that this is what one is 'meant' to do (Waterman, 1990).

In light of this critique, Ryff (1989, 2014) proposed six dimensions of psychological well-being: *self-acceptance* (a positive attitude towards oneself), *positive relationships* (feelings of mutual empathy, affection, and love with others), *autonomy* (an internal locus of causality), *environmental mastery* (the ability to manipulate or create environments and to take advantage of environmental opportunities), *purpose in life* (a sense of directedness and intentional goal pursuit), and *personal growth* (being open to experience and the ability to develop and realise one's potentialities). The Ryff (1989) Scales of Psychological Well-Being are widely used to measure these six dimensions. Although studies have provided evidence for this framework (e.g. Ryff & Singer, 2006), other research has failed to demonstrate independent variation among these six factors (Springer & Hauser, 2006), which may be reflective of the underlying theory, the measurement instruments, or both (Springer et al., 2006). These critiques have themselves been superseded and scientific debate continues (Ryff, 2014; Springer, Pudrovska & Hauser, 2011).

Alongside the development of Ryff's work, Waterman and colleagues (Huta & Waterman, 2014; Waterman et al., 2010) drew further attention to the distinction between hedonic well-being (HWB) versus eudaimonic well-being (EWB). In particular, contemporary understanding of eudaimonia should not only include the pursuit of worthy life goals, but also the outcomes and experiences that accompany these strivings. It is also recognised that hedonic and eudaimonic states may be compatible and the pursuit of both may produce greater well-being than either alone (Huta & Ryan, 2010). The two states may also be intertwined; for example, self-realisation may lead to positive affect (Huta & Waterman,

2014). EWB can be assessed using the multidimensional Questionnaire for Eudaimonic Well-Being (Waterman et al., 2010), while the overlap between HWB and the affective element of SWB means the PANAS (Watson et al., 1988) is often used to measure hedonic well-being.

Within the theoretical frameworks described, most attention has been afforded to well-being as opposed to ill-being. There is increasing evidence to suggest that ill-being is not merely the absence of wellness. Positive and negative affect have been shown to be independent dimensions of HWB with low correlations and distinct correlates (e.g. Diener, 2012; Ryff et al., 2006; Watson et al., 1988). Sport research frequently employs negative affect as a hedonic measure of ill-being in coach and athlete samples (e.g. Quested & Duda, 2010; Stebbings, Taylor & Spray, 2011), and we often see attention placed on burnout in sport, which comprises a reduced sense of accomplishment, emotional and physical exhaustion, and devaluation of an activity (Raedeke, 1997; Tashman, Tenenbaum & Eklund, 2010). These burnout dimensions would seem to provide interesting indicators of ill-being to contrast with eudaimonic perspectives of well-being, although this is not acknowledged within the major well-being paradigms. It would be of interest to explore whether burnout has foundations which directly oppose EWB, such as discrepancies between coaches' true self and their coaching behaviour.

To summarise, there are a range of substantiated theoretical frameworks that can provide solid foundations for the exploration of coach well- and ill-being. In particular, Ryff's (2014) six dimensions of well-being warrant attention, and consideration of eudaimonic and hedonic aspects seems necessary. As is shown in the following sections, however, coaching-based researchers rarely adopt these perspectives.

Review of the literature

Potential antecedents of coaches' well- and ill-being

A considerable portion of the research exploring well- and ill-being in athlete and coach populations is grounded within self-determination theory (Ryan & Deci, 2001). It is worth noting, then, that self-determination theorists draw heavily from the work of Waterman and Ryff by distinguishing between HWB and EWB. Advocates of SDT, however, posit that environmental mastery, autonomy, and positive relations with others (elements of Ryff's definition of well-being) do not reflect well-being itself, but are fundamental psychological requirements necessary for well-being to occur (Ryan & Deci, 2001). That is, the needs for competence, autonomy and relatedness are universal and innate, and satisfaction is essential for the maintenance of psychological well-being. In contrast, when competence, autonomy, and relatedness are overtly frustrated, psychological ill-being will ensue (Deci & Ryan, 2000).

Research has demonstrated the associations between basic psychological need satisfaction and thwarting on well- and ill-being in athlete populations (e.g.

Bartholomew, Ntoumanis, Ryan, Bosch & Thøgersen-Ntoumani, 2011; Quested & Duda, 2010). Until recently, however, the call for an increased focus on the psychological needs and health of coaches (Giges, Petitpas & Vernacchia, 2004) was largely ignored. In a cross-sectional study of 443 coaches from a variety of sports, satisfaction of coaches' competence and autonomy was positively associated with well-being, as indexed by positive affect and subjective vitality (a positive feeling of aliveness, vigour and energy emanating from the self; Ryan & Frederick, 1997; Stebbings et al., 2011). Relatedness need satisfaction was not a significant predictor of well-being. Extending these findings by incorporating measures of ill-being, Stebbings, Taylor, Spray and Ntoumanis (2012) investigated two distinct pathways of psychological functioning. Results demonstrated that coaches' psychological need satisfaction (measured as a composite variable, rather than independent needs) positively predicted well-being (positive affect and subjective vitality), and the active frustration of the psychological needs positively predicted ill-being (negative affect and emotional and physical exhaustion). These relationships were also found to be invariant across coaches working at different competitive levels.

In a study of United States high school athletic directors (staff members responsible for the administration of athletics and hiring of coaches), only competence psychological need satisfaction (not autonomy or relatedness) was indirectly and negatively associated with elements of burnout, via self-determined motivation towards the role (Sullivan, Lonsdale & Taylor, 2014). This coincides with qualitative and quantitative work with Australian coaches, in which self-determination to coach has been implicated in fostering higher well-being, as well as lower stress and burnout (McLean & Mallett, 2012; McLean, Mallett & Newcombe, 2012). Relatedly, US swim coaches who were characterised by increasing levels of entrapment (i.e. decreasing attraction to coaching but maintaining their involvement because they feel they have to continue) demonstrated substantial increases in exhaustion over a one-year period (Raedeke, 2004). Overall, this research implicates psychological need satisfaction (particularly competence need satisfaction) and self-determined motivation in the facilitation of well-being in coaches, albeit the evidence does not demonstrate causal effects. The lack of association found between relatedness satisfaction and well-being in coaches and directors is also noteworthy and requires further exploration. It would be rash to suggest that relatedness is not important for well-being development, given the weight of evidence opposing this conclusion (e.g. Baumeister & Leary, 1995; Leary, 2010).

Building on this work, researchers have attended to elements of coaches' social contexts which support (or thwart) these processes. In qualitative work, high performance coaches expressed that their psychological needs were satisfied when their sport organisations offered education, training, and practical experience (Allen & Shaw, 2009). Formal accreditation pathways, opportunities to observe and work with other high performance coaches, and the provision of feedback from athletes, other coaches, and mentors were perceived to be particularly valuable. Educational development and interaction with other coaches has also been highlighted by successful Olympic coaches as a path to more effective coaching (Olusoga, Maynard, Hays & Butt, 2012). In contrast, coaches perceived their needs to be frustrated when formal education opportunities were not readily available, development pathways were unclear, and organisations did not help overcome personal and financial constraints to development (Allen & Shaw, 2009).

Given the achievement-oriented culture of modern sport, coaches are often faced with extreme pressure to perform and their jobs are frequently contingent on the performance of their athletes (Giges et al., 2004; Potrac, Jones & Armour, 2002; Thelwell, Weston, Greenlees & Hutchings, 2008). Consequently, coaches often experience stressors associated with contract renewal, future employment, and being able to provide for their families (Fletcher & Scott, 2010; Olusoga, Butt, Hays, & Maynard, 2009). Work–life conflict may also hinder coaches' psychological health, because the coaching profession can interfere with family and social life (Kelley & Baghurst, 2009). Coaches are often required to undertake multiple managerial, mentoring and administrative roles alongside their primary coaching duties and undertake long working days, weekend work, and long-distance travel away from home. This may result in a lack of free time to spend with family and friends, disrupted or sacrificed holidays, difficulties in managing and maintaining personal relationships, and an inability to 'switch off' from coaching (Giges et al., 2004; Olusoga et al., 2009; Thelwell et al., 2008).

Tying these ideas together, Stebbings et al. (2012) established that greater opportunities for professional development, job security and an absence of work–life conflict were positively associated with coaches' psychological need satisfaction, which was in turn associated with psychological well-being (i.e. positive affect and subjective vitality). The relationship between an absence of work–life conflict and psychological need satisfaction was only found in high competitive level coaches (regional competitive level and above). Coaches working at lower levels reported coaching for fewer than ten hours per week, meaning work–life conflict may not have been a salient issue for them. Results also suggested that, for all coaches, higher work–life conflict and fewer opportunities for development were associated with thwarted psychological needs and psychological ill-being (i.e. negative affect and emotional physical exhaustion).

Several other factors associated with sports organisations have been highlighted in interviews as important in maintaining coaches' psychological health, including recognition of coaches' individual strengths, a supportive attitude towards family commitments, and regular debriefing and evaluation discussions (Allen & Shaw, 2009). Factors undermining coaches' psychological health included having no input into organisational decisions, competing with other coaches for positions, being required to function in isolation, and dealing with administrative problems surrounding budgeting and preparation for events (Allen & Shaw, 2009).

As well as general organisational pressures, specific individuals can also exert influence on coaches' well-being. For example, managers' autonomy-supportive interpersonal style (taking into account feelings and perspectives, offering opportunities for input and decision making, and providing a rationale for tasks; Mageau & Vallerand, 2003) was a positive predictor of athletic directors' competence, autonomy and relatedness satisfaction. A psychologically controlling style (pressuring the coach into thinking, feeling, or behaving in specific ways by utilising controlling feedback, task-contingent rewards, punishments and criticism; Bartholomew, Ntoumanis & Thøgersen-Ntoumani, 2010) was a negative predictor of all three needs (Sullivan et al., 2014). Pressure from coaching colleagues and club administrators has also been negatively associated with coaches' psychological functioning (Rocchi, Pelletier & Couture, 2013).

The evidence described above suggests that the organisational climate and individuals within it may have a significant impact upon coach psychological well-being. Of course, a psychologically healthy environment should not be created at the expense of a climate where competitiveness and a winning mentality are encouraged. These two environments are not opposite ends of a continuum, but are symbiotic dimensions of successful sport environments.

Potential consequences of coaches' well- and ill-being

The research literature has largely regarded psychological well-being as the end product, attempting to define the precursors of this optimal state. Seventeen articles studying psychological health in competitive athletes reviewed by Lundqvist (2011) all included well- or ill-being as the dependent variable. There has been some work investigating the potential outcomes of a psychologically healthy coach, particularly focusing on their interpersonal behaviours and coaching practices. Coaches experiencing greater feelings of personal accomplishment reported more effective coaching (e.g. better communication, use of praise, empathy, and less autocracy), whereas coaches reporting symptoms of burnout reported less effective coaching (Price & Weiss, 2000; Vealey, Armstrong, Comar & Greenleaf, 1998). Contrary to theoretical predictions, higher emotional and physical exhaustion have also been related to greater democratic and lower autocratic decision-making (Price & Weiss, 2000).

Utilising a longitudinal design across a one-year period with 195 coaches, Stebbings, Taylor and Spray (2015) assessed the relationship between coaches' psychological health and their interpersonal behaviours at the within-person level (variability in a participant's reports across different occasions) and individual difference level (variability between participants' average levels) of analysis. Stebbings and colleagues demonstrated that positive affect and integrated functioning (the degree to which coaches behave in accordance with their true self; used as a measure of EWB) were positively associated with provision of autonomy support at both levels of analysis. Negative affect was positively associated with use of a controlling interpersonal style at both levels. In other words, the psychological well-being of coaches was linked to adaptive coaching practices and ill-being associated with poor quality coaching. Despite assessing whether devaluation of coaching (a dimension of burnout employed as an index of ill-being) was associated with controlling interpersonal behaviours, no significant relationships were found. Based on research from the educational context in which teachers' burnout was associated with a lack of energy and willingness to invest effort in work (Hakanen, Bakker & Schaufeli, 2006), and an argument that burnt out coaches may adopt a "I don't care, whatever" attitude (Price & Weiss, 2000), the authors speculated that coaches who devalue their role may adopt a laissez-faire approach, instead of a controlling style. A laissez-faire interpersonal style is defined as passive non-leadership, in which a coach is hesitant to take action, abdicates their responsibilities, fails to use their authority when required, does not follow up requests for assistance, lacks involvement during critical junctures, and is resistant to expressing their views on important issues (Bass & Avolio, 1990).

This hypothesis was explicitly tested in a follow-up study with coach–athlete dyads from individual sports (Stebbings, Taylor & Spray, in press). Specifically, the relationship between coaches' well- and ill-being before a training session and subsequent coaching practices during the session was tested. In addition, this study included perceptions of athletes as opposed to a sample of coaches only. A series of actor–partner interdependence models (Kenny, Kashy & Cook, 2006) indicated that coaches' pre-session burnout was positively associated with coaches' and athletes' perceptions of the coaches' in-session laissez-faire coaching. In two further models, coaches' pre-session negative affect positively predicted coaches' and athletes' perceptions of coaches' controlling interpersonal behaviour, and positive affect was implicated in the subsequent use of autonomy supportive practices. In sum, the two studies propose that the well- and ill-being of the coach has important consequences for the quality of coaching, as reported by the coaches and the athletes.

Well- and ill-being contagion

Emotions are not just felt internally but are socially expressed (Van Kleef, 2009). Individuals often read and react to each other's displays, altering their own emotions and behaviour to coordinate with each other's actions and preferences, (i.e. a contagion effect; Hatfield, Cacioppo & Rapson, 1994; Johnson, 2008; Reis & Collins, 2004). Bakker and Schuafeli (2000) reported evidence of burnout contagion between colleagues in a sample of high school teachers, and links between the mood of players and their teammates were demonstrated in professional cricketers (Toterdell, 2000). Although emotional contagion research typically advocates the automatic transfer of emotions, other work suggests that interpersonal behaviour may also function as a mechanism for the transfer of psychological states between individuals (Radel, Sarrazin, Legrain & Wild, 2010). In the same way, the psychological health of coaches and athletes may also be transferred. Coach well- and ill-being influences their behaviour towards athletes (Price & Weiss, 2000; Stebbings et al., 2015, in press; Vealey et al., 1998), which, in turn impacts upon athlete well- and ill-being (e.g. Bartholomew et al., 2011; Quested & Duda, 2010). There is also potential for the reciprocal transfer from athlete to coach. Athletes' functioning influences coaches' autonomy-supportive behaviour (Rocchi et al., 2013). In turn, providing autonomy support has benefits for the provider (Deci, La Guardia, Moller, Scheiner & Ryan, 2006; Cheon, Reeve, Yu & Jang, 2014), a proposal supported in a sample of coaches using an experimental design during the London 2012 Paralympic games (Cheon, Reeve, Lee & Lee, 2015).

Stebbings and colleagues' (in press) explored these contagion effects with coach–athlete dyads. Coaching style during a training session acted as a mechanism for the transfer of positive and negative affect from coaches to athletes. These findings were demonstrated after controlling for athletes' pre-session levels of affect. A third model did not fully support the hypothesis that burnout was contagious and the reciprocal athlete-to-coach contagion process was not evidenced. This implies that, in dyads where one member has authority over the other, the contagion of psychological health may only be unidirectional. Coaches may not have acknowledged (explicitly or implicitly) athletes' well- and ill-being prior to the session to enough of an extent to influence their interpersonal behaviour and well- and ill-being. Nonetheless, coaches' perceptions of their own coaching style were associated with their well- and ill-being after the training session. This supports the proposal that providing athletes with a psychologically supportive training environment has additional benefits for the coach. For example, a coach who provides athletes with input into the session and opportunities for open discussion and decision-making (i.e. autonomy support), may feel pleased with the coaching session and fulfilled in their role.

Implications for future research

Methodologically speaking, well-designed longitudinal work with several time points, diary studies across multiple training sessions, as well as experimental studies and interventions aimed at establishing cause and effect, would provide stronger information regarding the strength and direction of the relationships demonstrated in the reviewed research.

Much of Lundqvist's (2011) critique of athlete well-being research can be applied to the coach research reviewed in this chapter. Psychological well-being is recognised as a complex multifaceted construct, with no clear and common consensus on definitions and structure of well-being. As we briefly stated earlier, theoretical paradigms do exist but the sport-based literature to date has often adopted ambiguous and inconsistent definitions of well- and ill-being. Researchers often use indicators of well- and ill-being, such as self-esteem and depression, but do not provide clarification on how these constructs relate to the wider paradigms. It is essential that the growing literature concerning coach psychological well- and ill-being addresses these issues by carefully selecting the appropriate theoretical perspective and providing a clear rationale for the choice. By taking this approach, coaching research may be able to offer new insight into the understanding of psychological well- and ill-being. At the same time, coaching research can learn from what is already known within the wider well- and ill-being research arenas.

When studying determinants of well-being, coach-based research has largely focused on how psychological needs can be satisfied within the coaching role (e.g. McLean & Mallett, 2012; McLean et al., 2012; Stebbings et al., 2011, 2012; Sullivan et al., 2014). Researchers could consider how coaches' needs may be satisfied within other contexts (e.g. alternative employment or familial roles), particularly when coaching represents only a part-time or voluntary role. Indeed, research with adolescents has shown that balanced basic psychological need satisfaction across life domains is important for psychological well-being (Milyavskaya et al., 2009).

Specific contextual factors may also suit future research exploration. For example, coaches often encounter pressures from parents, fans and governing bodies, experience a lack of social support, and suffer concerns about long working hours, salary and financial support. Coaches also highlight unclear expectations and a lack of agreed evaluation criteria to be particularly stressful (e.g. Knight, Read, Selzler & Rodgers, 2013; Olusoga et al., 2009; Thelwell et al., 2008). The nature of competitive events has also been shown to increase stress, arousal, unpleasant emotions and physiological markers of stress (Hudson, Davison & Robinson, 2013). Now that these factors have been highlighted as deleterious for coaches' psychological health, focused intervention studies within these areas are an interesting research direction. There is also a lack of measurement tools available to accurately assess these elements of the coaching context which needs to be addressed.

The associations among coaches' well- and ill-being and interpersonal behaviour also opens up interesting research questions. For instance, does the act of engaging in poor quality, psychologically controlling coaching represent a compensatory substitute to fill a void left by coaches' own needs being unfulfilled or thwarted (see Vansteenkiste & Ryan, 2013)? An unfulfilled coach who is experiencing ill-being may look to exert power over his or her athletes, for example. Similarly, a laissez-faire coaching style may be a form of coping attribution for expected failure that manifests when suffering from ill-being (e.g. 'my coaching ability wasn't the reason for failure, I just couldn't be bothered to put effort in'). With regards to contagion effects, future research could investigate different mechanisms through which well-being is transferred, such as non-verbal communication. Identifying moderators of the contagion effect may identify whether some coach–athlete relationships are more sensitive to transference than others. Interpersonal behaviour should also continue to be a focus, perhaps with network analyses to assess the contagion processes within teams of multiple coaches and support staff.

Implications for applied practice

Given the number of coaches who operate in organised sport at all levels and the fact that coaches have been described as performers in their own right (Gould, Greenleaf, Guinan & Chung, 2002), it is important that the focus of sport psychology practice does not attend to the development of athletes at the expense of coaches. The literature reviewed in this chapter offers some important implications for how sporting organisations (and significant individuals within these environments, such as performance directors, club managers, head coaches and sport psychologists) can help coaches flourish. For example, head coaches and club managers could provide coaches with regular non-controlling feedback regarding their coaching practices, and could also encourage them to seek feedback from athletes and parents. Moreover, performance directors (in conjunction with coaches) could develop clear and achievable goals to work towards. Coaches' thoughts and ideas should be readily acknowledged and discussed, and coaches should also be provided with opportunities to have an input into the organisation. Coaching partnerships could also be created in which two or more coaches share expertise and responsibilities for preparing athletes for tournaments, allowing for negotiation and peer support. In sum, interventions and educational programmes are warranted to enhance awareness of the importance of coach psychological health, and to develop strategies to help coaches attain an optimal psychological state.

The reviewed research also highlights some of the specific environmental conditions that are necessary for the well-being of coaches (e.g. Allen & Shaw, 2009; Stebbings et al., 2012; Sullivan et al., 2014). Organisations can highlight the availability of formal accreditation pathways and education prospects, offering financial assistance and flexible working hours in order for coaches to attend. Informal mentoring programmes may also allow coaches to engage in peer learning and mutual encouragement. Additionally, employers should aim to work alongside coaches in facilitating coaches' job security, by sharing future directions of the organisations and discussing how coaches' roles will fit within these plans. In terms of work–life conflict, employers should discuss with coaches their individual needs to lessen demands on their time and resources. For example, governing bodies could make available opportunities for coaches to bring families to competitions, provide childcare facilities and remain as flexible as possible when allocating coaches' working hours and responsibilities. Individuals who are managing coaches should ensure an autonomy-supportive interpersonal style is adopted when interacting with coaches – for example, acknowledging coaches' ideas and allowing input into coaching strategies.

The coach-based literature discussed has established that coaches' psychological health is related to their interpersonal behavioural styles towards athletes (e.g. Stebbings et al., 2012). Hence, coaches themselves need to be aware of how fluctuations in their well- and ill-being may influence how they interact with their athletes at the daily level within a training session, and also more generally. This is important for coaches and the athletes they work with, as the interpersonal environment coaches create allows for the transfer of their well- and ill-being to their athletes. Interventions based on the principles of emotional regulation training, or mindfulness techniques aimed at enhancing coaches' self-awareness, could be promoted to help coaches minimise the negative effects of ill-being on their interpersonal interactions. Additionally, a key strategy could be to educate coaches on the benefits of creating a psychologically healthy environment (i.e. providing autonomy support and limiting controlling and laissez-faire styles) for the benefit of both coach and athlete. Such education programmes should also allow coaches to experience techniques and strategies that comprise these interpersonal styles, so that coaches become aware of the exact practices that are favourable. Existing research in the educational domain has indicated that an autonomy-supportive interpersonal style is teachable (e.g. Cheon, Reeve & Moon, 2012; Reeve, 1998), and sport-based research has demonstrated some positive effects of coach education interventions (Langan, Blake, & Lonsdale, 2013).

Notes

1 University of Birmingham, UK
2 Loughborough University, UK

References

Allen, J. B., & Shaw, S. (2009). Women coaches' perceptions of their sport organizations' social environment: Supporting coaches' psychological needs? *The Sport Psychologist, 23*, 346–366.

Bakker, A. B., & Schaufeli, W. B. (2000). Burnout contagion processes among teachers. *Journal of Applied Social Psychology, 30*, 2289–2308.

Bartholomew, K. J., Ntoumanis, N., Ryan, R. M., Bosch, J. A. & Thøgersen-Ntoumani, C. (2011). Self-determination theory and diminished functioning: The role of interpersonal control and psychological need thwarting. *Personality and Social Psychology Bulletin, 37*, 1459–1473.

Bartholomew, K. J, Ntoumanis, N., & Thøgersen-Ntoumani, C. (2010). The controlling interpersonal style in a coaching context: Development and initial validation of a psychometric scale. *Journal of Sport and Exercise Psychology, 32*, 193–216.

Bass, B. M., & Avolio, B. J. (1990). *Transformational leadership development: Manual for the multifactor leadership questionnaire*. Palo Alto, CA: Consulting Psychologists Press.

Baumeister, R., & Leary, M. R. (1995). The need to belong: Desire for interpersonal attachments as a fundamental human motivation. *Psychological Bulletin, 117*, 497–529.

Busserri, M. A. & Sadava, S. W. (2011). A review of the tripartite structure of subjective well-being: Implications for conceptualization, operationalization, analysis, and synthesis. *Personality and Social Psychology Review, 15*, 290–314.

Cheon, S. H., Reeve, J., Lee, J. & Lee, Y. (2015). Giving and receiving autonomy support in a high-stakes sport context: A field-based experiment during the 2012 London Paralympic Games. *Psychology of Sport and Exercise, 19*, 59–69.

Cheon, S. H., Reeve, J. & Moon, I. S. (2012). Experimentally based, longitudinally designed, teacher-designed, teacher-focused intervention to help physical education teachers be more autonomy supportive. *Journal of Sport and Exercise Psychology, 34*, 365–396.

Cheon, S. H., Reeve, J, Yu, T. H. & Jang, H. R. (2014). The teacher benefits from giving autonomy support during physical education instruction. *Journal of Sport and Exercise Psychology, 36*, 331–346.

Deci, E. L., & Ryan, R. M. (2000). The 'what' and 'why' of goal pursuits: Human needs and the self-determination of behavior. *Psychological Inquiry, 11*, 227–268.

Deci, E. L., & Ryan, R. M. (2008). Hedonia, eudaimonia, and well-being: An introduction. *Journal of Happiness Studies, 9*, 1–11.

Deci, E. L., La Guardia, J. G., Moller, A. C., Scheiner, M. J. & Ryan, R. M. (2006). On the benefits of giving as well as receiving autonomy support: Mutuality in close friendships. *Personality and Social Psychology Bulletin, 32*, 313–327.

Diener, E. (1984). Subjective well-being. *Psychological Bulletin, 95*, 542–575.

Diener, E. (1994). Assessing subjective well-being: Progress and opportunities. *Social Indicators Research, 31*, 103–157.

Diener, E. (2012). New findings and future directions for subjective well-being research. *American Psychologist, 67*, 590–597.

Fletcher, D., & Scott, M. (2010). Psychological stress in sports coaches: A review of concepts, research, and practice. *Journal of Sports Sciences, 28*, 127–137.

Giges, B., Petitpas, A. J. & Vernacchia, R. A. (2004). Helping coaches meet their own needs: Challenges for the sport psychology consultant. *The Sport Psychologist, 18*, 430–444.

Gould, D., Greenleaf, C., Guinan, D. & Chung, Y. (2002). A survey of US Olympic coaches: Variables perceived to have influenced athlete performances and coach effectiveness. *The Sport Psychologist, 16*, 229–250.

Hakanen, J. J., Bakker, A. B. & Schaufeli, W. B. (2006). Burnout and work engagement among teachers. *Journal of School Psychology, 43*, 495–513.

Hatfield, E., Cacioppo, J. & Rapson, R. L. (1994). *Emotional Contagion.* New York: Cambridge University Press.

Hudson, J., Davison, G. & Robinson, P. (2013). Psychophysiological and stress responses to competition in team sport coaches: An exploratory study. *Scandinavian Journal of Medicine and Science in Sport, 23*, 279–285

Huta, V., & Ryan, R. M. (2010). Pursuing pleasure or virtue: The differential and overlapping well-being benefits of hedonic and eudaimonic motives. *Journal of Happiness Studies, 11*, 735–762.

Huta, V., & Waterman, A. S. (2014). Eudaimonia and its distinction from hedonia: Developing a classification and terminology for understanding conceptual and operational definitions. *Journal of Happiness Studies, 15*, 1425–1456.

Johnson, S. K. (2008). I second that emotion: Effects of emotional contagion and affect at work on leader and follower outcomes. *The Leadership Quarterly, 19*, 1–19.

Kelley, B. C., & Baghurst, T. (2009). Development of the coaching issues survey (CIS). *The Sport Psychologist, 23*, 367–387.

Kenny, D. A., Kashy, D. A. & Cook, W. L. (2006). *Dyadic data analysis.* New York: Guilford.

Knight, C. J., Reade, I. L., Selzler, A. & Rodgers, W. M. (2013). Personal and situational factors influencing coaches' perceptions of stress. *Journal of Sports Sciences, 31*, 1054–1063.

Langan, E., Blake, C. & Lonsdale, C. (2013). Systematic review of the effectiveness of interpersonal coach education interventions on athlete outcomes. *Psychology of Sport and Exercise, 14*, 37–49.

Leary, M. R. (2010). Affiliation, acceptance, and belonging: The pursuit of interpersonal connection. In S. T. Fiske, D. T. Gilbert, & G. Lindzey (Eds.), *Handbook of social psychology* (Vol. 2, pp. 864–897). Hoboken: Wiley.

Lundqvist, C. (2011). Well-being in competitive sports – The feel-good factor? A review of conceptual considerations of well-being. *International Review of Sport and Exercise Psychology, 4*, 109–127.

Mageau, G. A., & Vallerand, R. J. (2003). The coach–athlete relationship: A motivational model. *Journal of Sports Sciences, 21*, 883–904.

McLean, K. N. & Mallett, C. J. (2012). What motivate the motivators? An examination of sports coaches. *Physical Education and Sport Pedagogy*, *17*, 21–35.

McLean, K. N., Mallett, C. J., & Newcombe, P. (2012). Assessing coach motivation: The development of the coach motivation questionnaire (CMQ). *Journal of Sport and Exercise Psychology*, *34*, 184–207.

Milyavskaya, M., Gingrad, I., Mageau, G. A., Koestner, R., Gagnon, H., Fang, J. & Boiché, J. (2009). Balance across contexts: Importance of balanced need satisfaction across various life domains. *Personality and Social Psychology Bulletin*, *35*, 1031–1045.

Olusoga, P., Butt, J., Hays, K. & Maynard, I. (2009). Stress in elite sports coaching: Identifying stressors. *Journal of Applied Sport Psychology*, *21*, 442–459.

Olusoga, P., Maynard, I., Hays, K. & Butt, J. (2012). Coaching under pressure: A study of Olympic coaches. *Journal of Sports Sciences*, *30*, 229–239.

Pavot, W., & Diener, E. (1993). Review of the satisfaction with life scale. *Psychological Assessment*, *5*, 164–172.

Potrac, P., Jones, R. & Armour, K. (2002). It's all about getting respect: The coaching behaviours of an expert English soccer coach. *Sport, Education and Society*, *7*, 183–202.

Price, M. S., & Weiss, M. R. (2000). Relationships among coach burnout, coach behaviors, and athletes' psychological responses. *The Sport Psychologist*, *14*, 391–409.

Quested, E., & Duda, J. L (2010). Exploring the social-environmental determinants of well- and ill-being in dancers: A test of basic needs theory. *Journal of Sport and Exercise Psychology*, *32*, 39–60.

Radel, R., Sarrazin, P., Legrain, P. & Wild, T. C. (2010). Social contagion of motivation between teacher and student: Analyzing underlying processes. *Journal of Educational Psychology*, *102*, 577–587.

Raedeke, T. D. (1997). Is athlete burnout more than just stress? A sport commitment perspective. *Journal of Sport and Exercise Psychology*, *19*, 396–417.

Raedeke, T. D. (2004). Coach commitment and burnout: A one-year follow up. *Journal of Applied Sport Psychology*, *16*, 333–349.

Reeve, J. (1998). Autonomy support as an interpersonal motivating style: Is it teachable? *Contemporary Educational Psychology*, *23*, 312–330.

Reis, H. T., & Collins, A. (2004). Relationships, human behavior, and psychological science. *Current Directions in Psychological Science*, *13*, 233–237.

Rocchi, M. A., Pelletier, L. G. & Couture, A. L. (2013). Determinants of coach motivation and autonomy supportive coaching behaviours. *Psychology of Sport and Exercise*, *14*, 852–859.

Ryan, R. M., & Deci, E. L. (2001). On happiness and human potentials: A review of research on hedonic and eudaimonic well-being. *Annual Review of Psychology*, *52*, 141–166.

Ryan, R. M., & Frederick, C. M. (1997). On energy, personality and health: Subjective vitality as a dynamic reflection of well-being. *Journal of Personality*, *65*, 529–565.

Ryff, C. D. (1989). Happiness is everything, or is it? Exploration on the meaning of psychological well-being. *Journal of Personality and Social Psychology*, *57*, 1069–1081.

Ryff, C. D. (2014). Psychological well-being revisited: Advances in the science and practice of eudaimonia. *Psychotherapy and Psychosomatics*, *83*, 10–28.

Ryff, C. D., & Singer, B. H. (2006). Best news yet on the six-factor model of well-being. *Social Science Research*, *35*, 1103–1119.

Ryff, C. D., Love, G. D., Urry, H. L., Muller, D., Rosenkranz, M. A., Friedman, E. M., Davidson, R. J. & Singer, B. (2006). Psychological well-being and ill-being: Do they have distinct or mirrored biological correlates? *Psychotherapy and Psychosomatics*, *75*, 85–95.

Springer, K. W., & Hauser, R. M. (2006). An assessment of the construct validity of Ryff's scales of psychological well-being: method, mode, and measurement effects. *Social Science Research, 35,* 1079–1101.

Springer, K. W., Hauser, R. M. & Freese, J. (2006). Bad news indeed for Ryff's six-factor model of well-being. *Social Science Research, 35,* 1120–1131.

Springer, K. W., Pudrovska, T. & Hauser, R. M. (2011). Does psychological well-being change with age? Longitudinal tests of age variations and further exploration of the multidimensionality of Ryff's model of psychological well-being. *Social Science Research, 40,* 392–398.

Stebbings, J., Taylor, I. M. & Spray, C. M. (2011). Antecedents of perceived coach autonomy supportive and controlling behaviors: Coach psychological need satisfaction and well-being. *Journal of Sport and Exercise Psychology, 33,* 255–272.

Stebbings, J., Taylor, I. M. & Spray, C. M. (2015). The relationship between psychological well- and ill-being, and perceived autonomy supportive and controlling interpersonal styles: A longitudinal study of sport coaches. *Psychology of Sport and Exercise, 19,* 42–29.

Stebbings, J., Taylor, I. M. & Spray, C. M. (in press). Interpersonal mechanisms explaining the transfer of well- and ill-being in coach–athlete dyads. *Journal of Sport and Exercise Psychology.*

Stebbings, J., Taylor, I. M., Spray, C. M. & Ntoumanis, N. (2012). Antecedents of perceived coach interpersonal behaviors: The coaching environment and coach psychological well- and ill-being. *Journal of Sport and Exercise Psychology, 34,* 481–502.

Sullivan, G. S. Lonsdale, C. & Taylor, I. M. (2014). Burnout in high school athletic directors: A self-determination theory perspective. *Journal of Applied Sport Psychology, 26,* 256–270.

Tashman, L., Tenenbaum, G. & Eklund, R. (2010). The effect of perceived stress on the relationship between perfectionism and burnout in coaches. *Anxiety, Stress, and Coping, 23,* 195–212.

Tatarkiewicz, W. (1976). *Analysis of happiness.* The Hague, Netherlands: Martinus Nijhoff.

Tay, L., & Diener, E. (2013). Needs and subjective well-being around the world. *Journal of Personality and Social Psychology,* 354–365.

Thelwell, R. C., Weston, N. J. V., Greenlees, I. A. & Hutchings, N. V. (2008). Stressors in elite sport: A coach perspective. *Journal of Sports Sciences, 26,* 905–918.

Toterdell, P. (2000). Catching moods and hitting runs: Mood linkage and subjective performance in professional sports teams. *Journal of Applied Psychology, 84,* 848–859.

Van Kleef, G. A. (2009). How emotions regulate social life: The emotions as social information (EASI) model. *Current Directions in Psychological Science, 18,* 184–188.

Vansteenkiste, M. & Ryan, R. M. (2013). On psychological growth and vulnerability: Basic psychological need satisfaction and thwarting as a unifying principle. *Journal of Psychotherapy Integration, 23,* 263–280.

Vealey, R. S., Armstrong, L., Comar, W. & Greenleaf, C. A. (1998). Influence of perceived coaching behaviors on burnout and competitive anxiety in female college athletes. *Journal of Applied Sport Psychology, 10,* 297–318.

Watson, D., Clark, L. A. & Tellegen, A. (1988). Development and validation of brief measures of positive and negative affect: The PANAS scales. *Journal of Personality and Social Psychology, 54,* 1063–1070.

Waterman, A. S. (1990). Personal expressiveness: Philosophical and psychological foundations. *Journal of Mind and Behavior, 11,* 47–74.

Waterman, A. S. (1993). Two conceptions of happiness: Contrasts of personal expressiveness (eudaimonia) and hedonic enjoyment. *Journal of Personality and Social Psychology, 64,* 678–691.

Waterman, A. S., Schwartz, S. J., Zamboanga, B. L., Ravert, R. D., Williams, M. K., Bede Agocha, V., Yeong Kim, S. & Brent Donnellan, M. (2010). The questionnaire for eudaimonic well-being: Psychometric properties, demographic comparisons, and evidence of validity. *The Journal of Positive Psychology, 5,* 41–61.

Part III
Working through coaches

13 Transformational leadership and the role of the coach

Calum A. Arthur[1] and Alan Lynn[2]

Introduction

It is widely acknowledged that the coach plays a significant role in shaping the athlete experience (see Smith & Smoll, 2007). Coach behaviours have been shown to impact a wide range of athlete outcomes including cognitions, affect and performance (e.g. Hollembeak & Amorose, 2005; Horne & Carron, 1985; Smith, Smoll & Cumming, 2007; Weiss & Friedrichs, 1986). The very nature of coaching entails that coaches will spend a considerable amount of time interacting with their athletes in various different situations that include formal settings (e.g. training and competition) and informal settings (e.g. travelling to matches, on tour). Thus it is not surprising that a considerable amount of research has been conducted in the sport-coaching domain that has sought to identify coach behaviours and map their impact on athlete outcomes. The coaching-related research has adopted a number of different paradigms to examine coaching, including observational analysis (e.g. Gallimore & Tharp, 2004; Partington & Cushion, 2013; Smith, Smoll & Hunt, 1977), qualitative approaches where either coaches or athletes are interviewed (e.g. Vallee & Bloom, 2005), and empirical approaches that focus on athlete reports of coach behaviours (e.g. Aoyagi, Cox & McGuire, 2008). A relatively recent development in the sport coaching research has been the inclusion of transformational leadership theory (Bass, 1985). The introduction of transformational leadership theory into the sport context opens up new avenues of research and practice that can help to generate a better understanding of the effects of 'great' coaches.

Key terms

Leadership has been claimed to be vital for effective organizational and societal functioning and is one of the most studied domains in the social sciences (Antonakis, 2004). However, despite the importance of leadership, researchers cannot agree on what leadership is; indeed, as long ago as 1971, Fiedler (1971) stated that, 'There are almost as many definitions of leadership as there are theories of leadership – and there almost as many theories of leadership as there are psychologists working in the field' (p. 1). In a similar notion, Bass and Bass

(2008) commented that 'the search for the one and only proper and true definition of leadership seems to be fruitless. Rather, the choice of an appropriate definition should depend on the methodological and substantive aspects of leadership' (p. 23). In this regard, the current chapter adopts a transformational leadership theory (Bass, 1985) perspective on the definition of leadership in a sport-coaching context.

Review of literature

Transformational leadership theory was first developed by Burns (1978) in the political domain and later brought into organisational psychology by Bass (1985) and is only relatively recently being explored in sport (see Arthur & Tomsett, 2015). Transformational leaders are proposed to inspire their followers via emotional appeals to transcend their own self-interest for the greater good. In doing this, transformational leaders are said to inspire their followers to achieve beyond expectations. The underlying influence process of transformational leadership is proposed to involve making followers more aware of the importance of task outcomes and inspiring them to transcend their own self-interest for the sake of the organization or larger polity. Transformational leadership is often described in relation to transactional leadership, in which rewards and punishments are used to gain compliance. Indeed, one of the central predictions of transformational leadership is that transformational leadership will predict variance in performance over and above that accounted for by transactional leadership. This is referred to as the augmentation hypothesis. It is important to note that Bass (1985) did not stipulate that transformational leadership replaced transactional leadership, but rather that transformational leadership operated in conjunction with transactional leadership. Indeed, Bass (1985) postulates that transactional leadership is necessary for transformational leadership to occur.

Transformational leadership has been described as a constellation of leader behaviours and attributes that affect followers' trust and loyalty towards the leader. However, exactly what these behaviours and attributes are, and how they should be measured, is the focus of some debate (see Table 13.1 for an overview of the different measures). The original and most widely used conceptualization stems from Bass's (1985) seminal works on transformational leadership. The original conceptualization consisted of: *charismatic leadership* – leadership that instils pride, faith, and respect, shows a special gift for seeing what is really important, and shows a sense of mission; *intellectual stimulation* – leadership that provides ideas which result in a rethinking of issues that had never been questioned before and that enables subordinates to think about old problems in new ways; and *individualized consideration* – leadership that delegates assignments to provide learning opportunities, gives personal attention to neglected members, and treats each subordinate as an individual. Bass (1985) also identified a cluster of items that emerged from the charismatic item pool that he referred to as *inspirational leadership*. Since this original conceptualization, Bass and colleagues have modified transformational leadership several times which resulted in the Full-Range Leadership Theory (FRLT) (Bass & Avolio, 1994). The FRLT consists of three broad factors: transformational leadership, transactional leadership, and laissez-faire leadership. The transformational factor consists of: *idealized influence (attributed)* – refers to the socialized charisma of the leader, whether the leader is perceived as being confident and powerful, and whether the leader is focussed on higher order ideals and ethics; *idealized influence (behaviours)* – refers to charismatic actions of the leader that are centred on values, beliefs, and a sense of mission; *inspirational motivation* – refers to the ways in which the leader energises his/her followers by viewing the future with optimism, stressing ambitious goals, projecting an idealized vision, and communicating to followers that the vision is achievable; *intellectual stimulation* – refers to getting followers to question the tried and true ways of solving problems and encourages them to question the methods they use to improve upon them; and *individualized consideration* – refers to understanding the needs of each follower and working continuously to get them to develop to their full potential. The transactional factor consist of: *contingent reward* – is based on economic and emotional exchanges, clarifying role requirements, and rewarding and praising desired outcomes; *management-by-exception active* – monitors deviations from the norm and provides corrective action – the leader actively watches for, and acts on, mistakes and errors; *management-by-exception passive* – similar to the active category, except leaders wait until deviations occur before intervening. Lastly, the laissez-faire category refers to an absence of leadership. The FRLT is measured by the Multifactor Leadership Questionnaire-5X (MLQ-5X). The MLQ-5X is the most widely used measure of transformational leadership in the organizational psychology literature. A key feature of Bass and colleagues' conceptualization of transformational leadership is that the separate subscales of the transformational elements of the MLQ-5X are normally collapsed to represent a single global construct of transformational leadership.

Although less used, alternative conceptualizations have also emerged in the literature. For example, Podsakoff, MacKenzie, Moorman and Fetter (1990) developed the Transformational Leadership Inventory (TLI) which includes: *identifying and articulating a vision* – behaviour on the part of the leader aimed at identifying new opportunities for his or her unit/division/company, and developing, articulating, and inspiring others with his or her vision of the future; *providing an appropriate role model* – behaviour on the part of the leader that sets an example for employees to follow that is consistent with the values espoused by the leader; *high performance expectations* – behaviour that demonstrates the leaders' expectations for excellence, quality, and/or high performance on the part of the follower; *fostering acceptance of group goals* – behaviour on the part of the leader aimed at promoting cooperation among employees and getting them to work together for the same goal; *intellectual stimulation* – behaviour on the part of the leader that challenges followers to re-examine some of their assumptions about their work and rethink how it can be performed; and *providing individualized support* – behaviour on the part of the leader that indicates that he/she respects followers and is concerned about their personal feelings and needs. The

TLI also included the transactional behaviour of *contingent reward* – behaviour on the part of the leader that praises followers for appropriate follower behaviour.

Based on Podsakoff et al.'s (1990) and Bass & Avolio's (1997) conceptualizations, Hardy et al. (2010) developed the Differentiated Transformational Leadership Inventory (DTLI). The sub-dimensions of transformational leadership included in the DTLI are: *Inspirational motivation* – developing and articulating a positive vision of the future and inspiring others to achieve that vision; *Providing an appropriate role model* – behaviour by the leader that sets an example for employees to follow which is consistent with the values that the leader/organization espouses; *Fostering acceptance of group goals and team work* – behaviour by the leader aimed at promoting cooperation among followers, getting them to work together towards a common goal, and developing teamwork; *High performance expectations* – behaviour by the leader that demonstrates his or her expectations for excellence in followers; *Intellectual stimulation* – behaviour by the leader that challenges followers to re-examine old problems in new ways; *Individual consideration* – behaviour by the leader that recognizes individual differences and demonstrates concern for the development of followers; and *Contingent reward* – provision of positive reinforcement to followers in return for appropriate follower behaviour. The DTLI has been modified to reflect a sporting context (Callow, Smith, Hardy, Arthur & Hardy, 2009), higher education (Mawn, Callow, Hardy & Arthur, 2012), and expedition context (McElligott, Arthur & Callow, 2012). A key factor of the DTLI is that it was designed as a context-specific differentiated measure of transformational leadership.

Other context-specific measures of transformational leadership have also been developed in the literature; these include the Safety Specific Transformational Scale (Barling, Loughlin & Kelloway, 2002), the Transformational Parenting Questionnaire (TPQ; Morton et al., 2011), and the Transformational Teaching Questionnaire (TTQ; Beauchamp et al., 2010). Broadly speaking, the various questionnaires can be categorized according to whether they were developed in a specific context (e.g. DTLI and TPQ) or were developed across contexts (e.g. MLQ-5X), and whether they measure transformational leadership as a global construct (e.g. MLQ-5X and TTQ) or as a differentiated construct (e.g. TLI and DTLI). Thus far the transformational leadership in sport research has made use of four different transformational leadership scales: MLQ-5X has been used in six papers, DTLI has also been used in six papers, and the TTQ and Global Transformational Leadership Scale (Tucker, Turner, Barling & McEvoy, 2010) have both been used once in the sport coaching transformational leadership research. Of the measures that have been used in sport, only the DTLI conceptualises transformational leadership as a differentiated construct and as yet no measure has been developed that targets specific behaviours or values in sport.

Transformational leadership has been demonstrated to be effective across a wide range of contexts including business (e.g. Barling, Weber & Kelloway, 1996; Podsakoff et al., 1990), military (e.g. Bass, Avolio, Jung & Berson, 2003; Hardy et al., 2010), higher education (e.g. Koh, Steers & Terborg, 1995),

Table 13.1 Summary of the behaviours used in various transformational leadership scales

	Charismatic leadership	Inspirational motivation	Vision	Idealized influence (attributed)	Idealized influence (behaviours)	Individualized consideration	Intellectual stimulation	Appropriate role modelling	High performance expectations	Inspirational communication	Supportive leadership	Transactional behaviours	Global or differentiated
Multi Factor Leadership Questionnaire (original)[a]	✓	✓				✓	✓					✓	G
Multifactor Factors Leadership Questionnaire-5X[b]		✓		✓	✓	✓	✓					✓	G
Transformational Leadership Inventory[c]		✓				✓	✓	✓	✓			✓	D
Rafferty & Griffin[d]			✓			✓	✓			✓	✓	✓	D
Differentiated Transformational Leadership Inventory[e]		✓				✓	✓	✓	✓	✓		✓	D
Safety Specific Transformational Leadership Scale[f]		✓		✓	✓	✓	✓						G
Transformational Parenting Questionnaire[g]		✓		✓	✓	✓	✓						G
Transformational Teaching Questionnaire[h]		✓		✓	✓	✓	✓						G

Sources: a Bass (1985), b Bass & Avolio (1997), c Podsakoff et al (1990), d Rafferty & Griffin (2004), e Hardy et al (2010), f Barling et al (2002), g Morton et al (2011), h Beauchamp et al (2010)

secondary education (Beauchamp et al., 2010), parenting (e.g. Morton et al., 2011), and the public sector (e.g. Rafferty & Griffin, 2004). It is thus not surprising that transformational leadership has also been demonstrated to be effective in the sport domain (e.g. Arthur, Woodman, Ong, Hardy & Ntoumanis, 2011; Charbonneau, Barling & Kelloway, 2001; Price & Weiss, 2013). While transformational leadership research is still relatively new to sport, there is a growing body of research in sport that demonstrates that transformational leader behaviours are influential in predicting important athlete outcomes (for review see Arthur & Tomsett, 2015). Indeed, the extant evidence in the sport psychology literature would suggest that athletes who rate their coaches as displaying more transformational leader behaviours are more intrinsically motivated (Charbonneau et al., 2001), have greater levels of well-being and need satisfaction (Stenling & Tafvelin, 2014), exert extra effort (Arthur et al., 2011) and have teams that are cohesive, with players willing to make greater sacrifices for the benefit of the team (Cronin, Arthur, Hardy & Callow, 2015).

To date, there has been a range of athlete outcomes that have been examined within the sport literature; these include variables such as cohesion (Callow et al., 2009; Cronin et al., 2015; Smith, Arthur, Hardy, Callow & Williams, 2013, communication (Smith et al., 2012), sacrifice (Cronin et al., 2015), developmental outcomes (Vella, Oades & Crowe, 2013), collective efficacy (Price & Weiss, 2013), intrinsic motivation (Charbonneau et al., 2001), well-being and need satisfaction (Stenling & Tafvelin, 2014), satisfaction with coach (Rowold, 2006), empowerment and organizational citizen behaviours (Lee, Kim & Joon-Ho, 2013), aggression (Tucker et al., 2010), self-report attendance (Rowold, 2006), and coach-rated performance (Charbonneau et al., 2001). From the above research, it appears that transformational leadership is effective in predicting individual affective and motivational outcomes as well as socially construed variables such as cohesion. However, a brief glance at the list of variables examined and it becomes strikingly apparent that there are some notable variables missing (e.g. anxiety, self-handicapping, coping, attribution styles, mental toughness etc.) and that there is a distinct lack of objective behavioural data. That is, the vast majority of the research in sport has relied almost entirely on self-report data in which common method bias is nearly always an issue (see Arthur & Tomsett (2015) for discussion of this issue).

Transformational leadership has been demonstrated to be effective across a variety of different sports, including youth soccer (e.g. Price & Weiss, 2013; Vella et al., 2013), ultimate Frisbee (e.g. Callow et al., 2009; Smith et al., 2012), handball (Lee et al., 2013), and floor ball (Stenling & Tafvelin, 2014). In mixed sport studies, transformational leadership has also been shown to be effective in predicting athlete outcomes. For example, Arthur et al. (2011) demonstrated that transformational leadership predicted athlete-reported effort in a mixed sport sample (e.g. soccer, netball, athletics and golf). Similar results have also been demonstrated with mixed sport samples with collegiate students in the USA (Cronin et al., 2015) and Canada (Charbonneau et al., 2001). The transformational leadership research has also been conducted in a variety of countries including the UK (e.g. Callow et al., 2009; Smith et al., 2013, Canada (e.g. Char-bonneau et al., 2001), USA (e.g. Cronin et al., 2015), Sweden (Stenling & Tafve-lin, 2014), Korea (Lee et al., 2013), Australia (e.g. Vella et al., 2013), Singapore (Arthur et al., 2011), and Germany (Rowold, 2006). With regard to age and level of participants, the majority of the samples come from youth- or university-level athletes, with very little representation from elite level athletes. However, recent qualitative research by Hodge, Henry and Smith (2014) with the All Blacks rugby team has begun to provide evidence of transformational leadership in elite sport.

Implications for future research

While the early indications are that transformational leadership has positive effects on athlete outcomes across sport types, nationality, age, and level, there is clearly a substantial amount of research still required within sport. First, there is a very real need to move beyond self-report data by including other report and behavioural data. Second, the research has been dominated by cross-sectional designs, with limited use of longitudinal and experimental designs. Third, there is a need to move beyond the simple main-effect paradigm by exploring poten-tial mediating and moderating variables – that is, identify and test under what conditions and with whom are transformational leader behaviours more (or less) effective (moderators). For example, high-trait anxious individuals selectively scan the environment and focus on threat related information (Spielberger, 1966). This raises at least two intriguing possibilities; one is that trait anxiety may influence what athletes see their coaches doing, with high trait anxious indi-viduals perhaps being inclined toward perceiving their coach's behaviour as less transformational. However, this suggestion may be countered with the notion that a component of transformational leadership is specifically about being aware of, and sensitive towards, the individual needs of their followers. Thus a trans-formational coach may be aware of their athlete's individual needs and adjust their behaviours accordingly with this athlete. Alternatively, trait anxiety may moderate the effectiveness of certain transformational leader behaviours, so that the more supportive behaviours (such as individual consideration and role modelling) may be more beneficial for high trait anxious individuals than their low trait anxious counterparts. Research exploring individual differences in the context of transformational leadership would help to extend the understanding of transformational leadership in sport.

Fourth, there has been no research in sport that has examined antecedent factors involved in the emergence of transformational leadership. That is, under what conditions are coaches likely to display transformational leader behaviours, and/or what personality variables are related to the emergence of transformational leadership in sport? The research that has examined ante-cedent factors in the organisational psychology has produced what one might describe as inconclusive results with regards to the Big Five personality traits and transformational leadership. In a meta-analysis, Bono and Judge (2004) found modest relationships between the Big Five and transformational leadership with extraversion having the strongest relationship. Outside the Big Five, there has been some recent research conducted on narcissism, leader emergence and transformational leadership. Ong, Roberts, Arthur, Woodman and Akehurst (2016) examined the temporal relationship between narcissism, leader emergence and leader effectiveness. The results indicated that, early on, narcissism was related to transformational leadership, but this relationship was not apparent later in the relationship. This suggests that narcissism is positively related to transformational leadership, but only in the early stages of the leader's tenure. This study points towards some interesting avenues of research in relation to sport coaching where the personality of the coach may have an impact on whether they are rated as being more or less transformational by their athletes. Intriguingly, however, this relationship may be moderated by the situation, and/or, context. Clearly, the antecedent factors involved with the emergence of transformational leadership in sport are likely to be fairly complex and urgently require research.

A final area of research that is worth noting is the methodological approach that is typically adopted to measure transformational leadership. To date, transformational leadership in sport has relied solely on athlete reports. It is important to note that this is not necessarily a weakness, but other methods of measurement might warrant exploration. For example, there is a tradition in sport-coaching research that utilizes behavioural observation methods, where coach's behaviours are observed and coded by trained observers (e.g. Bloom, Crumpton & Anderson, 1999; Gallimore & Tharp, 2004; Lacy & Darst, 1984; Partington & Cushion, 2013; Smith et al., 1977). These approaches typically either observe and code behaviours of a number of different coaches (e.g. Smith & Cushion, 2006) or observe individual coaches that have been identified as being *great*, for example, John Wooden (Gallimore & Tharp, 2004) and Pat Summitt (Becker & Wrisberg, 2008). Several behavioural observation systems have been developed; these include the Coach Behavioral Assessment System (Smith, Smoll & Hunt, 1977), and Arizona State University Observation Instrument (Lacy & Darst, 1984). These behavioural assessment systems have identified a large number of coach behaviours that can be observed by a third party. However, as yet no observational research has been applied to the transformational leadership research. Indeed, it could be argued that observational methods are not appropriate for transformational leadership because transformational leadership effects are often described as an attributed characteristic that is made by followers who receive the leadership. Thus, one needs to have directly received the leadership in order to determine whether transformational effects have occurred or not. Nonetheless, it would seem that a combination of follower report and observer report might help to shed more light on the broader coaching process. Follower reports will be best placed to ascertain the emotional component of leadership whereas observer reports maybe better placed to code the frequency of behaviours. The observational methodologies can document and quantify what a coach does in terms of the classic behavioural typologies of instruction, feedback, praise etc., but they can also code behaviours in relation to discernable preceding events or determine the order in which behaviours are displayed. For example, in the CBAS, behaviours are coded in relation to responses to specific preceding events such as desirable performance, mistake error, and misbehaviours. This is important contextual and situational information that can help to place the coach behaviour in context. Follower reports cannot do this as they typically ask followers about their coach's normal/usual behaviors. Of course, if one were to adopt a critical incident technique (for a review of critical incident techniques, see Butterfield, Borgan, Amundson & Maglio, 2005) to follower reports by asking followers to rate their leader in relation to a critical incident (e.g. the last time they *misbehaved*) then this would help to provide information about the context in which the leader behaviour occurred. However, critical incident techniques have yet to be applied to the transformational leadership literature in sport. To sum up, it would appear that the adoption of observer reports into the transformational leadership literature would be able to provide a fuller picture of coach behaviours in which transformational leadership may be considered as a quasi-indicator of the quality of behaviour, and the observational methodologies of the frequency of behaviour and the specific context in which the behaviour was delivered. In this way, research can start to examine the combined effects of frequency and quality of behaviour. The adoption of multiple methodologies may also allow for research to begin exploring order effects of different coach behaviours. That is, in what order should coaches display different types of behaviours to maximize motivation and learning. For example, when delivering instructions, the coach may precede this with a motivational type speech or rationale of why it is important.

To sum up, it appears that transformational leadership theory offers a sound theoretical platform to build on for future coaching-related research. Transformational leadership offers much promise with regard to exploring the inspirational effects of great coaches and thus can inform best coaching practice which will help to develop better coaches. However, the sole adoption of transformational leadership theory and/or the sole adoption of follower perspective are not recommended, just as the sole adoption of observational approaches is not recommended. A balanced approach that adopts multiple perspectives would seem to offer the optimum way forward for coaching-related research. Indeed, this sentiment has been articulated in the sport coaching literature in which the use of observational methods combined with qualitative methods has been encouraged and used in research (e.g. Potrac, Brewer, Jones, Armour & Hoff, 2000; Smith & Cushion, 2006). In this light, no one theory, model, or methodological approach can possibly uncover the entire area of effective coaching. Thus researchers should consider ways to work together to bring these disparate silos of coaching research together in order to further coaching theory and practice – that is, explore ways in which observational techniques can be coupled with athlete perceptions of their coach's transformational behaviours.

Implications for applied practice

When conducting research, and developing models and theories for coaches to use in their day to day work, it is important to make the information as easy to understand and apply as possible. The acquisition of knowledge is relatively straightforward when compared to the application of that knowledge, especially in pressured environments. Coaching is essentially a doing occupation that operates in real time with real people; there is no pause or rewind button. Many hundreds of interactions with athletes occur on a daily basis, with some immediate decisions having to be made and often under intense pressure. Being able to succinctly and accurately articulate the latest theory and research from psychology may not necessarily help the coach (of course it might) but ultimately the translation of this knowledge into what it looks like on a day-to-day basis is crucial. Langan, Blake and Lonsdale (2013) discuss the challenge of translating knowledge acquisition into knowledge application in coach education programmes. They draw a distinction between short-term memory retention and long-term knowledge application in real-life complex situations. Within the context of the application of knowledge and theory to real life situations, in this case the application of transformational leadership theory to an applied context, the Vision, Support and Challenge Model (Arthur, Hardy & Woodman, 2012; Hardy et al., 2010) was developed. The primary purpose of the VSC Model is to make transformational leadership more accessible in applied contexts; thus, transformational leadership was articulated as a means to provide followers with three easily understood and intuitive outcomes.

The meta-cognitive VSC model was developed by Hardy and Arthur in a military leadership intervention context (Arthur & Hardy, 2014; Hardy et al., 2010) and was later articulated in a sport setting by Arthur, Hardy and Woodman (2012). The VSC model was developed as a meta-cognitive model that was theorised to represent what it is that transformational leaders provide their followers with. Thus the VSC model takes a follower-centric approach to leadership, whereby the primary outcomes of transformational leadership are specified as follower outcomes. The model posits that *great* coaches inspire their athletes by: creating an inspirational *vision* of the future; providing the necessary *support* to achieve the vision; and providing the *challenge* to achieve the vision. The underlying proposition is that the vision provides meaning and direction for athletes' effort. That is, in a high performance context, the vision serves as the beacon towards which all the sweat, pain and sacrifice is directed. The premise that underpins the VSC model is that, all other things being equal, the person who is motivated to practise longer and train harder will fulfil more of their potential and that the strength of the vision, and amount of support and challenge in the environment will play a crucial role in this.

A key distinction that the VSC model makes is that it differentiates what the coach does (i.e. coach behaviours) and the direct consequences of coach behaviours (i.e. athlete's meta-cognitions) in the same model. In this light a clear causal pathway can be theoretically developed and tested between *what*

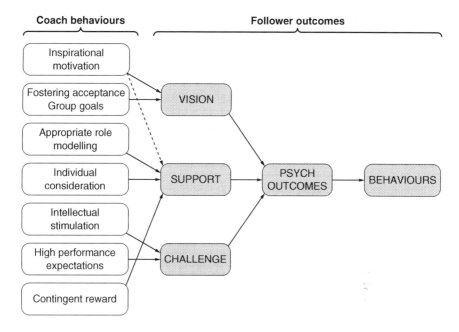

Figure 13.1 Vision, Support and Challenge Model. The above is a pictorial representation of the Vision Support and Challenge Model. While it is recognised that contingent reward is not a transformational leader behaviour, it is an important element of the support dimension within the model. The Psych outcomes box refers loosely to individual and team outcomes that are favourable in terms of encouraging appropriate behaviours – for example, factors such as self-confidence, anxiety, group cohesion, sacrifice, satisfaction.

the coach does and *athlete cognitions and affect*. Therefore, the VSC model is measured and conceptualised at the athlete level in terms of the strength of the vision they have, how much support they perceive is available and the extent to which they feel challenged. Vision is defined as the extent to which athletes have an inspirational and meaningful future image of themselves in their sport. Support is defined as the extent to which emotion, esteem, information, and tangible support is provided, or is perceived as being available, when needed. Challenge is defined as an understanding of what needs to be done in order to achieve goals and the gap between the current state and a future desired state, with the implicit assumption that the larger the discrepancy the more challenged followers are.

In order for the vision to serve optimally as a motivating agent (i.e. have potential inspirational effects) it will need to be meaningful to the athlete. It will also have to be perceived as challenging but achievable, probably via a lot of hard work and effort. The perception of hard work and effort is part of the challenge element of the model, and the belief that it is achievable is part of the support aspect of the model. These are discussed later. From a transformational leadership perspective, the content of the vision will be best served if it is tied to an underpinning set of values that are worthwhile and important to the athlete. The underpinning values are related to what it is that makes this team/sport/nationality different – for example, what it means to be part of this club/sport/team. It can also include a superordinate purpose, such as who we represent or some greater cause that transcends the individual. That is not to say that the individual is not important; quite the contrary, the individual will need to perceive that they have a key role in achieving the vision for the team and themselves. Regardless of whether they are a reserve player, a regular first team player, or part of the support staff, they will need to perceive that they have a key role in determining the success of the team and are thus a valued part of the team. In an elite sport setting, Hodge, Henry and Smith (2014) related the 'Better people' part of the 'Better people make better All Blacks' philosophy to the inspirational motivation component of transformational leadership. In relation to the current model, the 'Better people' aspect relates to a vision that is tied to a set of values on 'being better people'. In this case, the vision is not only about being the best in the world, but also speaks to something deeper and perhaps more profound. Thus it might stimulate the activation of higher order ideals and values in the athletes. In a practical sense, in order to maximize the motivational impact of the vision, it needs to be meaningful and tied to a set of underlying values or philosophy: 'what it means to be part of this team/play this sport'. The transformational leader's behaviours that are theorized to predict vision are inspirational motivation and fostering acceptance of group goals.

Regardless of the meaning and nature of the vision, if individuals do not believe it is possible it will not serve as a motivational tool. Rather, individuals will disengage from it, unless they feel sufficiently confident that it is achievable. This is where the role of support comes in: the vision might be a wonderful thing to dream about, but, if sufficient support and belief is not present, then it will be unlikely to generate the motivation, effort and persistence that is required to achieve great things. The provision of support by the leader is recognized as a key element of transformational leadership (Bass, 1985) and has been shown to have positive effects on a number of follower outcomes (Podsakoff et al., 1990). It is hypothesized that the transformational behaviours of individual consideration, appropriate role modelling and an element of inspirational motivation will serve to provide followers with perceptions of support. It is also hypothesized that contingent reward, although not a transformational leader behaviour, will also provide followers with perceptions of being supported. That is, when followers receive praise for a job well done or the exertion of effort, this will contribute towards them feeling supported.

Inherent within transformational leadership is the notion of challenge. Indeed, Bass and Bass (2009) stated that 'transformational leaders motivate their followers to do more than the followers originally intended and thought possible. The leader *sets challenging expectations* and achieves higher standards of performance [emphasis added]' (p. 618). The perception of challenge is also theorized to be fundamental to maximizing the motivational effects of the vision. That is, without the perception of challenge, there is unlikely to be a strong drive to consistently put maximum effort into training. This is summed up nicely by Hodge et al. (2014) who stated that, within the All Blacks, the challenge element was encapsulated by the performance expectation of 'Being the best in the world every day'. Paradoxically, if there is not enough perception of challenge in the environment, the objectives and goals become somewhat less worthy. The notion here is that perceptions of challenge ameliorate against coasting. The assumption underpinning the challenge is that elite levels of performance or increasing one's own personal bests, fitness levels, skills etc. require a lot of hard work and effort. Great achievements by their very nature cannot be easy: indeed, a pre-requisite of greatness is likely to be that it has to be very challenging: if it is easy, greatness is unlikely to be ascribed to the deed. It is important to note that very hard work and/or being highly challenged is not necessarily inherently enjoyable at the time; indeed, it often entails dealing with a lot of pain and sacrifice over a prolonged period of time. Therefore, challenge on its own is likely to predict negative affective outcomes. It may also predict effort over a short period of time, but this is likely to be short lived and lead to burn out and withdrawal if support and an inspirational vision are not also present. In the VSC model, it is proposed that the perception of challenge in the environment is proportional to the level of perceived support. The major prediction with regard to support and challenge is that optimum motivation will occur when high levels of both are present in the environment. Of course the impact of support and challenge will only be optimized in the presence of a vision that is sufficiently inspirational.

Whilst the VSC model is predominately about the coach provision of these components, the relative levels that the coach needs to provide of vision, support and challenge will be determined by the individual and context. Some environments will be inherently very challenging: for example, when an athlete is selected to the next level (e.g. regional level to national level) will likely be very challenging in their own right. Therefore, in this situation the coach may not need to provide additional challenge as the environment takes care of the challenge; rather, the coach may wish to find ways to support the athlete's transition. Of course, the personality of the athlete will also be likely to have an impact on the amount of support they require for optimum motivation. For example, in the trait anxiety illustration given earlier, athletes with high trait anxiety may require more supportive behaviours from the coach. The VSC model provides a useful and intuitive applied model of transformational leadership in sport, but it is important to note that the propositions here have yet to be empirically tested. There is evidence emerging from some qualitative research in a high performance/ world class context that supports the presence of VSC in these environments (e.g. Hodge et al., 2014). However, there is a need to test empirically the predictions and antecedents of the VSC model proposed here.

Notes

1 University of Stirling, UK
2 National Coach, Scottish Swimming, UK

References

Antonakis, J., Cianciolo, A. T. & Sternberg, R. J. (2004). Leadership, past, present, and future. In J. Antonakis, A. T. Cianciolo & R. J. Sternberg (Eds.), *The nature of leadership* (pp. 3–15). New York. Sage.

Aoyagi, M. W., Cox, R. H. & McGuire, R. T. (2008). Organizational citizenship behavior in sport: Relationships with leadership, team cohesion, and athlete satisfaction. *Journal of Applied Sport Psychology, 20*, 25–41.

Arthur, C. A., & Hardy, L. (2014). Transformational leadership: A quasi-experimental study. *Leadership and Organization Development Journal, 35*, 38–53.

Arthur, C. A., & Tomsett, P. (2015). Transformational leadership behaviour in sport. In S. D. Mellalieu & S. Hanton (Eds.), *Contemporary advances in sport psychology* (pp. 175–201) London: Routledge.

Arthur, C. A., Hardy, L. & Woodman, T. (2012). Realising the Olympic dream: Vision, support, and challenge. *Reflective Practice International and Multidisciplinary Perspectives, 13*, 399–406.

Arthur, C. A., Woodman, T., Ong, C. W., Hardy, L. & Ntoumanis, N. (2011). The role of athlete narcissism in moderating the relationship between coaches' transformational leader behaviors and athlete motivation. *Journal of Sport and Exercise Psychology, 33*, 3–19.

Barling, J., Loughlin, C. & Kelloway, E. K. (2002). Development and test of a model linking safety-specific transformational leadership and occupational safety. *Journal of Applied Psychology, 87*, 488–496.

Barling, J., Weber, T. & Kelloway, E. K. (1996). Effects of transformational leadership training on attitudinal and financial outcomes: A field experiment. *Journal of Applied Psychology, 81*, 827–832.

Bass, B. M. (1985). *Leadership and performance beyond expectations* (4th edn). New York: Free Press.

Bass, B. M. & Avolio, B. J. (1997). *Full range leadership development: Manual for the multifactor leadership questionniare.* Palo Alto, CA: Mindgarden.

Bass, B. M., & Bass, R. (2009). *The Bass handbook of leadership: Theory, research, and managerial applications.* New York: Free Press.

Beauchamp, M. R., Barling, J., Li, Z., Morton, K. L., Keith, S. E. & Zumbo, B. D. (2010). Development and psychometric properties of the transformational teaching questionnaire. *Journal of Health Psychology, 15*, 1123–1134.

Becker, A. J., & Wrisberg, C. A. (2008). Effective coaching in action: Observations of legendary collegiate basketball coach Pat Summitt. *Sport Psychologist, 22*, 197–211.

Bloom, G. A., Crumpton, R. & Anderson, J. E. (1999). A systematic observation study of the teaching behaviors of an expert basketball coach. *Sport Psychologist, 13*, 157–170.

Bono, J. E., & Judge, T. A. (2004). Personality and transformational and transactional leadership: A meta-analysis. *Journal of Applied Psychology, 89*, 901–910.

Burns, J. M. (1978). *Leadership.* New York: Harper and Row.

Butterfield, L. D., Borgen, W. A., Amundson, N. E. & Maglio, A. T. (2005). Fifty years of the critical incident technique: 1954–2004 and beyond. *Qualitative Research, 5*, 475–497.

Callow, N., Smith, M. J., Hardy, L., Arthur, C. A. & Hardy, J. (2009). Measurement of transformational leadership and its relationship with team cohesion and performance level. *Journal of Applied Sport Psychology, 21*, 395–412.

Charbonneau, D., Barling, J. & Kelloway, E. K. (2001). Transformational leadership and sports performance: The mediating role of intrinsic motivation. *Journal of Applied Social Psychology, 31*, 1521–1534.

Cronin, L. D., Arthur, C. A., Hardy, J. & Callow, N. (2015). Transformational leadership and task cohesion in sport: The mediating role of inside sacrifice. *Journal of Sport and Exercise Psychology*, *37*, 23–36.

Fiedler, F. E. (1971). Leadership. Morristown, NJ: General Learning Press.

Gallimore, R., & Tharp, R. (2004). What a coach can teach a teacher, 1975–2004: Reflections and reanalysis of John Wooden's teaching practices. *Sport Psychologist*, *18*, 119–137.

Hardy, L., Arthur, C. A., Jones, G., Shariff, A., Munnoch, K., Isaacs, I. & Allsopp, A. J. (2010). The relationship between transformational leadership behaviors, psychological, and training outcomes in elite military recruits. *Leadership Quarterly*, *21*, 20–32.

Hodge, K., Henry, G. & Smith, W. (2014). A case study of excellence in elite sport: Motivational climate in a world champion team. *Sport Psychologist*, *28*, 60–74.

Hollembeak, J., & Amorose, A. J. (2005). Perceived coaching behaviors and college athletes' intrinsic motivation: A test of self-determination theory. *Journal of Applied Sport Psychology*, *17*, 20–36.

Horne, T., & Carron, A. V. (1985). Compatibility in coach–athlete relationships. *Journal of Sport Psychology*, *7*, 137–149.

Koh, W. L., Steers, R. M. & Terborg, J. R. (1995). The effects of transformational leadership on teacher attitudes and student performance in Singapore. *Journal of Organizational Behavior*, *16*, 319–333.

Lacy, A. C., & Darst, P. W. (1984). Evolution of a systematic observation system: The ASU coaching observation instrument. *Journal of Teaching in Physical Education*, *3*, 59–66.

Langan, E., Blake, C. & Lonsdale, C. (2013). Systematic review of the effectiveness of interpersonal coach education interventions on athlete outcomes. *Psychology of Sport and Exercise*, *14*, 37–49.

Lee, Y., Kim, S. & Joon-Ho, K. (2013). Coach leadership effect on elite handball players' psychological empowerment and organizational citizenship behavior. *International Journal of Sports Science and Coaching*, *8*, 327–342.

Mawn, L., Callow, N., Hardy, J. & Arthur, C. (2012). Transformational leadership in higher education: Developing a measure. *International Journal of Psychology*, 47 Supplement 1.

McElligott, S. J., Arthur, C. A. & Callow, N. (2012). The impact of transformational leadership behaviors on self-esteem in the youth expedition context. *Journal of Sport and Exercise Psychology*, *34*, S260–S261.

Morton, K. L., Barling, J., Rhodes, R. E., Mâsse, L. C., Zumbo, B. D. & Beauchamp, M. R. (2011). The application of transformational leadership theory to parenting: Questionnaire development and implications for adolescent self-regulatory efficacy and life satisfaction. *Journal of Sport and Exercise Psychology*, *33*, 688–709.

Ong, C. W., Roberts, R., Arthur, C. A., Woodman, T. & Akehurst, S. (2016). The leader ship is sinking: A temporal investigation of narcissistic leadership. *Journal of Personality*, *84*, 237–247.

Partington, M., & Cushion, C. (2013). An investigation of the practice activities and coaching behaviors of professional top-level youth soccer coaches. *Scandinavian Journal of Medicine and Science in Sports*, *23*, 374–382.

Podsakoff, P. M., MacKenzie, S. B., Moorman, R. H. & Fetter, R. (1990). Transformational leader behaviors and their effects on followers' trust in leader, satisfaction, and organizational citizenship behaviors. *The Leadership Quarterly*, *1*, 107–142.

Potrac, P., Brewer, C., Jones, R., Armour, K. & Hoff, J. (2000). Toward an holistic understanding of the coaching process. *Quest*, *52*, 186–199.

Price, M. S., & Weiss, M. R. (2013). Relationships among coach leadership, peer leadership, and adolescent athletes' psychosocial and team outcomes: A test of transformational leadership theory. *Journal of Applied Sport Psychology, 25*, 265–279

Rafferty, A. E., & Griffin, M. A. (2004). Dimensions of transformational leadership: Conceptual and empirical extensions. *Leadership Quarterly, 15*, 329–354.

Rowold, J. (2006). Transformational and transactional leadership in martial arts. *Journal of Applied Sport Psychology, 18*, 312–325.

Smith, M., & Cushion, C. J. (2006). An investigation of the in-game behaviours of professional, top-level youth soccer coaches. *Journal of Sports Sciences, 24*, 355–366.

Smith, M. J., Arthur, C. A., Hardy, J. T., Callow, N. & Williams, D. (2013). Transformational leadership and task cohesion in sport: The mediating role of intra-team communication. *Psychology of Sport and Exercise, 14*, 249–257.

Smith, R. E., & Smoll, F. L. (2007). Social-cognitive approach to coaching behaviors. In S. Jowett & D. Lavallee (Eds.), *Social psychology in sport* (pp. 7–90). Champaign, IL: Human Kinetics.

Smith, R. E., Smoll, F. L. & Cumming, S. P. (2007). Effects of a motivational climate intervention for coaches on young athletes' sport performance anxiety. *Journal of Sport and Exercise Psychology, 29*, 39–59.

Smith, R. E., Smoll, F. L. & Hunt, E. (1977). System for behavioral-assessment of athletic coaches. *Research Quarterly, 48*, 401–407.

Spielberger, C. D. (1966). Theory and research on anxiety. In C. D. Speilberger (Ed.), *Anxiety and behaviour* (pp. 3–22). New York: Academic Press.

Stenling, A., & Tafvelin, S. (2014). Transformational leadership and well-being in sports: The mediating role of need satisfaction. *Journal of Applied Sport Psychology, 26*, 182–196.

Tucker, S., Turner, N., Barling, J. & McEvoy, M. (2010). Transformational leadership and children's aggression in team settings: A short-term longitudinal study. *Leadership Quarterly, 21*, 389–399.

Vallee, C. N., & Bloom, G. A. (2005). Building a successful university program: Key and common elements of expert coaches. *Journal of Applied Sport Psychology, 17*, 179–196.

Vella, S. A., Oades, L. G. & Crowe, T. P. (2013). The relationship between coach leadership, the coach–athlete relationship, team success, and the positive developmental experiences of adolescent soccer players. *Physical Education and Sport Pedagogy, 18*, 549–561.

Weiss, M. R., & Friedrichs, W. D. (1986). The influence of leader behaviors, coach attributes, and institutional variables on performance and satisfaction of collegiate basketball teams. *Journal of Sport Psychology, 8*, 332–346.

14 Enhancing coaching efficacy in the psychosocial development of athletes

Chris Harwood[1]

Introduction

If there were a single notable insight about the coaching profession over the past 15 years, it would most probably be that the roles and responsibilities of the modern day coach have widened exponentially. Coaches face an ever more complex set of responsibilities in order to be holistically effective with respect to athlete development (Camiré, Forneris, Trudel & Bernard, 2011). There is a global premium placed on increasing and sustaining general sport participation across the lifespan as a healthy lifestyle choice, as much as there is commercial and corporate value in the coaching, nurturing and protection of young talent. The vast majority of young athletes in competitive sport programs will not transition into a sustainable, professional career. Therefore, coaches are being challenged to pay careful attention to maximising personal development experiences in young athletes in conjunction with nurturing psychological qualities most associated with performance enhancement (see Johnston, Harwood & Minniti, 2013; Vella, Oades & Crowe, 2011). To achieve this range of coach-facilitated athlete outcomes requires an extensive degree of confidence in one's coaching – an intrapersonal concept referred to in the literature as coaching efficacy. The aim of this chapter is to focus on research that has explored the antecedents and outcomes of coaching efficacy, before detailing recent intervention attempts to enhance coaches' confidence in influencing positive psychosocial responses and behaviours in young athletes. In addition, the chapter presents future research directions in terms of the role of the coach in athlete psychosocial development, and specifies the need to target applied coaching efficacy research at more micro- and situational levels across a range of sports.

Key terms

Inspired by Bandura's (1977) self-efficacy theory and Denham and Michael's (1981) multidimensional model of teacher efficacy, the concept of *coaching efficacy* has been defined as the extent to which coaches believe they have the capacity to influence the learning and performance of their athletes (Feltz, Chase, Moritz & Sullivan, 1999). Traditionally, the construct of coaching efficacy has been multi-dimensional, divided into technique, motivation, game strategy and character-building efficacies, and quantitatively assessed via the Coaching Efficacy Scale (CES; Feltz et al., 1999). Technique efficacy is the belief coaches have in their instructional/diagnostic skills when working with athletes; motivation efficacy is the confidence coaches possess in their ability to affect the psychological skills and motivational/mood states of their athletes; game strategy efficacy is the confidence coaches have in their ability to coach during competition and lead their athletes to a successful performance; finally, character-building efficacy is the confidence coaches possess in their ability to influence an athlete's positive attitude towards sport. When revising the CES for use with high school team sports, Myers, Feltz, Chase, Reckase and Hancock (2008) introduced a fifth dimension of physical conditioning efficacy, representing the confidence that coaches have in their ability to prepare their athletes physically for participation in sport.

Although the coaching efficacy model embraces certain psychological components through a quantitative focus on a coach's motivation and character-building efficacy, it does so at a generic, higher-order level. The CES items do not focus on the coach's beliefs about influencing specific psychological or social skills at a more micro-level of attention. In recent years within youth sport, there has been a growing interest in more specific *psychosocial assets* (and allied life skills) that stem from the field of positive youth development (PYD). Schulman and Davies (2007) define PYD as 'the acquisition of all the knowledge, skills, competencies and experiences required [by young people] to successfully transition from adolescence to adulthood' (p. 4), a definition which champions the idea of psychological, social and emotional development of young people through their experiences and interactions with significant others in their environment. One of the primary frameworks in this field is Benson's developmental assets framework with 20 'internal' developmental assets characterising young people's commitment to learning, positive values, social competencies and positive identity (Benson, 1997). The terms 'coaching efficacy', 'psychosocial assets' and 'positive youth development' are important in this chapter as the responsibilities for youth coaches [to athletes] are no longer restricted to knowledge around game strategy, technique and physical fitness, but extend to facilitating a potentially much wider range of psychosocial outcomes through their coaching.

Review of literature

Research on the coaching efficacy model

Feltz and colleagues (1999) proposed a coaching efficacy model (see Figure 14.1) that sought to explain how sources of coaching efficacy information influenced the four (and later five) dimensions of coaching efficacy beliefs which, in turn, predicted coach, athlete and team outcomes. Coaching experience/preparation, prior success, the perceived skill of athletes and social support from parents, administrators and the community were posited as antecedent sources of coaching efficacy beliefs, and a sizeable body of research has explored these predictions (see Chase & Martin, 2012). When considering these sources for the purpose of intervention research, the most controllable factor with respect to proactive change is coaching experience and preparation. Social support is potentially open to manipulation and change as an environmental factor, whereas prior success and the skill level of athletes are less controllable factors. With relevance placed on controllable factors, several studies have explored the impact of coaches' engagement in coach education programmes on coaching efficacy beliefs. Malete and Feltz (2000) noted positive differences in coaching efficacy in those coaches who participated in a short-term coach education program compared to non-participants. Coaches in the experimental group attended 12 hours (two six-hour sessions, one week apart) of education through the Program for Athletic Coach Education (PACE; Seefeldt & Brown, 1990). This program met certified national standards for coach education and included attention to the role of the coach in respect of motivational, psychological and social skills. Small post-intervention improvements were noted in all efficacy dimensions, with the greatest differences reported in game strategy and technique efficacy. A similar finding emerged for Lee, Malete and Feltz (2002) when examining groups of certified coaches (i.e. those who had followed educational courses) versus non-certified coaches in Singapore. Studies by Campbell and Sullivan (2005) and Malete and Sullivan (2009) drew similar conclusions about the role of coach education and coach certification. With respect to coaching experience, research has generally been supportive of a positive relationship between years of experience and coaching efficacy (Fung, 2002), with Marback, Short, Short and Sullivan (2005) noting key influences on motivation, game strategy and character-building efficacies, and Kavussanu, Boardley, Jutkiewicz, Vincent and Ring (2008) reporting higher technique-coaching efficacy in a range of individual and team sports.

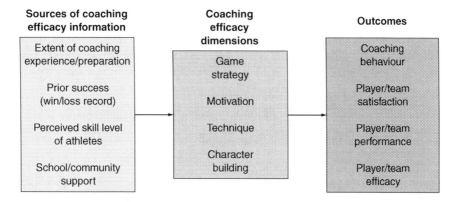

Figure 14.1 Feltz and colleagues' (1999) conceptual model of coaching efficacy.

Further avenues of research into the coaching efficacy model have examined the influence of coaching efficacy beliefs on coach and athlete outcomes. Such outcomes include coaching behaviour (e.g. leadership style), player/team satisfaction and performance as well as player and team efficacy beliefs. In their initial study, Feltz and colleagues (1999) found that coaches who reported higher coaching efficacy used more praise and encouragement and less organisational and instructional behaviours (as measured by the Coaching Behaviour Assessment System (CBAS); Smith, Smoll & Hunt, 1977) than lower efficacy coaches. These findings were complemented by Sullivan and Kent (2003) in their investigation of US and Canadian collegiate coaches' perceptions of coaching efficacy and self-vs-ideal leadership styles. Both motivation and technique efficacy predicted coaches' perceptions of a preferred leadership style encompassing positive feedback and training and instruction. The authors proposed that, where coaches were more confident in their roles as motivators and teachers, they were closer to their image of the ideal leader with respect to using positive feedback and appropriate training and instruction, and engaged in these behaviours to a greater extent (Sullivan & Kent, 2003).

Coaches reporting higher compared to lower coaching efficacy have also been linked to greater perceptions of athlete satisfaction on their teams (Feltz et al., 1999; Myers, Vargas-Tonsing & Feltz, 2005). This relationship holds for team performance with respect to links between levels of coaching efficacy and team win:loss records. Interestingly, among collegiate coaches (Myers et al., 2005), it was the dimensions of motivation and character-building efficacy that were associated with higher winning records. These two dimensions of coaching efficacy were also found to predict athletes' perceptions of team efficacy in a sample of high-school volleyball players (Vargas-Tonsing, Warners & Feltz, 2003). Finally, using a modified CES, Boardley, Kavussanu and Ring (2008) assessed athletes' perceptions of their coach's abilities in the four original efficacy dimensions, revealing a number of key relationships with athlete outcomes. Specifically, athletes' evaluations of their coach's motivation effectiveness predicted effort, commitment and enjoyment; their perceptions of their coach's technique effectiveness predicted their own levels of self-efficacy; and their evaluation of the coach's character-building effectiveness predicted their own self-reported prosocial behaviour. As a totality, these findings reinforce the important role of motivation, technique and character-building efficacy and that, where coaches (or athletes) possess belief in their ability to influence athletes in positive psychological and social manners, positive athlete/team perceptions, experiences and outcomes may follow.

Psychosocial coaching-efficacy interventions

The vast majority of research focused on the coaching efficacy model has been quantitative and cross-sectional in nature, with a focus on examining model predictions and improving measurement scales for specific sport populations, including high school and youth sport teams (see Myers, Chase, Pierce &

Martin, 2011; Myers et al., 2008). There still remains limited field-based intervention research that has targeted specific aspects of coaching efficacy in natural coaching contexts or situations. Longitudinal fieldwork is particularly lacking, whereby interventions track improvements in coaching efficacy over time as a result of ongoing education, support, practice and self-reflection. Indeed, Malete and Feltz (2000) acknowledge the limitation of a short intensive bout of formal education over a two-weekend period, and contemplate how:

> a longer program could have greater effects ... and could also include more time for mastery experiences for coaches, where they could have opportunities for practicing positive feedback techniques, effective instruction of a skill, or maintaining control during a simulated practice.
>
> (p. 416)

The CES assesses a coach's general beliefs about their abilities related to the five efficacy dimensions, without a clear focus on the coaching context (i.e. training, pre-match, post-match, during performance); it does not target situation-specific confidence in integrating particular skills or influencing specific athlete behaviours, responses or outcomes in training sessions. Indeed, with respect to more situation-specific coaching efficacy in their use of psychology, Gould, Damarjian and Medbery (1999) reported how tennis coaches lacked confidence in terms of integrating psychological elements into typical coaching sessions. Coaches cited insufficient information, salience (i.e. value) and knowledge of psychological skills, as well as a lack of access to user-friendly examples (i.e. to help 'know how') and limited concrete hands-on resources as key reasons for this lack of confidence. Recent applied research has adopted a more fine-grained approach to investigating how longitudinal interventions can impact on more specific coaching efficacies and psychosocial responses in athletes. Such research has also employed methodologies focused on individual (as opposed to group) coach experiences and targeted more prolonged engagement with coaches to assess their developments in confidence.

In 2008, I reported on the consulting initiatives and intervention research that I had undertaken when working with coaches at an English professional football academy (Harwood, 2008). My goal as a scientist–practitioner at the academy was to improve the psychological provisions and services for player development and create an emphasis on psychosocial development beyond the predominant focus on physical, technical and tactical elements. During the process of building rapport with the academy coaches, I observed how coaches valued psychology but lacked awareness in terms of the process and structure of employing psychological principles in their coaching (Gould et al., 1999). This lack of awareness resulted in uncertainty about applying psychology in their role and constrained their confidence to systematically deliver training sessions focused on facilitating psychological outcomes for players.

In formulating the intervention, I was interested in targeting psychosocial coaching efficacy, which essentially reflected the confidence the coach possessed in applying coaching strategies and behaviours that would influence key psycho-social behaviours in players. In terms of specific psychosocial constructs, the research was influenced by Fraser-Thomas and colleagues' notion of an applied sport-programming model (Fraser-Thomas, Côté & Deakin, 2005) based on Bronfenbrenner's (1999) bio-ecological model of youth development. Fraser-Thomas et al. contended that youth development occurred within a dynamic environment that promoted key internal assets (e.g. commitment to learning, interpersonal competence, restraint and self-esteem) through the influence of coaches and significant others. To strike a balance between psychological attributes perceived as relevant to both personal development and performance in youth football (Thelwell, Greenlees & Weston, 2006), I presented a frame-work to coaches referred to as 'the 5Cs': namely, commitment, communication, concentration, control, and confidence. Important for the subculture within which I was working, I perceived these terms to be user friendly for coaches and reflective of psychology language that coaches understood (Harwood, 2008). With acknowledgement of nurturing youth development through sport, such constructs reflected certain internal assets from PYD (Benson, 1997; Lerner, Fisher & Weinberg, 2000) and shared similarities with the psychosocial compe-tencies viewed as important for successful talent transition in youth soccer (Holt & Dunn, 2004).

In terms of achieving greater contextual and ecological precision in coaching efficacy and its assessment, I considered motivational, interpersonal and self-regulatory behaviours and responses that would represent positive player dem-onstrations of the 5Cs in coaching sessions. Psychosocial coaching efficacy reflected the belief that coaches possessed in developing and executing sessions that would influence players to produce or demonstrate such behaviour linked to each 'C'. In other words, rather than coaches reporting on their overall motiva-tion or character-building efficacy, coaches were to be assessed on their beliefs about their specific coaching strategies linked to specific psychosocial outcomes in a specific coaching context (i.e. training/practice). The original CES (Feltz et al., 1999; Malete & Feltz, 2000) contained 24 items measured on a Likert scale in terms of efficacy strength, ranging from *not at all confident* (0) to *extremely confident* (9). Items begin with the stem question: "How confident are you in your ability to …?". For the purposes of the 5C intervention, the CES was fully adapted based on the sport psychology literature, personal experiences in youth football, and consultation with the academy director at the professional club. Three player behaviours associated with each of the 5Cs (i.e. 15 behaviours in total) in training sessions were selected to represent positive psychosocial attributes in the young player. Therefore, using this study-specific coaching effi-cacy measure, each coach responded to the stem question: 'How much confi-dence do you possess in employing behaviours or strategies that actively help players to …' for each of the 15 items on the same 10-point Likert scale as the CES. Specific items included: persist at skills in the face of mistakes (commit-ment); encourage, praise and instruct teammates clearly and confidently (com-munication); stay focused on key components of a drill without being distracted (concentration); recover quickly after mistakes without a negative reaction or emotion (control); and want the ball with no fear of mistakes (confidence).

In order to assess changes in psychosocial coaching efficacy, I employed a quasi-single case, multiple baseline design with multiple treatments methodology (see Barker, McCarthy, Jones & Moran, 2011). Coaches at the football academy completed a single pre-intervention assessment of their current 5C (i.e. psychosocial) coaching efficacy prior to engagement in a 15-week coach education and practice intervention programme during the season. Their psychosocial coaching efficacy was then individually re-assessed at four further time points during the intervention as the education-to-practice implementation format moved from one C to the next.

In terms of the precise 5C coaching efficacy intervention, an organisational empowerment/supervisory consulting approach was employed (Smith & Johnson, 1990) whereby 'I worked with the coaches to work with the players'. The intervention drew on achievement goal theory (AGT; Nicholls, 1989), self-determination theory (SDT; Deci & Ryan, 2005), attention control training (Nideffer & Sharpe, 1978) and self-efficacy theory (Bandura, 1977) to inform the 5C work with coaches. The workshop model was influenced by personal consulting experience and past coach education initiatives including Smith and Smoll's (1997) Coaching Effectiveness Training (CET) program.

In brief, the 5C program incorporated cycles of awareness and education, application, and evaluation. Coaches at the academy were introduced to each C in separate 90-minute workshops in which awareness was raised around core principles and practical applications associated with that specific psychosocial construct. Coaches discussed strategies, coaching behaviour and squad social interactions that would facilitate players to respond with appropriate behaviours associated with that C in a given session. An important element of these workshops became the reminder for coaches to consider eight directives or guidelines that would help them to plan, structure and be appropriately proactive and reactive in terms of the coaching sessions. These eight directives have subsequently been refined into the mnemonic 'PROGRESS' (Harwood & Anderson, 2015) and they assist coaches in their planning, monitoring and evaluation of coaching related to each C (see Figure 14.2). After each workshop, coaches practised the application of coaching strategies related to each C in their coaching sessions with their age group squads. They also reflected on their application of such behaviours and strategies following each session as well as the responses of their players. Following three weeks of coaching sessions, coaches' levels of psychosocial efficacy were reassessed prior to commencing the educational workshop on the next C in the series. This cycle of education–application–evaluation continued until the principles, practices and behaviours associated with each of the 5Cs had been explored with academy coaches. The order of workshops was carefully considered and started with a focus on motivational and interpersonal attributes in the form of commitment and communication, followed by self-regulatory qualities represented by concentration and control. Confidence was the focus of the final workshop due to the content of the prior

Promote the 'C' in the same way that coaches would introduce and value a technical or tactical skill. Provide the rationale for the C and how important it is to football.

Role-model the 'C' through the appropriate model behaviour as a coach. Bring the meaning of C to life by demonstrating or referring to excellent examples, versus bad examples from football, or other sports.

Ownership of their learning. Involve players in decisions within the session about how they can demonstrate a 'C'; allow them options to work at their own pace and to benefit from favourite drills and practices that showcase their strengths.

Grow the 'C' by providing players with opportunities to practise the C, and then to train it in more open game situations when 'pressure' can be added to test players.

Reinforce the 'C' by praising those players who respond by demonstrating the chosen C skill or behaviour, and by making courageous decisions.

Empower peer support by encouraging players to praise each other for positive efforts related to each 'C' in order to build individual and collective confidence.

Support the supporter by acknowledging those players who praise a fellow peer, thereby closing the loop on a supportive peer climate around each of the 'C's.

Self-Review. Check-in with players on their levels of the 'C' and empower them to keep working hard; use monitors to review collective efforts, and apply self-reflection and learning points at the end of the session.

Figure 14.2 Guidelines for making PROGRESS with the 5Cs in coaching (adapted from Harwood and Anderson, 2015).

workshops supporting many of the principles that would further underpin the development of self-efficacy in players (Bandura, 1977).

With respect to assessing the outcomes of the 5Cs coaching efficacy program, the study reported not only the quantitative single-case journeys of coaches, but also their continuous perceptions of their squad's psychosocial responses and qualitative social validation data from post-program interviews (Harwood, 2008). Overall, positive increases in psychosocial coaching efficacy were reported by coaches in several areas with the 'communication' and 'commitment' coaching phases being particularly influential on the confidence of coaches. Interestingly, after coaches implemented their learning from the communication workshop in subsequent coaching sessions, a number of coaches not only reported higher communication coaching efficacy but also enhanced beliefs in influencing players' concentration, control and confidence-related behaviour. In other words, the influence of a C-related education and practice phase was not limited solely to the target 'C' under attention. Crossover effects were evident. Coaches' quantitative perceptions of their squad's 5C responses reinforced a similar message, in that they perceived their players to demonstrate improved levels of commitment, concentration, self-control and confidence-related behaviour when they spent time understanding the value of communication and were practising communicating better with others. Through the social validation data captured in the study, one coach stated:

> I think communication has been the biggest improvement personally for this age group. We gave them silent drills; we gave them drills where only one player could communicate; and drills where everybody communicated but at certain levels. I can see a big improvement in 5 of our players. I hear positive communication – 'well done that was a great pass, that was' and I hear encouragement – 'don't worry about that pass, you'll get it better'. It's good to see a 9-year-old coming out with things like that.
>
> (p. 126)

However, despite reporting improvements in process knowledge and 'know how' (Gould et al., 1999), coaches in the program also cited difficulties and uncertainty in implementing the more advanced control and concentration-related coaching elements discussed in educational sessions. This reinforced how coaches needed time to develop their confidence in integrating basic 'in session' strategies around the 5Cs before considering more advanced practices. A further coach in the study noted:

> My knowledge of these 5C areas was very, very limited and having gone through the sessions, I've learnt a lot more. Now I'm focusing more on these qualities in sessions and really putting the point across as opposed to just being general ... and I can see the development in the lads.
>
> (p. 126)

Summarising this specific program of work, several elements of the intervention may have served as important sources of coaching efficacy information for coaches (Chase & Martin, 2011). First, the continuous bouts of education and practice during the season may have helped coaches to attain more mastery experiences, particularly given the time for coaches to plan and prepare each session. Second, coaches reflected on each session and such a process may have helped them to reconsider or reinforce ideas and strategies from which to garner enhanced beliefs. Third, the intervention involved prolonged engagement with a supervisory coach educator/consultant in a group setting with age-group coaches at the same academy. This may have fostered a greater sense of social and peer support (e.g. we are in this program together for the good of our players), an important factor in the coaching efficacy model (Feltz et al., 1999). Finally, the general congruence between self-reported coaching efficacy related to the 5Cs and the coach's perceptions of their squads' behaviour in sessions suggests that coaches were positively buoyed by the responses of their charges. The perceived skill levels of athletes is believed to be further source of coaching efficacy (Feltz et al., 1999) and, when coaches notice their players developing specific (psychosocial) skills, they may make internal stable attributions for such improvements in their charges. Such attributions to their own personal coaching strategy may serve to strengthen beliefs in their work.

Implications for future research

As noted earlier, traditional coaching efficacy research in sport psychology has largely focused on examinations of the coaching efficacy model in different populations (particularly North American high school and collegiate coaches). By employing the CES to yield a general broad understanding of coaching efficacy, antecedents and outcomes of coaching efficacy beliefs have been the main targets of such research. When considering the purely psychological and social roles of a coach for a moment, few studies (if any, beyond Harwood, 2008) have gone beyond general quantitative assessments of motivation and character-building efficacy; nor have studies examined more situation or context-specific coaching efficacy vis-à-vis influencing psychosocial outcomes (e.g. coaching session, during vs post-match behaviour). Chase and Martin (2011) note that future research in coaching efficacy should consider the different developmental levels of sport (e.g. recreational, developmental, performance, elite) where the demands placed on the coach and the athlete mean that coaching roles and responsibilities change. The sources, efficacy dimensions and outcomes of coaching efficacy may be highly specific to their coaching context (Chase & Martin, 2011) (e.g. recruitment efficacy; managerial efficacy for elite level coaches).

Beyond the attention to technical and game strategy efficacy, this chapter has specified a focus on psychosocial issues because there has been much greater attention to the importance of athlete psychosocial development in recent years (Camiré et al., 2011; Strachan, Côté & Deakin, 2011; Jones & Lavallee, 2009). Indeed, in drawing from Lerner et al.'s (2000) 6Cs of PYD, Côté and Gilbert (2009) define coaching expertise as the consistent application of sport specific, interpersonal and intrapersonal knowledge to improve athletes' competence, confidence, connection and character (their 4Cs) in specific coaching contexts (p. 316). Although it is patently obvious that there are a number of models promoting psychosocial constructs beginning with the letter 'C', the key issue here is how much coaches truly have the confidence and belief in influencing such psychosocial factors. Indeed, how much do coaches actually perceive this to be their role, beyond the more traditional technical, tactical and psychological performance-based duties?

Recently, Johnston et al., (2013) explored the psychosocial assets that were perceived to be relevant to personal and talent development in the context of youth swimming. Seventeen different assets emerged through content analysis and expert validation, grouped within five higher order categories of self-perceptions, behavioural skills, social skills, approach characteristics, and emotional competence. A further quantitative investigation (Johnston, 2014) revealed that coaches and parents both placed greater value on the more intrapersonal assets that were contained within the self-perceptions, approach characteristics and behavioural skills groups, while the interpersonal assets contained within the social skills and emotional competence groups appeared to receive lesser value. Furthermore, self-reported levels of behavioural attention paid to developing these assets by coaches and parents were significantly lower than the cognitive value placed on them. Such findings suggest that, although coaches may appear to place value in assets associated with PYD outcomes, when it comes to matters of priority in sport, some assets may be more compromised than others.

An implication for future research therefore lies in a continued fine-grained approach to investigating psychosocial coaching efficacies through a wider range of sports. Harwood's (2008) consulting and applied research in football targeted education, coaching and session management strategies, as well as reinforcement techniques that would facilitate positive intrapersonal and interpersonal behaviour in players. Beyond the 5Cs, other athlete competencies may include conflict resolution, negotiation, discipline, organisation, self-appraisal, and caring/connection, which may be developed through different sport experiences. How much do coaches possess confidence in helping athletes to develop these psychosocial attributes and skills through their interactions and contextual involvement? Although research questions such as this make sense for coaches in development and recreation-focused sport programs, it is at the more performance-based end of the coaching spectrum where research such as this carries more curious appeal. Elite performance coaches may ask questions such as 'Is my job to produce a fine young man/woman, or a fine young athlete?' 'Where do I find the time and the skills to produce both?' Although these are perhaps matters of coaching philosophy, organisational values and commercial mandates, where a coach or a sport system values psychosocial outcomes in young athletes, research is required to understand (a) from what sources coaches have gained coaching efficacy for achieving such outcomes? and/or (b) how can coaching efficacy be enhanced to facilitate such psychosocial development in athletes?

From a methodological perspective, the CES (and its variations) is valuable as an empirically validated assessment tool, and perhaps more longitudinal (as opposed to cross-sectional) intervention research could offer greater insight into the development of motivation and character-building efficacies – the most psychosocial dimensions of the scale. Indeed, although a strength of the Harwood (2008) study was the specific and sustained attention to psychosocial coaching efficacy in training, the research was limited by its use of measures that had not undergone any psychometric testing. Future research may seek to conduct a 5Cs intervention with coaches but employ relevant dimensions of the CES to determine whether motivation and character-building efficacy develop. Further, in line with Boardley et al.'s (2008) method, researchers should assess athlete improvements in psychosocial behaviour or competency (see Harwood, Barker & Anderson, 2016) and request athlete evaluations of their coach's ability or influence to develop such qualities. Additionally, beyond group-based, pre/ post interventions and large-scale quantitative research designs, researchers will extend applied knowledge by considering single-case design methods that allow for individual scrutiny of coaches' experiences and development journeys. This endeavour might also be facilitated by considering how Bandura's (1997) micro-level approach to measurement can be applied beyond the generic dimensions of the CES. At present, the CES appears to measure 'level' of coaching efficacy in rather broad subcomponents, and does not tap into 'strength' of efficacy on specific coaching tasks or roles in specific contexts (i.e. training, competition, post-competition). Finally, greater qualitative research may also yield much needed practical knowledge on how certain coaches have built confidence in influencing psychosocial outcomes, with recent research offering some initial insights into this process (see Camiré et al., 2011; Gould, Collins, Lauer & Chung, 2007).

Implications for applied practice

When it comes to enhancing coaching efficacy for psychosocial development, the responsibilities lie not only with the coach, but with national governing bodies and organisations in terms of providing a supportive climate for coach education and athlete personal development. A key premise of positive youth development in sport is the provision of external assets (i.e. coaches and parents of athletes) to influence intrapersonal and interpersonal assets though positive interactions and support. However, research suggests that, although many coaches acknowledge the value of psychosocial development, there remains a lack of understanding as to how to integrate this developmental objective into their coaching style and programmes. Lacroix, Camiré and Trudel (2008) interviewed 16 high school coaches and revealed that, even though coaches could generally present an ideal representation of what school sports should be, they were often unable to provide concrete examples of activities and methods that they employ to foster youth development. Allied with the behavioural gap between perceived asset value and reported asset attention noted by Johnston (2014), McCallister, Blinde and Weiss (2000) also found inconsistencies between youth sport coaches' stated philosophies and the actual implementation of these philosophies.

Past research has noted that coaches benefit from applied knowledge and 'know how' as they seek to become comfortable with processes of integration that help them to overcome uncertainty (Gould et al., 1999; Harwood, 2008). Therefore, any program designed to enhance psychosocial coaching efficacy should be empowering in terms of educational content, strong on user-friendly ideas and strategies, and high on consultant support. Following the PROGRESS directives employed in Harwood's (2008) study, psychosocial coach education and support might consider (a) helping coaches understand the definition and principles of a specific psychosocial construct, (b) demonstrating how they can convey the principles to young athletes through modelling and use of real world examples, (c) integrating behavioural strategies, conditions and reinforcement schemes that foster the value of a psychosocial construct in athletes, and (d) encouraging reflective practice in coaches and self-reflection in athletes. In line with Fraser-Thomas and colleagues' (2005) focus on a coherent and supportive environment, such work with coaches should not exist in a vacuum. Allied initiatives with parents and other stakeholders in the sport organisation (that reinforce the same value messages) are important in creating a community of practice around the development of relevant psychosocial competencies. In conclusion, coaching efficacy is an important contemporary construct in the psychology of coaching; there is a great deal of opportunity and currency for applied researchers to consider the mechanics of psychosocial coaching efficacy, and the importance of innovative interventions that may enhance both the self-belief of coaches and the personal development of athletes.

Note

1 Loughborough University, UK

References

Bandura, A. (1977). Self-efficacy: Toward a unified theory of behavioral change. *Psychological Review, 84*, 191–215.

Bandura, A. (1997). *Self-efficacy: The exercise of control*. New York: W. H. Freeman.

Barker, J. B., McCarthy, P. J., Jones, M. V. & Moran, A. (2011). *Single-case research methods in sport and exercise psychology*. London: Routledge.

Benson, P. L. (1997). *All kids are our kids: What communities must do to raise caring and responsible children and adolescents*. San Francisco: Jossey-Bass.

Boardley, I. D., Kavussanu, M. & Ring, C. (2008). Athletes' perceptions of coaching effectiveness and athlete-related outcomes in rugby union: An investigation based on the coaching efficacy model. *The Sport Psychologist, 22*, 269–287

Bronfenbrenner, U. (1999). Environments in developmental perspective: Theoretical and operational models. In S. L. Friedman & T. D. Wachs (Eds.), *Measuring environment across the life span: Emerging methods and concepts* (pp. 3–28). Washington, DC: American Psychological Association.

Camiré, M., Forneris, T., Trudel, P. & Bernard, D. (2011). Strategies for helping coaches facilitate positive youth development through sport. *Journal of Sport Psychology in Action, 2*, 92–99.

Campbell, T., & Sullivan, P (2005). The effect of a standardized coaching education program on the efficacy of novice coaches. *Avante, 11*, 38–45.

Chase, M. A., & Martin, E. (2012). Coaching efficacy beliefs. In J. Dennison, P. Potrac & W. Gilbert (Eds.), *Handbook of Sports Coaching*. London: Routledge.

Côté, J., & Gilbert, W. (2009). An integrative definition of coaching effectiveness and expertise. *International Journal of Sports Science and Coaching, 4*(3), 307–323.

Deci, E. L. & Ryan, R. M. (1985). *Intrinsic motivation and self-determination in human behavior*. New York: Plenum Press.

Denham, C. H., & Michael, J. J. (1981). Teacher sense of efficacy: A definition of the construct and a model for further research. *Educational Research Quarterly, 5*, 39–63.

Feltz, D. L., Chase, M. A., Moritz, S. A. & Sullivan. P. J. (1999). A conceptual model of coaching efficacy: Preliminary investigation and instrument development. *Journal of Educational Psychology, 91*, 765–776.

Fraser-Thomas, J., Côté, J. & Deakin, J. (2005). Youth sport programs: An avenue to foster positive youth development. *Physical Education and Sport Pedagogy, 10*, 19–40.

Fung, L. (2002). Task familiarity and task efficacy: A study of sports coaches. *Perceptual and Motor Skills, 95*, 367–372.

Gould, D., Collins, K., Lauer, L. & Chung, Y. (2007). Coaching life skills through football: A study of award winning high school coaches. *Journal of Applied Sport Psychology, 19,* 16–37.

Gould, D., Damarjian, N. & Medbery, R. (1999). An examination of mental skills training in junior tennis coaches. *The Sport Psychologist, 13,* 127–143.

Harwood, C. G. (2008). Developmental consulting in a professional football academy: The 5Cs coaching efficacy program, *The Sport Psychologist, 22,* 109–133.

Harwood, C. G., & Anderson, R., (2015). *Coaching psychological skills in youth football: Developing the 5Cs.* London: Bennion-Kearney.

Harwood, C. G., Barker, J. B. & Anderson, R. (2016). Psychosocial development in youth soccer players: Assessing the effectiveness of the 5Cs intervention program. *The Sport Psychologist, 29,* 319–334.

Holt, N. L., & Dunn, J. G. H. (2004). Toward a grounded theory of the psychosocial competencies and environmental conditions associated with soccer success. *Journal of Applied Sport Psychology, 16,* 199–219.

Johnston, J. (2014). Positive youth development in swimming: The roles of coaches and parents. Unpublished manuscript. School of Sport, Exercise and Health Sciences, Loughborough University, Loughborough, UK.

Johnston, J., Harwood, C. & Minniti, A. M. (2013). Positive youth development in swimming: Clarification and consensus of key psychosocial assets. *Journal of Applied Sport Psychology, 25,* 392–411.

Jones, M. I., & Lavallee, D. (2009). Exploring the life skills needs of British adolescent athletes. *Psychology of Sport and Exercise, 10,* 159–167.

Kavussanu, M., Boardley, I. D., Jutkiewicz, N., Vincent, S. & Ring, C. (2008). Coaching efficacy and coaching effectiveness: Examining their predictors and comparing coaches' and athletes' reports. *The Sport Psychologist, 22,* 383–404.

Lacroix, C., Camiré, M. & Trudel, P. (2008). High school coaches' characteristics and their perspectives on the purpose of school sport participation. *International Journal of Coaching Science, 2,* 23–42.

Lee, K. S., Malete, L. & Feltz, D. L. (2002). The strength of coaching efficacy between certified and noncertified Singapore coaches. *International Journal of Applied Sports Sciences, 14,* 55–67.

Lerner, R. M., Fisher, C. B. & Weinberg, R. A. (2000). Toward a science for and of the people: Promoting civil society through the application of developmental science. *Child Development, 71,* 11–20.

Malete, L., & Feltz, D. L. (2000). The effect of a coaching education program on coaching efficacy. *The Sport Psychologist, 14,* 410–417.

Malete, L. & Sullivan, P. J. (2009). Sources of coaching efficacy in coaches in Botswana. *International Journal of Coaching Science, 3,* 17–28.

Marback, T. L., Short, S. E., Short, M. W. & Sullivan, P. J. (2005). Coaching confidence: An exploratory investigation of sources and gender differences. *Journal of Sport Behavior, 28,* 18–34.

McCallister, S. G., Blinde, E. M. & Weiss, W. M. (2000). Teaching values and implementing philosophies: Dilemmas of the coach. *Physical Educator, 57,* 35–45.

Myers, N. D., Chase, M. A., Pierce, S. W. & Martin, E. (2011). Coaching efficacy and exploratory structural modeling: A substantive-methodological synergy. *Journal of Sport and Exercise Psychology, 33,* 779–806.

Myers, N. D., Feltz, D. L., Chase, M. A., Reckase, M. D. & Hancock, G. R. (2008). The Coaching Efficacy Scale II – High School Teams. *Educational and Psychological Measurement, 68,* 1059–1076.

Myers, N. D., Vargas-Tonsing, T. M. & Feltz, D. L. (2005). Coaching efficacy in collegiate coaches: Sources, coaching behavior, and team variables. *Psychology of Sport and Exercise, 6,* 129–143.

Nicholls, J. G. (1989). *The competitive ethos and democratic education.* Cambridge, MA: Harvard University Press.

Nideffer, R. M., & Sharpe, R. (1978). *Attention control training.* New York: Wyden Books.

Schulman, S., & Davies, T. (2007). *Evidence of the impact of the 'Youth Development Model' on outcomes for young people – A literature review.* London: The National Youth Agency: Information and Research.

Seefeldt, V., & Brown, E. (1990). *Program for Athletic Coach Education (PACE).* Carmel, IN: Benchmark Press:

Smith, R. E., & Johnson, J. (1990). An organizational empowerment approach to consultation in professional baseball. *The Sport Psychologist, 4,* 347–357.

Smith, R. E., & Smoll, F. L. (1997). Coaching the coaches: Youth sports as a scientific and applied behavioral setting. *Current Directions in Psychological Science, 6,* 16–21.

Smith, R. E., Smoll, F. L. & Hunt, E. B. (1977). A system for the behavioral assessment of athletic coaches. *Research Quarterly, 48,* 401–407.

Strachan, L., Côté, J. & Deakin, J. (2011). A new view: Exploring positive youth development in elite sport contexts. *Qualitative Research in Sport, Exercise and Health, 3,* 9–32.

Sullivan, P. J., & Kent, A. (2003). Coaching efficacy as a predictor of leadership style in intercollegiate athletics. *Journal of Applied Sport Psychology, 15,* 1–11.

Thelwell, R., Greenlees, I. & Weston, N. (2006). Using psychological skills training to develop soccer performance. *Journal of Applied Sport Psychology, 18,* 254–270.

Vargas-Tonsing, T. M., Warners, A. L. & Feltz, D. L. (2003). The predictability of coaching efficacy on team efficacy and player efficacy in volleyball. *Journal of Sport Behavior, 26,* 396–407.

Vella, S., Oades, L. & Crowe, T. (2011). The role of the coach in facilitating positive youth development: Moving from theory to practice. *Journal of Applied Sport Psychology, 23,* 33–48.

15 Antecedents and impacts of effective and inspirational coach communication

Matthew J. Smith,[1] *Sean G. Figgins*[1] *and Christopher N. Sellars*[2]

Introduction

Communication is key to effective coaching (La Voi, 2007). If effectively utilised, communication can have positive impacts on the interaction between coaches and athletes in individual and/or team contexts, by aiding coaches to provide technical and tactical instruction, build positive working relationships, and offer support and encouragement to their athletes. Bloom, Schinke and Salmela (1997) found that the ability to communicate effectively was a distinguishing characteristic of elite coaches. While communication occurs in many forms (verbal, non-verbal) and is clearly two-way and interactional, researchers (Trudel & Côté, 1994; Trudel, Côté & Bernard, 1996) found coaches communicate with athletes only a small percentage of total coaching time. Thus, coaches need to consider how they might utilise the time spent communicating with athletes effectively in order to have the greatest impact possible.

This chapter outlines the important role of communication in coaching athletes, and considers how a coach can communicate effectively, with a specific focus on how coaches can use their communications to inspire their athletes. Anecdotally, there are many examples of athletes who report being inspired in their sport, with Arthur, Hardy and Woodman (2012) highlighting how 'the sporting arena is replete with examples and anecdotes of inspirational coaches that have led teams to success' (p. 1). Recent research (e.g. Thrash & Elliot, 2003; Thrash, Elliot, Maruskin & Cassidy, 2010) has shown that inspiration can be activated, manipulated, and can have a major effect on important life outcomes. Thus, in this chapter, we consider how coaches can communicate in a way that inspires athletes, as well as considering the consequences of such inspirational communication. We first review research that has used different theoretical underpinnings and various methodological approaches to examine the way a coach might communicate in an effective manner. We then provide a rationale for specifically investigating the concept of inspiring athletes in a coaching context which builds on the existing coaching and leadership literature. Following this, we draw on theory from organisational and social psychology literature that has examined the concept of inspiration, before reviewing research literature that has examined how coaches might communicate in a way that has an inspirational impact on their athletes. Finally, we consider implications for future research and provide suggestions for applied practice.

Key terms

Everything a coach does or says in their interactions with athletes can be considered as communication (La Voi, 2007). This can include verbal communication, in terms of the words spoken by a coach, and non-verbal communication, such as the coach's actions or body language. *Effective* communication would refer to interactions with athletes that result in positive outcomes such as sport skill development, increased motivation, and enhanced levels of performance. Inspiration is proposed to be a highly emotive state in which an individual can move beyond the mundane to the extraordinary by transcending their everyday experiences and limitations (Thrash, Moldovan, Oleynick & Maruskin 2014). Specifically, inspiration is associated with 'illumination' or 'insight', whereby illumination refers to an epistemic event in which one hears or apprehends something that is deeply important. Furthermore, Thrash and Elliot (2003) proposed a tripartite conceptualisation of inspiration, characterised by transcendence, evocation, and approach motivation, which can be applied to the way a coach communicates and interacts with athletes. Transcendence refers to how inspiration orients people toward something that is better than their normal concerns so that they see better possibilities; evocation refers to how inspiration is evoked by an external stimulus, such as a person or idea; and approach motivation refers to the desire to express that which is newly apprehended, such as an athlete being compelled to actualise their new vision or idea. Thus, in this chapter, we consider how coaches might communicate in a way that evokes inspiration in their athletes.

Review of the literature

Effective coach communication

Preferences for coach communication

Researchers examining the effective communication of coaches have considered athlete preferences for coach communication. For example, Aly (2014) surveyed 14 head coaches and 208 college athletes about their perceptions of coach communication, such as on the development of communication, communication styles and timing. The results revealed a variety of findings concerning coach communication in a variety of different contexts and situations. For example, the male coaches in the study reported that their communication was much more verbal whereas athletes felt that their male coach's communication style was much more non-verbal. Aly highlighted that the implications of these findings are that athletes are being influenced by aspects of their coaches' communication of which the coaches themselves are unaware. In terms of athlete preferences, Aly found gender differences in their preferences for the coach getting a message across quickly during a game. Male participants reported their coach might use verbal or visual communication, but female athletes reported a preference for visual communication, such as signs or gestures.

Observation of coaches' communication strategies

Trudel and Côté (1994) summarised research evidence concerning the communication of coaches in training sessions. The authors estimated athletes listened to instructions 6 per cent of the time and received feedback from coaches for approximately 4 per cent of the time. In a further study using observational methods to examine the behaviours of ice hockey coaches, Trudel, Côté and Bernard (1996) found coaches on average spent 11 per cent of the time on instructional behaviours, with over 50 per cent of the time on observing without communication. Erickson, Côté, Hollenstein and Deakin (2011) observed two synchronised swimming teams, and assessed the interactions between coaches and athletes in training sessions. Erickson et al. found that the more successful team had more consistent patterns of interactions, with coaches in this team more effectively pairing technical instruction with positive reinforcement.

Observational methods have also been used to examine the coaching and communication of expert coaches. Tharp and Gallimore (1976) used systematic observation to analyse the coaching behaviours of John Wooden, a legendary college basketball coach. The researchers observed Wooden's practice sessions, and used a formal observational tool to record and code the coaching behaviours exhibited. In a subsequent study, Gallimore and Tharp (2004) summarised how Wooden's verbal communications during practice were 'short, punctuated, and numerous. There were no lectures, no extended harangues' (p. 120). In another observation study, Becker and Wrisberg (2008) observed the practice behaviours of Pat Summit. Becker and Wrisberg described Summit as 'the winningest collegiate basketball coach in NCAA Division I history' (p. 198). Throughout the season, Summitt's verbal and nonverbal behaviours were video-recorded during six practices. After coding the behaviours, the results revealed that the single most common action was the communication of instructions, which happened 48 per cent of the time, followed by praise, which was displayed 14 per cent of the time. Thus, as the majority of Summit's actions involved instruction, Becker and Wrisberg suggest coaches might focus their communication on this element in practice, as this is arguably a clear indicator of expert coaching. Summitt was also seen to be able to communicate in a way that provided an equal distribution of feedback to both the starters and non-starters on her teams.

Coaches' perspectives of effective communication

Early research examining effective coach communication used retrospective interviews to examine coaches' perspectives and experiences. For instance, Bloom, Schinke and Salmela (1997) interviewed expert basketball coaches, and found that the communication styles of the coaches changed as their coaching careers developed through to elite level. Specifically, coaches reported using a more autocratic style with younger athletes, but this changed to a two-way communication style when they worked with elite international athletes. In addition, Bloom and Salmela (2000) interviewed 16 high level coaches from a range of sports to investigate the coaches' perceptions of their own effective personal characteristics. The results of this study revealed how expert coaches perceived that the ability to communicate effectively is a key part of their role. For instance, when communicating information that players do not wish to hear, the coaches discussed the importance of communicating in a way that demonstrates empathy to their players. This suggests that effective communication includes consideration of what is being communicated and why; subsequently, coaches adapt communication, content and delivery accordingly. Vallee and Bloom (2005) interviewed five Canadian female university coaches in seeking to understand how coaches build successful athletic development programmes. Vallee and Bloom found that the coaches possessed various personal attributes enabling them to display appropriate leadership behaviours, including the way they communicate, that best results in players buying into the vision the coach espouses.

Athletes' perspectives of effective coach communication

In recent years, researchers have sought to understand effective coach communication from the athletes' perspective. For example, Becker (2009) conducted interviews with elite athletes to examine their perceptions of great coaching. Becker found a variety of aspects that referred to communication in the categorisation of the athletes' experiences of elite coaching. Participants reported that coaches communicated in a way that demonstrated passion, and that coaches communicated in an emotional way in game situations, but this emotion was controlled. Participants also described coaches creating an environment that encouraged one-on-one communication, with experienced coaches described as being not only open to conversation, but also good listeners. In addition, participants reported coaches communicating in a variety of ways, such as offering basic performance information, explaining player roles, and articulating a common team vision. Participants highlighted the quality of coaches' communication as being clear, consistent, and honest. Effective communication was seen as being in a manner that was appropriate and positive, and athletes also discussed how their coaches' communication was well timed, with high-quality communication described as the coaches knowing what to say and, also, when to say it.

Researchers have also investigated the communication of coaches in prematch team talks, using experimental (e.g. Gonzalez, Metzler & Newton, 2011; Vargas-Tonsing & Bartholomew, 2006) and qualitative (e.g. Breakey, Jones, Cunningham & Holt, 2009; Vargas & Short, 2011) methods. Vargas-Tonsing and Bartholomew (2006) asked participants to imagine they were participating in a championship game, and then they listened to one of three audio-recorded speeches created by the authors. Findings revealed that the speech containing emotional messages enhanced the participants' feelings of team efficacy compared to the speeches that had either uniform and field information, or game strategy information. Subsequently, Vargas-Tonsing and Guan (2007) considered whether the competitive setting was the reason for the differences in athletes' preferences for pre-game speech content. Participants were given examples of informational content (e.g. game plans, technique information) and emotional content (e.g. arousing phrases, appeals to emotions such as pride or anger) and were asked to describe the situation in which they would prefer to hear such content. The results showed that participants preferred more emotional speeches before a championship game, when competing against a higher-ranked opponent, and when they were considered an underdog. Alternatively, more informational speeches were preferred when competing against an opponent against whom they had narrowly lost on a previous occasion, or when they were competing against an unknown opponent.

Using qualitative methods, Vargas and Short (2011) surveyed elite soccer players concerning their perceptions of their managers' pre-game speeches. Participants were asked to answer seven questions after games to assess features of their managers' speeches, their preferences for these speeches, and perceptions of how speeches impacted upon them. Participants reported liking the speeches, and reported impacts that included greater focus, arousal levels, and performance. Breakey et al. (2009) used a case-study methodology to investigate the speeches of the male manager of a successful Canadian university women's hockey team. Twenty female hockey players from the team were each interviewed twice, in the days following separate home games. Participants identified a number of positively and negatively perceived aspects of the manager's speech. Positive aspects included when the manager conveyed genuine emotion in his voice, when short, meaningful messages were provided, and when the manager referred to team values. Negatively perceived aspects included when players disagreed with what the manager was saying, and when information was omitted, or players were surprised with unexpected information. The above focus on effective communication is included here as it is argued that it is an important consideration when considering how coach communication can inspire athletes. We will now explore the notion of inspiration and how effective communication can contribute to it.

Leadership theory and effective coach communication

Over the last decade, much research that has considered the impact of coach behaviours on athlete outcomes has been underpinned by transformational leadership theory (Bass, 1985). Researchers have found that, if coaches act in a transformational way, then this will result in a range of positive athlete outcomes, including individual outcomes such as extra effort (Rowold, 2006), and team outcomes such as greater task cohesion (Callow, Smith, Hardy, Arthur & Hardy, 2009). However, this research is not without its limitations. Indeed, in a recent critique of leadership research, van Knippenberg & Sitkin (2013) highlight confusion surrounding the way terms such as transformational, inspirational and charismatic are used interchangeably, even though these terms are proposed to be distinct constructs (e.g. Barbuto, 1997). To further our understanding of effective leadership (and coaching), Van Knippenberg and Sitkin suggested that researchers should examine specific elements of charismatic–transformational leadership theory, in order to explain further the mechanisms through which leaders can impact on their athletes.

Given that the ability to inspire is proposed to be at the heart of effective leadership (Clemens & Mayer, 1999), exploring inspiration in the sport-leadership context (e.g. coaching) is of great potential benefit to coaches and sport psychology researchers. To highlight, inspiration is considered to be central to transformational leadership. Indeed, Bass, Avolio, Jung & Berson (2003) suggest that a transformational coach builds relationships with followers based on personal, emotional, and *inspirational* exchanges, with the intention of developing followers to their fullest potential, and Yukl (2006) described transformational leadership as 'inspiring, developing, and empowering followers' (p. 287). However, despite the strong emphasis on leaders being the source of inspiration for followers, to date, there is little knowledge on the process by which transformational leaders inspire others (Mio, Riggio, Levin & Reese, 2005). Considering the links between inspiration and leadership theory, and in line with van Knippenberg and Sitkin's contentions, it appears that one way to further enhance the leadership literature is to understand more fully the concept of inspiration, and to consider how coaches communicate in a way that inspires athletes, and, in turn, the effects inspiration has on athletes.

Inspiration

In a study asking 332,860 managers, peers, and subordinates what skills have the greatest impact on a leader's success, Zenger and Folkman (2014) found that inspiring and motivating others was the most highly rated leadership skill. Examination of terms used to define different theories of effective leadership demonstrates that inspiration has been synonymous with leadership for many years (Searle & Hanrahan, 2011). For instance, Clemens and Mayer (1999) proposed motivation, inspiration, sensitivity and communication to be integral facets of effective leadership.

Tripartite Conceptualisation

Research in the social psychology domain has focussed on the conceptualisation of inspiration as a distinct psychological process. Thrash and Elliot (2003) proposed a tripartite conceptualisation of inspiration, which specifies the three core characteristics of the state of inspiration, which are sufficient to distinguish inspiration from other states. First, evocation relates to how inspiration is evoked and unwilled – that is, when an individual is inspired by something outside of the self (e.g. a coach communicating with an athlete regarding their future potential). Second, transcendence refers to how an individual (e.g. an athlete) has been oriented towards something that surpasses their normal concerns, making them aware of new or better possibilities (e.g. future potential in their sport). Third, approach motivation refers to an individual being compelled to express that which is newly apprehended, such as an athlete being compelled to actualise their new vision or idea (e.g. by dedicating more time or effort into their training).

Component Processes

While the tripartite conceptualisation specifies three core characteristics of the state of inspiration, Thrash and Elliott (2004) considered how the conceptualisation explains the distinct processes of an episode of inspiration. Thrash and Elliott highlighted how inspiration is associated with 'illumination' or 'insight', suggesting that illumination is an epistemic event in which one hears or apprehends something that is deeply important, and defining illumination as the mechanism that exerts a press on the individual to express or actualise what has been apprehended. Thus, transmission involves two processes: an illuminating trigger object; and a target object towards which the inspiring qualities are extended. Using this description, a coach might provide the illuminating trigger (through words or actions) which leads to the athlete being inspired to action (e.g. training harder to achieve their newfound goals). Furthermore, Thrash and Elliott (2004) describe two component processes of being inspired. Being 'inspired by' involves appreciating and accommodating the value of the evocative object (in this case, the words or actions of the coach). Being 'inspired to' involves motivation to transmit the qualities exemplified by the evocative object. This conceptualisation can be used to further explain the process through which coaches inspire their performers to achieve outcomes such as greater levels of commitment and motivation.

Transmission Model

In addition to conceptualising inspiration in terms of core characteristics and component processes, Thrash, Moldovan, Fuller and Dombrowski (2014), suggest that inspiration might be conceptualised in terms of the function it serves. Thrash et al. suggest how intrinsically valued qualities presented by an evocative stimulus object induce inspiration, which, subsequently, motivates the inspired individual to extend the intrinsically valued qualities to a new object. In particular, the way the sources of inspiration produce changes in behaviour and performance may be explained by the three forms of transmission (see Thrash, Moldovan, Fuller et al., 2014). These are *replication*, where one is inspired by the qualities of a pre-existing object (e.g. dedication to improvement displayed by a coach) in the environment and seeks to reproduce these qualities in a new object (e.g. showing greater dedication to one's own training and development); *actualisation*, which refers to the appreciation of a compelling seminal idea which enters awareness during a moment of insight (e.g. a leader outlining an athlete's future potential) and, as such, the individual is energised (e.g. athletes experience an increase in motivation and set new goals in order to reach their potential) by the possibility of bringing the idea into fruition; and *expression*, whereby actualisation is facilitated by a compelling idea which is already well formed when it enters awareness (e.g. specific technical or tactical advice provided in order to counter a difficult situation) and is acted upon immediately (Thrash, Moldovan, Oleynick et al., 2014). Taking this into account, it appears there would be great value in more fully understanding how coaches might evoke an experience of inspiration in athletes.

Inspiration in non-sport settings: antecedents and consequences

A limited number of studies have examined the construct of inspiration in organisational settings. Hart (1998) provided the first empirical study of inspiration, analysing 70 in-depth interviews that revealed four main phenomenological characteristics of inspiration: having a sense of connection, being open and receptive, experiencing clarity, and energy. Lockwood and Kunda (1999) investigated the antecedents of inspiration, and found that, when participants were exposed to high-achieving role models, this led participants to adopt more positive self-conceptions and inspired them to set higher aspirations. In addition, Thrash and Elliot (2003) found the personality characteristics/dispositions of openness to experience, positive affect, optimism, self-esteem, work mastery and creativity to be antecedents of inspiration. In a further set of studies, Thrash and Elliot (2004) found evidence that inspiration is triggered for individuals who are able to put aside habitual patterns of thought and engage in a receptive way to the stimulus environment.

Research has also examined the consequences of inspiration. Within the social psychology literature, researchers have shown inspiration to be associated with a range of positive outcomes, including increased self-determination and work-mastery motivation (Thrash & Elliot, 2003), improved well-being (Thrash, Elliot et al., 2010), increased goal progress (Milyavskaya, Ianakieva, Foxen-Craft, Colantuoni & Koestner, 2012), and increased productivity (Thrash & Elliot, 2004). For example, Thrash, Maruskin et al. (2010) examined the role of inspiration in the actualisation of creative ideas (the writing process) and found evidence that inspiration enhanced well-being, as well as enhancing a range of variables including creativity, productivity, and efficiency. Given such beneficial consequences of inspiration in contexts where individuals' perceive there to be high intrinsic value (e.g. potential for self-growth), it is a surprise that limited research attention has been paid to how coaches might inspire athletes in sport, where individuals often compete for intrinsic reasons.

Inspiration in a sporting context

While researchers have advanced our understanding of the process of inspiration in social psychology, only a small number of studies have explored this process in a sporting context. Using a sporting stimulus, Thrash, Elliot et al. (2010) randomly assigned (non-sporting) participants to a 'Jordan' or control condition, in which they were required to watch video clips of either Michael Jordan expertly performing a series of basketball skills or a computer screen saver of abstract shapes. The results revealed that participants in the Jordan condition experienced higher levels of inspiration, which in turn enhanced a number of well-being variables, such as positive affect, life satisfaction, vitality, and self-actualisation. Using a sport-specific participant sample, Gonzalez et al. (2011) found that collegiate football players who viewed a film clip of a coach giving an inspirational speech were more inspired after viewing this footage, compared to a control clip. In the experimental condition, Gonzalez et al. used a clip from the film *Any Given Sunday* and used footage of a coach giving game instructions in the control condition. Findings revealed that participants in the experimental condition showed increased levels of inspiration to compete, play, and perform well, and also reported a rise in the emotion of dominance.

Interestingly, Gonzalez et al. found the inspirational video clip did not differentially influence athletes' levels of pleasure, arousal, intrinsic motivation, externally regulated motivation, or overall autonomous motivation relative to the control condition. The findings suggest that it is possible to influence athletes' feelings of inspiration using a video clip, but these elevated levels of inspiration do not necessarily relate to athletes' levels of motivation. Furthermore, in an elite team sport context, Smith, Young, Figgins and Arthur (in press) found limited evidence of coaches communicating in an inspiring way. Smith et al. interviewed nine professional cricketers, to examine and illustrate the leadership behaviours of their coaches. The results showed participants struggled to verbally recall instances where they were explicitly inspired by their coaches, despite having rated the coach highly on the *inspirational motivation* subscale of the leadership measure. These findings concerning inspiration suggested that, while the participants could not consciously recall being inspired by their coaches, this does not necessarily mean the coaches were not inspirational. It might not just be classic speeches or highly charismatic leaders that instil inspiration, but rather it is in the daily interactions that leaders have in which trust and loyalty are built up over time that might enable coaches to have inspirational effects.

In a further study which included the concept of inspiration, Gucciardi, Jackson, Hanton and Reid (2015) examined the motivational correlates of mental toughness, and included measures of inspiration frequency and intensity in their measures. Gucciardi et al. surveyed 347 adolescent tennis players and found inspiration frequency predicted mental toughness – that is, the tennis players who experienced inspiration on a regular basis were more likely to behave in a mentally tough manner. However, the strength of inspiration experience showed no predictive relationship with mental toughness behaviours. This finding was in contrast to the work of Thrash and Elliot, whose research in a non-sporting context found significant relationships between both the intensity and frequency dimensions of inspiration and important outcomes such as intrinsic motivation and positive affect.

Leaders'/coaches' perspectives of inspiration

While a limited number of studies have provided some evidence that leaders can provide inspiration in a sporting context, they have yet to provide a coherent body of research to explain the process of inspiring others. Searle and Hanrahan (2011) aimed to extend the research by examining the phenomenon of leaders inspiring followers in a range of contexts. In-depth interviews were conducted to investigate seven inspiring leaders from a range of contexts (e.g. CEO of high level company and Olympic level coach), to examine their personal experiences of leading to inspire others. The findings revealed five key dimensions of leading to inspire others, which included: the importance of a connection between the leader and the follower; aspects concerning the 'inspirees' (followers being inspired); the actions occurring as a result of inspiration; and the context in which inspiration took place. In line with these findings, Searle and Hanrahan proposed a model to summarise the process of inspiring others that included various active processes occurring prior to a moment of inspiration, with the primary antecedent being the connection between the leader and follower. Then the 'inspiring moment' happens, which leads to the 'inspiree' taking 'action'.

In a study conducted within the sporting context, Poynor, Arthur and Gibas (2012) aimed to understand more about coaches as a source of inspiration for athletes. Interviews were conducted with five elite soccer coaches who had experienced leading their sides either at international level, or in the English

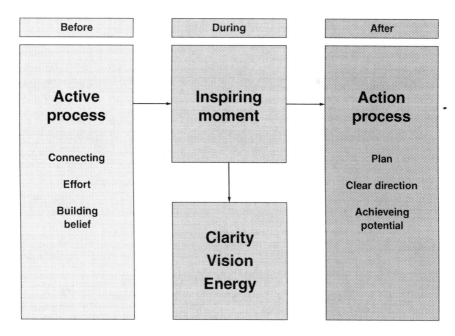

Figure 15.1 A model to show the process of inspiring others (adapted from Searle & Hanrahan, 2011).

Premier League. The results revealed seven themes of behaviours that the coaches considered to have an inspirational impact on their athletes, which were vision, communicating the vision, charisma, need for change, follower empowerment, risk taking and leader reliability (which included providing protection and pressure relief). The results appear to have some similarity and overlap with transformational leadership (Bass, 1985) and charismatic leadership (Conger & Kanungo, 1987). For example, conceptualisations of transformational leadership typically contain factors such as role modelling, articulation of a vision, empowering and developing followers (e.g. Hardy et al., 2010). However, themes emerged from the data that are not contained within typical charismatic or transformational approaches to leadership, such as providing protection, pressure relief, risk taking, and vulnerability. Other theories of leadership might explain these factors: for example, taking personal risks is often described as a core component of sacrificial leadership (e.g. Choi & Mai-Dalton, 1999; Cremer, Mayer, van Dijke, Schouten & Bardes, 2009). The results of the Poynor et al. (2012) study would appear to suggest that no one theory of leadership can fully account for the inspirational effects of leadership; rather, a combination of different theories might have to be adopted. Clearly more research is needed into this important area of inspiration and specifically the leader's role in inspiring their followers.

Athletes' perspectives of inspiration

Figgins, Smith, Sellars, Greenlees, and Knight (2016) aimed to expand on the inspiration literature by understanding the experiences of followers who have been inspired in a sporting context, as these are the only people who can actually say when and why they were inspired. In an initial data collection, 95 athletes wrote about an experience of being inspired in sport. The results identified three main sources of inspiration: (i) personal performance, thoughts, and accomplishments (e.g. producing an unexpected successful performance); (ii) interacting with and watching role-models (e.g. viewing an elite athlete's ability to perform under extreme pressure); and (iii) demonstrations of leadership (e.g. a coach's emotional half-time team talk). Demonstrations of leadership emerged as the most common and potentially potent source of inspiration (49 participants wrote about being inspired by leaders).

Building on these findings, Figgins et al. (2016) interviewed 17 athletes to understand in greater depth their experiences of being inspired by leaders. The findings revealed the athletes to be inspired by a range of leadership behaviours and actions, such as demonstrations of belief (e.g. outlining an athlete's long-term potential), providing an example to follow (e.g. displaying exceptional effort), providing opportunities to be inspired (e.g. setting up meetings with higher-level athletes), and showing the way forward (e.g. providing technical or tactical instruction to enable an athlete to understand how to improve). In addition, the results built on the earlier work of Searle and Hanrahan (2011) by shedding some light on the contexts in which inspirational leadership occurred.

Specifically, where inspiration was experienced in a range of, mainly negative, situations (e.g. following poor performance, where an athlete was uncertain regarding how to overcome difficult competitive circumstances, and conflict between an athlete and a coach), athletes experienced negative cognitions (e.g. decrease in confidence) and emotions (e.g. worry and anger). Inspirational experiences were seen to impact on athletes' awareness of their own capabilities (e.g. athletes thought they could reach a higher level of performance), lead to increased confidence and motivation, and perceptions of group dynamics (e.g. increased cohesion within the group), and subsequently drive behaviour (e.g. athletes reported increasing effort in training in order to improve).

Implications for future research

Research in the social psychology literature has provided evidence of a range of positive outcomes of being inspired, such as increased self-determination and intrinsic motivation (Thrash & Elliot, 2003), greater goal attainment and persistence (Milyavskaya et al., 2012), and improved productivity (Thrash, Maruskin et al., 2010). Given the potential benefits of being inspired, research is needed to create a greater understanding of how coaches can communicate in a way that inspires athletes. Thus, future research should aim to explain how coaches can exert an inspirational influence on their athletes. In doing this, a model of the inspirational process of leadership should be developed that has the potential to provide a framework to help direct future research examining the concept and guide applied practice. In addition, as much of the literature reported above uses retrospective recall, future researchers should consider the development of experimental studies to test the effectiveness of specific facets of communication within defined contexts.

While Searle and Hanrahan (2011) provide some suggestions concerning the process of inspiring others, there is more we need to understand about the process of inspiring athletes in a sporting context. For instance, research should aim to explain more fully the way coaches inspire athletes (e.g. how coaches specifically articulate belief in an athlete's future potential); the longer-term impacts of inspiration; and which characteristics determine the likelihood an athlete is inspired by a leader. Also, research (e.g. Searle & Harahan, 2011; Poyner, Arthur, & Gibas, 2012) to date has focussed on coaches' perspectives of providing inspirational communication; thus, further qualitative research is needed to investigate the perceptions of the athletes with regard to inspirational coach communication.

Researchers might explore different sporting contexts and use a range of methods to understand inspirational communication more fully. For example, research might examine the way a coach communicates across team and individual sports, and how inspiration impacts for athletes of different ages, genders and experience in sport. Different situational circumstances that could impact on inspiration might be explored, such as the sense of hope at the start of a season, the position in the league or morale levels during a season. In terms of methods utilised, recordings of coaches communicating to athletes might be used to stimulate recall (e.g. Mackenzie & Kerr, 2012), which might lead to more accurate recollections of inspiration occurring. In addition, diaries over a season could be used to capture inspirational moments over time, to capture further interesting details about the process of inspiring athletes. Another approach might include examining individual dyadic interactions and exploring the inspirational nuances thereof. Furthermore, much of this research is North American in origin, and future research might consider cultural differences (e.g. Gill & Kamphoff, 2009) in examining athlete perceptions of effective coach communication.

In terms of measuring inspiration, Thrash and Elliot (2003) developed and validated a trait measure of inspiration, the Inspiration Scale (IS). The IS was completed by two independent undergraduate student samples. Confirmatory factor analyses revealed the measure to consist of two internally consistent four-item factors, labelled as intensity and frequency subscales. Thrash and Elliot (2003) also reported excellent psychometric properties of the measure after finding good convergent, construct, and predictive validity. In the two studies that used measures of inspiration in a sporting context, Gucciardi et al. adapted Thrash and Elliot's measure, while Gonzalez et al. used their own three-item measure. Gucciardi and his colleagues reported adequate internal reliability estimates for inspiration intensity ($\rho = 0.90$), and inspiration frequency ($\rho = 0.91$). However, they also reported a large overlap ($r = 0.86$) between these two inspiration dimensions, and further suggested that the adolescent athletes in their study may not have been able to easily distinguish between the two inspiration components. Gonzalez et al. created a three-item measure, which included, 'I am experiencing inspiration', 'I encountered or experienced something that inspires me', and 'I feel inspired'. However, the validity of this scale is yet to be established. In summary, while a validated measure of inspiration exists (Thrash & Elliot, 2003), it was developed in a student population and may not capture the full nature of the experience of inspiration in sport (Gonzalez et al., 2011). Future research might look to develop a more suitable measure of inspiration in a sporting context. In addition, research might also consider developing a measure which captures the elements of Thrash and Elliot's (2003) tripartite conceptualisation or the transmission model.

Once we know more about how coaches can inspire athletes in different contexts, and a suitable measure of inspiration has been developed, then experimental and longitudinal designs might be utilised to identify causal relationships between inspirational coach communication and athlete-outcomes. In addition, future research might examine whether leaders can be trained to behave in a way that has an inspirational impact on their athletes.

Implications for applied practice

Our review of literature could justify various applied recommendations for coaches concerning effective communication strategies. Coaches should consider the communication preferences of their athletes (Chelladurai & Saleh,

1980), including possible gender preferences, such as men favouring verbal and visual communication, while women prefer nonverbal approaches (Aly, 2014). In order to communicate effectively, coaches should consider how they communicate messages to athletes and the appropriate timing of when to deliver messages (Becker, 2009). In team sports, the findings of Erickson et al. (2011) suggest coaches might work to develop a more consistent pattern of interactions with their athletes. In terms of delivering pre-match communication, coaches might consider adapting their communication to the situation. For example, if it is an important game, or one against a higher-ranked opponent, coaches might communicate in an emotional manner to arouse players (Vargas-Tonsing & Bartholomew, 2006; Vargas-Tonsing & Guan, 2007). At the elite level in team sports, coaches might keep their communication short and to the point (Tharp & Gallimore, 1976), and, during practice, coaches might offer more instruction, and ensure there is equality with respect to time communicating with each player (Becker & Wrisberg, 2008). In summary, key considerations for coaches include knowing their athletes and considering the context.

In terms of coaches communicating in a way that inspires their athletes, as little research has been conducted in the sporting context, it is difficult to make applied suggestions due to the lack of supporting evidence. Searle and Hanrahan's (2011) research offers some considerations for coaches, such as ensuring a positive connection between coaches and athletes to make inspiration more likely. Furthermore, researchers have found a variety of antecedents of inspiration in the social psychology literature, such positive affect, optimism, self-esteem, and for individuals who are open to experience or high in receptive engagement (Thrash & Elliot, 2003, 2004). This suggests that coaches could strive to build athletes' belief, in general, which may improve the likelihood that an athlete views their communication as inspirational. However, more research would be needed to understand the process of inspiration in sport to allow us to have confidence in making such applied suggestions concerning how coaches might communicate to inspire athletes.

Notes

1 Department of Sport and Exercise Sciences, University of Chichester, UK
2 Institute of Sport, University of Wolverhampton, UK

References

Aly, E. (2014). Communication management among athletes and coaches. *European Scientific Journal*, 3, 1857–1881.

Arthur, C. A., Hardy, L., & Woodman, T. (2012). Realising the Olympic dream: vision, support and challenge. *Reflective Practice*, *13*(3), 399–406.

Barbuto, J. E. (1997). Taking the charisma out of transformational leadership. *Journal of Social Behavior and Personality*, *12*(3), 689–697.

Bass, B. M. (1985). *Leadership and performance beyond expectations*. New York: Free Press.

Bass, B. M., Avolio, B. J., Jung, D. I. & Berson, Y. (2003). Predicting unit performance by assessing transformational and transactional leadership. *Journal of Applied Psychology*, *88*(2), 207–218.

Becker, A. (2009). It's not what they do, it's how they do it: Athlete experiences of great coaching. *International Journal of Sports Science and Coaching*, *4*(1), 93–119.

Becker, A. J., & Wrisberg, C. A. (2008). Effective coaching in action: Observations of legendary collegiate basketball coach Pat Summit. *The Sport Psychologist*, *22*(2), 197–211.

Bloom, G. A., & Salmela, J. H. (2000). Personal characteristics of expert team sport coaches. *Journal of Sport Pedagogy*, *6*, 56–76.

Bloom, G. A., Schinke, R. J. & Salmela, J. H. (1997). The development of communication skills by elite basketball coaches. *Coaching and Sport Science Journal*, *2*(3), 3–10.

Breakey, C., Jones, M., Cunningham, C. T. & Holt, N. (2009). Female athletes' perceptions of a coach's speeches. *International Journal of Sports Science and Coaching*, *4*, 489–504.

Callow, N., Smith, M. J., Hardy, L., Arthur, C. A. & Hardy, J. (2009). Measurement of transformational leadership and its relationship with team cohesion and performance level. *Journal of Applied Sport Psychology*, *21*(4), 395–412.

Chelladurai, P., & Saleh, S. D. (1980). Dimensions of leader behavior in sports: Development of a leadership scale. *Journal of Sport Psychology*, *2*, 34–45.

Choi, Y., & Mai-Dalton, R. R. (1999). The model of followers' responses to self-sacrificial leadership: An empirical test. *The Leadership Quarterly*, *10*(3), 397–421.

Clemens, J. K., & Mayer, D. (1999). *The classic touch: Lessons in leadership from Homer to Hemingway*. Raleigh, NC: Contemporary Books.

Conger, J. A., & Kanungo, R. N. (1987). Toward a behavioral theory of charismatic leadership in organizational settings. *Academy of Management Review*, *12*(4), 637–647.

De Cremer, D., Mayer, D. M., van Dijke, M., Schouten, B. C. & Bardes, M. (2009). When does self-sacrificial leadership motivate prosocial behavior? It depends on followers' prevention focus. *Journal of Applied Psychology*, *94*(4), 887.

Erickson, K., Côté, J., Hollenstein, T. & Deakin, J. (2011). Examining coach–athlete interactions using state space grids: An observational analysis in competitive youth sport. *Psychology of Sport and Exercise*, *12*(6), 645–654.

Figgins, S. G., Smith, M. J., Sellars, C. N., Greenlees, I. A. & Knight, C. J. (2016). 'You really could be something quite special': A qualitative exploration of athletes' experiences of being inspired in sport. *Psychology of Sport and Exercise*, *24*, 82–91.

Gallimore, R., & Tharp, R. (2004). What a coach can teach a teacher, 1975–2004: Reflections and reanalysis of John Wooden's teaching practices. *The Sport Psychologist*, *18*, 119–137.

Gill, D. L., & Kamphoff, C. S., (2009). Cultural diversity in applied sport psychology. In R. Schinke & S. J. Hanrahan, (Eds.), *Cultural sport psychology*. Champaign, IL: Human Kinetics.

Gonzalez, S. P., Metzler, J. N. & Newton, M. (2011). The influence of a simulated 'pep talk' on athlete inspiration, situational motivation, and emotion. *International Journal of Sports Science and Coaching*, *6*(3), 445–459.

Gucciardi, D. F., Jackson, B., Hanton, S. & Reid, M. (2015). Motivational correlates of mentally tough behaviours in tennis. *Journal of Science and Medicine in Sport*, *18*(1), 67–71.

Hardy, L., Arthur, C. A., Jones, G., Shariff, A., Munnoch, K., Isaacs, I. & Allsopp, A. J. (2010). A correlational and an experimental study examining the sub-components of transformational leadership. *Leadership Quarterly*, *21*, 20–32.

Hart, T. (1998). Inspiration: Exploring the experience and its meaning. *Journal of Humanistic Psychology*, *38*(3), 7–35.

La Voi, N. M. (2007). Interpersonal communication and conflict in the coach–athlete relationship. In S. Jowett & D. Lavallee (Eds.), *Social psychology in sport* (pp. 29–40). Champaign, IL: Human Kinetics.

Lockwood, P., & Kunda, Z. (1997). Superstars and me: Predicting the impact of role models on the self. *Journal of Personality and Social Psychology, 73*(1), 91–103.

Mackenzie, S. H., & Kerr, J. H. (2012). Head-mounted cameras and stimulated recall in qualitative sport research. *Qualitative Research in Sport, Exercise and Health, 4*(1), 51–61.

Milyavskaya, M., Ianakieva, I., Foxen-Craft, E., Colantuoni, A. & Koestner, R. (2012). Inspired to get there: The effects of trait and goal inspiration on goal progress. *Personality and individual differences, 52*(1), 56–60.

Mio, J. S., Riggio, R. E., Levin, S. & Reese, R. (2005). Presidential leadership and charisma: The effects of metaphor. *The Leadership Quarterly, 16*(2), 287–294.

Poynor, R., Arthur, C. A. & Gibas, D. (2012). Inspirational coaches: An underdeveloped phenomenon in sport psychology. *Journal of Sport and Exercise Psychology, 34*, S273–S273.

Rowold, J. (2006). Transformational and transactional leadership in martial arts. *Journal of Applied Sport Psychology, 18*(4), 312–325.

Searle, G. D., & Hanrahan, S. J. (2011). Leading to inspire others: Charismatic influence or hard work? *Leadership and Organization Development Journal, 32*(7), 736–754.

Smith, M. J., Young, D., Figgins, S. & Arthur C. A. (in press). Transformational leadership in elite sport: A qualitative analysis of effective leadership behaviors in cricket. *The Sport Psychologist.*

Tharp, R. G., & Gallimore, R. (1976). What a coach can teach a teacher. *Psychology Today, 9*, 74–78.

Thrash, T. M., & Elliot, A. J. (2003). Inspiration as a psychological construct. *Journal of Personality and Social Psychology, 84*(4), 871–889.

Thrash, T. M., & Elliot, A. J. (2004). Inspiration: Core characteristics, component processes, antecedents, and function. *Journal of Personality and Social Psychology, 87*(6), 957–973.

Thrash, T. M., Elliot, A. J., Maruskin, L. A. & Cassidy, S. E. (2010). Inspiration and the promotion of well-being: Tests of causality and mediation. *Journal of Personality and Social Psychology, 98*(3), 488–506.

Thrash, T. M., Maruskin, L. A., Cassidy, S. E., Fryer, J. W. & Ryan, R. M. (2010). Mediating between the muse and the masses: Inspiration and the actualization of creative ideas. *Journal of Personality and Social Psychology, 98*(3), 469–487.

Thrash, T. M., Moldovan, E. G., Fuller, A. K. & Dombrowski, J. T. (2014). Inspiration and the creative process. In J. C. Kaufman (Ed.), *Creativity and Mental Illness* (pp. 343–362). New York: Cambridge University Press.

Thrash, T. M., Moldovan, E. G., Oleynick, V. C. & Maruskin, L. A. (2014). The psychology of inspiration. *Social and Personality Psychology Compass, 8*(9), 495–510.

Trudel, P., & Côté, J. (1994). Sports education and learning conditions. *Childhood, 47*, 285–298.

Trudel, P., Côté, J. & Bernard, D. (1996). Systematic observation of youth ice hockey coaches during games. *Journal of Sport Behavior, 19*(1), 50–66.

Vallée, C. N., & Bloom, G. A. (2005). Building successful university programs: Key and common elements of expert coaches. *Journal of Applied Sport Psychology, 17*(3), 179–196.

van Knippenberg, D., & Sitkin, S. B. (2013). A critical assessment of charismatic–transformational leadership research: Back to the drawing board? *The Academy of Management Annals, 7*(1), 1–60.

Vargas, T. M., & Short, S. E. (2011). Athlete's perceptions of the psychological, emotional, and performance effects of coaches' pre-game speeches. *International Journal of Coaching Science*, 5(1), 27–43.

Vargas-Tonsing, T. M., & Bartholomew, J. B. (2006). An exploratory study of the effects of pregame speeches on team efficacy beliefs. *Journal of Applied Sport Psychology*, 36, 918–933.

Vargas-Tonsing, T. M., & Guan, J. (2007). Athletes' preference for informational and emotional pre-game speech content. *International Journal of Sports Science and Coaching*, 2, 171–180.

Yukl, G. A. (2006). *Leadership in organizations* (6th ed.). Upper Saddle River, NJ: Pearson Prentice Hall.

Zenger, J., & Folkman, J. (2014). The skills leaders need at every level. *Harvard Business School Blogs*. https://hbr.org/2014/07/the-skills-leaders-need-at-every-level.

16 Developing resilience through coaching

Mustafa Sarkar[1] *and David Fletcher*[2]

Introduction

Why is it that some athletes and teams are able to withstand the pressures of competitive sport and attain peak performances, whereas others succumb to the demands and under perform? It is the study of psychological and team resilience that aims to address this question. A burgeoning body of empirical evidence points to the importance of psychological and team resilience for success in sport (see, e.g., Fletcher & Sarkar, 2012; Galli & Vealey, 2008; Morgan, Fletcher, & Sarkar, 2013, 2015; White & Bennie, 2015). Moreover, there is emerging research evidence in other domains of psychology regarding the benefits of resilience training through coaching (see Grant, Curtayne, & Burton, 2009; Sherlock-Storey, Moss, & Timson, 2013). Drawing on the existing body of knowledge in these areas, this chapter presents an evidence-based foundation for the development of resilience through coaching and outlines what coaches can do to develop resilience in their athletes and teams.

Key terms

Psychological resilience

Over the past three decades, numerous definitions of resilience have been proposed in the psychology research literature based on alternative conceptualizations of resilience as a process or a trait (see, for a review, Fletcher & Sarkar, 2013; Windle, 2011). To illustrate, psychological resilience has been defined as a 'dynamic process encompassing positive adaptation within the context of significant adversity' (Luthar, Cicchetti, & Becker, 2000, p. 543) and 'the positive role of individual differences in people's response to stress and adversity' (Rutter, 1987, p. 316). Building on these perspectives, Fletcher and Sarkar defined psychological resilience as 'the role of mental processes and behavior in promoting personal assets and protecting an individual from the potential negative effect of stressors' (2012, p. 675, 2013, p. 16). This definition extends previous conceptual work in this area in a number of ways. First, the focus on *psychological* resilience delimits the scope of the description, by definition, to 'mental processes and behavior' and excludes other types of resilience such as physical, molecular, and structural resilience. Second, this definition encapsulates aspects of both trait and process conceptualizations of resilience (see Fletcher & Sarkar, 2012, 2013). Regarding the trait conceptualization, the 'mental processes and behavior' enable individuals to adapt to the circumstances they encounter (see Connor & Davidson, 2003). The process conceptualization of resilience recognizes that it is a capacity that develops over time in the context of person–environment interactions (Egeland, Carlson, & Stroufe, 1993). Central to the definition is the focusing of the conceptual lens on the role that psychological-related phenomena play – rather than the mental processes and behaviour per se – in avoiding negative consequences. Third, the emphasis is placed on the more neutral term 'stressor' rather than the negative value-laden term 'adversity' (see Fletcher & Sarkar, 2013). Fourth, the focus is on 'promoting personal assets and protecting an individual from the potential negative effect of stressors' rather than positive adaptation per se, because resilience generally refers to the ability of individuals to maintain normal levels of functioning rather than the restoration or enhancement of functioning (see Bonanno, 2004).

Team resilience

Resilience researchers, in various domains of psychology, have recently shifted their attention from individuals toward the study of groups and teams (see, e.g., Alliger, Cerasoli, Tannenbaum, & Vessey, 2015; Bennett, Aden, Broome, Mitchell, & Rigdon, 2010; Morgan et al., 2013, 2015; Rodriguez-Sanchez & Vera Perea, 2015; Stephens, Heaphy, Carmeli, Spreitzer, & Dutton, 2013). Reinforcing the need to consider group level resilience, Bennett et al. (2010) remarked that 'resilience may be viewed as much [as] a social factor (existing in teams and groups) as an individual trait' (p. 225). In a similar fashion to the construct of psychological resilience, a variety of definitions of team resilience have been proposed in the psychology research literature over the past five years. West, Patera, and Carsten (2009) defined team resilience as 'the capacity to bounce back from failure, setbacks, conflicts, or any other threat to well-being that a team may experience' (p. 253). Similarly, when measuring team resilience, Stephens et al. (2013) constructed items to assess 'a team's capacity to bounce back from a setback' (p. 27). In a recent review examining team factors that may build team resilience, Rodriguez-Sanchez and Vera Perea (2015) defined team resilience as 'a capacity that teams have in order to overcome crisis and difficulties' (p. 30). Elsewhere, in another recent review of team resilience exploring how teams flourish under pressure, Alliger et al. (2015) defined team resilience as 'the capacity of a team to withstand and overcome stressors in a manner that enables sustained performance; it helps teams handle and bounce back from challenges that can endanger their cohesiveness and performance' (p. 177).

Drawing on the psychological and team resilience literatures in sport and coaching psychology, in this chapter we present an evidence-based foundation for the development of resilience through coaching. To this end, the narrative is divided into three main sections. The first section reviews the literature regarding psychological resilience in sport, team resilience in sport, and resilience training through coaching. The second section proposes implications for future research regarding the development of resilience through coaching. The third section concludes with some implications for applied practice.

Review of the literature

Psychological resilience in sport

A growing body of evidence points to resilience as an important psychological phenomenon for attaining high levels of sport performance (see, e.g., Gould, Dieffenbach, & Moffett, 2002; Holt & Dunn, 2004; Johnston, Harwood, & Minniti, 2013; Mills, Butt, Maynard, & Harwood, 2012; Weissensteiner, Abernethy, & Farrow, 2009). In their study examining the psychosocial competencies associated with soccer success, Holt and Dunn (2004) identified resilience as one of the four factors that was central to success in elite youth soccer. Interestingly, in 2004, Holt and Dunn observed that 'resilience has yet to be extensively examined in sport' (p. 214), despite the construct being related to high levels of athletic achievement. Indeed, it is only in the last decade or so that there has been an attempt to specifically investigate psychological resilience in sport performers (see, e.g., Fletcher & Sarkar, 2012; Galli & Vealey, 2008; Martin-Krumm, Sarazzin, Peterson, & Framose, 2003; Mummery, Schofield, & Perry, 2004; Schinke, Peterson, & Couture, 2004; White & Bennie, 2015).

In one of the initial sport-related resilience studies, Martin-Krumm et al. (2003) examined the relationship between explanatory style and resilience in a group of recreational basketball players, using an experimental approach. Following failure feedback in a dribbling task, optimistic participants were found to be more confident, to be less anxious and to perform better than pessimistic participants. Adopting a more ecologically valid approach, Mummery et al. (2004) explored the impact of three protective factors (namely, self-concept, social support, coping style) against three performance-related outcomes (i.e. initially successful performance; resilient performance involving an initial failure followed by subsequent success; non-resilient performance involving an initial failure followed by subsequent failure) in a National swimming championship. Findings revealed that resilient performers had higher self-perceptions of physical endurance but lower perceptions of social support than the other two groups. Moreover, the initially successful performers had higher perceptions of peaking under pressure and coping with adversity than the other groups. In an attempt to translate empirical evidence into practice, Schinke and colleagues (Schinke & Jerome, 2002; Schinke et al., 2004) described the implementation of a resilience training program for national team athletes and coaching staff. Specifically, based on the University of Pennsylvania resilience training protocol, the authors provided an overview of three general optimism skills (namely, evaluating personal assumptions, disputing negative thoughts, de-catastrophizing) that were taught to elite athletes to help them improve their performance in adverse competitive situations. Although the work in this area from 2002 to 2004 provided an initial insight into resilience in sport performers, it is worth noting that the research focused on a limited number of psychological characteristics (namely, optimistic explanatory style, self-concept, social support, coping style) that precluded participants from providing a broader insight into the trait and process elements of resilience.

Taking a more holistic approach to resilience inquiry, Galli and Vealey (2008) interviewed college and professional athletes about their perceptions and experiences of resilience, using Richardson (2002) and Richardson and colleagues' (1990) resiliency model as a guiding theoretical framework. Four different adversities were identified: injury, performance slump, illness, and career transition. Moreover, five general dimensions emerged that described the resilience experience of the athletes: breadth and duration of the resilience process, agitation (i.e. the use of a variety of coping strategies to deal with a wide range of unpleasant emotions and mental struggles), personal resources (e.g. positivity, determination, competitiveness, commitment, maturity, persistence, and passion for the sport), sociocultural influences (e.g. social support and cultural factors), and positive outcomes (e.g. learning, perspective, realization of support, and motivation to help others). Although there has been some support for Richardson's model in relation to health promotion (e.g. Walker, 1996), it is not without its limitations, including the linear stage framework evident within its structure, the absence of meta-cognitive and emotive processes, and its bias toward coping-orientated processes (see Fletcher & Sarkar, 2013). These drawbacks are of particular concern since 'the resiliency model (Richardson, Neiger, Jensen, & Kumpfer, 1990) served to drive and direct … [our] study' (Galli & Vealey, 2008, p. 321).

In an attempt to address the limitations of Galli and Vealey's (2008) work, several groups of researchers (e.g. Fletcher & Sarkar, 2012; White & Bennie, 2015) have employed inductive qualitative designs to explore resilience free from the constraints of a preconceived model. To illustrate, Fletcher and Sarkar (2012) developed a grounded theory of psychological resilience in Olympic champions. They interviewed twelve Olympic gold medallists to explore and explain the relationship between psychological resilience and optimal sport performance. The findings revealed that numerous psychological factors (relating to a positive personality, motivation, confidence, focus, and perceived social support) protected the world's best athletes from the potential negative effect of stressors by influencing their challenge appraisal and meta-cognitions. These constructive cognitive reactions promoted facilitative responses that led to the realization of optimal sport performance.

To clarify how sport can cultivate resilience, White and Bennie (2015) recently investigated gymnast and coach perceptions about the development of resilience through gymnastics participation. Underpinned by a qualitative design, 22 female gymnasts and seven gymnastics coaches participated in semi-structured interviews. Data analysis revealed that aspects of the gymnastics environment created stress and exposed gymnasts to many challenges in training and competition. Features of the sport environment, such as interpersonal relationships and positive coach behaviours, supported gymnasts through these challenges and encouraged them to overcome failure. Gymnastics participation was perceived to develop resilience, as well as life skills, self-efficacy, and self-esteem. These findings support the notion that youth sport may be an appropriate avenue for the development of resilience and have implications for future coaching practice. The implications of these findings for applied practice will be discussed later.

Team resilience in sport

As mentioned earlier, resilience researchers, in various domains of psychology, have lately turned their focus to the group level (see, e.g., Alliger et al., 2015; Bennett et al., 2010; Morgan et al., 2013, 2015; Rodriguez-Sanchez & Vera Perea, 2015; Stephens et al., 2013). Within the sport psychology literature, Morgan et al. (2013) conducted the first study of team resilience in sport. Employing focus groups with members of five elite sport teams, a definition of team resilience was developed and the resilient characteristics of elite sport teams were identified. Specifically, team resilience was explained as a 'dynamic, psychosocial process which protects a group of individuals from the potential negative effect of the stressors they collectively encounter. It comprises of processes whereby team members use their individual and collective resources to positively adapt when experiencing adversity' (p. 552). Team resilience was described as a dynamic phenomenon with participants stating that it was 'dependent upon what time of the season it is' or 'whether there is an injury in the team'. In terms of its protective function, the participants described team resilience as akin to 'having a barrier around you' and 'having a thick skin'. Furthermore, the participants emphasized that team resilience involved a shared experience of stressors (e.g. team disruptions, low team morale) and this was revealed through comments such as 'we have been through so many setbacks together'. Four resilient characteristics of elite sport teams emerged from this study: group structure (i.e. conventions that shape group norms and values), mastery approaches (i.e. shared attitudes and behaviours that promote an emphasis on team improvement), social capital (i.e. the existence of high-quality interactions and caring relationships within the team), and collective efficacy (i.e. the team's shared beliefs in its ability to perform a task).

The recent developments in resilience research have advanced our knowledge of the nature, meaning, and scope of team resilience. In the sport psychology literature, Morgan et al.'s (2013) study extended resilience research by providing greater definitional clarity of resilience at the team level (i.e. what team resilience is) and proposing a framework to profile the resilient characteristics of elite sport teams (i.e. what resilient teams 'look' like). Although such knowledge provided descriptive information about the factors that enable teams to withstand stressors, these characteristics do not explain how resilient teams function.

Morgan et al. (2013) described team resilience as a 'dynamic, psychosocial process' (p. 552), which points to operational aspects of this construct and how it changes over time. They went on to argue that 'due to the contextual and temporal nature of team resilience, future studies should aim to identify the processes that underpin the resilience characteristics' (p. 558). To address this gap in our understanding of team resilience, Morgan et al. (2015) subsequently explored the psychosocial processes underpinning team resilience in elite sport. Using narrative inquiry, Morgan et al. (2015) analysed the autobiographies of eight members of the 2003 England rugby union World Cup winning team. Findings revealed five main psychosocial processes underpinning team resilience: transformational leadership, shared team leadership, team learning, social identity, and positive emotions. The results indicated that these processes enabled the England rugby team to effectively utilize their cognitive, affective, and relational resources to act as leverage points for team resilience when facing stressors. Furthermore, the findings of this study revealed that team resilience was illuminated through a progressive narrative form. This was portrayed by team members evaluating stressors in a positive fashion and focusing on moving forward as a team despite setbacks.

Resilience training through coaching

Drawing on the psychological and team resilience literatures, resilience-building programs have increasingly been adopted to improve well-being and performance. While the benefits of such programs are now starting to be recognized, their efficacy as a whole has remained unclear since a comprehensive review of existing primary literature had not been undertaken to date. In order to address this limitation in the literature, Robertson, Cooper, Sarkar, and Curran (2015) recently provided a systematic review of work-based resilience training interventions. Their review identified 14 studies that investigated the impact of resilience training on personal resilience and four broad categories of dependent variables: (1) mental health and subjective well-being outcomes, (2) psychosocial outcomes, (3) physical/biological outcomes, and (4) performance outcomes. Findings indicated that resilience training can improve personal resilience and is a useful means of developing mental health and subjective well-being outcomes in employees. They also found that resilience training has a number of wider benefits that include enhanced psychosocial functioning and improved performance.

Interestingly, a couple of resilience training studies identified in Robertson et al.'s (2015) review were based on coaching-related principles (namely, Grant et al., 2009; Sherlock-Storey et al., 2013). In Grant et al.'s (2009) randomised controlled study, 41 executives in a public health agency received 360-degree feedback, a half-day leadership workshop, and four individual coaching sessions over 10 weeks. The coaching sessions used a cognitive–behavioural solution-focused approach. Quantitative and qualitative measures were taken. Compared to controls, coaching enhanced goal attainment, increased resilience and workplace well-being, and reduced depression and stress. Qualitative responses indicated participants found coaching helped increase self-confidence and personal insight, build management skills, and helped participants deal with organisational change. Findings indicated that short-term coaching can be effective, and that evidence-based executive coaching can be valuable as an applied positive psychology in helping people deal with the uncertainty and challenges inherent in organisational change.

Most recently, Sherlock-Storey et al. (2013) piloted a brief resilience coaching programme and explored the impact on participants' reported levels of resilience and attitudes towards organizational change. An opportunity sample of 12 middle managers from a UK public sector organization experiencing significant organizational change participated in the study. A program of three 90-minute coaching sessions was delivered at three-weekly intervals over a six-week period. The coaching program was designed to support individuals in developing and demonstrating resilient behaviours in the face of organizational changes and progressing their well-being and/or resilience-related goals. The coaching approach used differed from that of Grant et al. (2009) in that it trialled a skills-based rather than an executive coaching approach. Luthans, Youssef, and Avolio (2007) Psychological Capital (Psycap) Questionnaire and questions relating to participants' confidence in dealing with organizational change were administered in a test/re-test design one week prior to the commencement of coaching and within two weeks of coaching conclusion. Statistical analyses supported both study questions, with participants reporting significant (positive) changes in resilience levels and confidence in dealing with organizational change following the coaching program. Increases in participants' psychological capital in the areas of hope and optimism were also found, although self-efficacy was not found to be significantly enhanced.

In this section, we have reviewed the literature regarding psychological resilience in sport, team resilience in sport, and resilience training through coaching. Overall, a convergence of evidence points to the importance of resilience in sport and coaching contexts. Nevertheless, the body of knowledge in this area remains at a nascent stage. Empirical examination of developing resilience through coaching is rather scant both in sport and coaching psychology. The landscape that has revealed itself to sport and coaching psychologists to explore is vast, the opportunities to elucidate the complex relationship between athletes, teams, and coaches are inviting, and the research agenda that beckons is exciting. In the remainder of this chapter, we propose implications for future research and conclude with some implications for applied practice.

Implications for future research

The literature reviewed in this chapter suggests that resilience is likely to be a fruitful avenue for sport researchers to explore. Here, we discuss two main areas that we believe will advance knowledge in this area in the context of developing resilience through coaching.

First, since coaches play an important role in promoting resilience (see White & Bennie, 2015; Young, 2014), future research should consider the perceptions

of coaches when further investigating psychological and team resilience in competitive sport. Building on the work of White and Bennie (2015), future studies
should investigate coach perceptions regarding the development of resilience
specifically to discover coaching behaviours and environmental aspects perceived to foster resilience in athletes and teams. Furthermore, since elite sport
coaches operate within complex, ever-changing environments that impose many
pressures on them (see, for a review, Fletcher & Scott, 2010), future research
should examine resilience in elite coaches and its impact on athlete behaviour
and performance. Specifically, due to the exploratory nature of this emerging
area of inquiry, researchers should initially seek to define and characterize coach
resilience (see Young, 2014) and subsequently strive to understand the development of resilience amongst coaches and how this impacts their ability to foster
resilience in their athletes and teams.

   Second, to advance knowledge of developing resilience, resilience intervention studies are needed in sport. As a caveat to this suggestion, Fletcher and
Sarkar (2012) argued that:

> From a research perspective ... it is important that such work is grounded in
> systematic resilience research programs rather than piecemeal and incom-
> plete strategies based on, for example, the mental toughness, hardiness or
> coping literatures. Such research programs, which should be underpinned by
> the conceptual and theoretical advances already made in this area in general
> psychology (see Fletcher & Sarkar, 2013) will provide the most rigorous
> and robust platform from which to develop resilience training in sport.
>
> (p. 676)

To provide an illustration, albeit in another performance context, the Comprehensive Soldier Fitness (CSF) program designed to develop resilience in soldiers
was adapted primarily from the Penn Resiliency Program (PRP; see, for a
review, Brunwasser, Gillham, & Kim, 2009). Notwithstanding the program's
foundation, Eidelson, Pilisuk, and Soldz (2011) voiced a number of conceptual
and ethical concerns about the CSF intervention. To illustrate, Eidelson et al.
contended that the resilience program's outcomes should have been convinc-
ingly demonstrated first in carefully conducted randomized controlled trials
before being rolled out under less controlled conditions, that the model on which
the CSF program is based was developed on dramatically different (non-
military) populations and therefore cannot be generalized to the challenges that
soldiers face in combat, and that the PRP's effects seemed to be unrelated to the
'resilience' theory underpinning the program. Ethically, Eidelson et al. argued
that 'resilience training could ... harm ... soldiers by making them more likely
to engage in combat actions that adversely affect their psychological health'
(Eidelson et al., 2011, p. 643). Moreover, they provided a general critique of
positive psychology that was the foundation of CSF. This included the failure of
positive psychology to appreciate the valuable functions played by 'negative'
emotions such as anger, guilt, and fear; its disregard for harsh societal realities

such as poverty and oppression; and its promotion of claims without sufficient scientific support (see Coyne & Tennen, 2010). In light of the criticisms of the CSF resilience program, sport psychologists attempting to develop similar interventions with coaches should ensure that a rigorous methodological design is employed (ideally a randomized controlled trial), that the intervention is underpinned by conceptual and theoretical context-specific knowledge of resilience, that the 'dark side' of resilience is considered, and that the program draws on humanistic and other perspectives that may not be covered in the field of positive psychology (see Robertson et al., 2015).

Implications for applied practice

In this final section, we conclude with some implications for applied practice based on the aforementioned literature on psychological resilience in sport, team resilience in sport, and resilience training through coaching.

Psychological resilience in sport

Fletcher and Sarkar's (2012) grounded theory provides coaches with a model to understand the impact of psychological resilience on the stress process in sport, and its relationship with optimal sport performance. Coaches operating in elite sport should identify and monitor the psychological factors (i.e. positive personality, motivation, confidence, focus, perceived social support) that an athlete needs to develop to exhibit resilience, and should intervene to attain the optimum levels of, and balance between, these factors. In addition, it is crucial that athletes' immediate environment is carefully managed to optimize the demands they encounter, in order to stimulate and foster the development of psychological factors that will protect them from negative consequences. Furthermore, educational programs in challenge appraisal and meta-reflective strategies, such as evaluating personal assumptions, minimizing catastrophic thinking, challenging counterproductive beliefs, and cognitive restructuring, should form a central part of resilience training (see Reivich, Seligman, & McBride, 2011; Schinke et al., 2004). To help support these initiatives, athletes should be exposed to various formal and informal psychosocial training and developmental experiences. Examples include personal mentoring, expert coaching provision, and performance enhancement training.

White and Bennie's (2015) study provides useful implications for future coach education and coaching practice in gymnastics. Specifically, their findings suggest that a positive training environment underpinned by supportive communication (e.g. praise, talking with coaches about topics other than gymnastics) may help gymnasts with emotional support and increased self-efficacy. Allowing gymnasts to make decisions regarding training activities may inspire them to act independently and problem solve when experiencing adversity. These strategies could be used when encountering challenges during competition where the coach has limited influence over the performance outcome. Coaches could also advise gymnasts to set realistic goals, since attaining goals increased gymnasts' motivation and was associated with the adoption of resilient approaches towards setbacks.

Team resilience in sport

The resilient characteristics identified in Morgan et al. (2013) provide coaches with a framework to enhance team resilience. To illustrate, using the group structure components, coaches could work with athletes to collectively develop a shared vision, based on core values and a clear sense of purpose. The use of group debriefings and reflections on key incidents, underpinned by the identified core values, would promote a setting for shared constructive sense making amongst team members about the lessons learnt after experiencing adversity. In relation to mastery approaches, coaches could employ simulation training exercises to enable teams to gain experience of adversity, and to promote adaptability and behavioural preparedness. Based on the social capital characteristic, positive relationships should be nurtured by ensuring opportunities are created for informal interactions and social activities to build a sense of camaraderie among team members and to reinforce a team identity via the use of images (e.g. logos, mottos). Finally, to build collective efficacy, coaches might hold small group meetings with athletes to reflect on the benefits of experiencing adversity and discovering whether there are new strengths to be gained. They may also consider how to optimize the impact of influential leaders to ensure that confidence is spread throughout the group during setbacks.

The findings of Morgan et al.'s (2015) study revealed five main psychosocial processes, underpinning the resilience of a world champion team, that offer coaches a framework to build team resilience during the course of a team's journey. During the early phase of team formation, the results suggest that transformational leadership strategies, such as articulating and reinforcing a compelling team vision, are important to focus on to protect groups of individuals from the potential negative consequences of stressors. During the middle phase, it appears that the creation of a leadership group (i.e. shared team leadership) becomes more of a priority to boost team resilience since it promotes connectivity, ensures that players are 'on the same wavelength' during setbacks, and enforces accountability by taking positive action. The facilitation of team learning also seems to be beneficial during this phase. To expedite team learning, coaches could hold meetings that require players to reflect on the new knowledge and benefits gained from experiences of adversity (e.g. evaluate stressors as an opportunity for group development and mastery) and consider how this information can be used in the future. During the latter period of a team's development, the findings suggest that displays of positive emotions are important to emphasize. Coaches should closely observe the behaviour of athletes during training for signals that may indicate lack of vitality. To stimulate humour, players could create a platform for banter through team rituals (e.g. celebrating moments of resilience) and 'storytelling' to explain successes and failures.

Resilience training through coaching

A number of implications for applied practice emerge from Grant et al.'s (2009) study. The study showed that as few as four coaching sessions can be effective. Executive coaching typically takes place over a greater number of sessions, with many experienced coaching practitioners recommending eight to ten sessions (Berman & Bradt, 2006). However, Burke and Linley (2007) found that just one coaching session improved goal self-concordance and commitment, although they did not measure goal attainment. The results of Grant et al.'s study extend Burke and Linley's (2007) work and suggest that short-term coaching interventions can indeed be effective. The quantitative results of the study provide support for the notion that executive coaching can increase goal attainment, enhance resilience, ameliorate depression and stress, and increase workplace well-being. The participants' qualitative responses support many of the quantitative findings and suggest that executive coaching may be a valuable tool in helping individuals deal with the uncertainty and challenges inherent in organizational change. Given that many organizational change initiatives are problematic (Stober, 2008), and such change failures can be costly in both business and human terms, sport organizations should consider using individual coaching as a support mechanism in conjunction with organizational-level change initiatives during times of significant change, thereby building resilience at both an organizational and individual level.

Sherlock-Storey et al.'s (2013) study provides encouraging support for brief, skills (behaviour) focused coaching as a potentially effective method for enhancing employee resilience and change orientation. Compared to development coaching approaches which typically require highly skilled, experienced and often costly coaching professionals, a program such as the one used in Sherlock-Storey et al.'s study may provide an accessible and affordable approach to employee support and development during change. The area of resilience offers a potentially promising topic of focus for coaches supporting individuals during organisational change. Although this area is often implicitly at the centre of coaching and coaching conversations, Sherlock-Storey et al.'s study provides support for the potential value of a more explicit and focused coaching emphasis on resilience that can enhance an individual's capacity to deal with change.

Concluding remarks

Resilience is viewed here as a prerequisite for success and a key area of development. In an attempt to help coaches gain a better practical understanding of resilience, this review has examined the literature with the specific intention to highlight the praxis of the current research. Specifically, it is hoped that this synthesis of literature will help coaches gain a better practical understanding of resilience in athletes and teams, while providing a rigorous and robust platform for the development of sport-specific interventions to facilitate resilience. In drawing together our observations, the emerging research examining resilience in sport has provided coaches with sport-specific frameworks for understanding what resilience at different levels of analysis is, how it develops, and what functions it serves. In addition, this review has also raised a number of implications for future research and applied practice regarding the development of resilience through coaching.

Notes

1 Department of Sport Science, Nottingham Trent University, UK
2 School of Sport, Exercise, and Health Sciences, Loughborough University, UK

References

Alliger, G. M., Cerasoli, C. P., Tannenbaum, S. I., & Vessey, W. B. (2015). Team resilience: How teams flourish under pressure. *Organizational Dynamics*, *44*, 176–184.

Bennett, J. B., Aden, C. A., Broome, K., Mitchell, K., & Rigdon, W. D. (2010). Team resilience for young restaurant workers: Research-to-practice adaptation and assessment. *Journal of Occupational Health Psychology*, *15*, 223–236.

Berman, W. H., & Bradt, G. (2006). Executive coaching and consulting: 'Different strokes for different folks'. *Professional Psychology: Research and Practice*, *37*, 244–253.

Bonanno, G. A. (2004). Loss, trauma and human resilience: Have we underestimated the human capacity to thrive after extremely aversive events? *American Psychologist*, *59*, 20–28.

Brunwasser, S. M., Gillham, J. E., & Kim, E. S. (2009). A meta-analytic review of the Penn Resiliency program's effect on depressive symptoms. *Journal of Consulting and Clinical Psychology*, *77*, 1042–1054.

Burke, D., & Linley, P. A. (2007). Enhancing goal self-concordance through coaching. *International Coaching Psychology Review*, *2*, 62–69.

Connor, K. M., & Davidson, J. R. T. (2003). Development of a new resilience scale: the Connor-Davidson resilience scale (CD-RISC). *Depression and Anxiety*, *18*, 76–82.

Coyne, J. C., & Tennen, H. (2010). Positive psychology in cancer care: Bad science, exaggerated claims, and unproven medicine. *Annals of Behavioral Medicine*, *39*, 16–26.

Egeland, B., Carlson, E., & Sroufe, L. A. (1993). Resilience as process. *Development and Psychopathology*, *5*, 517–528.

Eidelson, R., Pilisuk, M., & Soldz, S. (2011). The dark side of Comprehensive Soldier Fitness. *American Psychologist*, *66*, 643–644.

Fletcher, D., & Sarkar, M. (2012). A grounded theory of psychological resilience in Olympic champions. *Psychology of Sport and Exercise*, *13*, 669–678.

Fletcher, D., & Sarkar, M. (2013). Psychological resilience: A review and critique of definitions, concepts, and theory. *European Psychologist*, *18*, 12–23.

Fletcher, D., & Scott, M. (2010). Psychological stress in sports coaches: A review of concepts, research, and practice. *Journal of Sports Sciences*, *28*, 127–137.

Galli, N., & Vealey, R. S. (2008). 'Bouncing back' from adversity: Athletes' experiences of resilience. *Sport Psychologist*, *22*, 316–335.

Gould, D., Dieffenbach, K., & Moffett, A. (2002). Psychological characteristics and their development in Olympic champions. *Journal of Applied Sport Psychology*, *14*, 172–204.

Grant, A. M., Curtayne, L., & Burton, G. (2009). Executive coaching enhances goal attainment, resilience and workplace well-being: A randomized controlled study. *Journal of Positive Psychology, 4*, 396–407.

Holt, N. L., & Dunn, J. G. (2004). Toward a grounded theory of the psychosocial competencies and environmental conditions associated with soccer success. *Journal of Applied Sport Psychology, 16*, 199–219.

Johnston, J., Harwood, C., & Minniti, A. M. (2013). Positive youth development in swimming: Clarification and consensus of key psychosocial assets. *Journal of Applied Sport Psychology, 25*, 392–411.

Luthans, F., Youssef, C. M., & Avolio, B. J. (2007). *Psychological capital*. New York: Oxford University Press.

Luthar, S. S., Cicchetti, D., & Becker, B. (2000). The construct of resilience: A critical evaluation and guidelines for future work. *Child Development, 71*, 543–562.

Martin-Krumm, C. P., Sarrazin, P. G., Peterson, C., & Famose, J. (2003). Explanatory style and resilience after sports failure. *Personality and Individual Differences, 35*, 1685–1695.

Mills, A., Butt, J., Maynard, I., & Harwood, C. (2012). Identifying factors perceived to influence the development of elite youth football academy players. *Journal of Sports Sciences, 30*, 1593–1604.

Morgan, P. B. C., Fletcher, D., & Sarkar, M. (2013). Defining and characterizing team resilience in elite sport. *Psychology of Sport and Exercise, 14*, 549–559.

Morgan, P. B. C., Fletcher, D., & Sarkar, M. (2015). Understanding team resilience in the world's best athletes: A case study of a rugby union World Cup winning team. *Psychology of Sport and Exercise, 16*, 91–100.

Mummery, W. K., Schofield, G., & Perry, C. (2004). Bouncing back: The role of coping style, social support, and self-concept in resilience of sport performance. *Athletic Insight, 6*, 1–18.

Reivich, K. J., Seligman, M. E., & McBride, S. (2011). Master resilience training in the US Army. *American Psychologist, 66*, 25–34.

Richardson, G. E. (2002). The metatheory of resilience and resiliency. *Journal of Clinical Psychology, 58*, 307–321.

Richardson, G. E., Neiger, B. L., Jensen, S., & Kumpfer, K. L. (1990). The resiliency model. *Health Education, 21*, 33–39.

Robertson, I., Cooper, C. L., Sarkar, M., & Curran, T. (2015). Resilience training in the workplace from 2003–2014: A systematic review. *Journal of Occupational and Organizational Psychology, 88*, 533–562.

Rodríguez-Sánchez, A. M., & Vera Perea, M. (2015). The secret of organisation success: A revision on organisational and team resilience. *International Journal of Emergency Services, 4*, 27–36.

Rutter, M. (1987). Psychosocial resilience and protective mechanisms. *American Journal of Orthopsychiatry, 57*, 316–331.

Schinke, R. J., & Jerome, W. C. (2002). Understanding and refining the resilience of elite athletes: An intervention study. *Athletic Insight, 4*, 1–13.

Schinke, R. J., Peterson, C., & Couture, R. (2004). A protocol for teaching resilience to high performance athletes. *Journal of Excellence, 9*, 9–18.

Sherlock-Storey, M., Moss, M., & Timson, S. (2013). Brief coaching for resilience during organisational change – an exploratory study. *The Coaching Psychologist, 9*, 19–26.

Stephens, J. P., Heaphy, E. D., Carmeli, A., Spreitzer, G. M., & Dutton, J. E. (2013). Relationship quality and virtuousness: Emotional carrying capacity as a source of individual and team resilience. *Journal of Applied Behavioral Science, 49*, 13–41.

Stober, D. R. (2008). Making it stick: Coaching as a tool for organizational change. *Coaching: An International Journal of Theory, Research and Practice, 1,* 71–80.

Walker, R. J. (1996). *Resilient reintegration of adult children of perceived alcoholic parents.* Unpublished doctoral dissertation, University of Utah.

Weissensteiner, J., Abernethy, B., & Farrow, D. (2009). Towards the development of a conceptual model of expertise in cricket batting: A grounded theory approach. *Journal of Applied Sport Psychology, 21,* 276–292.

West, B. J., Patera, J. L., & Carsten, M. K. (2009). Team level positivity: Investigating positive psychological capacities and team level outcomes. *Journal of Organizational Behavior, 30,* 249–267.

White, R. L., & Bennie, A. (2015). Resilience in youth sport: A qualitative investigation of gymnastics coach and athlete perceptions. *International Journal of Sports Science and Coaching, 10,* 379–394.

Windle, G. (2011). What is resilience? A review and concept analysis. *Reviews in Clinical Gerontology, 21,* 152–169.

Young, J. A. (2014). Coach resilience: What it means, why it matters, and how to build it. *Coaching & Sport Science Review, 22,* 10–12.

17 Integrating decision-making into training

Matt Dicks[1] *and Mark Upton*[2]

Introduction

The beneficial impact of research in different sports science disciplines is exemplified through advances in the performance of elite athletes across a range of team and individual sports. New technologies and training practices have produced more agile and powerful athletes, resulting in faster game-play leading to arguably more exciting and marketable sports events. The evolution of increasingly fast and dynamic sports does, however, potentially present an additional challenge to the technical and tactical demands of performance. Specifically, a hallmark of fast-ball sports (e.g. rugby and football) is that performers are required to adapt to – and perform successfully in – complex and dynamic situations that offer increasingly less time for perception and action. For example, analysis of penalty kicks executed in international competitions has highlighted that ball flight-times from the moment of penalty-taker foot-ball contact have decreased from a range of 400–800 ms in the 1980s (Kuhn, 1988) to a mean flight-time of 344 ms in the 2002 FIFA World Cup (Morya, Bigatão, Lees & Ranvaud, 2005). The implication of this finding is that now, more than ever before, sportspeople require skill in 'reading the game' in order to adapt to such time constraints. One way that researchers believe that athletes overcome the spatio-temporal demands is through expertise in anticipation and decision-making skills (Williams, Ford, Eccles & Ward, 2011). Moreover, a developing body of literature has begun to provide evidence on a variety of methods that can be implemented with the aim of improving these aspects of performance (Farrow, 2013).

Given research advances, one would expect to observe an increase in the application of decision-making findings into applied practice. However, a recently highlighted concern is that research evidence has been under-applied across different sports (Steel, Harris, Baxter, King & Ellam, 2014). For example, observation of association football coaching practices delivered by UEFA A and B Licensed coaches working within professional youth academies has highlighted that a gap appears to exist between the applied recommendations that stem from skill acquisition research and actual coaching behaviours (Ford, Yates & Williams, 2010). In addition, the stated intention of qualified coaches to deliver practices that have the aim of creating 'decision-makers' is somewhat contradicted by the actual behaviours and practices utilised by coaches (Partington & Cushion, 2013). For example, personal correspondence between one of the authors and coaches at a category 1 football academy in England revealed that high value was placed on spending significant time doing repetitive drills that place very little demand on perceptual and decision-making processes (see Ford et al., 2010).

With the current gap between practice and research in mind, an aim of this chapter will be to consider the applied implications that stem from the extant literature on decision-making and perceptual skill. Moreover, we will reflect on some of our experiences on the challenges of integrating decision-making training into practice. We begin by introducing some key terms before providing an overview of some of the experimental approaches and associated findings in the decision-making literature. We then focus our review on some of the different approaches used to train decision-making. Within this section, we will also describe some examples from our own experiences of working in elite sport. Finally, we consider future research questions that build upon existing gaps in the research literature and then summarise the implications for coaches.

Key terms

The term decision-making, as typically considered in the sport psychology literature to date, reflects the ability of sport performers to select the correct response – from a number of possibilities – in a given situation. For example, in the context of team sports such as basketball, rugby, and hockey, the player in possession is, among other possibilities, required to decide whether they should pass or run with the ball. With every unfolding moment, information in the environment (e.g. position of teammates and opponents) will alter, inviting a new set of possible actions. An array of factors, have been highlighted that can potentially impact upon the decision-making process. Arguably, the most developed (inter-related) facet of the decision-making literature is the research that has examined visual anticipation, which concerns the study of *advance* visual information exploited by performers in order to anticipate the outcome of a forthcoming event. Research aimed at addressing this question is particularly important, as the majority of methodological developments in the study (and training) of decision-making stem from the visual anticipation literature. In this chapter, we will therefore consider the wider body of perceptual skill literature, which includes both visual anticipation and decision-making studies.

In order to gain understanding of the information exploited during the decision-making process, researchers have interpreted participant responses alongside gaze behaviour measures. Eye movement systems record point-of-gaze, which provides a measure of the location of information pick-up in foveal (central) vision (Williams, Davids & Williams, 1999). Dependent measures utilised in the literature include the location and duration of fixations (Vaeyens, Lenoir, Williams, Mazyn & Philippaerts, 2007; Williams & Davids, 1998) and scan-paths (visual search strategies) that reveal the spatio-temporal distribution of gaze patterns (Dicks, Button & Davids, 2010; Ripoll, Kerlizin, Stein & Reine, 1995). Gaze behaviour technologies have developed in recent years, meaning that an increasing amount of research is moving from the lab to the field, and such paradigms are often referred to as being *in situ* (for reviews, see Dicks, Davids & Button, 2009; Vickers, 2007).

In this chapter, we will consider Gibson's (1979) ecological approach as a framework to study the mechanisms that underpin perceptual skill in sport (see also van der Kamp, Rivas, van Doorn & Savelsbergh, 2008). A central proposal within Gibson's approach is that a person's behaviour is visually guided by the perception of *affordances* (Gibson, 1979). The perception of an affordance entails the perception of what the environment offers a performer relative to his/her movement capabilities (for a review, see Fajen, Riley & Turvey, 2009). Broadly speaking, Gibson's theory of affordances is one that can help us to understand 'embodied' decisions – that is, decisions that are grounded in one's own abilities (Wilson & Golonka, 2013). In the exact *same* situation, the decision-making possibilities may vary markedly from one player to the next, depending on his/her abilities. For example, where one rugby player with an excellent kicking ability may perceive an opportunity to kick the ball to touch, another player who is incredibly agile may perceive an opportunity to make a quick break through the opposing team's defensive line. It has been argued that such embodied decisions, which are a hallmark of elite sport, and emerge in dynamic and constantly changing game situations, are not well captured by extant theories that have been developed to explain behaviour in other domains (e.g. economics) (see Cisek & Pastor-Bernier, 2014). An important implication for sport is that variation in player abilities means that the correct decision for one player will not necessarily be correct for another. From our own experience of working in applied sport, such insight resonates with coaches working at an elite level, where there is growing interest in decision-making research and recognition of differences in this aspect of skill from player to player, a point we will consider further in this chapter.

Review of literature

Off-field decision-making

An established body of existing research supports the idea that skilled performance in complex and dynamic team sports is founded upon accurate decision-making (Travassos et al., 2013). Studies have tended to examine decision-making using video simulation paradigms that allow the control of extraneous variables (Roca, Ford, McRobert & Williams, 2011). These simulations have typically required participants to respond to video presentations of either a competitive (Lorains, Ball & MacMahon, 2013) or training situation (Vaeyens, Lenoir, Williams, et al., 2007). The video presentations used have contained a controlled number of players and are edited to conclude at selected moments during a

252 M. Dicks and M. Upton

sporting event (e.g. when a pre-determined player gains possession of the ball). Participants are then required to select the action (e.g. pass, dribble or shoot) that they would perform if they were the pre-determined player. Once selected, the decision is typically communicated by participants via a verbal response, a hand-written mark on a sheet of paper or a simulated movement (see Dicks et al., 2009). The accuracy of decision-making for video-based tests of decision-making are typically evaluated against the a priori decision of a panel of quali-fied coaches who determine what they believe the correct decision is for each situation (e.g. Williams & Davids, 1998). Thus, unlike embodied decision-making perspectives considered in the previous section, there appears to be an underlying assumption in typical approaches that there is an optimal decision for any given scenario that is universal across all athletes (and coaches), irrespective of individual abilities.

Typical of the approach described above, Vaeyens, Lenoir, Williams et al. (2007) measured the scan paths and decision-making behaviours of association football players while they responded to video simulations of small-sided games that consisted of a different numbers of attackers and defenders (i.e. 2 vs 1, 3 vs 1, 3 vs 2, 4 vs 3 and 5 vs 3). Participants were required to make decisions as though they were one of the attacking players in the film. The trend of results suggested that the time until a movement response increased and response accu-racy decreased as the number of players within the training drill increased. Spe-cifically, the higher the proportion of attacking players relative to defenders in the video, the faster the response time and the more accurate the decision. Sim-ilarly, there was a change in gaze behaviours between conditions, with more fix-ations of shorter duration occurring for the 3 vs 2, 4 vs 3 and 5 vs 3 scenarios in comparison with 2 vs 1 and 3 vs 1. These findings suggest that an important con-straint on decision-making is the complexity of the configuration of players pre-sented in the video display. The gaze patterns described reflect a high search rate (high number of fixations of short duration) when there are a large number of players to attend to. In comparison, lower search rates (small number of fixations of long duration) tended to occur during instances when there were fewer players in the display (see also Williams & Davids, 1998).

Further to the observation of changes in scan paths with different task com-plexities, research conducted by Roca and colleagues (e.g. Roca et al., 2011) has highlighted how gaze behaviours can vary as a function of player skill levels. During the observation of video simulations of 11 vs 11 football scenarios, skilled players tended to search the display by using a greater number of fixa-tions of shorter durations than lesser skilled players. Primarily, the less-skilled players tended to fixate the ball and player in possession on the display. In con-trast, the better skilled players tended to search more areas of the display, includ-ing peripheral players that were not immediately in possession of the ball. Despite the congruency in findings between the respective studies of Vaeyens, Lenoir, Williams et al. (2007) and Roca et al. (2011), it should be noted that the video footage used in each study was presented to participants from different viewing perspectives. The former study presented footage filmed from an aerial perspective whereas the latter was filmed from a pitch perspective. There has been a long-held concern that decision-making processes may vary relative to the experimental task constraints sampled in a study (Abernethy, Thomas & Thomas, 1993). In response to such concern, Mann and colleagues (Mann, Farrow, Shuttleworth & Hopwood, 2009) compared the response accuracy and gaze behaviours of skilled youth footballers when viewing footage of the same training drill from an aerial and pitch-side (player) perspective. Participants made more accurate decisions when viewing the aerial footage in comparison with the pitch-side view. Furthermore, differences in gaze control emerged, with players utilising more fixations of shorter duration when viewing the aerial perspective. As with findings that have revealed that scan paths are adapted to changes in game complexity (Vaeyens, Lenoir, Williams, et al., 2007), the results from the study of Mann et al. (2009) suggest that changes in the experimental task will also effect the decision-making process. As we will consider in more detail in the section on training decision-making, it is commonplace for coaches to show footage from an aerial perspective during team performance analysis interventions (Mackenzie & Cushion, 2013). It follows that the decision-making processes developed as part of such training may not significantly improve the acquisition of skills needed in game contexts.

On-field decision-making

The body of literature considered in the previous section points to the importance of decision-making in sport as a domain of expertise. An important consideration is whether videos adequately sample the competitive performance environments towards which researchers are aiming to generalise findings. Specific concerns over the disparity between video simulations and on-field performance settings have been conveyed in the literature since the mid-to-late 1990s (Abernethy et al., 1993; Williams et al., 1999). Researchers (e.g. Vaeyens, Lenoir, Philippaerts & Williams, 2007) have acknowledged that it is currently unknown 'whether the decision-making skills that researchers observe in the laboratory are related to those observed in the actual competitive setting' (p. 406). Significantly, it has been highlighted that the mechanisms underpinning performance during video-based decision-making tasks that require participants to make a prediction about the outcome of an event are likely to differ markedly from the mechanisms underpinning on-field decision-making that require the real-time control of actions (Cisek & Pastor-Bernier, 2014; van der Kamp et al., 2008).

In sport psychology, van der Kamp et al. (2008) introduced a framework with which to understand the perception–action processes that underpin the control of decision-making. Van der Kamp et al.'s perspective is grounded in theory from ecological psychology (Gibson, 1979) and neuroscience (Milner & Goodale, 1995). Milner and Goodale (2008) drew together neuroscientific evidence that two neuroanatomically separate, but interconnected, streams exists within the visual cortex – dorsal vision-for-action and ventral vision-for-perception. The dorsal system specialises in the use of visual information for the control of movements (i.e. action), whereas the ventral system is concerned with the use of visual information to obtain knowledge about objects, events, and places (i.e. perception). Furthermore, action entails the online pick-up of information to instantaneously control the on-going movement, while vision for perception does not involve a time constraint, with information used to obtain knowledge about the environment exploited over long time intervals (Nortje, Dicks, Coopoo & Savelsbergh, 2014). In line with such a distinction, there is increasing evidence in the broader visual perception literature that people utilise different information between visual judgment and visual perception–action tasks (van Doorn, van der Kamp, de Wit & Savelsbergh 2009). Specific to perceptual skill in sport, Mann, Abernethy and Farrow (2010) reported that expertise effects in cricket batsman decision-making were most clearly elicited for an interceptive action response compared with verbal, foot movement and simulated batting. Moreover, Dicks and colleagues (Dicks, Button, et al., 2010) reported distinct differences in the timing and location of gaze behaviours of goalkeepers relative to different response requirements when facing penalty kicks. Goalkeepers fixated the ball earlier and for a longer duration when attempting to save kicks in real-time in comparison with judgment-oriented response conditions (i.e. verbal and simplified body movements). Together, these results point to the fact that much of the current understanding on decision-making stems almost exclusively from judgment-oriented conditions that do not permit participants the opportunity to fully exploit the rapid control mechanisms that define expert decision-making (van der Kamp et al., 2008).

A further example of the differences between real-time perception–action and judgment decision-making is provided by the study of Paterson and colleagues (Paterson, van der Kamp, Bressan & Savelsbergh, 2013). Skilled football players were asked to make decisions as to their intended action prior to free-kick execution on field and also for a video simulation of the same task that took place in a laboratory. During the on-field task, participants were required to execute kicks at a constant distance of 18.9 m from the goal in response to varying configurations of defensive wall and goalkeeper location. Prior to execution of the kick, participants were also asked to state the area of the goal they intended to aim towards. In the video task, participants viewed images of the *same* situation from the *same* perspective on a computer screen before providing a written response indicating which area of the goal they would aim at in order to have the best chance of scoring. Participants indicated that they would aim towards different, more challenging, goal locations in the video task in comparison with the on-field condition. Moreover, even though decisions were more cautious during the on-field task, the success of players in accurately executing kicks to their intended location only occurred in roughly 24.8 per cent of trials. It was interpreted that the different decisions were due to the on-field decision-making task being grounded in the players' action capabilities (i.e. players had to execute kicks), which was not a requirement for the laboratory task. Such findings point to a further important aspect of van der Kamp et al.'s (2008) framework, which draws upon a central aspect of Gibson's (1979) ecological approach – namely, the theory of affordances.

As considered in the key terms section of this chapter, affordance perception entails the perception of what the environment offers a performer relative to his/ her movement capabilities (Fajen et al., 2009). In an array of different day-to-day contexts, research has demonstrated that the decisions people make are grounded in their ability to act on properties of the environment. For instance, the decision on whether stairs of different heights are climbable or not is scaled to an individual's leg-length and range of motion around the hip joint (Konczak, Meeuwsen & Cress, 1992), while the decision on whether one can pass through a gap or not is scaled to a person's shoulder width (Warren & Whang, 1987). In the context of sport, research has demonstrated that the ability of American football players to regulate their running trajectories through a defensive gap (Higuchi et al., 2011) and the catching behaviours of baseball outfielders (Oudejans, Michaels, Bakker & Dolné, 1996) are predicated on the accurate perception of affordances (for a review, see Gray, 2014). Differences in the action capabilities of skilled athletes can also impact upon accuracies in perceptual skill. Dicks and colleagues (Dicks, Davids & Button, 2010) reported that experienced goalkeepers scaled the timing of their diving movements relative to their action capabilities when attempting to save penalty kicks. The more agile the goalkeeper, the later the diving action was likely to be initiated relative to penalty taker foot–ball contact. Analyses of the movement kinematics of penalty takers have revealed that the information that unfolds in the final moments of the kicking action has a high congruency with the final kicking direction (Lopes, Jacobs, Travieso & Araújo, 2014). Specific to the study of Dicks and colleagues, the slower goalkeepers who moved earlier exploited kinematic information from the penalty taker's action that led to a fewer number of saves and a greater likelihood of being deceived (see also Brault, Bideau, Kulpa & Craig, 2012). Thus, being able to calibrate movements to later information appeared to support more successful performance.

Training decision-making

A recognised challenge for coaches working with elite athletes is the need to strike a balance between the time spent in physical training, competition, and recovery (see Farrow, 2013). Depending on the physical stressors associated with competition, athletes will require a necessary duration of rest in order to reduce risk of injury. A number of researchers have postulated on the potential benefits that video-based decision-making training may give athletes as this mode of practice can be carried out in conjunction with regular practice at no additional physical cost (Memmert, Hagemann, Althoetmar, Gepperet & Seiler, 2009; Starkes & Lindley, 1994). An aim for some researchers has been to understand how video – and more recently virtual reality technologies – can be used as part of a non-physical, off-field, training intervention to supplement on-field practice. It follows that findings from video simulation studies of decision-making have tended to provide a starting point for decision-making training studies (Williams et al., 2011).

Research by Starkes and Lindley (1994) provides an early example of a video-based intervention, where they studied the effect of this mode of training on the performance of skilled female basketball players. Decision-making was measured via a series of video clips of competitive basketball matches. The video stopped just before the ball-handler's action, and participants were required to select whether the best decision for the player in possession would be to shoot, dribble or pass the ball. Half of the participants undertook six video training sessions prior to a post-test, with results indicating that decision-making improved marginally for the video training group in comparison with a control. Participants also completed a transfer test in which they viewed real-time play sequences from the side of the court. Unlike the video-based test, there were no improvements in decision-making for the video training group. The results therefore indicated that video training might only improve accuracy on video-based decision-making tasks.

An important applied question raised in the article by Starkes and Lindley (1994) is whether a period of video training can lead to an on-field improvement in decision-making. There have been an increasing number of studies that have begun to explore a range of methods for training decision-making with video technology (Williams et al., 2011). On the whole, research largely demonstrates that novices who undertake video-based training do not improve their response accuracies in comparison with placebo groups (for a review, see Dicks, van der Kamp, Withagen & Koedijker, 2015). Following van der Kamp et al.'s (2008) framework considered in this chapter, it appears that video-training protocols may only improve a performer's ability to make a judgment about a sporting event (vision for perception), rather than facilitating the skill utilised during the control of decision-making behaviour (vision for perception–action). Unfortunately, the majority of research developments in the area of decision-making training have tended to focus on the evaluation of video interventions using off-field measures. There have been some efforts to assess performance away from the confines of the laboratory; however, many of these approaches have only measured performance using judgment-based measures of decision-making that do not offer participants the opportunity to produce requisite actions relative to ball-flight and opponent information (see Dicks, Button et al., 2010; van der Kamp et al., 2008). Moreover, rather than interventions examining the potential benefits of video training as an additional form of (non-physical) practice, many studies have examined the impact of video training as a stand-alone intervention.

Recent developments in video interventions have seen this mode of training used as a supplementary form of practice, with on-field measures of decision-making used to examine the effect of the intervention. For example, Lorains et al. (2013) studied the impact of a video-based above real time training (ARTT) intervention on the on-field and off-field decision-making accuracy of elite Australian football (AF) players. As defined by Lorains and colleagues, 'ARTT involves playing video faster than normal time in order to increase the required processing speed for decisions' (p. 670). During ARTT, the elite players viewed aerial footage of AF matches that were edited to play at 1.5 times normal speed.

The intervention lasted five weeks and participants watched 12 video-clips per week. Further to the ARTT, a normal training group watched the same clips that were played at the original video speed and a control group just completed pre-, post-, and retention tests. Off-field video decision-making results revealed that both the ARTT and normal speed training groups improved performance in a post-test compared to the control group. Furthermore, in a two-week retention test after the end of training, the ARTT group performed better than the normal speed training group. However, although all groups were found to improve on-field decision-making, there were no significant differences between groups. Therefore, comparable with the earlier observations of Starkes and Lindley (1994), although video-based training appeared to improve decision-making in comparison to a control group in a video-based test, there were no apparent positive transfer effects to on-field decision-making.

The lack of additional improvements in on-field decision-making in the study of Lorains et al. (2013) could be reconciled by the significant differences in decision-making behaviours for aerial and pitch perspective video footage (Mann et al., 2009). Hopwood, Mann, Farrow and Nielsen (2011) reported that a six-week player-perspective video training intervention improved the fielding performance of highly skilled cricketers. Importantly, the training was supplementary to regular fielding practice. Thus, while the benefits of video-training are inconclusive, it would appear that any intervention should ensure that the footage is from a player perspective and additional to regular practice (see also Causer, Holmes & Williams, 2011). The lack of findings for aerial video training have implications for the added value of 'video review' sessions that are commonly used in team sport settings, in which footage from an elevated/aerial view tends to be used as part of player performance evaluations (for a review, see Mackenzie & Cushion, 2013). While moving further away from the perspective that players encounter on the pitch may be useful for highlighting game structures, there is no clear evidence that this type of off-field practice directly enhances on-field decision-making (see also Williams & Manley, 2014). When previously working with an international coach, one of the authors learnt that little value was placed in the benefits of such off-field intervention. Nevertheless, video review sessions were used as part of a multidisciplinary approach to developing decision-making, which brought together sport science staff, coaches, and players. Video-review was primarily used to help reinforce the *same* coaching points as on-field practice.

This insight points to the observation that coaches acknowledge that relatively small – statistically insignificant – performance improvements may nevertheless lead to practical significance in elite sport (Hopwood et al., 2011; Hopkins, Marshall, Batterham & Hanin, 2009). From our experience, even though the benefits of video training are far from conclusive, it is a mode of practice that coaches apply as a supplementary training tool. By way of example, one of the authors has found that using 'behind the goals' (pitch-side) video footage with young elite athletes in a lengthy systematic training schedule led to improvements in off-ball decision-making, as rated subjectively by the team's coaches. Similarly, elite player exposure to a training program that simulated decision-making when entering the attacking third of the pitch using 'player-perspective' life-size footage, also received positive feedback from players in terms of 'feeling like we were on the pitch'. Hopwood and colleagues (2011) highlighted that the coach of the highly skilled players trained in their study 'acknowledged the value of combining perceptual training with regular on-field practice, emphasising increased exposure to a variety of fielding situations that the players would not have otherwise experienced during *traditional* [emphasis added] centre wicket fielding practice' (p. 533). Although evidence is inconclusive, and far more research is needed, there are at least indications that the use of video training as a supplement to physical practice may facilitate performance improvements in elite athletes. Most importantly, the need for physical practice alongside off-field training would appear to be essential to allow for any changes in information pick-up to be calibrated (scaled) to movements (see van Lier, van der Kamp & Savelsbergh, 2011). That is, accuracy in perceptual skill is predicated on reciprocal perception–action (van der Kamp et al., 2008).

Implications for future research

Methodological advances in the decision-making literature have revealed that the mechanisms that underpin on-field performance may not be equivalent to the mechanisms tested during (off-field) judgment tasks (van der Kamp et al., 2008). Unfortunately, aside from some of the examples provided in this chapter, there have been few attempts to evaluate the efficacy of video-based decision-making training using transfer tests and measures (Dicks et al., 2015). A primary requirement for future research is therefore to fully utilise adequate real-time *in situ* tests of decision-making to fully understand whether training interventions bring about performance improvements. To emphasise, such measures should place priority on the assessment of decision-making via requisite actions rather than simulated judgments. As we have briefly considered in this chapter, the development of perceptual skill appears to be grounded in the calibration of actions to the pick-up of visual information (e.g. van Lier et al., 2011). Research is needed to ascertain whether the benefits of video training are only apparent when used as a supplementary tool to practice (Causer et al., 2011; Hopwood et al., 2011) or if performance improvements can be elicited from video training alone.

There remains real scope for improving the design of practice sessions so that perception–action processes are developed in an integrated manner. Given the gap between research and practice highlighted at the outset of this chapter (e.g. Ford et al., 2010), an important focus in future research should be to identify appropriate methods for the dissemination of coach education material to support the development of skilled coach behaviours. Following Davids (2012), a fruitful starting point would be to examine whether coaches benefit from developing a (theoretical) model of the learner and learning process. Davids (2012) proposed the importance of an ecological dynamics perspective for the development of decision-making, with emphasis placed on understanding skilled behaviour as 'self-organized and emergent under interacting constraints' (p. 11). Learning from this perspective emphasises the development of skills that support the continual adaptation of a performer to dynamically changing sport environments. There are, of course, other theoretical perspectives that have been used to explain decision-making in sport (e.g. Williams et al., 2011), which could prove valuable to coaches in developing a model of the learner. The significant message emphasised by Davids (2012) though is that a theoretical understanding may benefit coaches in helping the integration of research evidence to facilitate the development of coaching skill-sets that, otherwise, may result in coaching the way that one was coached. Research is needed to identify methods for the dissemination of theoretical and research content that will be both accessible and relevant to coaches to facilitate the development of coaching practices (Williams & Manley, 2014).

From our own experiences, there would appear to be particular gains in knowledge dissemination to coaches working at talent and youth development levels, where the immediate pressures of results and up-coming matches are not as great as in the professional environment. On-field practice design may be best facilitated through the 'manipulation of task constraints' (for a review, see Renshaw, Davids & Savelsbergh, 2010). The design of practice through the manipulation of task constraints would place emphasis on adapting games to guide the development of different perceptual–motor skills that underpin decision-making. For instance, implementation of coaching practices from this view in team sports could include variations placed on the number of players, pitch size, equipment and rules, all with the aim of inviting different behaviours. While a number of studies have examined the effect of different task constraints on physiological variables (Hill-Haas, Dawson, Impellizzeri & Coutts, 2011), a key issue for future research is to understand which task manipulations are most beneficial for developing decision-making. For example, in a series of studies, Memmert and colleagues (e.g., Memmert & Roth, 2007) found that decision-making and creativity skills in young children can be developed via forms of practice that emphasise deliberate play through adaptive games. Moreover, research indicates that increasing the variability of conditions in practice can enhance accuracy in perceptual skill by forcing learners to search for and exploit different information (Smeeton, Huys & Jacobs, 2013). The use of variable practice via manipulation of task constraints also has the potential to cater for individual differences in perceptual skill, rather than aiming to train all performers to replicate the same decision in the same situation (e.g. Lorains et al., 2013).

As highlighted earlier in this chapter, our combined experiences have pointed to the interest from coaches in the need to better understand the individual differences that underpin decision-making. We have considered the theory of affordances as a possible starting point to address this research requirement. The current empirical approach in extant research to measure decision-making against the judgments of a panel of coaches may present a misleading picture on performance accuracies as this fails to take into account the abilities of individual athletes (Dicks, Davids et al., 2010; Paterson et al., 2013). There is a real need to better understand the relationship between the decisions that sportspeople make and their abilities to act on properties of the environment. Such research emphasis would necessitate a move towards the measurement of a person's action capabilities and an understanding of how such intrinsic properties of a performer are scaled to measurable properties of the environment (Warren, 1984). This research approach could include understanding on how a performer's agility influences the timing of actions relative to an opponent's/teammate's action (Dicks, Davids et al., 2010), how passing options over different distances are scaled to a performer's passing ability (Bruce, Farrow, Raynor & Mann, 2012), and how a person's level of fatigue or anxiety influences the perception of possible actions (Pijpers, Oudejans & Bakker, 2007). Understanding of such questions would make an important contribution to the development of theory and research in the broader psychology literature, where there is recognition that, in any given instance, the environment is not a manifold of *neutral* action possibilities (Withagen, de Poel, Araújo & Pepping, 2012). Exciting advances that potentially hold important implications for understanding of decision-making in sport, include acknowledgment that there are multiple factors that interact to shape a constantly changing 'field of affordances' (Bruineberg & Rietveld, 2014).

Implications for applied practice

This chapter has provided an overview of the literature that has examined decision-making in sport. A major theme of the research to date has been the use of video technologies to study and train decision-making. Unfortunately, one of the consequences of this empirical approach is that only limited inferences can be made regarding on-field decision-making. What is increasingly clear is that the processes that underpin on-field decision-making appear to be different in comparison with passively making judgments about a simulated environment (Cisek & Pastor-Bernier, 2014; Dicks et al., 2015; van der Kamp et al., 2008). Based on current knowledge, the implication for coaches is that there may be a real opportunity to make significant gains in the development of on-field training interventions that are specifically targeted towards improving decision-making. Adaptive games appear to be a fruitful means to guide the development of decision-making and creativity skills (Memmert & Roth, 2007). Increasing the variability of conditions in practice via the manipulation of task constraints in adaptive games can enhance accuracy in decision-making, while also holding potential to cater for individual differences in perceptual skill (Dicks et al., 2015). It is therefore essential to understand which coaching manipulations will bring about improvements in decision-making via longitudinal training practices. A move towards such understanding will hopefully prove beneficial in bridging the gap between research and practice.

Pertinent to this matter, there would appear to be particular gains in knowledge dissemination to coaches working at talent and youth development levels. To this end, investment – where money is available – is likely to be best spent on developing coach education and mentoring interventions that will better support the development of skilled coach behaviours at all levels of athlete development. Focus should be placed on identifying methods for the dissemination of theoretical and research content that will be both accessible and relevant to coaches (Williams & Manley, 2014). Finally, this review has highlighted that video technologies have been used to train decision-making but with some mixed success. What is increasingly clear is that, if video technologies are to be used as a form of practice, they should be an addition to on-field training and not a replacement (Hopwood et al., 2011). When used, video should also be presented from a player's perspective, rather than using aerial footage (Mann et al., 2009). This points to the need for any off-field training to accurately create/sample situations in practice that replicate game contexts (Dicks, Davids & Araújo, 2008).

Notes

1 Department of Sport and Exercise Science, University of Portsmouth, UK
2 English Institute of Sport, Bisham Abbey National Sports Centre, UK

References

Abernethy, B., Thomas, K. T. & Thomas, J. T. (1993). Strategies for improving understanding of motor expertise (or mistakes we have made and things we have learned!). In J. L. Starkes & F. Allard (Eds.), *Cognitive issues in motor expertise* (pp. 317–356). Amsterdam: Elsevier.

Brault, S., Bideau, B., Kulpa, R. & Craig, C. M. (2012). Detecting deception in movement: the case of the side-step in rugby. *PLoS One*, *7*(6), e37494–e37494.

Bruce, L., Farrow, D., Raynor, A. & Mann, D. (2012). But I can't pass that far! The influence of motor skill on decision making. *Psychology of Sport and Exercise*, *13*(2), 152–161.

Bruineberg, J., & Rietveld, E. (2014). Self-organization, free energy minimization, and optimal grip on a field of affordances. *Frontiers in human neuroscience*, *8*(599).

Causer, J., Holmes, P. S. & Williams, A. M. (2011). Quiet eye training in a visuomotor control task. *Medicine and Science in Sports and Exercise*, *43*(6), 1042–1049.

Cisek, P., & Pastor-Bernier, A. (2014). On the challenges and mechanism of embodied decisions. *Philiosophical Transactions of the Royal Society B, 5.*

Davids, K. (2012). Learning design for nonlinear dynamical movement systems. *The Open Sports Sciences Journal*, *5*(1), 9–16.

Dicks, M., Button, C. & Davids, K. (2010). Examination of gaze behaviors under in situ and video simulation task constraints reveals differences in information pickup for perception and action. *Attention, Perception, & Psychophysics*, *72*(3), 706–720.

Dicks, M., Davids, K. & Araújo, D. (2008). Ecological psychology and task representativeness: implications for the design of perceptual-motor training programmes in sport. In Y. Hong & R. Bartlett (Eds.), *Handbook of biomechanics and human movement science* (pp. 129–139). New York: Routledge.

Dicks, M., Davids, K., & Button, C. (2009). Representative task designs for the study of perception and action in sport. *International Journal of Sport Psychology*, *40*(4), 506–524.

Dicks, M., Davids, K. & Button, C. (2010). Individual differences in the visual control of intercepting a penalty kick in association football. *Human Movement Science*, *29*(3), 401–411.

Dicks, M., van der Kamp, J., Withagen, R. & Koedijker, J. (2015). 'Can we hasten expertise by video simulations?' Considerations from an ecological psychology perspective. *International Journal of Sport Psychology*, *46*, 109–129.

Fajen, B. R., Riley, M. A. & Turvey, M. T. (2009). Information, affordances and the control of action in sport. *International Journal of Sport Psychology*, *40*, 79–107.

Farrow, D. (2013). Practice-enhancing technology: a review of perceptual training applications in sport. *Sports Technology*, *6*(4), 170–176.

Ford, P., Yates, I. & Williams, A. M. (2010). An analysis of practice activities and instructional behaviours used by youth soccer coaches during practice: exploring the link between science and application. *Journal of Sports Sciences*, *28*(5), 483–495.

Gibson, J. J. (1979). *The ecological approach to visual perception*. Boston, MA: Houghton Mifflin.

Gray, R. (2014). Embodied perception in sport. *International Review of Sport and Exercise Psychology*, *7*(1), 72–86.

Higuchi, T., Murai, G., Kijima, A., Seya, Y., Wagman, J. B. & Imanaka, K. (2011). Athletic experience influences shoulder rotations when running through apertures. *Human Movement Science*, *30*, 534–549.

Hill-Haas, S. V., Dawson, B., Impellizzeri, F. M. & Coutts, A. J. (2011). Physiology of small-sided games training in football. *Sports Medicine*, *41*(3), 199–220.

Hopkins, W. G., Marshall, S. W., Batterham, A. M. & Hanin, J. (2009). Progressive statistics for studies in sports medicine and exercise science. *Medicine and Science in Sports and Exercise*, *41*(1), 3–13.

Hopwood, M., Mann, D., Farrow, D. & Nielsen, T. (2011). Does visual-perception training augment the fielding performance of skilled cricketers? *International Journal of Sports Science and Coaching*, *6*, 523–536.

Konczak, J., Meeuwsen, H. J. & Cress, M. E. (1992). Changing affordances in stair climbing: the perception of maximum climbability in young and older adults. *Journal of Experimental Psychology: Human Perception and Performance*, *18*(3), 691.

Kuhn, W. (1988). Penalty kick strategies for shooters and goalkeepers. In T. Reilly, A. Lees, K. Davids & W. J. Murphy (Eds.), *Science and football* (pp. 489–492). London: E. & F. N. Spon.

Lopes, J. E., Jacobs, D. M., Travieso, D. & Araújo, D. (2014). Predicting the lateral direction of deceptive and non-deceptive penalty kicks in football from the kinematics of the kicker. *Human Movement Science*, *36*, 199–216.

Lorains, M., Ball, K. & MacMahon, C. (2013). Expertise differences in a video decision-making task: speed influences on performance. *Psychology of Sport and Exercise*, *14*(2), 293–297.

Mackenzie, R., & Cushion, C. (2013). Performance analysis in football: A critical review and implications for future research. *Journal of Sports Sciences*, *31*(6), 639–676.

Mann, D. L., Farrow, D., Shuttleworth, R. & Hopwood, M. J. (2009). The influence of viewing perspective on decision-making and visual search behaviour in an invasive sport. *International Journal of Sport Psychology*, *40*(4), 546–564.

Mann, D. L., Abernethy, B. & Farrow, D. (2010). Action specificity increases anticipatory performance and the expert advantage in natural interceptive task. *Acta Psychologica*, *135*, 17–23.

Memmert, D., & Roth, K. (2007). The effects of non-specific and specific concepts on tactical creativity in team ball sports. *Journal of Sports Sciences*, *25*(12), 1423–1432.

Memmert, D., Hagemann, N., Althoetmar, R., Geppert, S. & Seiler, D. (2009). Conditions of practice in perceptual skill learning. *Research Quarterly for Exercise and Sport*, *80*(1), 32–43.

Milner, A. D., & Goodale, M. A. (1995). *The visual brain in action.* Oxford: Oxford University Press.

Milner, A. D., & Goodale, M. A. (2008). Two visual systems re-viewed. *Neuropsychologia, 46,* 774–785.

Morya, E., Bigatão, H., Lees, A. & Ranvaud, R. (2005). Evolving penalty kick strategies: World Cup and club matches 2000–2002. In T. Reilly, J. Cabri & D. Araújo (Eds.), *Science and football V* (pp. 237–242). London: Taylor & Francis.

Nortje, L., Dicks, M., Coopoo, Y. & Savelsbergh, G. J. P. (2014). Put your money where your moth is: verbal self-reported tactical skills versus on-line tactical performance in soccer. *International Journal of Sports Science and Coaching, 9*(2), 321–333.

Oudejans, R. R. D., Michaels, C. F., Bakker, F. C. & Dolné, M. A. (1996). The relevance of action in perceiving affordances: perception of catchableness of fly balls. *Journal of Experimental Psychology: Human Perception and Performance, 22*(4), 879–891.

Partington, M., & Cushion, C. (2013). An investigation of the practice activities and coaching behaviors of professional top-level youth soccer coaches. *Scandinavian Journal of Medicine and Science in Sports, 23,* 374–382.

Paterson, G., van der Kamp, J., Bressan, E. & Savelsbergh, G. J. P. (2013). The effects of perception-action coupling on perceptual decision-making in a self-paced far aiming task. *International Journal of Sport Psychology, 44,* 179–196.

Pijpers, J. R., Oudejans, R. R. & Bakker, F. C. (2007). Changes in the perception of action possibilities while climbing to fatigue on a climbing wall. *Journal of Sports Sciences, 25*(1), 97–110.

Renshaw, I., Davids, K. & Savelsbergh, G. J. P. (Eds.). (2010). *Motor learning in practice: A constraints-led approach.* London: Routledge.

Ripoll, H., Kerlizin, Y., Stein, J.-F. & Reine, B. (1995). Analysis of information processing, decision making, and visual strategies in complex problem solving sport situations. *Human Movement Science, 14*(3), 325–349.

Roca, A., Ford, P. R., McRobert, A. P. & Williams, A. M. (2011). Identifying the processes underpinning anticipation and decision-making in a dynamic time-constrained task. *Cognitive Processing, 12,* 301–320.

Smeeton, N. J., Huys, R. & Jacobs, D. M. (2013). When less is more: reduced usefulness training for the learning of anticipation skill in tennis. *PLoS ONE, 8*(11), e79811.

Starkes, J. L., & Lindley, S. (1994). Can we hasten expertise by video simulations? *Quest, 46,* 211–222.

Steel, K. A., Harris, B., Baxter, D., King, M. & Ellam, E. (2014). Coaches, athletes, skill acquisition specialists: a case of misrecognition. *International Journal of Sports Science and Coaching, 9*(2), 367–378.

Travassos, B., Araújo, D., Davids, K., O'Hara, K., Leitão, J. & Cortinhas, A. (2013). Expertise effects on decision-making in sport are constrained by requisite response behaviours – A meta-analysis. *Psychology of Sport and Exercise, 14,* 211–219.

Vaeyens, R., Lenoir, M., Philippaerts, R. M. & Williams, A. M. (2007). Mechanisms underpinning successful decision making in skilled youthful soccer players: an analysis of visual search behaviors. *Journal of Motor Behavior, 39*(5), 395–408.

Vaeyens, R., Lenoir, M., Williams, A. M., Mazyn, L. & Philippaerts, R. M. (2007). The effects of task constraints on visual search behavior and decision-making skill in youth soccer. *Journal of Sport and Exercise Psychology, 29,* 147–169.

van der Kamp, J., Rivas, F., van Doorn, H. & Savelsbergh, G. (2008). Ventral and dorsal contributions in visual anticipation in fast ball sports. *International Journal of Sport Psychology, 39*(2), 100–130.

van Doorn, H., van der Kamp, J., de Wit, M. & Savelsbergh, G. J. P. (2009). Another look at the Müller-Lyer illusion: different gaze patterns in vision for action and perception. *Neuropsychologia, 47*, 804–812.

van Lier, W. H., van der Kamp, J. & Savelsbergh, G. J. (2011). Perception and action in golf putting: Skill differences reflect calibration. *Journal of Sport and Exercise Psychology, 33*(3), 349.

Vickers, J. N. (2007). *Perception, cognition, and decision training: The quiet eye in action.* Champaign, IL: Human Kinetics.

Warren, W. H. (1984). Perceiving affordances: visual guidance of stair climbing. *Journal of Experimental Psychology: Human Perception and Performance, 10*(5), 683.

Warren, W. H., & Whang, S. (1987). Visual guidance of walking through apertures: body-scaled information for affordances. *Journal of Experimental Psychology: Human Perception and Performance, 13*(3), 371–383.

Williams, A. M., & Davids, K. (1998). Visual search strategy, selective attention, and expertise in soccer. *Research Quarterly for Exercise and Sport, 69*(2), 111–128.

Williams, A. M., Davids, K. & Williams, J. G. (1999). *Visual perception and action in sport.* London: E. & F. N. Spon.

Williams, A. M., Ford, P. R., Eccles, D. W. & Ward, P. (2011). Perceptual-cognitive expertise in sport and its acquisition: implications for applied cognitive psychology. *Applied Cognitive Psychology, 25*, 432–442.

Williams, S., & Manley, A. (2014). Elite coaching and the technocratic engineer: thanking the boys at Microsoft! *Sport, Education and Society*, (ahead-of-print), 1–23.

Wilson, A. D., & Golonka, S. (2013). Embodied cognition is not what you think it is. *Frontiers in Psychology, 4*(58).

Withagen, R., de Poel, H. J., Araújo, D. & Pepping, G. J. (2012). Affordances can invite behaviour: Reconsidering the relationship between affordances and agency. *New Ideas in Psychology, 30*, 250–258.

18 Pulling the group together

The role of the social identity approach

Andrew. L. Evans,[1] *Matt. J. Slater,*[2]
Pete Coffee,[3] *and Jamie B. Barker*[2]

Introduction

How do coaches successfully pull a group together? This chapter focuses on the role and importance of creating and maintaining social identities for group functioning and performance. Research documenting the role and importance of social identities has increased considerably over recent years, with over 200 research articles published across a variety of psychological domains in 2012 alone (Haslam, 2014). Given the wealth of empirical studies available, we have chosen to focus on key research articles within our review of social identity literature to highlight the role and importance of social identities in coaching contexts. Ultimately, social identity researchers recognise that groups are dynamic and have the capacity to change individuals, which means that groups and organisations are much more than an aggregation of their individual parts (Haslam, 2004). Therefore, the key to successfully pulling a group together from a social identity perspective lies in the understanding and promotion of a shared sense of social identity among group members. For a coach to understand their role in optimising group functioning and performance, the social identity approach to leadership (Haslam, Reicher, & Platow, 2011) contains four principles that can be implemented within coaching practice. This chapter will also explore each principle of social identity leadership for a coaching audience.

Key terms

According to the social identity approach, individuals can define themselves in terms of personal or social identities (Haslam, 2004). A personal identity reflects the unique attributes and characteristics that define an individual (Fransen et al., 2015). On the other hand, a social identity represents the sense of belongingness and emotional significance an individual feels towards a particular group (Slater, Evans, & Barker, 2013). In sport, an athlete may develop or maintain a social identity with a team (e.g. the England soccer team) and/or an organisation (e.g. United Kingdom [UK] Sport). To illustrate the distinction between personal and social identities, consider the case of Mark – a cricket batsman. Mark is creative, extroverted, and energetic as an individual, which are characteristics that define

Mark as a person ('I am Mark, a creative, extroverted, and energetic individual'). Mark also belongs to a cricket team with other athletes that share the same goals and interests (e.g. to win cricket matches). Mark's membership to a cricket team additionally defines Mark as a person. A social identity should not be confused with the term 'cohesion' – a predominant group-level psychological factor – which represents the tendency of individuals to stick together and remain united when pursuing goals and objectives (Carron, 1982). Although social identity and cohesion are significantly and positively related (Evans, Coffee, Barker, Allen, & Haslam, 2015a), social identity reflects the psychological significance of groups to individuals whilst cohesion represents a group-oriented behaviour. The notion that individuals with a strong sense of social identity share goals and interests highlights that social identities are meaningful to individuals. The meaning (or reason) individuals attach to their social identity is commonly termed as the content of social identity (Turner, 1985). Arguably, the most common contents of social identity prevalent in elite sport centre on achievement or excellent performance (Evans, Slater, Turner, & Barker, 2013; Slater, Barker, Coffee & Jones, 2015).

Given the importance of social identities for group functioning and performance, the social identity approach to leadership provides coaches with four main principles that make for effective leadership. The first principle of social identity leadership suggests that leaders should be an in-group prototype. An in-group represents a group that an individual has formed a social identity with, whereas an out-group signifies a group that an individual has not formed a social identity with. Being in-group prototypical therefore means that coaches should aim to represent the values of the group to which they belong. The second principle asserts that leaders should be an in-group champion. Being an in-group champion means that coaches should be solely motivated to further the collective interests of the group to which they belong. The third principle explains that leaders should be entrepreneurs of social identity. In other words, coaches should seek to construct meaningful in-group values that mobilise collective action. Finally, the fourth principle suggests that leaders should be embedders of social identity. Being an embedder of social identity means that coaches should aim to make in-group values a reality.

From this point, this chapter will: review research on the role and importance of social identities, the content of social identities, and social identity leadership; suggest future research; and outline applied recommendations for coaches aiming to pull groups together through the harnessing of social identities.

Review of the literature

The social identity approach

The social identity approach is a psychological framework incorporating several predictions about cognition, emotion, and behaviour that are communicated through two theories: social identity theory (Tajfel & Turner, 1979) and self-categorisation theory (Turner, 1999). Ultimately, the social identity approach recognises that the psychology and behaviour of group members is not simply determined by the ability of individuals to think, feel, and act as individuals (as 'I' or 'me'). The psychology and behaviour of group members is also influenced by the capacity of individuals to define themselves as belonging to meaningful social groups (as 'we' or 'us'; Fransen et al., 2015). Initially, the social identity approach stipulates that an individual will be inclined to categorise themselves as a member of a group (i.e. self-categorisation) when the differences between themselves (e.g. cricketers) and members of one group (e.g. a cricket team) are smaller than the differences between themselves and members of other groups (e.g. other cricket teams) within a particular context (e.g. a league). This process is commonly known as comparative fit (Turner, 1999). An individual will also be inclined to categorise themselves as a member of a group when their beliefs about in-group values (e.g. to win) are consistent with actual in-group values. This process is commonly known as normative fit (Turner, 1999). Self-categorisation then initiates a process of depersonalisation in which individuals view themselves and other in-group members as interchangeable representatives of the attributes and qualities associated with their group (Hornsey, Dwyer, Oei, & Dingle, 2009). Depersonalisation means that individuals do not view themselves and other in-group members as a collection of idiosyncratic individuals. Depersonalisation causes individuals to define themselves and others as belonging to a collective entity (e.g. *we* are a cricket team) rather than being defined through more personal forms of identity. At the point of depersonalisation, an individual has formed a social identity with their respective group. Depersonalisation then triggers a final process known as self-stereotyping where in-group members adopt forms of attitude and behaviour prescribed by in-group values (Turner, 1999). So, self-stereotyping would suggest that athletes will exert high levels of effort when being hard-working as a group is a valued component of social identity. The main implication of self-stereotyping is that in-group members will bring their attitude and behaviour into conformity with their in-group prototype while generating positive attitudinal consensus and behavioural uniformity (Hogg, 1992). Based on the social identity approach, the development of a social identity would appear to be an important pre-requisite for group-oriented thinking and behaviour (see Figure 18.1).

The importance of social identities

A critical mass of research across psychological domains has demonstrated that a strong sense of social identity significantly predicts a range of outcomes including morale, self-esteem, burnout, stress, satisfaction, and commitment (Haslam, Jetten, & Waghorn, 2009; Haslam, O'Brien, Jetten, Vormedal, & Penna, 2005; Haslam et al., 2007. One explanation for the positive effects of social identity on stress-related outcomes (e.g. self-esteem) suggests that social support emanating from a shared sense of social identity buffers against stressful experiences. Haslam (2004) suggested that a social identity serves as a basis for individuals to receive and benefit from support that fellow in-group members

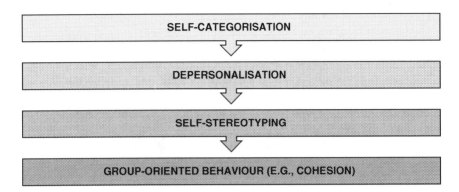

Figure 18.1 The development of social identities leading to group-oriented behaviour through the processes of self-categorisation, depersonalisation, and self-stereotyping.

can provide. Indeed, Haslam et al. (2005) demonstrated that social support mediated the relationship between social identity and stress, while social identity influenced the perception of how stressful different modes of work were for individuals. Applied to Lazarus's Cognitive–Motivational–Relational Theory (CMRT; Lazarus, 2000), a strong sense of social identity would appear to be a resource that would increase the coping potential of in-group members when appraising encounters with the environment. Emerging research within sport also supports the notion that social identities are important determinants of group-level outcomes. In a longitudinal study, Evans et al. (2015a) measured social identity, cohesion, collective efficacy, and team performance at the start, middle, and end of a season in all eight rugby league teams competing within one Rugby League Premier Division. Using multilevel modelling procedures, data indicated that higher levels of social identity (between-athletes) were associated with higher levels of cohesion, collective efficacy, and team performance. Higher levels of social identity (within-athletes) were also associated with higher levels of collective efficacy. Data appear logical when considering social identity theory. The main premise of social identity theory suggests that individuals will form social identities with groups that make a positive contribution to self-esteem (Haslam, 2004). Accordingly, individuals will feel inclined to behave in the best interests of their group (rather than their own personal interests) because individuals strive to see their group as different to (and better than) other groups to experience positive self-esteem (Haslam, 2004). In other words, individuals will strive to achieve in-group distinctiveness when a social identity has been formed. Social identities therefore motivate individuals towards group-level outcomes because the fate of the group will decide the psychological fate of individuals who have undergone processes of self-categorisation, depersonalisation, and self-stereotyping (van Knippenberg, 2000).

The content of social identities

The potential for social identity content to influence cognition and behaviour was highlighted in the process of self-stereotyping explained earlier (Turner, 1999). That is, once individuals have depersonalised the perception of themselves, in-group members take on forms of attitude and behaviour associated with their social identity. Livingstone and Haslam (2008) provided support for the effects of social identity content upon the cognition and behaviour of in-group members. Data revealed that Catholic and Protestant religious groups only acted antagonistically towards each other when the content of their religious identity was focused on being hostile and conflictual to opposing religious groups. The potential for social identity content to influence athletes was exemplified during the London 2012 Paralympic Games. During the final lap of the women's H1–3 hand-cycling road race, TeamGB athletes Karen Darke and Rachel Morris were set to contest a sprint finish for the bronze medal position. Fifty metres from the finish line, Darke and Morris held hands and crossed the finish line together in an attempt to finish equal third. From a social identity perspective, the behaviour of Darke and Morris could have been attributable to the strong sense of shared identity experienced between two teammates. Additional comments from Darke suggested that both athletes felt it wrong for one to cross the finish line without the other because both athletes had worked equally hard together preparing for the race (BBC Sport, 2012). Ultimately, a TeamGB hand-cycling identity focused strongly on excellent interpersonal relationships and respect between teammates appeared to encourage thoughts and actions aligned to the content of Darke and Morris' social identity. Nevertheless, preliminary research by Evans et al. (2015a) generally revealed that two components of social identity content pertinent to sport (i.e. achieving excellent results and exhibiting excellent friendships) failed to significantly predict ratings of cohesion and collective efficacy. However, correlational analyses did reveal that the relationship between league position and a social identity content focused on exhibiting excellent friendships was moderately high, significant, and positive over time. The authors argued that perhaps athletes changed the meaning attached to their social identity over time (a strategy known as social creativity) in response to threatened social identity content which prevented significant effects from emerging.

The effects of threat to social identity content

From a social identity perspective, threat arises when a situation or event causes an in-group to be negatively distinguished from another group. Examples of negatively distinguished in-groups include in-groups that are low in status compared to another group (e.g. a poorer performing in-group vs a high performing out-group) or in-groups that have received negative evaluation on a specific factor (e.g. 'we have performed poorly'). Across two experimental studies, Evans, Coffee, Barker, and Haslam (2015b) explored: the effects of threatening social identity content on social identity-related variables; and the role of social identity content during episodes of relevant content threat. Following a sustained period of threat to results content only, data revealed that members of a results-content condition (where social identities were focused on achieving excellent results) reported significantly lower social identity and in-group prototypicality than members of a support-content condition (where social identities were focused on being supportive of one another). Post-threat, members of the results-content condition also reported significantly higher out-group prototypicality and expressed a significantly stronger desire to move to another group (a strategy known as social mobility). Accordingly, in experiment two, participants were assigned to dual content conditions (in which social identities were focused on achieving excellent results and being supportive of one another). In condition one, results content was threatened through false performance feedback that suggested repeated failure on five performance trials. In condition two, support content was threatened through false supportive feedback that suggested poor willingness to support in-group members across all trials. Members of both conditions reported higher social identity and in-group prototypicality (post-threat) than members of the results-content condition in experiment one. Members of both conditions also reported lower out-group prototypicality and social mobility (post-threat) than members of the results-content condition in experiment one. Interestingly, members of both dual content conditions showed evidence of social creativity in response to social identity content threat. Specifically, members of each condition significantly reduced the emphasis placed on the threatened aspect of their social identity content while maintaining the focus placed on the unthreatened aspect of their social identity content. These experimental findings suggest that broadening the repository of social identity content within groups may protect important social identity processes and group-oriented behaviour when an aspect of social identity content is threatened. For example, groups that value achieving excellent results and supporting one another as a group are likely to be protected when the group experiences a period of poor form. Drawing on social identity theory, having unthreatened elements of social identity content available would mean that social identities contribute to the achievement of positive self-esteem (Haslam, 2004).

The social identity approach to leadership

The social identity approach to leadership has attracted growing research attention due to its appreciation of contextual influences and group dynamics within leadership. Essentially, the social identity approach to leadership proposes four principles that coaches can work through to harness social identities within groups (see Figure 18.2).

Leaders as in-group prototypes

The first principle of social identity leadership suggests that coaches should be in-group prototypes. Coaches who are in-group prototypical are more likely to be categorised as in-group members through the principles of comparative and

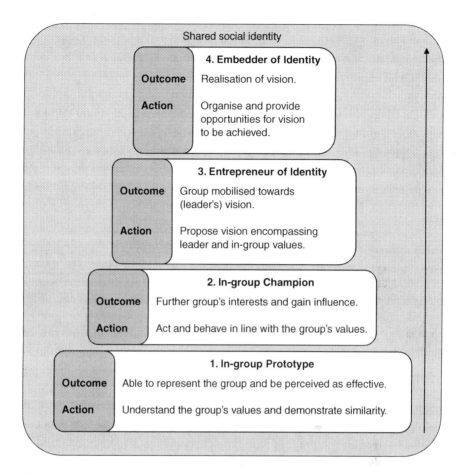

Figure 18.2 A hierarchical model of actions and outcomes for social identity leadership in sport. Taken from Slater et al., 2014.

normative fit. For instance, coaches are more likely to be categorised as an in-group member when their beliefs about in-group values are consistent with the actual values of their in-group (i.e. normative fit). Slater, Coffee, Barker, and Evans (2014) described how being in-group prototypical as a leader is akin to person-centred counselling procedures (Rogers, 1980) used by counsellors during applied practice to develop strong working alliances with clients. During person-centred counselling, effective working alliances are created when counsellors show key counselling skills (e.g. empathy) to their clients (Slater et al., 2014). Being in-group prototypical as a coach also relates to being co-oriented (i.e. when athletes' and coaches' thoughts are interconnected) within the 3C+1 model for building an effective coach–athlete relationship (Jowett, 2007). An example of a leader in sport who can be considered highly prototypical of their in-group is Sir David Brailsford. Throughout the London 2012 Olympic Games, Brailsford was motivated towards achieving cycling success for TeamGB cyclists (e.g. through the use of key performance indicators), which encapsulated the motivation of TeamGB to achieve their best medal haul at an Olympic Games (Slater et al., 2013). Research has found that being in-group prototypical as a leader benefits a host of outcomes including gaining trust, support, and the ability to influence in-group members (for a review, see van Knippenberg, 2011). Understanding in-group values as a coach is therefore imperative. Consider Alex Ferguson. When arriving at Manchester United football club in 1986, Ferguson spent considerable time understanding the values of Manchester United before implementing managerial activities (Bolton & Thompson, 2015). Research also suggests that understanding in-group values is critical for mobilising in-group members towards collective action. In the BBC prison experiment conducted by Reicher and Haslam (2006), volunteers were randomly assigned to the role of prisoner or guard within a mock prison. On the sixth day of the experiment, a new prisoner (who had a background working as a trade union official) was introduced into the prison regime to encourage collective action and develop an equal set of relations between prisoners and guards. Before articulating a shared vision for prisoners and guards, the new prisoner spent time reflecting on the current prison regime (e.g. with prisoners) to understand the prison regime. The ability to reflect on in-group values is therefore critical to becoming in-group prototypical as a coach.

Leaders as in-group champions

The second principle of social identity leadership suggests that coaches should be in-group champions. Using the social identity approach, coaches who enhance the interests of their group will help their group achieve positive distinctiveness in comparison to other groups, which means in-group members will be more likely to experience positive self-esteem (Haslam, 2004). Research has demonstrated that leaders must carefully consider context when attempting to enhance in-group interests. For example, Platow, Nolan, and Anderson (2003) asked Australian citizens to rate their support for leaders who either favoured their in-group over out-groups or treated all groups equally during the Sydney 2000 Olympic Games (a context that promotes inclusivity and fairness). Data indicated that, in the context of the Olympics, leaders who favoured their in-group over other groups were endorsed less than leaders who treated all groups equally. Platow et al. confirmed that the thoughts and actions within a coach's interest will be dependent on how in-group members define their social identity. Similarly, Slater et al. (2015) found that TeamGB's vision for achieving excellent performance at the London 2012 Olympic Games dictated decisions made around optimising peak performance (e.g. choice of team kit).

Recent research by Slater, Coffee, Barker, Haslam, and Steffens (under review) examined how leaders may best champion in-group interests in relation to the concept of power. Using an experimental design, participants were led by either a power-through leader or a power-over leader. The power-through leader sought to engage with the group to understand their social identity content and propose a vision that encompassed the group's shared social identity. The power-over leader sought to exert power in a top-down manner by outlining to the group what their social identity content was going to be. Slater et al. (under review) found that members of the power-through condition reported significantly higher levels of shared social identity, trust in the leader, and mobilised effort (assessed via time spent on a practice task) compared to members of the power-over condition. Data suggest that coaches who lead in a manner that works with and through (rather than against and over) their group will increase the effectiveness of their leadership practice.

Leaders as entrepreneurs of social identity

The third principle of social identity leadership implies that coaches should be entrepreneurs of social identities. As self-categorisation theory suggests, in-group functioning is determined by in-group values. Coaches may therefore aim for in-group members to take on in-group values that align with the coach's vision (Slater et al., 2014). Recent evidence (Slater et al., under review) has outlined the importance of coaches creating shared values rather than creating values independently. Across four experimental conditions, athletes' social identity content was either identical or dissimilar to the social identity content of a sports coach. Members of two shared content conditions reported significantly higher social identity with the team and coach, trust in their leader, and intentional mobilisation (assessed by hours dedicated to an additional task set by the coach) compared to members of two unshared content conditions. Overall, creating shared values underpins the development of a shared social identity, while the specific content of social identity that is shared may be less important that the act of sharing content itself.

Creating shared values requires time and involves change. Although group members can be resistant to change (Bovey & Hede, 2001), leaders have been shown to instigate a change in group values through various social identity-related methodologies. For example, in the BBC prison experiment, the prisoner introduced on day six encouraged prisoners and guards to view themselves under a new set of values while belonging to one group (i.e. a prison group vs prisoner and guard groups). The new prisoner instigated a change in group values and the conceptualisation of social identity by drawing on participant clothing and using collective language to emphasise a new shared social identity. Reicher and Haslam (2006) suggested that creating newly formed social identities enabled the new prisoner to gain support and mobilise the prison group towards his vision. Steffens and Haslam (2013) provided further evidence that using collective language can mobilise in-group members towards a newly articulated vision. Successful Australian Prime Ministerial candidates were found to use more collective pronouns in comparison to their unsuccessful counterparts across 43 election campaigns. Those successful candidates used collective language every 79 words, compared to every 136 words for unsuccessful candidates. For coaches, it seems imperative to be mindful of rhetoric used: 'together, *we* will achieve great things' triumphs over '*I* will lead you to great things'.

Leaders as embedders of social identity

The fourth principle of social identity leadership suggests that coaches should be embedders of social identity. A good example of a leader embedding social identities is Sir David Brailsford. Leading up to the London 2012 Olympic Games, Brailsford talked about how the values of TeamGB cycling were focused on being creative in achieving success (Slater et al., 2013). Brailsford sought innovation for TeamGB by recruiting expert professionals (e.g. bike technicians) and acquiring information that would assist TeamGB in making their vision a reality. For example, Brailsford consulted surgeons about washing hands thoroughly to reduce illness, while learning about improving the sleeping behaviour of athletes. Evans, Edwards, and Slater (2015c) corroborated the principle of embedding social identities as a leader by randomly assigning 74 members of team sports to one of two conditions. Participants in both conditions were given the same scenario of belonging to a sports team, having a strong connection with a coach, and sharing in-group values based around being innovative as a team. In condition one, the coach was described as helping the in-group realise its vision (a leader embedder) by seeking innovation for the team. In condition two, the coach was described as a leader non-embedder by not helping the in-group realise its vision. After reading their vignette, participants in the leader embedder condition reported significantly higher leader prototypicality, trust in their leader, leader influence, mobilisation, and expected realisation of in-group vision in comparison to participants in the leader non-embedder condition.

In a second experiment, Evans et al. (2015c) explored whether social identity processes change in response to either becoming a leader embedder or failing to sustain a leader embedder approach in a real-world setting. Across two conditions, soccer athletes were introduced to a soccer coach (week one), made aware of shared in-group values (week two), and completed four soccer activities over four separate weeks (week three to week six). After each activity, athletes completed a series of measures including mobilisation, realisation of vision, trust, influence, and conflict. In condition one, the coach embedded social identities during week three and week four by delivering soccer activities aligned to in-group values. The coach failed to embed social identities in week five and week six by delivering soccer activities inconsistent with in-group values. In condition two, the coach failed to embed social identities in week three and week four before embedding social identities in week five and week six. Data indicated that ratings of social identification and identity with the coach within each condition at baseline were significantly different from zero. Perceptions of the coach as a leader embedder were lower when the coach delivered soccer activities inconsistent with in-group values. When the coach delivered soccer activities aligned to in-group values, athletes reported higher mobilisation, trust in their leader, anticipated realisation of vision, and ability of their leader to influence the group. Athletes also reported lower levels of conflict with their leader when the coach delivered soccer activities aligned to in-group values. Overall, Evans et al. (2015c) demonstrated that coaches can improve social identity-related processes by becoming an identity embedder. Data also documented that failing to sustain an identity embedder approach will harm social identity-related processes. Therefore, the sustainability of effective leadership seems to rest in a coach's proactive capacity to embed what matters most to their group into reality.

Implications for future research

While social identity research in sport is beginning to emerge (e.g. Evans et al., 2015a), continuing to investigate the principles of the social identity approach in sport would benefit coaching practice. Current social identity research in sport has focused on exploring the relationships between two aspects of social identity content (i.e. results and friendships content) pertinent to sport (see Evans et al., 2015a). Future researchers could adopt qualitative methodologies to explore the various forms of social identity content that exist within sport. Accordingly, the relationships between aspects of social identity content (above and beyond results and friendships content) and a wider set of outcome variables (e.g. resilience, achievement goal orientation) could be examined. Current applied research in sport has documented the effects of two forms of Personal-Disclosure Mutual-Sharing (PDMS: relationship-oriented and mastery-oriented) on social identities and aspects of social identity content amongst athletes. PDMS is a communication-based intervention whereby individuals prepare and publicly disclose previously unknown information to members of their team or group (Barker, Evans, Coffee, Slater, & McCarthy, 2014). During relationship-oriented PDMS, individuals share information focused on relationships. During mastery-oriented PDMS, individuals share information based around best sporting performances. Future researchers could also demonstrate the effectiveness of alternative forms of PDMS (e.g. coping-oriented PDMS) or other group-based interventions in manipulating social identities and aspects of social identity content beyond those prescribed in current literature. It also remains to be seen whether PDMS (or other group-based interventions) can manipulate the social identities and social identity content of other group members (e.g. coaches, parents, key stakeholders) within an athlete's support network. Increasing the volume of applied social identity research would help to close the chasm that currently exists between social identity theorists and applied practitioners, which can potentially explain the difficulties researchers and practitioners have faced when attempting to apply the social identity approach to psychology and performance.

The majority of research studies exploring the four principles of social identity leadership within sport have adopted experimental research designs. To increase the external validity of research findings, future researchers could draw on real-life sporting groups when testing the four principles of social identity leadership. For coaches, having a structured intervention procedure or pro-gramme of workshops to base their social identity leadership practice around would also be useful. Existing research into the four principles of social identity leadership has had the propensity to focus on testing differences between experimental conditions that are faced with a specific type of leader. Future research could examine the importance of incorporating the four principles of social identity leadership into coaching practice within specific scenarios. For example, researchers could explore whether implementing the social identity approach to leadership can protect social identity processes (e.g. social mobility) during times of organisational change (e.g. a change in organisational strategy). Perhaps most importantly, however, social identity research in sport would benefit from the development of sport-specific measures of social identity, social identity content, and social identity leadership to assist researchers in their endeavours to advance current research findings.

Implications for applied practice

Primarily, research presented within the literature review suggests that it is important for coaches to build and maintain a shared sense of social identity among group members to encourage collective thinking and action (e.g. cohesion, collective efficacy) that may benefit performance. To promote a shared sense of social identity, coaches could increase group members' awareness of how their in-group is positively distinguished from other groups so that group members can achieve positive distinctiveness through their in-group membership (Haslam, 2004). For example, coaches could emphasise that their group is more creative, more successful, or friendlier in comparison to rival out-groups.

Applied research is also beginning to emerge that suggests social identities can be created or strengthened through group-based interventions. PDMS is a group-based intervention that would enable coaches to create or strengthen social identities within groups. Broadly, relationship-oriented PDMS activities have been found to increase the sense of social identity from pre-intervention to post-intervention (Barker et al., 2014; Evans et al., 2013). Mastery-oriented PDMS activities have been shown to maintain ratings of social identity from pre-intervention to post-intervention (Barker et al. 2014). As a coach, it would appear fruitful to encourage greater understanding between group members through group-based interventions (such as PDMS) to increase or maintain the emotional significance and sense of belongingness athletes feel towards their group.

PDMS research has also shown that the type of information shared within PDMS sessions can develop particular in-group values. For example, Evans et al. (2013) and Barker et al. (2014) found that disclosing information based around relationships significantly enhanced the value athletes placed upon friendships within their team (i.e. friendships identity content). Barker et al. also documented that disclosing information centred on best performances significantly enhanced the value athletes placed on the results achieved by their team (i.e. results identity content). Coaches could therefore ask athletes to share information around a specific theme (e.g. best performances) when aiming to improve certain performance-related outcomes (e.g. collective efficacy). Indeed, Barker et al. found that a single bout of mastery-oriented PDMS significantly enhanced collective efficacy beliefs from pre-intervention to post-intervention. Additionally, encouraging athletes to share information around a diverse set of themes (e.g. relationships, best performances, coping with stressors) could enable coaches to develop groups with multiple contents of social identity. As a coach, asking group members questions to generate discussion about in-group values (e.g. 'what type of group would *we* like to become?') would appear profit-able to begin moulding shared and meaningful social identities that empower group members towards collective thinking and action.

To implement the four principles of social identity leadership into coaching practice, Haslam et al. (2011) presented the 3Rs of social identity leadership (Reflection, Representation, and Realisation). Reflection involves coaches taking an interest in the group's identity and values through active listening, discussion, and observation. Reflecting with group members is important so that coaches do not misinterpret social identities, resulting in the advancement of alien identities (Haslam, 2004). Representation involves coaches making decisions and behav-ing in a manner consistent with the shared and multiple characteristics of their group. For example, if a group is founded on its togetherness, a coach should seek to represent that group by championing the importance of togetherness (e.g. organising inclusive group meetings). Realisation involves coaches organising opportunities for their group to behave in line with the group's social identity content, which enables group members to progress towards their collective vision. For instance, support staff (e.g. sports scientists) with a history of discov-ering modern-day innovation could be employed when in-group values are focused on being innovative as a group. Slater, Evans, and Turner (2015) suggest that a fourth 'R' (Reappraisal) may also be important to incorporate into leader-ship practice. It has been postulated that social identity can enhance resource appraisals (e.g. perceptions of control) and/or reduce demand appraisals (e.g. uncertainty) through the social support emanating from social identities. In turn, in-group members will approach stressful situations in a challenge state (i.e. a positive appraisal state) rather than a threat state (i.e. a negative appraisal state; see Slater et al., 2014).

Despite the collective-oriented nature of the social identity approach, it is not always the case that an inclusive approach to leadership is required. This approach was evident in the 2014 Ryder Cup golf tournament. European Ryder Cup captain Paul McGinley decided to assign certain athletes to leadership roles. More senior golfers (e.g. Ian Poulter, Lee Westwood, and Graeme McDowell) were to 'blood the rookies' (i.e. those less experienced European golfers) and socially support the rookies in their preparation and performance. Turner, Slater, and Barker (2015) explained that McGinley's decision was effective because 'the selected players represented the team ideal and epitomised the values of team Europe. In social identity terms, Poulter, Westwood, and McDowell are prototypical leaders' (p. 277). Ultimately, McGinley's decision to assign more senior golfers to specific leadership roles was particularly effective because this decision was made in the best interests of the team (Turner et al., 2015).

In conclusion, this chapter has highlighted the importance of attending to social identities as a coach when aiming to pull a group together. Social identities influence the way group members think and behave, so it makes sense for coaches to work on developing a shared sense of social identity within groups. Social identities are also meaningful to group members. When social identities incorporate multiple meanings, they can protect groups when faced with considerable strain. Coaches have a vital role to play in building and strengthening the social identities of group members. Being prototypical, championing the in-group, being an entrepreneur, and embedding in-group identities undoubtedly serve as useful principles that can assist coaches in their leadership activity.

Notes

1 Centre for Health Sciences Research, Salford University, UK
2 Centre for Sport, Health, and Exercise Research, Staffordshire University, UK
3 School of Sport, University of Stirling, UK

References

Barker, J. B., Evans, A. L., Coffee, P., Slater, M. J., & McCarthy, P. J. (2014). Consulting on tour: A multiple-phase personal-disclosure mutual-sharing intervention and group functioning in elite youth cricket. *The Sport Psychologist, 28*(2), 186–197.

BBC Sport (2012). Paralympics: Rachel Morris and Karen Darke try to share bronze. Accessed on 30 June 2015: www.bbc.co.uk/sport/0/disability-sport/19519150.

Bolton, B., & Thompson, J. (2015). *The entirepreneur: The all-in-one entrepreneur–leader–manager.* Oxon: Routledge.

Bovey, W. H., & Hede, A. (2001). Resistance to organisational change: The role of defence mechanisms. *Journal of Managerial Psychology, 16*(7), 534–548.

Carron, A. V. (1982). Cohesiveness in sport groups: Interpretations and considerations. *Journal of Sport Psychology, 4*, 123–138.

Evans, A. L., Coffee, P., Barker, J. B., Allen, M., & Haslam, S. A. (2015a). *The importance of social identity and social identity content for psychology and performance in sport.* Unpublished manuscript. Staffordshire University.

Evans, A. L., Coffee, P., Barker, J. B., & Haslam, S. A. (2015b). *When the going gets tough: The role of group meanings in response to social identity content threat.* Unpublished manuscript. Staffordshire University.

Evans, A. L., Edwards, M., & Slater, M. J. (2015c). *Embedding social identity principles into leadership practice.* Unpublished manuscript. Nottingham Trent University.

Evans, A., Slater, M. J., Turner, M. J., & Barker, J. B. (2013). Using personal-disclosure mutual-sharing (PDMS) to enhance group functioning in a professional soccer academy. *The Sport Psychologist, 27*(3), 233–243.

Fransen, K., Haslam, S. A., Steffens, N. K., Vanbeselaere, N., De Cuyper, B., & Boen, F. (2015). Believing in 'us': Exploring leaders' capacity to enhance team confidence and performance by building a sense of shared social identity. *Journal of Experimental Psychology: Applied, 21*(1), 89–100.

Haslam, S. A. (2004). *Psychology in organizations: The social identity approach.* (2nd ed.). Thousand Oaks, CA: Sage Publications.

Haslam, S. A. (2014). Making good theory practical: Five lessons for an applied social identity approach to challenges of organizational, health, and clinical psychology. *British Journal of Social Psychology, 53*(1), 1–20.

Haslam, S. A., Jetten, J., & Waghorn, C. (2009). Social identification, stress and citizenship in teams: A five-phase longitudinal study. *Stress and Health, 25*, 21–30.

Haslam, S. A., O'Brien, A., Jetten, J., Vormedal, K., & Penna, S. (2005). Taking the strain: Social identity, social support, and the experience of stress. *British Journal of Social Psychology, 44*, 355–370.

Haslam, S. A., Reicher, S. D., & Platow, M. J. (2011). *The new psychology of leadership: Identity, influence and power.* Hove: Psychology Press.

Haslam, S. A., Ryan, M. K., Postmes, T., Spears, R., Jetten, J., & Webley, P. (2007). Sticking to our guns: Social identity as a basis for the maintenance of commitment to faltering organizational projects. *Journal of Organizational Behavior, 27*, 607–628.

Hogg, M. A. (1992). *The social psychology of group cohesiveness: From attraction to social identity.* London: Harvester Wheatsheaf.

Hornsey, M. J., Dwyer, L., Oei, T. P. S., & Dingle, G. A. (2009). Group processes and outcomes in group psychotherapy: Is it time to let go of "cohesiveness"? *International Journal of Group Psychotherapy, 59*(2), 267–278.

Jowett, S. (2007). Interdependence analysis and the 3+1Cs in the coach–athlete relationship. In S. Jowett & D. Lavallee (Eds.), *Social psychology in sport* (pp. 15–28). Champaign, IL: Human Kinetics.

Lazarus, R. (2000). Cognitive-motivational-relational theory of emotion. In Y. L. Hanin (Ed.), *Emotions in sport.* (pp. 39–63). Champaign, IL: Human Kinetics.

Livingstone, A., & Haslam, S. A. (2008). The importance of social identity content in a setting of chronic social conflict: Understanding intergroup relations in Northern Ireland. *British Journal of Social Psychology, 47*(1), 1–21.

Platow, M. J., Nolan, M. A., & Anderson, D. (2003). *Intergroup identity management in a context of strong norms of fairness: Responding to in-group favouritism during the Sydney 2000 Olympics.* Unpublished manuscript. The Australian National University.

Reicher, S. D., & Haslam, S. A. (2006). Rethinking the psychology of tyranny: The BBC prison study. *British Journal of Social Psychology, 45*, 1–40.

Rogers, C. R. (1980). *A way of being.* Boston, MA: Houghton Mifflin.

Slater, M. J., Barker, J. B., Coffee, P., & Jones, M. V. (2015). Leading for gold: Social identity leadership processes at the London 2012 Olympic Games. *Qualitative Research in Sport, Exercise, and Health, 7*(2), 192–209.

Slater, M. J., Coffee, P., Barker, J. B., & Evans, A. L. (2014). Promoting shared meanings in group memberships: A social identity approach to leadership in sport. *Reflective Practice: International and Multidisciplinary Perspectives, 15*(5), 672–685.

Slater, M. J., Coffee, P., Barker, J. B., Haslam, S. A., & Steffens, N. (under review). Leaders mobilize followers by cultivating a sense of shared social identity content. *European Journal of Social Psychology.*

Slater, M. J., Evans, A. L., & Barker, J. B. (2013). Using social identities to motivate athletes towards peak performance at the London 2012 Olympic Games: Reflecting for Rio 2016. *Reflective Practice: International and Multidisciplinary Perspectives, 14*(5), 672–679.

Slater, M. J., Evans, A. L., & Turner, M. J. (2015). Implementing a social identity approach for effective change management. *Journal of Change Management.*

Steffens, N. K., & Haslam, S. A. (2013). Power through 'Us': Leaders' use of we-referencing language predicts election victory. *PLoS ONE, 8*(10), 1–6.

Tajfel, H., & Turner, J. C. (1979). An integrative theory of intergroup conflict. In W. G. Austin & S. Worchel (Eds.), *The social psychology of intergroup relations* (pp. 33–47). Monterey, CA: Brooks/Cole.

Turner, J. C. (1985). Social categorization and the self-concept: A social cognitive theory of group behaviour. In E. J. Lawler (Ed.), *Advances in group processes.* (pp. 77–122). Greenwich, CT: JAI Press.

Turner, J. C. (1999). Some current issues in research on social identity and self-categorization theories. In N. Ellemers, R. Spears, & B. Doosje (Eds.), *Social identity: Context, commitment, content* (pp. 6–34). Oxford: Blackwell.

Turner, M. J., Slater, M. J., & Barker, J. B. (2015). A commentary on Simon Jenkins' article: Winning formula, man management and the inner game: Commonalities of success in the Ryder Cup and Super Bowl. *International Journal of Sports Science and Coaching, 10*(2+3), 275–279.

van Knippenberg, D. (2000). Work motivation and performance: A social identity perspective. *Applied Psychology, 49*(3), 357–371.

van Knippenberg, D. (2011). Embodying who we are: Leader group prototypicality and leadership effectiveness. *The Leadership Quarterly, 22*, 1078–1091.

Index

Printed in the United States
By Bookmasters